GW00716383

SUMMER JOBS ABROAD 2002

EDITORS
Ian Collier
David Woodworth

Published annually by
Vacation Work, 9 Park End Street, Oxford.
www.vacationwork.co.uk

Thirty Third edition

SUMMER JOBS ABROAD

ISBN 1 85458 261 5 (hardback)
ISBN 1 85458 260 7 (softback)

ISSN 0308 7123

Statement for the purposes of
The Employment Agencies Act 1973:
The price of the Directory of Summer Jobs Abroad is £15.95 (hardback)
or £9.99 (softback) and is for the book and the information contained
therein; it is not refundable.

Cover design by Miller Craig and Cocking Design Partnership

Typeset by WorldView Publishing Services

Printed by Wm Clowes Ltd., Beccles, Suffolk, UK.

Contents

page

Introduction 5
Opting for a Summer Job Abroad 7

WORLDWIDE
Agricultural Work 24
Hotel Work & Catering 25
Industrial & Office Work 28
Sports, Couriers & Camping 31
Sports: Ski Resorts 49
Voluntary Work & Archaeology 49
Work With Children 67
Work at Sea 67
Other Employment Abroad 68
Au Pairs, Nannies, Home Helps and Exchanges 73

WESTERN EUROPE
Andorra 82
Austria 82
Belgium 88
Denmark 92
Finland 96
France 97
Germany 138
Great Britain 157
Greece 157
Ireland 166
Italy 173
Luxembourg 184
The Netherlands 187
Norway 191
Portugal 194
Spain 196
Sweden 210
Switzerland 212

EASTERN EUROPE
Belarus 225
The Czech Republic 225
Hungary 227
Latvia 227
Malta 229
Poland 229
Russia 231
Slovenia 232

Turkey..232
The Ukraine..235
Yugoslavia 235

AFRICA AND THE MIDDLE EAST
Egypt 236
Ghana 237
Israel 239
Kenya...243
Morocco...244
Nigeria 246
South Africa..246
Tanzania..247
Togo...248

THE AMERICAS
Brazil 249
Canada 249
Colombia..252
Costa Rica..252
Cuba...254
Ecuador..255
Mexico...256
Peru..257
USA 257

ASIA
China 267
India...267
Japan..270
Nepal 273
Thailand...275

AUSTRALASIA
Australia 277
New Zealand..283

USEFUL PUBLICATIONS 286

Introduction

We are delighted that once again this new edition of *Summer Jobs Abroad* not only includes details of more employers than ever before but also contains its largest ever range of jobs. Different people want different things from a summer job: some need to earn money, while others are more concerned with finding interesting work: some need employment for the whole summer, while others are free for only a few weeks. We have tried to fill *Summer Jobs Abroad* with a range of opportunities to suit everyone, whether they want to work in Europe, Australasia or Africa.

As always, most of the book consists of individual entries for specific employers and agencies who are able to offer full-time work overseas: the information in these entries has been supplied by the organisations themselves, and is included at their request. Entries covering opportunities in a number of countries are in the *Worldwide* chapter at the beginning of the book; others are listed in the relevant country chapter. At the start of each country chapter there are some general notes on employment prospects and regulations on work permits, entry visas etc.

Where there are few opportunities for paid employment – in, for example, developing countries – we have given details of voluntary organisations willing to accept unskilled workers for short periods of time. Even in those countries where paid employment is available, voluntary work has a number of advantages. Hours of work are likely to be shorter. leaving more time available for recreational and cultural activities, which are generally regarded to be an integral part of workcamp life. In most cases, volunteers are drawn from a number of countries, so that contact is made not only with local residents, but also with young people from all over the world.

David Woodworth
Oxford, October 2001

The editors would like to thank Fiona Kelcher, Anke Büttner and Harveys of
Lewes for their assistance in the preparation of this edition.

Opting for a Summer Job Abroad

The reasons why young people look for alternatives to the conventional summer job in their hometown are many and varied. Often it is just a case of itchy feet. Travelling abroad to do a holiday job is one of the best ways to shake off the boredom and routine of living at home and working locally. Whereas months of slogging at a local burger bar will allow you to save some money, time spent working abroad may alter your view of where you are headed in life.

Many students cite positive reasons for choosing to work abroad: to experience a foreign culture from the inside rather than as an onlooker, to fill a gap in their life's timetable in a productive way, **to improve their knowledge of foreign languages** and cultures, to **gain practical skills**. Usually there is an element of all these at work.

Working abroad is one of the means by which students and others can afford to stay overseas for an extended period, to have a chance to **absorb a foreign culture**, to meet foreign people on their own terms and to gain a better perspective on their own culture and habits. Sweeping generalisations about the valuable cultural insights afforded by working in a foreign land should be tempered with a careful consideration of the reality of doing a job abroad. In most cases, the expression 'working holiday' is an oxymoron like 'cruel kindness'. Jobs are jobs wherever you do them, and there is little scope for developing a social life and exploring museums if you are stranded in an obscure industrial town teaching English six days a week or manning reception in a damp caravan for a camping holiday operator. After perusing the jobs listed in this volume, it will be necessary to ask yourself whether you think you are sufficiently adaptable to work for a season in a Swiss hotel, Latvian summer camp, Danish strawberry farm or whatever catches your eye.

Earning and saving during the summer vacation have become crucially important to the vast majority of students since grants for higher education have been whittled away. A secondary consideration for some is that a summer job might **enhance a future CV** and allow you to gain useful experience or new skills. Jobs abroad can fulfil both these requirements. Some areas of career interest can just as easily be served by a summer job abroad as at home in fields as diverse as archaeology and social services, teaching and agriculture.

Employers have been shown to favour candidates who have demonstrated initiative and spent their time productively using a broad range of skills and working abroad will help you to fulfil these criteria. This does not necessarily mean finding an internship with a New York investment bank. Increasingly, employers are becoming open-minded to the fact that high-flying summer work is hard to come by and that transferable skills are what matter. For instance, those people who attain the position of barge manager on the French waterways will have demonstrated language and communication skills, leadership abilities, client service and a hardy stomach. Someone who works as a bar attendant may well have demonstrated these same skills plus a degree of numeracy and a faculty for working long hours under pressure. Undoubtedly there are some drawbacks as well. It is more difficult to land a job when you are not available for interview and when you are not fluent in the dominant language of the region. Then there is the hassle and cost of getting abroad and possible administrative formalities such as visas and insurance. You will have to sever yourself temporarily from your commitments at home (boyfriends/girlfriends, pets, teams and clubs). One of the main drawbacks of a summer job abroad is that if anything goes wrong, you are a long way from the safety net of home. Job descriptions may sound more glamorous than the reality (as is true with jobs anywhere) so that a job serving cocktails in paradise may turn out to be clearing ashtrays in a seedy discotheque.

Certain obstacles in the mind of the irresolute must be overcome: Can I possibly afford it? What jobs can I get? Do I need specific skills? What if I only speak English? This introductory section sets out to allay anxieties and to encourage readers to peruse details of the thousands of summer jobs available. Those who have shed their unrealistic expectations are normally exhilarated by the novelty and challenge of finding and doing a summer job abroad.

Finding a summer job abroad may strike you as a daunting task. However this book leads you through the process in a systematic way and provides sufficient listings to help you find a job suited to your needs. Some jobs listed pay very well and come with room and board; others are voluntary and therefore unpaid. Some last for the whole season (June to September or longer); others are just for a couple of weeks. Working abroad for a short period will enable the dream to become a reality, of being immersed in a different culture, meeting new friends and earning money at the same time.

Where to Go and What to Do

At the risk of oversimplifying the choices, the seeker of a summer job abroad must either fix up a definite job before leaving home or take a gamble on finding something on arrival. There is a lot to recommend prior planning, especially for people who have seldom travelled abroad on their own and who feel some trepidation at the prospect.

If you have no predisposition to choose one country over another based on previous holidays, language studies at school or information from friends or relatives who live abroad, you are free to consider any job listed in this book. It will soon become apparent that there are far fewer listings in developing countries, simply because paid work in the developing world is rarely available to foreigners. Yet many students arrange to live for next to nothing doing something positive (see the section on Volunteering below).

Some organisations and employers listed in this directory accept a tiny handful of individuals who satisfy stringent requirements; others accept almost anyone who can pay the required fee, for example agencies that recruit paying volunteers for conservation work in exotic places or to teach English. Some work schemes and official exchanges require a lot of advance planning since it is not unusual for an application deadline to fall three to six months before departure.

The kind of job you find will determine the stratum of society in which you will mix and therefore the content of the experience. The traveller who spends a few weeks picking olives for a Cretan farmer will get a very different insight into Greece from the traveller who looks after the children of a wealthy Athenian shipping magnate. And both will probably have more culturally worthwhile experiences than the traveller who settles for working at a beach café frequented only by his or her partying compatriots.

The more unusual and interesting the job the more competition it will attract.

For example it can be safely assumed that only a small percentage of applicants to the American Scandinavian Foundation is accepted as engineering trainees in Finland and only a few of the many British students who would like to spend the summer working in a British embassy abroad actually get to participate in the Foreign Office scheme. On the other hand, less glamorous options can absorb an almost unlimited number of people, for example working as a counsellor on an American children's summer camp or volunteering to work on a kibbutz in Israel. All these possibilities are included in this book.

The question of work permits and visas must be tackled by British students who plan to work in a country outside Europe. The standard situation among all European Union countries (plus Iceland, Liechtenstein and Norway) is that nationals of any member state have the right to work (or look for work) for up to three months. Before the end of that period they should apply to the police or the local authority for a residence permit, showing their passport and job contract, a process that can be more bureaucratic and difficult than the legislation would indicate.

Work permits and residence visas outside Europe or for North American job-seekers worldwide are not readily available in many countries and for many kinds of job. In most cases, the job-seeker from overseas must find an employer willing to apply to the immigration authorities on his or her behalf well in advance of the job's starting date, while they are still in their home country. A more accessible alternative is to join an organised exchange programme like the ones administered by Council Exchanges and BUNAC, where the red tape is taken care of by a sponsoring organisation. Britons who want to work outside Europe must investigate possibilities country-by-country (see sections on Red Tape in the country chapters).

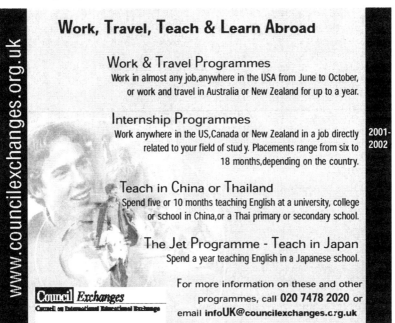

Seasonal Work Available

The Tourist Industry

The tourist industry is a mainstay of summer job seekers. The seasonal nature of hotel and restaurant work discourages a stable working population, so that hotel proprietors often rely on foreign and student labour during the busy summer season. Also, many tourist destinations are in remote places; young people have ended up working in hotels in some of the most beautiful corners of the world from high in the Alps to national parks in the USA.

In a few cases, agencies (see entries for Jobs in the Alps or the Swiss Hotels Association) can place eligible British students in continental hotels for the season. But mostly it is a case of applying to individual hotels. Only in a few cases can agencies and leisure groups place people without any relevant experience (e.g. in a café or takeaway in your hometown) or knowledge of the relevant language.

The earlier you decide to apply for seasonal hotel work the better are your chances. Hotels often recruit months before the summer season, and it is advisable to write to as many hotel addresses as possible by March, preferably in their own language. A knowledge of more than one language is an immense asset for work in Europe. If you have an interest in working in a particular country and want to cast your net wider than the hotels listed in this directory, get a list of hotels from their tourist office in London or from the internet and contact the largest ones.

If you secure a hotel job without speaking the language of the country and lack relevant experience, you will probably be placed at the bottom of the pecking order, e.g. in the laundry or washing dishes. Reception and bar jobs are usually the most sought after and highly paid. However the lowly jobs have their saving graces. The usual hours of chamber staff (7am-2pm) allow plenty of free time and of course you do not have to deal with guests. The same complaints crop up again and again among people who have worked in hotel kitchens: long and unsociable hours, low wages, dodgy accommodation and food, and hot working conditions.

But there are benefits as well. The vast majority of hotels provide their staff with accommodation and meals; a deduction will be made from wages for living expenses but in most cases this will not be unreasonable. Excellent camaraderie and team spirit, the opportunity to learn a foreign language, beautiful surroundings and the ease with which wages can be saved, including the possibility of an end-of-season bonus, are further incentives to consider a season in a foreign hotel.

Resorts and Holiday Centres

Camping tour operators employ a huge number of students and young people for the summer season. The Holidaybreak group, which includes Eurocamp and Keycamp, alone recruits up to 1,500 campsite couriers and children's couriers. The courier's job is to clean the tents and caravans between visitors, greet clients and deal with difficulties (particularly illness or car breakdowns) and introduce clients to the attractions of the area or even arrange and host social functions and amuse the children. All of this will be rewarded with on average £90-£100 a week in addition to free tent accommodation. Many companies offer half-season contracts April to mid-July and mid-July to the end of September. Setting up and dismantling the campsites in March/April and September (known as *montage* and *démontage*) is often done by a separate team. The work is hard but the language requirements are nil. The majority of vacancies is in France, though the major companies employ people from Austria to Denmark.

Successful couriers make the job look easy, but it does demand a lot of hard work and patience. Occasionally it is very hard to keep up the happy, smiling, never-ruffled courier look, but most seem to end up enjoying the job since it provides accommodation, a guaranteed weekly wage and the chance to work with like-minded people.

The big companies interview hundreds of candidates and have filled most posts by the end of January. But there is a high dropout rate and vacancies are filled from a reserve list, so it is worth ringing around the companies later on for cancellations. Despite keen competition, anyone who has studied a European language and has an outgoing personality stands a good chance if he or she applies early and widely enough.

Many specialist tour companies employ leaders for their clients (children and/or adults) who want a walking, cycling, watersports holiday, etc. Any competent sailor, canoeist, diver, climber, rider, etc. should have no difficulty marketing their skills abroad. A list of special interest and activity tour operators (to whom people with specialist skills can apply) is available from AITO, the Association of Independent Tour Operators (33A St Margaret's Road, Twickenham TW1 1RG). In the US, consult the *Specialty Travel Index* (305 San Anselmo Ave, San Anselmo, CA 94960; www.specialtytravel.com); the directory is issued twice a year at a cost of $10 in the US, $22 abroad.

For people who are pursuing a career in travel and tourism, it would be worth looking at another Vacation-Work Publications title *Working in Tourism* (£11.95).

Agriculture

Farmers from Norway to Tasmania (with the notable exception of developing countries) are unable to bring in their harvests without assistance from outside their local community and often reward their itinerant labour force well. Finding out where harvesting jobs can be found is a matter of doing some research (for example in the book *Work Your Way Around the World*) and asking around for instance at hostels and the pubs frequented by farmers. Small-scale farmers are less inclined to publicise vacancies in a directory like this one than hoteliers, though this book contains details of interesting farm work schemes in Switzerland and Norway, and some large Danish and Dutch farms are listed.

The organic farming movement is a very useful source of agricultural contacts. Organic growers everywhere take on volunteers to help them minimise or abolish the use of chemicals and heavy machinery. Various co-ordinating bodies go under the name of WWOOF - World Wide Opportunities on Organic Farms. National WWOOF co-ordinators compile and sell a worklist of their member farmers willing to provide free room and board to volunteers who help out and who are genuinely interested in furthering the aims of the organic movement. Each national group has its own aims, system, fees and rules but most expect applicants to have gained some experience on an organic farm in their own country first. WWOOF is an exchange: in return for your help on organic farms, gardens and homesteads, you receive meals, a place to sleep and a practical insight into organic growing. (If the topic arises at immigration, avoid the word 'working'; it is preferable to present yourself as a student of organic farming organising an educational farm visit or a cultural exchange.)

WWOOF has a global website www.wwoof.org with links to the national offices in the countries that have a WWOOF co-ordinator. WWOOF organisations exist in Ireland, Denmark, Finland, Norway, Germany, Italy, Ivory

Coast, Sweden, Switzerland, Austria, Hungary, Australia, New Zealand, USA, Canada, Ghana and Togo. Individual farm listings in other countries, i.e. those with no national organisation, are known as WWOOF Independents. It is necessary to join WWOOF before you can obtain addresses of these properties.

If you are starting in Britain, send an s.a.e. to the UK branch of WWOOF (PO Box 2675, Lewes, Sussex BN7 1RB) who will send you a membership application form. Membership costs £15 per year and includes a subscription to their bi-monthly newsletter which contains small adverts for opportunities both in Britain and abroad.

Teaching English

There are areas of the world where the boom in English language learning seems to know no bounds, from Ecuador to Slovenia, Lithuania to Vietnam. In some private language institutes, being a native speaker and adopting a professional manner are sometimes sufficient qualifications to get a job. But for more stable teaching jobs in recognised language schools, you will have to sign a contract (minimum three months, usually nine) and have some kind of qualification which ranges from a university degree to a certificate in education with a specialisation in ELT (English Language Teaching is now the preferred label).

To fix up a job in advance, make use of the internet and check adverts in the Education section of the *Guardian* every Tuesday. In a few cases, a carefully crafted CV and enthusiastic personality are as important as EFL training and experience. There is also increasing scope for untrained but eager volunteers willing to pay an agency to place them in a language teaching situation abroad (for example, see entries for i-to-i and Teaching Abroad in the *Worldwide* chapter).

Native speaker teachers are nearly always employed to stimulate conversation rather than to teach grammar. Yet a basic knowledge of English grammar is a great asset when more advanced pupils ask awkward questions. The wages paid to English teachers are usually reasonable, and in developing countries are quite often well in excess of the average local wage. In return you may be asked to teach some fairly unsociable hours since most private English classes take place after working hours, and so schedules split between early morning and evening are commonplace.

Most language institutes operate throughout the academic year and close for the summer though some run summer courses or more commonly are affiliated with residential summer language camps where English and sports are taught to children and teenagers. These create jobs for monitors and counsellors as well as for EFL teachers. (See for example entries for A.C.L.E. Summer Camps in Italy chapter, Village Camps in the Worldwide chapter and APASS in the Poland chapter).

A good source of information about the whole topic of English teaching is the 2001 edition of *Teaching English Abroad* by Susan Griffith (Vacation-Work, £12.95).

Au Pairs, Nannies & Mothers' Helps

Young women and (increasingly) young men can arrange to live with a family, helping to look after the children in exchange for pocket money. The terms au pair, mother's help and nanny are often applied rather loosely, since all are primarily live-in jobs concerned with looking after children. Nannies may have some formal training and take full charge of the children. Mother's helps work full-time and undertake general housework and/or cooking as well as childcare. Au pairs are supposed to work fewer hours and are expected to learn a foreign language (except in the USA) while living with a family. The Council of Europe guidelines stipulate that au pairs should be aged 18-27 (though these limits are flexible), should be expected to work about five hours a day, five days per week plus a couple of evenings of babysitting, must be given a private room and full board, health insurance, opportunities to learn the language and weekly pocket money of £40 to £50 in most cases plus board and lodging.

A number of agencies both in the UK and in the destination countries are described in this book. After satisfying an agency that you are a suitable candidate for a live-in childcare position, you will have to wait until an acceptable match can be made with a family abroad. Make enquiries as early as possible, since there is a shortage of summer-only positions. In the first instance contact several agencies to compare terms and conditions. If your requirements are very specific as regards location or family circumstances, ring around some agencies and ask them to be blunt about their chances of being able to fix you up with what you want. In the UK agencies are permitted to charge a fee of up to £40 plus VAT only after a placement has been verified.

The advantage of a summer placement is that the au pair will accompany the family to their holiday destination at the seaside or in the mountains; the disadvantage is that the children will be out of school and therefore potentially a full-time responsibility. Most language classes close for the summer so au pairs are unlikely to be able to attend formal lessons.

Anyone interested in finding out about all aspects of live-in childcare should consult *The Au Pair & Nanny's Guide to Working Abroad* (Vacation-Work, £11.95).

Volunteering

Charities and aid organisations offer a range of structured and unstructured voluntary opportunities around the world. For example, enterprising summer workers have participated in interesting projects from helping a local native settlement to build a community centre in Arctic Canada, to working with hill tribes in the state of Haryana in northern India.

Every year the international workcamps movement mobilises thousands of volunteers from many countries to join a programme of conflict resolution and community development. As well as providing volunteers with the means to live cheaply for two to four weeks in a foreign country, workcamps enable unskilled volunteers to become involved in what is usually useful work for the community (e.g. buildiing footpaths, working with disabled people), to meet people from many different backgrounds and to increase their awareness of other lifestyles and social problems.

When starting your research for a longer stint abroad as a volunteer, it is important to maintain realistic expectations. Ideally, your research should begin well in advance of your intended departure so that applications can be lodged, sponsorship money raised, language courses and other preparatory courses attended, and so on. When you receive the literature or check the website of voluntary organisations, consider the tone as well as the content. For example, profit-making commercial companies that charge high fees for participating in their programs are more likely to produce glossy brochures that read almost like a tour operator's, whereas underfunded charities or small grassroots organisations with no publicity budget will probably duplicate their information on an ancient photocopier.

Many voluntary agencies require more than idle curiosity about a country; they require a strong wish to become involved in a specific project and in many cases an ideological commitment to a cause. Almost without exception, volunteers must be self-funding, which serves to deter all but the committed.

For anyone with a green conscience, numerous conservation organisations throughout the world welcome volunteers for short or long periods. Projects range from tree-planting to gibbon counting. Unfortunately the more glamorous projects such as helping to conserve a coral reef or accompanying scientific research expeditions into wild and woolly places charge volunteers a great deal of money for the privilege of helping.

For a specialist directory of opportunities, consult *Green Volunteers: The World Guide to Voluntary Work in Nature Conservation* published in Italy and distributed by Vacation Work Publications in Europe (£10.99 plus £1.50 postage). Related titles from the same publisher are *Working with the Environment* and *Working with Animals*. Also look at the website for the Ecovolunteer Programme of wildlife and conservation projects worldwide (www.ecovolunteer.org.uk).

Several organisations assist scientific expeditions by supplying fee-paying volunteers. For details of scientific expedition organisations which use self-financing volunteers, see entries for Coral Cay Conservation, Earthwatch and Trekforce among others in the Worldwide chapter.

Maximise Your Chances

Plan of Attack
Remember that most employers prefer to take on a person to work for the whole of the season rather than several people to work for shorter periods. If you are able to work for longer than the minimum period quoted, let the employer know at an early stage since this is often a deciding factor.

2. Most employers like to make their staff arrangements in good time so try to apply early, but not earlier than the date mentioned in the job details or later than the closing date for applications, if given. Some of the biggest employers may maintain reserve lists to cover late staff cancellations, so it might pay off to apply after the deadline, but don't be disappointed if you receive no reply.

3. Apply as widely as possible. If more than one job seems to be suitable or appeals to you, apply for all of them. Make sure that you are qualified for the position for which you are applying. Check minimum age and work period requirements and any special qualifications needed, particularly if a good knowledge of another language is called for. If there is any shortfall, emphasise other skills and qualifications that may be useful.

4. Compose a short formal letter, explaining which position interests you, when you are available and why you think you are suitable. If possible produce this letter on a computer; if not, take care to make it legible. Always mention that the job has been seen in this book: employers can be wary as to the origin of information about themselves but most of them have a long-standing and trusting relationship with Vacation Work and its publications.

5. Try to address the potential employer in his or her language. It is not only polite to do so, but there is a possibility that he or she is unable to speak English.

6. Enclose with your letter a standard *Curriculum Vitae* (CV or resumé) on a single A4 sheet covering the following points and any other details you consider relevant:

Personal details (name, address, nationality, age, date of birth, marital status).
Previous work experience, especially of similar type of work.
Special qualifications, especially when they have some relevance to the job in question, e.g. canoe instructor's certificate, typing speeds or fluency in another language.
Education (brief details of type of education, examinations passed)

7. Enclose a small recent passport-sized photo of yourself. (This may not be necessary when applying to a voluntary organisation.)

8. Employers are more likely to reply promptly if you enclose an international reply coupon, available at any post office. This will not guarantee a reply, but it will make one more likely.

9. If there is no reply from the employer within a reasonable period of time (say two weeks), it may be advisable to follow up the written application with a telephone call or an e-mail. The employer may be impressed by your initiative and perseverance if it is matched by enthusiasm and politeness. Otherwise, he/she may feel hassled. In a few cases it is expected that applicants should make themselves available for an interview or visit the employer in person. Where this is the case, the applicant is likely to find more success if he can back up claims of suitability with a written CV and references.

10. When a job is offered to you, check details of wages, hours and other conditions of work with the employer. Do not be afraid to negotiate; you are always entitled to ask whether or not different terms are possible.

12. Please note that wages are normally quoted in sterling but will usually be paid in foreign currency: exchange rates may vary. The details given in the Directory have been supplied by the employer and will normally be correct, but it is wise to obtain written confirmation of them before taking up the position. You should insist that you receive a contract of employment before you set off for your job if the journey involves any great expense, or if the employer seems at all vague about the details of the work you will do.

13. When you are offered a job, please confirm acceptance or otherwise as quickly as possible. Do not accept more than one job. If you need to juggle possible outcomes, keep the prospective employers informed of your intentions and the expected timescale. If plans change and you do not want to take up a job you have already accepted, it is only fair to let the employer know immediately.

14. If you are offered more than one job, decide quickly which one you prefer and inform both employers of your decision as promptly as possible.

15. Those who contact employers and apply for positions via e-mail should bear in mind that small businesses will not necessarily welcome e-mails with CVs added as large attachments. It will always come across as polite to e-mail and ask in advance as this also gives an opportunity to find out what word-processing software they use. A CV in an unreadable electronic format is worse than useless. You should also note that certain programmes are susceptible to viruses so make sure that your machine is clean before endeavouring to seek employment via cyberspace; a hotel is highly unlikely to employ an applicant who has disabled their computer system!

The Internet

An increasing number of job vacancies (summer or permanent) is now available on the internet. Yet the plethora of resources can be bewildering and not infrequently disappointing. Because many sites are in their infancy, they often seem to promise more than they can deliver and you may find that the number and range of jobs posted fall short of the claims. No employer looking for two waitresses and a bellhop for the summer wants to publicise this fact through cyberspace since they are bound to be inundated with applications from Merseyside to Mongolia. The internet as a job-finding tool works best for those with specific experience and skills, for example people looking for TEFL jobs abroad.

Still, internet surfers will find a host of potentially useful links on the web. Many websites promise to provide free on-line recruitment services for travellers. These include www.hotrecruit.co.uk, Jobs Abroad Bulletin (www.payaway. co.uk), www.coolworks.com (recommended for seasonal work in the North American tourist industry), www.anyworkanywhere.com, www.summerjobseeker. com, ww.travelrecruit.com, www.jobmonkey.com and so on. Elsewhere on the web, committed individuals around the world manage non-commercial sites on everything from kibbutzim to bar-tending. The Vacation-Work website (www.vacationwork.co.uk) has a regularly updated section listing job vacancies for travellers both in Britain and abroad.

A Europe-wide employment service called *EURES* (EURopean Employment Service) operates as a network of about 450 EuroAdvisers who can access a database of jobs within Europe. Most vacancies are long-term though a few are for shorter periods. Language skills are almost always a requirement. Ask at your local Jobcentre how to contact your nearest EuroAdviser. The websites http://europa.eu.int/jobs/eures and http://eu.int/europedirect have extensive information for Euro-jobseekers.

BEFORE YOU GO: Essential Preparation

Travel

Student travellers can take advantage of a comprehensive range of special discounts both at home and abroad which enable them to go almost anywhere in the world on the cheap. To qualify for a range of discounts on train, plane and bus fares, on selected accommodation, admission to museums, etc., you need an International Student Identity Card (ISIC) which is recognised all over the world. The card is obtainable from local student travel offices for £6 or by post for £6.50 from ISIC Mail Order, PO Box 48, Horndean, Waterlooville, Hants. PO8 0FJ. The ISIC card is valid for 16 months from September 1st. All full-time students are eligible (though some flight carriers do not offer discounts to students over the age of 31); applications should include proof of student status, a passport photo, full name, date of birth, nationality, address and a cheque or postal order.

Americans can obtain an International Student Identity Card at scores of student travel outlets throughout the country. The two major agencies in the field are Council Travel (1-800-2COUNCIL; www.counciltravel.com) and STA Travel (1-800-781-4040; www.sta-travel.com). To find your nearest location use their websites or the telephone directory. The ISIC fee of $22 comes with a basic accident/sickness insurance package. An alternative card is the International Student Exchange Identity Card available from ISE Cards, 5010 East Shea Blvd, A-104, Scottsdale, AZ 85254 (1-800-255-8000; www.isecard.com) at a cost of

$25. They also sell student discount flights.

Valuable discounts are also available for air travel. Student and youth discount flights are operated by the major student travel organisations under the umbrella of the Student Air Travel Association. Most of the flights are open to ISIC card holders under 30 (some have different age restrictions) together with their spouses and dependent children travelling on the same flight or to young persons with a valid EURO<26 or Go 25 card.

Specialist youth and student travel agencies are an excellent source of information for just about every kind of discount. Staff are often themselves seasoned travellers and can be a mine of information on budget travel in foreign countries. But check out your High Street, local independent travel agent and no-frills airlines as well to compare prices before making a final decision.

The two leading youth and budget travel specialists in the UK are STA Travel and usit-Campus Travel, both of which can organise flexible deals, domestic flights, overland transport, accommodation and tours. Both publish brochures-cum-magazines which survey travel options for students; pick up STA's *The Guide* and usit-Campus's *Hit the Ground*. STA (www.statravel.co.uk; 0870 160 6070) is a major international travel agency with 250 branches worldwide. Usit Campus (www.usitcampus.co.uk; 0870 240 1010) is Britain's largest student and youth travel specialist with 49 branches in high streets, at universities and in YHA Adventure Shops. As well as worldwide airfares, they both sell discounted rail and coach tickets, budget accommodation and insurance and many other packaged products.

In America, in addition to the major student travel agencies Council Travel and

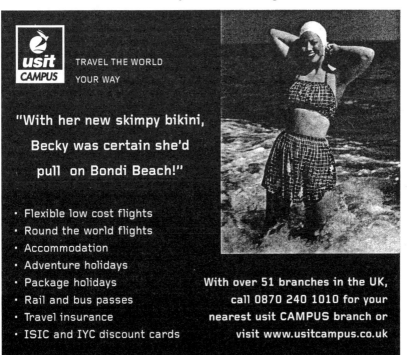

STA Travel mentioned above in the context of student cards, discount tickets are available online on a standby basis from agencies like Air-Tech at 588 Broadway, Suite 204, New York, NY 10012 (212-219-7000; www.airtech.com), Air Treks (442 Post St, Suite 400, San Francisco, CA 94102; 1-800-350-0612; www.AirTreks.com) and Air-hitch (1-800-326-2009; www.airhitch.org). The cheapest fares from the US are available to people who are flexible about departure dates and destinations; the passenger chooses a block of possible dates (up to a five-day 'window') and preferred destinations. The company then tries to match these requirements with empty airline seats being released at knock-down prices.

From the UK to Europe it is often cheaper to fly on one of the new no-frills ticketless airlines shuttling between Stansted or Luton and many European destinations than it is by rail or bus. Note that quoted prices do not include taxes which can add up to £30 to the fare. These airlines do not take bookings via travel agents so it is necessary to contact them directly:

Buzz – 0870-240 7070; www.buzzaway.com. Stansted to Berlin, Bordeaux, Geneva, Helsinki, La Rochelle, Milan, Vienna and a number of others.

Easyjet – 0870-600 0000; www.easyjet.com. If you book over the internet, you can save £5 per return flight. Flies from Luton to Scotland, Nice, Barcelona, Amsterdam, Madrid, Malaga, Palma de Mallorca, Athens, Geneva and Zurich.

GO – 08456-054321; www.go-fly.com. The British Airways-linked airline flies from Stansted to Rome, Milan, Venice, Copenhagen, Lisbon, Munich, Madrid, Bilbao, etc.

Ryanair – 0870-333 1231; www.ryanair.com. To Irish airports and dozens of European cities. Amazing bargains on the internet such as return fares from £10.

Virgin Express – 020-7744 0004; www.virgin-express.com. From Gatwick or Heathrow to Shannon, Brussels, Copenhagen, Barcelona, Madrid, Malaga, Milan, Nice and Rome, often with a layover in Brussels.

Cheap rail travel is dependent chiefly upon age and is generally open to everyone under the age of 26. Inter-Rail is available on a zonal basis - from £129 for a 22-day 1 zone pass to £229 for a month long all-zones pass covering all 28 countries on the network as well as entitling you to discounts on Eurostar and cross-Channel travel. Inter-Rail passes are available from youth travel agencies and from Rail Europe (179 Piccadilly, London W1V 0BA; 08705 848848; www.raileurope.co.uk).

Europe's largest scheduled coach operator *Eurolines* (4 Cardiff Road, Luton, Bedfordshire LU1 1PP; 0990 143219/ www.eurolines.co.uk) offers a 10% discount to passengers under 26. It pays to compare prices carefully between coach and rail because the differences are sometimes less than you might expect.

One of the most interesting revolutions in independent and youth travel has been the explosion of backpackers' bus services which are hop-on hop-off coach services following prescribed routes. These can be found in New Zealand, Australia, USA, Canada, South Africa and Russia as well as on the continent and in Britain. For example a month long coach pass on *Busabout Europe* (258 Vauxhall Bridge Road, London SW1V 1BS; 020-7950 1661/ www.busabout.com) costs £279 for those under 26. Alternatively you can buy a Flexi-pass; for example 15 days of travel in two months costs £329. In North America trips run by *Green Tortoise* (494 Broadway, San Francisco, California 94133; 800-867-8647; www.greentortoise.com) use vehicles converted to sleep about 35 people and make interesting detours and stopovers.

What to Pack

Even if you are travelling directly to your place of work, don't load yourself down with excess baggage. Most people who go abroad for a summer job want to do at least some independent travelling when their job ends and will find themselves seriously hampered if they are carrying around a 60 pound rucksack. When you're buying a backpack/rucksack in a shop try to place a significant weight in it so you can feel how comfortable it might be to carry on your back, otherwise you'll be misled by lifting something usually filled with foam.

While aiming to travel as lightly as possible you should consider the advantage of taking certain extra pieces of equipment. For example a Swiss army knife is often invaluable (if only for its corkscrew) and a comfortable pair of shoes is essential since most summer jobs will involve long hours on your feet whether in a hotel dining room or in a farmer's field. Ideally, talk to someone who has done the job before who might recommend an obscure piece of equipment you'd never think of, for example a pair of fingerless gloves for cold-weather fruit-picking or dental floss which can be used as strong twine for mending backpacks, hanging up laundry, etc.

You might allow yourself the odd lightweight luxury, such as a favourite cassette tape, a short-wave radio or a jar of peanut butter. You can always post some belongings on ahead, with the employer's permission. Try to leave at home anything of either monetary or sentimental value.

Good maps and guides always enhance one's enjoyment of a trip. If you are in London, visit the famous map shop *Edward Stanford Ltd.* (12-14 Long Acre, Covent Garden, WC2E 9LP; 020-7836 1321) and *Daunt Books for Travellers* (83 Marylebone High Street, W1M 4DE; 020-7224 2295). *The Map Shop* (15 High St, Upton-on-Severn, Worcestershire WR8 0HJ; 01684 593146/ themapshop@ btinternet.com) does an extensive mail order business and will send you the relevant catalogue. Two other specialists are the Inverness-based *Traveller's Companion* (www.travellerscompanion.co.uk) and *Maps Worldwide*, PO Box 1555, Melksham, Wilts. SN12 6XJ (01225 707004/ www.mapsworldwide. co.uk). There are dozens of travel specialists throughout North America, including the *Complete Traveller Bookstore* (199 Madison Ave, New York, NY 10016; 212-685-9007/fax 212-481-3253/ completetraveller@ worldnet.att.net) which also issues a free mail-order catalogue and, in Canada, *Wanderlust* (1929 West 4th Avenue, Kitsilano, Vancouver, BC, V6J 1M7; 604-739-2182/fax 604-733-9364/ wanderlust@uniserve.com).

Visas and Red Tape

Up-to-date visa information is available from national consulates in London/ Washington or on the internet. For example the visa agency Thames Consular Services in London (www.thamesconsular.com) allows you to search visa requirements and costs for individual countries. The health consultancy *MASTA* now operates a Visa and Passport line charged at £1 a minute (0906 5 501100) providing accurate and comprehensive visa information for all destinations.

As mentioned earlier, the free reciprocity of labour within the European Union means that the red tape has been greatly simplified for European nationals wanting to work in Europe. The standard situation among all EU countries (plus Norway and Iceland which belong to the European Economic Area or EEA) is that nationals of any EU state have the right to look for work in another member state for up to three months. At the end of that period they should apply to the police or the local authority for a residence permit, showing their passport and job contract.

Outside Europe, obtaining permission to work is next to impossible for short periods unless you are participating in an approved exchange programme where the red tape is taken care of by a sponsoring organisation. The same applies to non-European students looking for seasonal jobs in Europe. Established organisations which run work abroad programmes are invaluable for guiding students and other young people through the red tape problems and for providing a soft landing for first time travellers.

For example *BUNAC* (16 Bowling Green Lane, London EC1R 0BD; 92907-251-3472) is a student club that helps British students to work abroad while BUNAC USA (PO Box 430, Southbury, CT06488; www.bunac.org) assists a large number of Americans to work in Britain for up six months and in the Antipodes. BUNAC in the UK has a choice of programmes in the United States, Canada, Australia, New Zealand, South Africa and Ghana, and in all cases assists participants to obtain the appropriate short-term working visas. In some programmes, participants have jobs arranged for them, for instance as counsellors or domestic staff at American children's summer camps; in others, it is up to individuals to find their own summer jobs once they arrive at their destination.

Council Exchanges (www.councilexchanges.org.uk) oversees work abroad programmes for Britons in the USA, Canada, Australia, Japan and China (52 Poland St, London W1F 7AB; 020-7478 2020. Council in New York does likewise for American students who want to work in Ireland, France, Germany, Canada, Australia, New Zealand, Japan or China: see their entry under the heading *Other Employment Abroad* in the *Worldwide* chapter. Many other youth exchange organisations and commercial agencies offer packages which help students to arrange work or volunteer positions abroad. For example *Camp America* and *Camp Counselors USA* are major recruitment organisations which arrange for thousands of young people to work in the US mostly on summer camps (see chapter on the USA). Other agencies specialise in placing young people (both women and men) in families as au pairs, as voluntary English teachers or in a range of other capacities.

Accommodation
Employers who regularly employ foreign young people will either provide accommodation or help their staff to arrange lodgings locally. The majority of jobs listed in this book come with accommodation. Always find out ahead of time what the deal is: how much do you lose from your wages to cover accommodation? What facilities (especially for self-catering) are provided? How close to your place of work is it? Will there be extra costs for food, utilities, etc.? Are staff allowed to move out if they find more congenial or cheaper accommodation? Much of the accommodation provided by employers for staff is very basic indeed and you should be prepared for something a lot more rustic than you are used to at home or at university. The only job which might provide more luxurious accommodation is as an au pair or any live-in job where you live in the employer's own house which may come with its own drawbacks.

If accommodation is not provided with the job, try to arrange something in advance, and certainly for the first couple of nights. If necessary make the journey to your destination several days early to fix up a suitable room. In cities, try universities which might rent out student accommodation which has been vacated for the summer or notice boards may include details of housing. In holiday resorts, accommodation may be at a premium and you will have to use your ingenuity to find something you can afford.

Membership of the *Youth Hostels Association* costs £12 if you're over 18, £6 if you're not; you can join at any YHA hostel or shop or at their HQ (Membership Department, Trevelyan House, 8 St. Stephen's Hill, St. Albans, Herts. AL1 2DY; 0870 870 8808; www.yha.org.uk). Seasonal demand abroad can be high, so it is always preferable to book in advance if you know your itinerary. You can pre-book beds over the internet on www.iyhf.org or through individual hostels and national offices listed in the *Hostelling International Guides*: Volume I covers Europe and the Mediterranean, Volume II covers the rest of the world. They can be ordered by ringing Customer Services on the above number and cost £8.50 each including postage.

Hostels of Europe and Hostels of America offer membership to a network of more than 500 Hostels on the best-travelled routes. Members get discounts of 5%-15% on accommodation, internet access, tours, etc. Information and on-line bookings can be made through www.hostels.net which is a searchable database of independent hostels in Europe, America and Downunder. A one-year membership costs £10 (15 Euros). Hostels worldwide employ young people for a variety of jobs during the summer. In exchange for their labour, staff normally receive free board and lodging and some pocket money. The wardens or managers of individual hostels normally recruit their own staff.

Money

The average budget of a travelling student is about £25 a day though many survive on half that. Whatever the size of your travelling fund, you should give some thought to how and in what form to carry your money. Travellers' cheques are much safer than cash, though they cost an extra 1% and banks able to encash them are not always near to hand. The most universally recognised brands are American Express, Thomas Cook and Visa. (Note that Thomas Cook travellers' cheques and foreign currency are sold free of commission on their website www.thomascook.co.uk.) It is advisable also to keep a small amount of cash. The easiest way to look up the exchange rate of any world currency is to check on the internet (e.g. www.xe.net/ucc or www.oanda.com) or to look at the Monday edition of the *Financial Times.*

Euro notes and coins will be introduced across most of Europe from January 2002. The countries that are replacing their currencies with the Euro are Austria, Belgium, Finland, France, Germany, Greece, Ireland, Italy, Luxembourg, the Netherlands, Portugal and Spain. National currency notes and coins will be withdrawn in these countries and replaced by the Euro. Please note that most wages etc in this book are quoted in English pounds sterling: exchange rates can fluctuate, so you are always advised to covert wages quoted at the current rate before accepting a job.

Ask your bank for a list of cash machines in the countries you intend to visit. Otherwise you can find these listed at www.mastercard.com or www.visaholiday-card.com. Theft takes many forms, from the highly trained gangs of gypsy children who artfully pick pockets in European railway stations to more violent attacks on the streets of American cities. Risks can be reduced by carrying your wealth in several places including a comfortable money belt worn inside your clothing, steering clear of seedy or crowded areas, remaining particularly alert in railway stations and moderating your intake of alcohol. If you are robbed, you must obtain a police report (often for a fee) to stand any chance of recouping part of your loss from your insurer (assuming the loss of cash is covered in your policy) or from your travellers' cheque company. Always keep a separate record of the cheque numbers you are carrying, so you will know instantly the numbers of the ones that have been taken.

If you do end up in dire financial straits and do not have a credit card, you should contact someone at home who is in a position to send money. You may contact your bank back home and ask them to wire money to you, often through the Swift service. This can only be done through a bank in the town you're in –

something you have to arrange with your own bank, so you know where to pick the money up. Sample charges might be £15-£20 though high street banks.

Western Union offers an international money transfer service whereby cash deposited at one branch can be withdrawn by you from any other branch or agency, which your benefactor need not specify. Western Union agents – there are 90,000 of them in nearly 200 countries – come in all shapes and sizes (e.g. travel agencies, stationers, chemists). The person sending money to you simply turns up at a Western Union counter, hands over the desired sum plus the fee, which is £8 for up to £25 transferred, £21 for £100-£200, £37 for £500 and so on. For an extra £7 your benefactor can do this over the phone with a credit card. In the UK, ring 0800 833833 for further details, a list of outlets and a complete rate schedule.

Thomas Cook, American Express and the Post Office offer a similar service called Moneygram. Cash deposited at one of their foreign exchange counters is available within ten minutes at the named destination or can be collected up to 45 days later. The fee for sending £500 (for example) is £33. Ring 0800 897198 for details.

Insurance and Health

The National Health Service ceases to cover British nationals once they leave the United Kingdom. If you are a national of the European Economic Area (UK, Ireland, Netherlands, Belgium, Liechtenstein, Luxembourg, Denmark, Germany, France, Italy, Spain, Portugal, Greece, Austria, Finland, Sweden, Norway and Iceland) and will be working in another EEA country, you will be covered by the European Community Social Security Regulations. Advice and the leaflet SA29 *Your Social Security Insurance, Benefits and Health Care Rights in the European Community* may be obtained free of charge from the Contributions Agency, International Services, Department of Social Security, Longbenton, Newcastle-upon-Tyne NE98 1ZZ (08459-154811/fax 08459-157800).

Those intending to work abroad can obtain further details by contacting the Contributions Agency with their national insurance number, name and address of their employer and their start date for work. Leaflet T6 (*Health Advice for Travellers*) available from post offices contains an application form to obtain form E111 (called the 'E-one-eleven') which is a certificate of entitlement to medical treatment in the EEA. The E-111 is not issued to EEA nationals who are going to work in another member country for less than 12 months and who continue to pay UK National Insurance contributions. Form E128 is now issued which gives entitlement to a full range of health care. This form also applies to students staying temporarily in another EEA country as part of their studies.

When British nationals begin work abroad they may be required to pay foreign social security contributions in order to be eligible for health cover. Leaflet T6 gives details of the special health agreements that the United Kingdom has with non-EU countries including Australia, the Channel Islands, Malta, New Zealand and several Eastern European countries which enable visitors to use their health services. In countries outside the EEA and not listed in leaflet T6 British citizens can use the public health service only if they are contributing to its Social Security scheme: for example, in Switzerland they must be paid-up members of a Swiss sickness insurance fund.

Foreign health services rarely offer as comprehensive a free service as the NHS does; while some offer free treatment, others will only subsidise the cost. The cost of bringing a person back to the UK in the case of illness or death is never covered under the reciprocal arrangements so it is wise to purchase private insurance. Ordinary travel insurance policies cover only those risks that a holidaymaker can expect to face and will not cover work-related injuries such as treating backs damaged while grape-picking, or burns caused by an overboiling goulash in a restaurant kitchen.

The following companies should be able to arrange insurance cover for most people going to work abroad, as long as they are advised of the exact nature of the physical/manual job to be undertaken:

Extrasure Travel Insurance Ltd, 16 St. Helen's Place, London EC3A 6DF (tel 020-7480 6871; fax 020-7480 6189). Specialist in travel policies; can arrange insurance for those working abroad for short or long periods (up to 12 months).

The Travel Insurance Agency, Suite 2, Percy Mews, 775B High Road, North Finchley, London N12 8JY (tel 020-8446 5414; fax 020-8446 5417; www.travelinsurers.com). Policies only for travellers, including those working abroad.

Worldwide Travel Insurance Services Ltd, The Business Centre, 1 Commercial Road, Paddock Wood, Tonbridge, Kent TN12 6YT (tel 01892-833338; fax 01892-837744; e-mail sales@worldwideinsure.com; www.worldwideinsure.com). Comprehensive policies for most work abroad from 5 days to 24 months. Manual labour cover can be purchased from overseas for an additional premium.

Endsleigh Insurance, Endsleigh House, Cheltenham, Glos GL50 3NR (01282-451166; 3NR; www.endsleigh.co.uk). Offices in most university towns. Twelve months of cover in Europe costs from £215, worldwide £338 (£299 and £485 respectively for a higher level of cover).

If you are planning to include developing countries on your itinerary, you will want to take the necessary health precautions, though this won't be cheap unless you are able to have your injections at your local NHS surgery where most injections are free or given for a minimal charge. Malaria poses an increasing danger and expert advice should be sought about which medications to take for the specific parts of the world you intend to visit.

Tap water is unsafe to drink in many parts of the world so it will be necessary to give some thought as to the method of water purification you will use (filtering, boiling or chemical additives). Remember that water used to wash vegetables, brush teeth or make ice cubes is also potentially risky. Tap water throughout Western Europe is safe to drink.

MASTA (Medical Advisory Service for Travellers Abroad) at the London School of Hygiene and Tropical Medicine, Keppel St, London WC1E 7HT; www.masta.org) maintains an up-to-date database on travellers' diseases and their prevention. You can ring their interactive Travellers' Health Line on 0906 822 4100 with your destinations (up to six countries) and they will send you a basic health brief by return, for the price of the telephone call (60p per minute).

Increasingly, people are seeking advice via the internet; check for example www.fitfortravel.scot.nhs.uk; www.tmb.ie and www.travelhealth.co.uk. The BBC's Health Travel Site www.bbc.co.uk/health/travel is a solid source of information about travel health ranging from tummy trouble to water quality to snake bites.

Many women are reluctant to travel alone though thousands do so with great pleasure. Sensible precautions include behaving with modesty and trusting your instincts about potentially suspect characters and situations. General advice on minimising the risks of independent travel is contained in the book *World Wise – Your Passport to Safer Travel* published by Thomas Cook in association with the Suzy Lamplugh Trust and the Foreign Office (www.suzylamplugh.org/worldwise; £6.95 plus £1 postage). Arguably its advice is over-cautious, advising travellers never to hitch-hike, ride a motorbike or accept an invitation to a private house. Travellers will have to decide for themselves when to follow this advice and when to ignore it.

Worldwide

Agricultural Work

AGRIVENTURE/IAEA: YFC Centre, NAC, Stoneleigh Park, Kenilworth, Warwickshire CV8 2LG (tel 02476-696578; fax 02476-696684; e-mail uk@agriventure.com; www.agriventure.com).

AgriVenture is run by the International Agricultural Exchange Association and arranges working exchanges to Australia, New Zealand, Canada, USA and Japan on farming or horticultural enterprises. Applicants must be aged 18-30, have no dependants, be British passport holders, have a full driving licence and good practical experience in agriculture/horticulture or in the home. Programmes depart spring to late summer for Australia and NZ for a minimum of 6^1/2 months and in February/March/April to USA and Canada. Wages are paid in accordance with local rates.

Programme costs start at £1,790 and include: return flights, full work insurance, work permits, job placement, departure information meeting, seminar in host country and full emergency back-up. For a free brochure freephone 0800-7832186 or e-mail your name and address.

Australian citizens can apply to: AgriVenture/IAEA, Suite 203, Level 2, 65 York Street, Sydney 2000 (tel 02-92995300; e-mail australia@agriventure.com).

New Zealand citizens can apply to: AgriVenture/IAEA, PO Box 20-113,Christchurch (tel 03-359 0407; e-mail nz@agriventure.com).

Canadian citizens can apply to: AgriVenture/IAEA, 105, 7710 5 Street SE, Calgary, Alberta, T2H 2L9 (tel 403-255 7799; e-mail canada@agriventure.com).

Citizens from Austria, Belgium, Czech Republic, Denmark, Finland, France, Germany, Iceland, Luxembourg, Netherlands, Norway, Sweden, and Switzerland can apply to: AgriVenture/IAEA, Lerchenbeorg Gods, 4400 Kalundborg, Denmark (tel +45 59 51 15 25; fax +45 59 51 05 07; e-mail europe@agriventure.com).

INTERNATIONAL FARM EXPERIENCE PROGRAMME: YFC Centre, National Agricultural Centre, Stoneleigh Park, Warwickshire CV8 2LG (tel 02476-857211; fax 02476-857229; e-mail ifep@nfyfc.org.uk).

IFEP is an international discovery programme open to anyone aged 18-30 with relevant agricultural experience in Britain and Eire. It offers a range of placements on farms in Europe from 3-6 months and in Australia, New Zealand, the USA, Canada and South Africa from 6-12 months. Placements may be connected with livestock production, soft and top fruit, equestrian, rural tourism, environmental and organic farms or tree and pot plant nurseries.

Assistance is given with all arrangements; travel, visas, insurance, accommodation, a guaranteed wage and in-country support. Language courses and university study may be arranged if relevant.

Candidates must pay a registration fee, their air fare and insurance and an additional seminar fee in some countries. For more details *contact* the above address.

WWOOF (Worldwide Opportunities on Organic Farms)

WWOOF exists to give people the opportunity of gaining first hand experience of organic farming and gardening in return for spending a weekend or longer working on a farm. Since WWOOF began in England in 1971, similar schemes have developed in other countries around the world. Each national group has its own aims, system, fees and rules. They are all similar in that they offer volunteers the chance to learn in a practical way the growing methods of their host. Each group will supply a worklist booklet to members from which volunteers can choose a farm. Most national organisations expect applicants to have gained experience on an organic farm in their own country before they help place them abroad. Where countries do not have a national WWOOF organisation, individual hosts are listed with WWOOF Independents.

For further information applicants should contact WWOOF (UK) (c/o Fran Whittle, P.O. Box 2675, Lewes, Sussex BN7 1RB), and WWOOF Independents (www.wwoof.org) for information on overseas projects and application forms. Please send an SAE/International Reply Coupon. For WWOOF information in the USA, see that chapter, or contact The New England Small Farm Institute, 275 Jackson St, Belchertown, MA 01007, USA (tel 413-323-4531; fax 413-323-9594; e-mail info@smallfarm.org; www.smallfarm.org). Details of other schemes in the USA can also be found in the publication *Educational and Training Opportunities in Sustainable Agriculture* available free from the Alternative Farming Systems Information Center, USDA, National Agricultural Library, Room 132, 10301 Baltimore Avenue, Beltsville MD 20705-2351, USA (tel 301-504-6559; fax 301-504-6927; e-mail: afsic@nal.usda.gov; www.nal.usda.gov).

WWOOF Australia and WWOOF Independents will shortly produce a combined list, (costing £10) giving details of over 600 farms needing help in over 50 countries without their own WWOOF groups of their own around the world: for details write to WWOOF (Australia), Buchan, Victoria 3885, Australia. Details of some individual national WWOOF groups can be found in the country chapters below. WWOOF Australia's own *Aussy Listings* costs £17 single/£18 couple and has over 1200 entries. (tel +61-3-5155 0218; fax +61-3-5155 0342; e-mail: wwoof@net-tech.com.au; www.wwoof.com.au).

Hotel Work and Catering

CHOICE HOTELS EUROPE: 112-114 Station Road, Edgware, HA8 7BJ (tel 020-8233 2001; fax 020-8233 2080; e-mail FBernardon@ChoiceHotelsEurope. com). Owns, manages and franchises over 400 hotels in 13 European countries. Positions are primarily for the UK, but guidance and advice can be given for other countries.

Receptionists, Chefs, Waiter/Waitresses, Bar Persons. Minimum period of work 6 months, 1 year in front office. 39 hours per week spread over 5 days. Salary in accordance with minimum wages regulations. Applications are considered all year round. Applicants should have a smart appearance, pleasant customer oriented personality and be over 18 years old. Priority given to those with hotel qualifications and/or experience and good English or French (fluent for front office). *Applications* in writing to Francoise Bernardon, Human Resources Officer, at the address above.

FIRST CHOICE SKI, LAKES & MOUNTAINS: Olivier House, 18 Marine Parade, Brighton, BN2 1TL (tel 0870-900300; fax 01273-600486; e-mail skijobs@firstchoice.co.uk). As well as being a Tour operator First Choice has a Hotels Divison which leases and runs 25 Clubhotels and 55 Chalets in European ski lakes and mountain resorts.

Hotel Managers/Assistant Managers, Chefs (all grades), **Chalet Cooks, General Assistants,** (500 in all). A job with First Choice provides an opportunity to travel, meet and make new friends, improve language skills and gain experience. Staff are encouraged to expand their knowledge of the Catering and Hospitality industry, and many current Hotel Managers have been bar or kitchen staff in previous seasons. An attractive package including travel to and from the resort, medical insurance, personal belongings insurance, food and accommodation is offered.

Applicants must have a National Insurance number and either EU passport or relevant EU work visa/permit. For more information *please send a SAE* to Overseas Human Resources Dept, First Choice Ski Lake & Mountains Division at the above address.

HOBO HOLIDAYS LTD: 1 Port Hill, Hertford, SG14 1PJ (tel 01992-550616; fax 01992-303434). Small, friendly company operating a Dutch barge as a cruising hotel in Europe and England. Passengers come from all over the world. Staff needed for cruising in Holland, Belgium, and France from April to September 2002.

Cook to live aboard and prepare meals for crew and up to 8 guests. Remuneration £140 per week plus tips.

Host/Hostess to live aboard and provide full-time general care of guests, serve meals, wash up, clean cabins and help Captain with sailing barge (mooring etc.). Wages £120 per week plus tips.

Car Driver to ferry passengers from airports etc. and take them on tours. Minimum age 25. £120 per week plus tips.

All positions come with full board and accommodation provided. Non-smokers preferred. *Applications to* Sheila Purdue, Director, at the above address.

OPENWIDE INTERNATIONAL LTD.: 7 Westmoreland House, Cumberland Park, London NW10 6RE (Tel 020-8962 3400; fax 020-8962 3440; www.openwideinternational.com). Openwide International is Europe's largest independent supplier of entertainers and all-round personalities to the mainstream leisure and tourism industry. Working with Openwide is an excellent way to develop professional skills and over 100 people are recruited annually to work in hotels.

Entertainers with bright, enthusiastic personalities and excellent PR and communication skills to work in hotels in Spain, Cyprus, Greece, Balearics, Turkey and the Canaries. A knowledge of Spanish, German or French would be an advantage but not essential. All successful applicants will be given full training on the running of daytime and evening entertainment programmes.

Positions are available all year round; minimum period of work 6 months with salaries between £130 and £225 per week plus meals, accommodation and flight. Main season is May to November. All applicants are invited to send CVs and *applications to* the Overseas Recruitment Department at Openwide International and also visit their website.

SCOTT DUNN: 12 Noyna Rd, London, SW17 7PH (tel 020-8767 0202; fax 020-8767 2026; e-mail antonia@scottdunn.com). A small, very professional company, which provides beautiful villas and chalets in stunning locations all over Europe.

Chalet and Villa Chefs/Cooks (20) required to plan the menu and cook to a very high standard for the clients in their exclusive villas and chalets. Applicants must have completed a six month cooking course, or have extensive experience and flair. Must be organised and outgoing.

Chalet and Villa Hosts (20) required to assist the chef, look after the guests, supervise the local maid and maintain the villa/chalet. No formal qualifications necessary, but applicants must be outgoing, organised and good with people.

Nannies (20) Required to care for our younger guests. Must have a recognised childcare qualification, at least one year's childcare experience and be organised, confident and outgoing.

Board and accommodation are provided free of charge. Wages and hours to be discussed at interview. Work is available during the winter and summer season. Knowledge of French, Spanish, Italian or Portugese useful, but not mandatory.

For summer positions *apply* January 2002, or for winter positions apply from July.

TRAVELBOUND: First Choice Ski, Lakes and Mountains, Olivier House, 18 Marine Parade, Brighton, East Sussex BN2 1TL (tel 0870 900 3200; fax 01273-600486; e-mail skijobs@firstchoice.co.uk). Activity/educational tour operator to Austria and France (Alps and Normandy), member of AITO.

Summer Staff (over 250) including resort reps, chalet and hotel staff (Chefs, General Assistants, Kitchen/Night Porters). Full season in Austria and French Alps lasts May-September and in Normandy February-October. Flexible contract lengths available. Applications are processed in January through to July. Minimum age for hotel positions 18, for Resort Representatives 21. Applicants must have EU passport and National Insurance number. An attractive package which includes food, accommodation, insurance and travel to/from resort. Winter work also available for Ski Season with First Choice Ski.

For more information please send an A4 SAE to Overseas Human Resources Dept. at the address above.

Industrial and Office Work

THE AMERICAN SCANDINAVIAN FOUNDATION: Scandinavia House, 58 Park Avenue, New York, NY 10016, USA (tel 212-879-9779; fax 212-249-3444; e-mail asf@amscan.org; www.amscan.org). A non-profit organisation set up in

1910 to promote educational and cultural exchange between the USA and Denmark, Finland, Iceland, Norway and Sweden. Through ASF reciprocal training programme young Americans aged over 21 are able to live and work in Scandinavia on a temporary basis.

ASF offers short term training placements to American students in the fields of: engineering, computer science, chemistry and business studies. Placements, primarily in Finland and Sweden, last from 8-12 weeks and occur from late Spring through to the Autumn. Applicants should be full-time students majoring in the field in which training is sought, with at least three years undergraduate study completed and some previous relevant work experience. Knowledge of a Scandinavian language is not required. Work permits are arranged by ASF. Trainees receive sufficient income from trainers to cover living expenses during their stay, but are expected to cover the cost of the round-trip airfare.

While some trainees may arrange a place for themselves outside of the ASF scheme, ASF offers help with arranging work permits. All that is required is written confirmation from the training firm specifying the dates of training, the income, type of work and the name of the training supervisor. A non-returnable application fee of $50 (£33 approx.) is charged but this includes a one year membership of the foundation.

Those interested should *contact* ASF at the above address.

FOREIGN AND COMMONWEALTH OFFICE: Room 2/98, Old Admiralty Building, Whitehall, London SW1A 2PA (tel 020-7008 0764; fax 020-7008 0638; e-mail pmd.fco@gtnet.gov.uk).

The Foreign and Commonwealth Office promotes and protects British interests overseas; presenting a positive image of the UK, helping British citizens and assisting British exporters. They also advise and support government ministers in the formulation and implementation of foreign policy.

The FCO offers a limited number of short term attachments to overseas Posts for undergraduates in their penultimate year. The attachments can last between two weeks and two months over the summer vacation period, depending on the student's and the FCO's circumstances.

Participants are expected to fund their own travel and living expenses although Posts overseas will provide either accommodation or pocket money whenever possible. *Applicants must be British citizens* and be seriously interested in a career in the Diplomatic Service.

Application forms can be downloaded from the Foreign and Commonwealth website on www.fco.gov.uk, or call 020-7008 0639 from October 2001.

IMI PLC: Box 216, Witton Birmingham B6 7BA (tel; 0121-356 4848; fax 0121-356 2877; e-mail grad.recruit@imi.plc.uk; www.imi.plc.uk). This major international engineering group operates in the field of fluid control and is divided into four main business areas. Each of these is focused on market requirements and linked by common technology and manufacturing techniques. IMI has offices in over 60 countries worldwide but predominantly in the UK, Switzerland and Germany. **Vacation Placements** are offered by IMI each year (approx.12) to penultimate year students who are studying for a degree in Mechanical, Manufacturing, or Electronic and Electrical Engineering.

Overseas Placements can be offered dependent on individual language skills and placement availability. Successful candidates should be able to work for a period of 8-12 weeks. Applicants should have a good working knowledge of the country's language. During their placements students are required to attend a two day Management Skills training course. The salary for a placement is £770 per month. On completion of a successful placements students will be offered sponsorship through their final year at university and a place on the IMI Graduate Engineering Training Scheme.

Application forms available from the above address and on the company website. Closing date for applications is Friday 22nd February 2002.

INTERNATIONAL ASSOCIATION FOR THE EXCHANGE OF STUDENTS FOR TECHNICAL EXPERIENCE (IAESTE): See below for addresses.

IAESTE operate an exchange scheme whereby students in degree level scientific and technical studies are offered **course-related traineeships** in industrial, business, governmental and research organisations in 80 countries. IAESTE selected trainees are employed on short term contracts, usually for up to 3 months, undertaking specific scientific, professional or manual tasks. Students are responsible for their own travel and insurance costs, but are paid a salary by the host employer.

Students should seek more information from the relevant address below. Special arrangements may be possible for sponsored students whose companies can arrange reciprocal placements for foreign students.

The British address for this body is IAESTE UK, 10 Spring Gardens, London SW1A 2BN (tel 020-7389 4114; www.iaeste.org.uk); the American equivalent is the Association for International Practical Training (AIPT), 10400 Little Patuxent Parkway, Suite 250, Columbia, MD 21044-3510, USA (tel 410-997 3068; e-mail aipt@aipt.org; www.aipt.org).

Sports, Couriers and Camping

3D EDUCATION AND ADVENTURE LTD: Business Support, Osmington Bay, Weymouth, Dorset DT3 6EG (tel 01305-836226; fax 01305-834070; e-mail darren@3d-education.co.uk). 3D is a specialist provider of activity and educational experiences for young people. Owned by Center Parcs, 3D has been operating since 1991 and gone from strength to strength year on year.

Activity Instructors (500) Employed and trained as either multi-activity instructor, field studies instructor, specialist watersports instructor or IT instructor, staff will work with children at specialist holiday centres across the south of England as well as across the UK and Europe with Pontins and Center Parcs.

Field studies instructors must hold or at least be gaining a relevant degree. IT instructors need to have a broad range of IT skills. Any sports coaching awards or national governing body awards are advantageous, if applying for Activity instructor and Watersports instructor postitions, although those with relevant experience will be considered. Training courses are held from late January through to July, so there is plenty of opportunity to develop your skills and qualifications.

Most important is an applicant's enthusiasm, personality and energy, coupled with a true desire to work in the outdoor leisure industry. Excellent accommodation and catering packages are offered with payment and working hours as covered by minimum wage and working time legislation. Minimum period of work 14 weeks.

Applicants should *telephone* 01305-836226 for a recruitment pack between September and June. Before employment all applicants must complete a residential training programme in the UK.

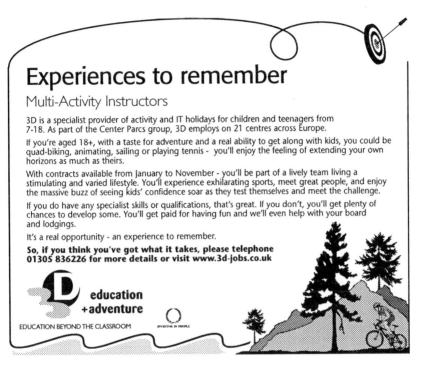

AIRTOURS HOLIDAYS LTD: Holiday House, Sandbrook Park, Sandbrook Way, Rochdale, Lancs OL11 5SA (tel 0870-241 2642; fax 01706-232328). Airtours Holidays, the UK tour division of Airtours plc, recruit staff to work in their overseas resorts.

Customer Services Representatives are responsible for providing a quality service to ensure customers have a successful holiday. Whether they are involved in accompanying coach transfers, welcome meetings, selling excursions or sorting out any problems that arise, they are responsible for making sure everything runs smoothly. Aged 21 and above, applicants must have previous experience of working in a customer service or sales background and the energy and enthusiasm to keep customers happy.

Customer Service Assistants meet the customers on arrival in resorts and accompany them on coaches to their accommodation to ensure everything runs smoothly. They also accompany customers returning to the airport at the end of their holiday. Based in Mallorca, Gran Canaria and Ibiza only.

Childrens' Club Leaders are responsible for organising and running daily activities for groups of children aged 3-15. Applicants must be aged 19 or over and have proven experience of working with children aged 3-15, in addition to some customer service experience.

Crèche Leaders are responsible for organising and running crèche facilities within the Family First programme. looking after children from newborn to 3 years old. Applicants must be aged 19 or over and have NNEB or equivalent qualifications in addition to proven experience of working with children of this age.

Overseas Administrators provide administrative support to the resort team to help ensure that the resort operation runs smoothly. Responsibilities range from dealing with flight lists and transfers to liaising with Head Office. Must be aged 21 or over with previous experience of working in a busy office environment dealing with customers and suppliers is essential. Computer literacy an advantage and a foreign language, especially Spanish, is beneficial.

Escapades Reps look after customers on Escapades Holidays - special holidays for the young and adventurous. Emphasis is placed on making sure that customers have a great time and applicants must have a keen sense of responsibility to make sure that everyone is looked after. Applicants must be aged at least 19, enjoy life to the full and get pleasure out of organising and getting involved in group activities.

Entertainers are responsible for providing a comprehensive day and evening entertainments programme in the Suncenter and all-inclusive properties. Must be aged at least 21 and have entertainments experience.

Golden Years Hosts plan, set up and manage a varied activities programme to enhance Golden Years winter holidays for the over 50s. Hosts are aged 21 and over with excellent customer service skills and proven experience of organising and participating in various activities and entertainments. Applications are also welcome from couples.

All employees of Airtours Holiday Team will receive a basic salary, accommodation, insurance cover and flights to and from the resort, plus there is the opportunity to earn commission in some posts. Full training is provided for all positions and flexibility is essential as employees are expected to help their colleagues. Employees work 6 days a week, hours can be long and unsociable; the ability to work under pressure is essential. Applicants for summer work must be available between March and October and for winter work from October to May; long-term career opportunities are available. For further information *contact* the Recruitment line 0870-241 2642 (24 hrs).

AMERICAN COUNCIL FOR INTERNATIONAL STUDIES (ACIS): AIFS (UK), 38 Queen's Gate, London SW7 5HR (tel 020-7590 7474; fax 020-7590 7475; e-mail tmdepartment@acis.com; www.acis.com). ACIS has been offering quality educational travel for 20 years. Tour managers are vital to the success of the company, and are given unequalled training and support.

Tour Managers (100) to lead American high school teachers and students on educational trips through Europe. The length of trips varies from 10 days to 2 weeks and may visit one or several countries. All trip details and itineraries are prearranged. Busiest periods are March/April and June/July. Tour Managers for both short and long periods are needed; minimum is 10 days. Tour Managers meet groups on arrival, travel with them, act as commentators and guides, keep accounts, direct bus drivers, troubleshoot etc. Fluency in French, Italian, German or Spanish is essential for trips outside the UK and Ireland. Applicants must be over 21, and either have or be studying for a university degree. Daily salary, accommodation provided with the groups in 3/4-star hotels, generous tips, insurance and back-up provided. *Contact* the above postal or e-mail address, or visit the website (address above) for an application form.

BOMBARD BALLOON ADVENTURES: Château de Laborde, Laborde Au Chateau 21200 Beaune France. (www.bombardsociety.com/jobs).

Since 1977, Bombard Balloon Adventures has provided complete luxury travel progammes including daily hot-air balloon flights to and international clientele **Ground Crew** (15) to work for a travel company operating hot air balloons mainly in France from May to October and in the Swiss Alps from mid January to mid February, but also occasionally in other European countries. Duties include the assembly, inflation, and deflation of balloons, equipment preparation, driving after balloons and participating in general household chores. Small salary plus food and lodging provided. Period of work by arrangement.

Must have a clean driving licence with at least one year's experience, a neat, clean-cut and cheerful appearance and be fit and able to get on with others. Knowledge of languages an advantage. Applicants should send a c.v. with a photo and photocopy of driving licence, details of height, weight and nationality and dates of availability to Mr Michael Lincicome at the above address, or apply by email to mike@bombardsociety.com.

CANVAS HOLIDAYS: East Port House, 12 East Port, Dunfermline, Fife KY12 7JG (tel 01383-629018; fax 01383-629071; www.canvas holidayscom). Canvas Holidays are looking for enthusiastic, resourceful people who enjoy a challenge and love the outdoor life. Main positions for 2002 include:
Campsite Courier. Varied responsibilities. Involves cleaning and preparation of customer accommodation, welcoming and looking after customers during their holiday and ensuring that they have the best holiday ever. As a campsite courier you will have new challenges every day which can lead to one of the most enjoyable summers you will ever have. Variable working hours.
Children's Courier. As a Canvas Holidays Children's Courier you will have had formal experience of working with children. You will organise and carry out a six day programme which involves four hours a day of Children's Club for children between the ages of 4 and 11. You will be prepared to help out with courier duties as and when requried. For many customers, the Children's Club is one of the main parts of the holiday. You will need to have the energy of a seven year old and the imagination of an eleven year old to succeed.

Remuneration package includes tented accommodation, medical insurance, full uniform and return travel to and from a UK port of entry. Positions are available from March until October. *Applications* are invited from individuals and couples. Contact Sandy, Karen or Michele at the above contact details for an application pack.

CASTERBRIDGE TOURS LTD: Salcombe House, Long Street, Sherborne, Dorset DT9 3BU (tel 01935-810810; fax 01935-815815; e-mail chiefguide@casterbridge-tours.co.uk). Casterbridge operate customised Group Tours throughout Britain and Europe. They have three specialist divisions: Student Educational Study Tours; Concert Tours for Performing Choirs, Orchestras and Bands; Adult Special Interest Tours.
Tour Managers/Guides to escort groups in Europe. Wages from £280 per week, with board and lodging provided. To work all hours necessary, seven days per week. Period of work by arrangement between March and August. Applicants are expected to attend a training course; knowledge of languages useful. Applications to the Chief Guide at the above address.

CLUB CANTABRICA HOLIDAYS LTD: 146/148 London Road, St. Albans, Herts AL1 1PQ (tel 01727-833141; fax 01727-843766 www.cantabrica.co.uk). Offer luxury coach, air and self-drive holidays on excellent sites in Austria,

Corfu, France, Italy and Spain. Opportunities also available for ski season positions in the Alps.

Resort Manager (15) to manage sites varying in size from 25-100 units. Must have previous campsite rep. experience and French, German, Italian or Spanish language skills. Wages between £75 and £110 per week, plus bonus.

Campsite Couriers (25) to work on camp sites in Corfu, France, Italy, and Spain. Work involves looking after clients, setting up and closing down site, tent and mobile home cleaning and maintenance, paper-work and excursion sales. Wages £75 per week plus commission and bonus.

Peak Season Courier (15) to cover same tasks as couriers but for June-September only. Minimum period of work 3 months. Wages £75 per week.

Childrens' Courier (13) to run Kids' Club on campsites, must have experience of working with children. Wages £75 per week.

Maintenance Staff (13) to carry out maintenance and upkeep work on tents and mobile homes. Applicants should have good practical skills. Wages £75-£100 per week.

Hotel Staff (32) includng **General Duties Rep.** and **Chef** to help run the Club Hotel in Chamonix Valley and Val Cenis - Fluent French and Italian speakers required.

Free accommodation provided. To work approximately 40 hours per 6 day week, from April to October, except Peak Season staff. Couriers should be enthusiastic and have plenty of stamina, with knowledge of languages an advantage. Applicants should be over 21 years old. Experience preferable.

Applications with curriculum vitae and stamped addressed envelope to the above address from December. Applicants can also e-mail iona.mccabe@ catabrica.co.uk

CLUB MED: Kennedy House, 115 Hammersmith Road, London W14 OQH (Tel 020-7348 3333; fax 020-7348 3336). Club Med reps take part in all aspects of village life and help to create the international atmosphere which makes Club Med holidays unique. Staff are required for Club Med villages in Europe and Africa.

Staff for children's clubs; should have NNEB qualifications and/or experience in working with children.

Sports Instructors: should have relevant qualifications and experience to teach sailing, water-skiing, scuba diving (BSCA-advanced, CMAS), tennis, windsurfing, aerobic fitness and golf.

Boutique, Receptionists: should have relevant experience and speak two or three European languages.

Applicants must possess excellent communication skills speak good French, be single, aged 18-30 and available for a period of 3 or 6 months. Applicants should send a cv and covering letter to Miss M Carlton, Recruitment Manager at the above address.

CRYSTAL HOLIDAYS: King's Place,12-42 Wood Street, Kingston-upon-Thames, Surrey KT1 1SH (tel 0870 888 0028; e-mail overseasrecruitment@s-h-g.co.uk; www.crystalholidays.co.uk). Crystal Holidays is incorporated within the Specialist Holidays Group. They recruit for Summer Lakes and Mountains staff throughout the year in many exciting European destinations.

Resort Representatives, Chalet Hosts, Chalet Assistants, Hotel Chefs, Hotel Assistants. Crystal Holidays recruit qualified and unqualified staff with a flexible and friendly attitude. Also needed is a good understanding of cutomer

Club Med

International Recruitment

We are looking for enthusiastic young people to join our international team of G.O.s (gentils organisateurs) for our forthcoming summer season in our European villages

Baby/Children's Clubs

NNEB/Experience in working with children

Hostess/Boutique

2 European languages

Receptionist/Cash Desk

2 European languages

Sports Instructors

Relevant Diplomas/Experience required
Golf, Tennis, Aerobics, Archery, Sailing, Windsurfing, Scuba Diving (BSAC Advanced, CMAS), Swimming, Waterskiing

Barman/Barmaid

Bar Experience

If you have experience in any of the above, speak French and are free from March/April for 4-6 months, send CV to:

**Club Med International Recruitment
Kennedy House
115 Hammersmith Road
London W14 0QH**

All positions are open to male and female applicants

requirements and the ability to work within a busy team. All employees must be aged 18 and over. A second European language is an advantage but not essential.

All roles are available for each season Summer Lakes and Mountains and Winter Ski. Summer Lakes and Mountains Season is from May to September. Winter Ski season is from November to April. It is possible to continue from one season to the next. For more information on the above jobs please contact the Overseas Recruitment Team on 0870-888 0028.

EQUITY LTD.: Dukes Lane House, 47 Middle Street, Brighton BN1 1AL (tel 01273-886901; fax 01273-203212; e-mail travel@equity.co.uk). Equity is a direct sale tour operator, organising ski holidays, educational tours and weekend breaks with the emphasis on customer service, quality and value for money.

Resort Representatives (2) to work with school groups on educational study courses in France, Germany and Austria. Each group spends 5 nights in a resort, and during this period the rep spends all his or her time assisting the group; there are generally a few days' gap between courses. Duties include liaison between the group, hotelier and coach driver and organisation of room assignment, excursions and medical emergencies. It also includes helping pupils with their projects among local people and assisting them with their language work or concert arrangements for musical tours.

Resort Representatives/Interpreters (2) to work with school groups on cuisine courses in France and Italy. Duties as for the above but also include interpreting for the chef during demonstrations, accompanying the group and translating during cookery-related excursions to bakers, markets, etc.

Wage £100-£150 per course plus full board, accommodation, travel expenses and insurance. Temporary positions are available for lengths of time varying from one week to a month between February and July, then again in October. Minimum age 21.

Applicants must be fluent French, German or Italian speakers, well organised, able to take responsibility and work on their own initiative, be able to relate to children (teaching experience would be an advantage) and ideally should have some experience of working with the public or in a service industry. Please send a c.v. with covering letter to Matthew Pavitt at the above address.

EUROCAMP: Overseas Recruitment Department (Ref SJ/02) (tel 01606-787522). Eurocamp is a leading tour operator in quality self-drive camping and mobile home holidays in Europe. Each year the company seeks to recruit up to 1,500 enthusiastic people for the following positions:

Campsite Courier: job involves cleaning and preparing customer accommodation, providing assistance, acting as an information service and an interpreter and performing some administrative duties. Couriers need to be flexible to meet the needs of the customer to provide them with excellent service. Minimum age 18 years. Applicants should be independent with plenty of initiative and relish a challenging and rewarding position. They should also possess a friendly and helpful personality. Some working knowledge of another European language is required and previous customer service experience would be an advantage. Applicants should be available to work from April/May to September.

Children's Courier: work involves organising a wide range of exciting activities for children aged 4-13. Applicants should possess initiative, imagination and enthusiasm along with good safety awareness. Previous childcare experience is essential. Minimum age is 18 years and applicants should be available from April/May to September. Languages are not a requirement but would be an advantage (in particular German).

Senior Couriers: required to work alongside a team of Campsite Couriers and organise their daily workload, as well as carrying out the normal day to day duties of a Campsite Courier. Applicants should have good language skills and experience of leading a team.

Site Managers: required to lead a large team of Campsite Couriers, organising their daily workloads and ensuring they provide the very best customer service. Applicants should be 21 or over, have proven managerial experience, excellent communication skills and language ability.

In all the above positions you should be be available for the full season commencing in April/May through to September. Comprehensive training is provided together with a competitive salary, insurance and return travel. Applications are accepted from September/October and *can only be accepted from UK/EU passport holders.* Interviews will be conducted in Hartford, Cheshire between October and April.

EUROPEAN SERVICES LTD: 54 Oakland Road Trading Estate, Rodley, Leeds, LS13 1LQ, England. (tel 0113-236 1577; fax 0113-236 1875; e-mail europserv@aol.com).

Staff to help with the installation and maintenance of mobile homes, tents and their storage and distribution. European Services operate in nine countries, with most work being in France, Italy (a growing market) and Spain. Wages and period of work by arrangement.

Applicants must be over 21 and must have a valid driving license. To *apply* or to obtain more information contact Norman Pickett, Personnel Officer at the above address.

EUROSITES: The Globe Centre, St James Sqaure, Accrington BB5 0RE (www.eurosites.co.uk).

Campsite and **Children's Representatives** in France, Germany, Holland, Italy and Spain. Duties include greeting and looking after customers, cleaning, solving problems and administration. Children's Representatvies organise a programme of acitivies. Applicants should be over 19, physically fit and have knowledge of another European language. A flexible approach to working hours is essential. Salary approximately £460 per month. Free accommodation provided. Duration of employment; mid-March to end of October. Written *applications* accepted between October and January, or e-mail kate.almond@eurosites.com.

EXPLORE WORLDWIDE: 1 Frederick Street, Aldershot, Hants., GU11 1LQ (tel 01252-760200; fax 01252-760207; e-mail info@explore.com; www.explore.com). Explore Worldwide is Europe's largest adventure tour operator.

Tour Leaders (110) to work 7 days per week for 3-6 months leading tour groups of 16 clients per group, to 96 countries around the world. Applicants with language skills and previous travel experience preferred. Wages by negotiation. Full training given.

Tour leaders are expected to be available all hours. Work is available throughout the year, with the minimum period of work being 3 months. Board and lodging are included.

Applications to the above address are accepted all year round.

FIRST CHOICE HOLIDAYS: London Road, Crawley, West Sussex, RH10 2GX (tel 01293-588-528; fax 01293-588-277). First Choice Holidays are a large, award winning tour operator with worldwide destinations.

Sovereign Service Executives (10). Applicants should have excellent customer service skills, be very attentive to details in order to provide a high level of service to customers, previous experience beneficial. Wages are £600 per month. Applicants should be at least 24 years old.

Resort Representatives (300). Applicants should have good customer service and sales experience and be at least aged 21. £400 per month.

20s Representatives (20) to perform the same duties as the Resort Representatives. Minimum age 20 years, wages £350 per month.

Children's Representatives (150). Applicants should have childcare experience, be able to work with groups and be able to provide varied and fun activities.

The above positions all require responsible people, willing to work long, unsociable hours. Sovereign, Resort and 20s reps can also earn commission on top of the wages listed above. All applicants must be confident, able to speak publicly to groups of varying sizes, and be sociable, committed, self-motivators.

For all positions, the period of work is flexible between March and October. Accommodation is provided free of charge, but board is not available. Recruitment takes place all year round, *EU applicants only*.

HALSBURY TRAVEL LTD.: 35 Churchill Park, Colwick Business Estate, Nottingham NG4 2HF (tel 0115-9404 303; fax 0115-9404 304; e-mail enquiries@halsbury.com; www.halsbury.com). Halsbury Travel is an ABTA Bonded Tour Operator, specialising in School Group, European and Worldwide Tours. Established in 1986 they are one of the leading UK student group tour operators.

Group Leaders (40), **Language Tutors** (20). Required to work with touring groups in France, Germany or Spain. Wage £150 per week.

Camp Supervisors (6). To work on camps in France or Spain. Wage £400 per month.

Telesales (20) Calling customers in France, Germany and Spain. Wage £600 per month.

All applicants should be fluent in the native language of the country they wish to work in. Most positions involve 8 hour days 6 days per week, working for a minimum period of 1 week. Board and accommodation is provided.

Applications are invited to the above address in May/June for the winter season, (skiing jobs), and in January or February for jobs in the summer season.

HAVEN EUROPE: Recruitment Team, HR Dept.,1 Park Lane, Hemel Hempstead HP2 4YL (tel 01442-203282/203954; fax 01442-241473; www.haveneurope.com). Haven Europe Ltd have provided self-drive family camping holidays for over 20 years and are part of Bourne Leisure, who are one of the world's leading leisure companies. They have job opportunities in throughout France, Italy and Spain from March to September/October.

Campsite Representatives, Children's Couriers, Entertainers, Grounds/Maintenance Staff, NPLQ qualified Lifeguards, Bar Servers and Cleaners. Minimum age 18. Customer service experience is essential although full training is given. Hours range from 35-46 per week over 5½ days. Salaries vary according to position. Staff receive free accommodation, travel, uniform and personal insurance plus use of various on-site facilities. *Applicants must be UK nationals*. For further information *please call or see their website* to request an information pack.

HOLIDAYBREAK: Hartford Manor, Greenbank Lane, Northwich, Cheshire, CW8 1HW (tel 01606-787522).

Montage/Demontage Team Leaders to supervise the Montage/Demontage Teams (see below) in the erection and dismantling of tents. Responsibilities include training allocated teams, liaising with campsite proprietors and couriers while adhering to a demanding schedule and maintaining a high standard of workmanship. Some training provided but the ability to think on your feet, be practical and use common sense are pre-requisites. Applicants should be at least 22 years old, have a good standard of spoken French, Italian or Spanish, a current driving licence, energy, confidence and relevant experience. Wages approx. £140 per week with accommodation and travel expenses provided. Period of work from approx. 15 April-15 May or 9th September-11 October.

Montage/Demontage Team Members to work under supervision in teams of about five people to set up and close down campsites, spending three to four days on each site. The work predominantly involves erecting and dismantling tents, long journeys and heavy lifting and this may be carried out in poor weather conditions. Wages approx. £100 per week with accommodation and travel expenses provided. Typical working hours 9am-6pm. Period of work from 15 April to early June or 9 September to 11 October. No special qualifications are needed but applicants must be fit, hardworking and able to work without supervision. Driving licence an advantage.

Couriers to clean and prepare tents and mobile homes, welcome clients, organise social activities and deal with any problems. Couriers are theoretically on call 24 hours a day. Minimum period of work 15 May to 15 July or 15 July to 30 September or full season, from 15 May to 30 September. Applications are invited from people of all ages; those with a good working knowledge of France, Germany, Italy and Spain and French, German, Italian or Spanish preferred. Previous camping/caravanning and customer serving experience an advantage. Wages range from £98-£130 per week depending on position.

For further details *contact* the Recruitment Department at the above address.

INGHAMS TRAVEL: 10-18 Putney Hill, London SW15 6AX (tel 020-8780 4400; fax 020-8780 8805; e-mail travel@inghams.com; www.inghams.co.uk). Inghams Travel is the largest independent operator of ski holidays in the UK with an excellent reputation built up over the last 70 years. We offer quality ski and lakes and mountains holidays to Europe and North America. We aim to attract the best staff in the industry and our salaries and conditions of employment refect this policy.

Representatives (approx.160) for client service, administration, sales, guiding of excursions and general problem solving. Salary £800-£1,200 per month including commission. Knowledge of French, German, Italian or Spanish is required. Minimum age 23.

Hotel Managers (5) for staff management, budgetary control, guest and supplier liaison, problem solving and menu planning. Wages £500-£800 per month. Applicants must have good man management and food and beverage experience within the hospitality industry. A good command of French or German is essential. Minimum age 24

Hostesses (20) to waitress, clean and liaise with guests. Salary £200-300 per month. Experience in waitressing and chambermaiding is required. Minimum age 18.

Chefs and **Assistant Chefs** required to cater for up to 80 guests. Recognised cooking qualifications required and the ability to budget and menu plan. Salary £400-800 per month. Minimum age 20.

All staff to work 6 days a week in one of the following countries: Andorra,

Austria, France, Italy and Switzerland. Minimum period of work 3-4 months from May to September. Free board and accommodation is provided. Applicants must be friendly, outgoing flexible team players with enthusiasm and a good sense of humour and must be customer care orientated and have a liking for the coutnry and culture.

Applications all year round to the above address.

JOB-EXPRESS: Postbus 1459, Randstad 22-117, NL-1300 BL Almere, The Netherlands (tel +31-36-530 2000; fax +31-36-530 0300; e-mail postmaster@ jobexpress.nl; www.jobexpress.nl). Dutch recruitment and international employment agency specialising in international positions worldwide.
Campsite Workers, Animation Staff, Bar/Restaurant Staff, and **Other Positions** are frequently available for Dutch speakers as well as English speakers with a foreign language (preferably German).

Job Express often have permanent positions available for English speakers with fluency in French, German, Italian or Spanish. Several information packs are available at low cost. Please see their website or contact them for details.

This agency seeks staff for a number of temporary and permanent jobs around Europe. The hours of work vary but are generally over a 6 day week. Board and lodging is available for these jobs and will be either free or at cost price according to the job. *Applications* are invited all year round for these positions, contact Job-Express at the above address for more details.

JMC: 6 Midford Place, London W1T 5BF (tel 0870-6070309; e-mail overseas.jobs:jmc.com). JMC is one of the UK's newest and largest tour operators, launched in September 1999, and part of the Thomas Cook Group. The company is looking for enthusiastic, responsible people to work overseas and help provide hassle-free, enjoyable holidays to its customers. As the face of JMC in resort, you must be hard working and approachable with a real customer focus.
Overseas Representatives: Responsible for ensuring that guests receive their promised hassle-free holiday. Customer facing experience, a genuine desire to help and stamina to work long, unsociable hours are all essential. Minimum age 20 years old.
Children's Representatives to supervise and entertain groups of children aged 3-16 years. Experience of working with large groups of children is essential. Minimum age 19 years old.
Crèche Representatives to look after younger children aged between 6 months and 2 years; a qualification in childcare is necessary. Minimum age 19 years.
Overseas Administrators: Their overseas offices are the nerve centre of JMC's whole operation. People needed with office experience, who are used to working under pressure. Sound experience of using MS Word, Excel and Outlook is essential. Minimum age 19 years old.
Contracts run from March until October with a possibility to continue throughout the winter. All applicants *must have a valid EEC or British passport*.
To *apply* telephone 0870 6070309 or e-mail overseas.jobs@jmc.com.

KEITH AND SHANAN MILLER: 53 Horsepool, Bromham, Chippenham, Wiltshire SN15 2HD (tel 01380-850383; fax 01380-859159 e-mail ksmillerbrom@btconnect.com). Organisers of adventure holidays worldwide for

over 25 years, Keith and Shanan Miller now operate walking and cycling holidays on behalf of two major UK companies on a sub-contract basis.
Tour Leaders/Support Drivers to accompany groups of up to 16 adults on mountain walking holidays in the Alps and Provence, low level walking holidays in Tuscany and Madeira and cycling holidays along the Loire. Food and accommodation are provided plus a wage of £120 per week on average. To work 7 days a week, but with free time built into itineraries. Period of work from early May to the end of September.

Applicants should be aged at least 23 and need some knowledge of French, German, Portugese or Italian language and culture as relevant plus experience/qualification in mountain walking and current first aid certificate. *Applications* to Shanan Miller, Partner, at the above address or e-mail ksmillerbrom@btconnect.com.

NEILSON: 120 St George's Road, Brighton, East Sussex, BN2 1EA (tel 01273-626281; fax 01273-626285; e-mail recruitment@neilson.com). Neilson is a holiday company committed to providing excellent quality activity holidays. They pride themselves on having a high staff/client ratio and the exceptional calibre of their overseas staff.
Child Minders (10) (NNEB, BTEC or equivalent preferred) to care for 0-5 year olds in the resorts. Summer and winter (ski) work is available. Working 6 days a week. Pay from £95 per week in local currency. Flights paid to and from resort, accommodation, insurance and uniform provided. Applicants should be at least 18 years old with experience of working with children, a sense of fun, and be creative team players.
Contact Karen McGill, Personnel Manager, at the above address or on recruitment@neilson.com

OPEN HOLIDAYS: The Guildbourne Centre, Chapel Road, Worthing, BN11 1LZ (tel 01903-201864; fax 01903-201225; e-mail donnaelias@openholidays.co.uk).
Overseas Representatives required between March/April and October. Staff look after holidaymakers staying with the company, hosting welcome meetings, checking properties. The working week is 43 hours over 6 days. Wages vary according to age and experience, but start at £750 (gross) per month, accommodation is provided at a cost of £150 per month.

Applicants must have a full driving licence and ideally be over 21. To *apply* contact the General Manager, Miss D. Elias, at the above address.

PANORAMA AND MANOS HOLIDAYS: Vale House, Vale Road, Portslade, East Sussex, BN41 1HG (tel 01273-427000; fax 01273-427149). Located on the sunny south coast, Panorama and Manos Holidays operate a wide range of short and long haul programmes. Recognised as an Investor in People, they actively encourage and give employees opportunity for self-development.
Overseas Representatives to work from May/June to September/October. Reps work a 6 day week, hours as required, with work including customer service/relations e.g. hosting welcome meetings, arranging transfers, duty times, excursions and informal events. The remuneration package includes £375 per month plus commission, accommodation, flights, insurance and uniform. Reps must be over 21 with customer service experience, languages are an advantage.
Children's Representatives and Assistants required from May/June to September/October. To work 6 days per week organising childrens' clubs with a full activity programme for a variety of ages. Wages £450 per month plus

accommodation, flights, insurance and uniform. Childrens Reps must be over 21 with NNEB or equivalent plus/or minimum of 2 years working with children.

Staff will be working in the Algarve, Cyprus, Fuerventura, the Greek Islands, Ibiza, Gran Canaria, Majorca, Malta, Morocco, Tenerife, Tunisia or Turkey.

Applications to Bianca Berry, Personnel and Training Executive, at the above address.

POWDER BYRNE: 250 Upper Richmond Road, London SW15 6TG (tel 020-8246 5310; fax 020-246 5321; www.powderbyrne.com). Powder Byrne is an exclusive tour operator offering tailor-made holidays, working alongside 4 and 5 star luxury hotels, to provide a top of the range holiday package. They are looking for highly motivated customer-focused team players to work in their summer resorts programme in exotic Mediterranean holiday destinations

Resort Managers required to manage a team of staff in resort, to provide a high calibre of services to Powder Byrne clients and to liaise with head office. Applicants should be 24+, have previous management experience, a professional approach and have the ability to think on their feet.

Drivers required to transport guests in exclusive company minibuses and assist the Resort Manager in providing a high level of customer service to Powder Byrne clients. Applicants should be 21+, good time-keepers, reliable and have customer service experience. Full, clean driving licence essential.

Nursery Nurses required to manage resort Crèches for children aged six months to four years. Applicants should have relevant experience and be NNEB qualified or equivalent. (Non-qualified assistants are also required).

Children's Club Co-ordinators to organise and run our kids' clubs for four to 14 year olds. Applicants must have child care experience and lots of energy (would suit teachers during the school holidays).

Accommodation, food, transport to resort insurance, uniform and competitive salary provided. Duration of contracts vary from six months to two weeks between April and October.

Applications taken on-line at www.powderbyrne.co.uk.

RAMBLERS' HOLIDAYS LTD: Box 43, Welwyn Garden City, Herts AL8 6PQ (tel 01707-331133; fax 01707-333276; e-mail mandy@ramblersholidays.co.uk). An established small tour operator, organising graded walking and sightseeing holidays worldwide. Their clients are mostly professional individuals or couples in small parties, with the emphasis being on the countryside or culture depending on the grade of the holiday.

Tour Leaders to lead walking and sightseeing holidays in Europe and beyond. Wages from £440 per month; to work approximately 8 hours per day, 6 days per week. Free board and accommodation. Minimum period of work 8 weeks between April and October.

Applicants should be over 24 years old and should have a working knowledge of a foreign language (French, German, Spanish, Italian or Greek), demonstrate leadership qualities, have a current first aid certificate and enjoy walking and map reading and/or have a cultural interest. *Applications* to the above address.

SHEARINGS HOLIDAYS: European Product Department, Miry Lane, Wigan, Lancs (tel 01942- 823416; fax 01942-829760). Shearings Holidays provide a quality service to ensure that their customers have an enjoyable holiday. The following positions are available for work in Europe.

Resort Representatives: to greet customers on arrival, host welcome meetings,

OVERSEAS REPRESENTATIVES

Europe's largest coach holiday operator, Shearings requires overseas staff for 2002. Positions include Resort based holiday representatives, TGV couriers (accompanying customers to and from resort, combined with resort representative duties when abroad) & Tour Managers, (fluent in Italian).

Experience in a customer service orientated role, (preferably as an overseas rep), common sense, the ability to work well under pressure, together with a professional and positive outlook are essential. A good working knowledge of French and/or Italian would be an advantage.

Flexible and adaptable, you must be over 21, have a genuine interest in people and a consistent commitment to the highest standards of customer care.

In return we can offer a competitive salary and genuine career prospects with a growing company.

To apply please write with full career details and a recent photograph to:
Sharon Ward, European Products,
Shearings Holidays, Miry Lane, Wigan WN3 4AG.

sell excursions and solve problems.

TGV Representatives: to accompany customers on the TGV Train and carry out resort rep. duties when abroad.

Tour Managers. To greet customers upon arrival, escorting and guiding tours throughout Europe and general liaison with the coach driver and hotels.

Applicants should have previous experience in a customer service orientated role, common sense and the ability to work under pressure, together with a professional and positive outlook. Those applying for the Tour Manager positions must be fluent in one or more languages.

Wages are dependant on experience and accommodation is provided. Period of work is likely to be May to October.

Applicants should *apply* in writing to the above address with a Curriculum Vitae and passport sized photograph.

ST PETER'S PILGRIMS: 87a Rushey Green, Catford, London, SE6 4AF (tel 020-8244 8844; fax 020-8697 2466; e-mail info@stpeter.co.uk; website www.stpeter.co.uk)

Representatives/Pilgrimage Leaders (2) to look after pilgrims and arrange hotel bookings, transfers, excursions and daily programmes. Most pilgrimages are in France, but there are also some in Israel, Italy and Portugal. A good knowledge of Christianity is required. Representatives will be paid c. £800 and will have full board, uniform and other extras provided.

Applications to Bob Metcalf at the above address.

SIMPLY TRAVEL: King's House, 12-42 Wood Street, Kingston-upon-Thames, Surrey, KT1 1SG (tel 020-8541 2227; fax 020-8541 2278; e-mail personnel@simply-travel.com; www.simply-travel.com). Simply Travel is part of the Specialist Holidays Group, providing holidays for the discerning traveller. Offering a selection of top Mediterranean destination as well as a winter ski programme in the top ski destinations.

Resort Representatives: seasonal and year-round. Working to very high company expectations, applicants should be hard working, self-motivated and have initiative. Simply Travel look for staff with excellent customer service and problem solving skills. A second European language and full clean driving licence are essential for all customer-facing positions. The representative's job is to ensure that customers have an enjoyable holiday exceeding their expectations. Period of work late March/April to October.

A competitive package including salary, accommodation, transport to and from resort and insurance is offered. Other roles available: **Chamber Persons, Drivers, Chefs, Watersports Instructors.**

For more information on the above please *contact* the Overseas Recruitment Department on 0870-888 0028.

SPECIALISED TRAVEL LTD: 12-15 Hanger Green, London, W5 3EL (tel 020-8799 8360; fax 020-8998 7965; e-mail admin@stlon.com) Established in 1955, a tour operator specialising in concert tours of mainland Europe and the UK for both amateur and professional musical groups (choirs, bands and orchestras). **Couriers/Tour Leaders**(1-2 per tour) to escort choirs, bands and orchestras from the USA on concert tours throughout the UK and Europe. To be responsible for all daily events, confirming accommodation, transportation, concert arrangements and leading sight-seeing excursions. Knowledge of touring and musical background is an advantage. Excellent organisational skills, leadership qualities and initiative required.

Work is available for a minimum of one tour in Spring and Summer. Work will be full time for the duration of each tour (usually 10-20 days). Board and accommodation is included for the duration of each tour. Wage level depends on the particular tour. Confidence in the native language of the country being toured is required.

Applications from *EU nationals only* are invited throughout the year to the above address.

SUNSAIL LTD: The Port House, Port Solent, Portsmouth, Hampshire PO6 4TH (tel 01705-222325; 24 hrs 01705-214330). Sunsail are the leaders in worldwide sailing holidays with 34 bases worldwide employing around 1000 staff; of these two thirds are seasonal workers, although career progression and training within the company is also available.

Flotilla Skipper. Must be RYA Yachtmaster/Coastal Skipper/Commercially Endorsed professional sailor with unlimited patience and a friendly personality. To be responsible for the organisation/safety of guests aboard up to 13 cruising yachts. Duties include navigational briefings/assistance in all sailing matters and excellent organisational skills. Considerable yacht skippering and people skills essential.

Yacht Technicians capable of diagnosing/repairing ancillary systems aboard flotilla and base charter yachts. Knowledge of mechanics, woodwork, fibreglass and practical skills essential to carry out maintenance and yacht repair. Previous knowledge of marine systems and sailing an advantage.

Hostess to work as part of a team of three staff to look after flotilla guests. Duties include basic accounts, organisational skills, dealing with local suppliers, organising BBQs/events and customer care. Knowledge of German/French particularly valued.

All the above positions require staff who are flexible and used to dealing with people.

Diesel Mechanics, Electronics Specialists, Sailmakers, Storepersons to work on a seasonal and full time basis in Greece and Turkey. Relevant qualifications and experience essential in order to join teams of experts maintaining fleets of charter yachts in the Mediterranean.

The following staff are also required for seasonal vacancies (March-October) to run Watersports Hotels for up to 200 guests:

Hotel Managers, Front of House/Food and Beverage Managers, 706/1/2 Chefs, Commis Chefs, Catering Assistants, Barpersons, Receptionists, Waiting Staff, Childcare Assistants (NNEB, BTech, RGN), Activities Organisers. In addition to the specific roles staff commit a great deal of time to socialising with and looking after guests.

Sailing Managers, RYA Qualified Yacht/Windsurfing/Dinghy and BWSF Water-Dki Instructors qualified to instruct and provide rigging assistance and rescue cover for beach operations.

Bosun/Engineers required to maintain outboards and yacht engines. Woodwork, GRP repair and all yacht maintenance skills are desirable for this work.

All positions to work 45-50 hour, 6 day week, plus socialising with guests in the evenings. Salary £45-£125 per week depending on position. Accommodation provided on yachts or sharing rooms ashore, where applicable. Insurance 50% of premium paid, food on site included, return flights on successful completion of contracted period. To work from March/April-October/November, certain vacancies also available for summer vacation periods. Staff must be aged between 20 and 35. Relevant qualifications and experience essential. Staff should be enthusiastic, hard working, loyal and honest with an outgoing personality.

Apply for a Recruitment Pack to the above address.

TALL STORIES: 67A High Street, Walton on Thames, Surrey KT12 1DJ (tel 01932-252002; fax 01932-225145; e-mail: info@tallstories.co.uk; www.tallstories.co.uk). Tall Stories offer adventure sports holidays in France, Spain, Austria or Corsica for people with no previous experience. Activities include rafting, mountain biking, trekking, kayaking, paragliding, snowboarding and many many more.

Representatives to work as sports reps for an adventure sports holiday company, acting as hosts to small groups of 8-16 clients in Austria, Corsica, France and Spain. Duties include airport transfers, organising hotels and sports as well as organising evening entertainment, and generally making the holidays of guests as good as possible. Reps are needed from mid-May to mid-September. Applicants should have outdoor sporting interests, speak French, Spanish or German, hold a clean driving licence (PSV licence an advantage) and get on with people. Must have experience of working with people: those with previous experience of rep work preferred. Must be aged 22 or over.

Chalet Persons to cater for groups of 10-16 people in France; work includes cooking breakfast and evening meals, budgeting, cleaning, and looking after the running of a chalet. Period of work from early June to mid September.

Wages for above positions from £120 per week, plus food, accommodation and travel. *Applications* should be sent to the Personnel Manager at the above address.

THOMSON: Human Resources Overseas, Greater London House, Hampstead Road, London NW1 7SD (tel 020-7387-9321; www.thomson-holidays.com/jobs). Thomson Holidays, Portland Direct, Skytours and Club Freestyle are all holiday products of Britain's No. 1 holiday company, Thomson Holidays Ltd, part of The Thomson Travel Group.

Representatives to be based abroad. The role involves meeting holiday makers on arrival, providing information about the resort and advice on how holiday makers can make the most of their holiday, including the recommending and selling of excursions. Other responsibilities include monitoring quality standards and providing excellent customer service whatever the situation.

Applicants should be 21+, willing to work in any destination, have at least 1 year's experience involving face to face customer contact and have a high standard of personal presentation. A second European language is desirable. Package includes salary and commission paid monthly in the UK, accommodation, uniform and other benefits.

Childrens' Representatives are also required to organise varied, imaginative and fun activities for 3-12 year olds. The role involves supervising daytime and evening activities. Aged 19+, applicants must hold a child care, infant teaching or nursing qualification, have at least 6 months practical experience working independently with large groups of children and a valid first aid certificate. Additionally, a friendly outgoing personality and a genuine liking for children is essential. Package includes: salary paid monthly in UK, accommodation, meals, uniform and other benefits.

Entertainment Representatives to organise a varied programme of daytime and evening entertainments and activities for guests. Applicants should be aged 20+ and have experience of entertaining an audience at either amateur or professional level or within a similar role in the leisure industry.

All positions require applicants to have lots of enthusiasm plus stamina, have a high degree of diplomacy and the ability to use initiative.

Applications for summer should be made between October and April. For further details and an application form send a large self addressed envelope.

TJM TRAVEL: Penhalveor East, Redruth, TR16 6NL (tel 01209-860000; fax 01209-860998; e-mail jobs@tjm-travel.co.uk). TJM run hotels and activity centres in France, Spain and the UK in the summer months, and they operate ski holidays from Alpine hotels in the winter.
Qualified Sailing, Canoe, Windsurfing, Snorkelling, Climbing, Mountain Biking Instructors, Hotel Staff; Manager, Chef, Bar, Waiting, Chamber, Kitchen Staff, Handymen. All required for hotel or activity centre work in France, Spain or the UK, all staff must have appropriate qualifications, experience and skills. Wages vary between £200 and £700 per month according to job and experience. Board and lodging provided. Staff work 7 hours a day per 6 day week, with the minimum period of work being 3-4 weeks. Working period is May to August.

Applicants can apply any time of year by letter, must include passport photos, full photo, current c.v. and copies of any relevant certificates.

TOP DECK TRAVEL: 7 Cambridge Court, 210 Sherperds Bush Road, London, W6 7NL (tel 020-7751 1204; fax 020-7751 1204; e-mail res@topdecktravel.co.uk). **Tour Leaders** (15), **Cooks** (15), **Coach Drivers** (15) with EU Licence.
To work for an adventure travel company, specialising in camping tours and hotel tours throughout Western and Eastern Europe. Countries visited include: Austria, Belarus, Britain, Bulgaria, Denmark, Finland, France, Germany, Greece, Hungary, Italy, the Netherlands, Norway, Romania, Russia, Spain, Switzerland and Turkey.

Salary from £110 per week. Hours of work spread over a seven day week. Peak period of work available June to September. Board and accommodation available when on tours. Minimum age 23. Knowledge of European history and languages. Applicants *apply* now.

TRACKS TRAVEL LTD: The Flots, Brookland, Romney Marsh, Kent TN29 9TG (tel 01797-344164; fax 01797-344135; e-mail info@tracks-travel.com; www.tracks-travel.com). A coach tour operator operating throughout Europe.
Drivers with a valid UK PCV Licence required.
Tour Managers must be good with a microphone, and confident in dealing with large groups.
Cooks: Must be able to cook for large groups. Relevant experience preferred.

Wage for all positions to be confirmed. Board and accommodation is available. Work is available throughout the year, but all applicants should be prepared to work for a minimum of 2 full seasons. Hours of work vary, depending on the nature of the tour. Knowledge of languages other than English is not required.

Applications should be made to the above address at any time of year.

UHURU SAFARIS LTD.: Rose Cottage, Summerleaze, Magor, Newport, Gwent NP26 3DE (tel 01633-880224; fax 01633-882128; e-mail: africaex@aol.com). Specialise in safaris and expectations in Africa. They offer a range of tours from 2-16 weeks all of which are based on camping and the outdoor way of life.

Expedition Leaders £130 per week after initial training period, usually 5 weeks. To run overland tours and safaris in East Africa, Morocco, and Southern Africa. Applicants must be diesel mechanics and speak fluent English.
Contact John Bogue at the above address for more information.

VENUE HOLIDAYS: 1 Norwood St, Ashford, Kent TN23 1QU (tel 01233-629950; fax 01233-634494; e-mail info@venueholidays.co.uk). Venue Holidays are a medium sized family run business supplying package camping and mobile home holidays. They offer the opportunity to live in a new environment, meet interesting people, travel and perhaps catch a tan.
Supervisors required for the period March to October. Must posess a clean driver's licence. Wages £700 per month.
Campsite Representatives (30) for work in Italy, France and Spain. Duties to include cleaning and maintaining holiday units, welcoming clients and looking after them during their stay, sorting out any problems, and liaising between the campsite's management and the UK office. Wage of £450 per month, with accommodation provided. To work hours as required. Minimum period of work June-August; the complete season runs from March to October. Applicants need to be fit, cheerful and to be able to work under pressure. Knowledge of French, German, Italian or Spanish would be advantageous but are not essential.
Applications should be sent to the above address from December.

WORLD CHALLENGE EXPEDITIONS: Black Arrow House, 2 Chandos Road, London NW10 6NF (tel 020-8728 7200; fax 020-8961 1551; e-mail: welcome@ world-challenge.co.uk; www.world-challenge.co.uk). World Challenge Expeditions, the educational training specialists, run four flexible programmes. Each of the programmes works to raise motivation through developing skills in leadership, team building, decision making and problem solving.
Expedition Leaders (300) World Challenge Expeditions requires male and female leaders for summer 2002 schools' educational expeditions to Central and South America, Africa, Himalayas and South East Asia. Fee negotiable and all expenses paid. Periods of work are four weeks between late June and late August. For application pack *apply* to Pauline Crossley on 01298-767900, or e-mail pcrossley@world-challenge.co.uk.

A WORLD OF EXPERIENCE EQUESTRIAN AGENCY: 52 Kingston Deverill, Warminster, Wiltshire (tel 01985-844022; fax 01985-844102; www.equestrian-recruitment.com). A small friendly specialist agency established in 1988. Overseas employers are all English-speaking and most jobs involve the care/exercise of valuable competition horses and travelling with them to national/international competitions.
Grooms, Head Grooms, Riding Instructors and **other stable staff** for vacancies all year round in about 20 countries in Europe and worldwide. Wages vary from £150-£250 or more per week plus free accommodation for an 8-12 hour day, 6 days per week.
Previous experience of full time employment with horses is strongly preferred; equine qualifications are essential for instructors but not for other posts. Applicants must be adaptable, aged at least 18, and available for at least 3 months. Advice is given on travel, insurance, visas and the differences which may be experienced working in other countries. Personal service with staff registration free.
For an application form *write* to the above address no earlier than 8 weeks before availability for work, enclosing a post-paid self-addressed envelope.

Sports: Ski Resorts

CLUB MED: Kennedy House, 115 Hammersmith Road, London W14 OQH (Tel 020-7348 3333; fax 020-7348 3336). Club Med reps take part in all aspects of village life and help to create the international atmosphere which makes Club Med holidays unique. Staff are required for Club Med villages in Europe and Africa.

Baby Club Reps to work as holiday reps and to be responsible for looking after children between 4 months and 4 years old; must have NNEB/Montessori or equivalent qualification/experience.

Children's Clubs Reps to work as holidays reps and look after children aged 4-16 years of age; should have good experience of working with children.

Bar Staff should have relevant experience in bars/hotels and ideally some knowledge of cocktail preparation.

Reception/Administration to work as holiday reps within the reception/boutiques/banks or planning departments. Must have experience in reception or administration.

All the above posts are well paid and include board and lodging. Minimum period of work 4 weeks, main working period December to April and/or April-September, as well as school holidays for children's reps and baby club staff. All staff will need to speak at least English and basic French.

Applicants should send c.v. and covering letter to the above address.

Voluntary Work and Archaeology

AFRICA AND ASIA VENTURE: 10 Market Place, Devizes, Wilts., SN10 1HT (tel 01380-729009; fax 01380-720060; e-mail av@aventure.co.uk; www. aventure.co.uk). Africa and Asia Venture run unpaid teaching or conservation projects with youth in Kenya, Tanzania, Uganda, Malawi, Botswana, India or Nepal. These projects are followed by the opportunity to travel and to go on safari.

Teachers and **Volunteers** needed to carry out work in the above countries. All applicants must be between $17^{1}/_{2}$ and 24 years of age and must either be undergraduates or school-leavers planning to go on to university. Placements all last for four months; the teaching projects in Africa depart in September, January and late April; in Nepal projects run from October and January; those in India begin in September and April. Conservation projects run from November to February, February to May and from May to August.

A place on one of the above projects costs £2,300, which includes selection, a training course, in-country support, food and accommodation and the safari. The air fare is not included; applicants should budget about £500 for this.

To *apply* write to the above address asking for an application form and giving information on when you are leaving school or university; suitable applicants will then be selected by interview.

AFRICAN CONSERVATION EXPERIENCE: PO Box 9706, Solihull, West Midlands, B91 3FF (tel 0870-241 5816; e-mail: info@afconservex.com; www. afconservex.com).

Voluntary Conservation Work Placements: lasting 4-12 weeks around the year for young people on game reserves in Southern Africa, including South Africa and Zimbabwe. Tasks may include darting rhino for relocation or elephant for fitting tracking collars. Game capture, tagging, assisting with wildlife veterinary work, game counts and monitoring may be part of the work programme. Alien plant control and the re-introduction of indigenous plants is often involved.

Applicants must have reasonable physical fitness and be able to cope mentally. Enthusiasm for conservation is essential. The programme may be of special interest to students of environmental, zoological and biological sciences, veterinary science and animal care.

Applicants are invited to attend an Introduction Weekend at a UK-based activity and training centre. Costs vary depending on reserve and time of year; support and advice are given on fund-raising. *Applications* to Lisa Hewston at the above address.

AFS INTERNATIONAL YOUTH DEVELOPMENT: Leeming House, Vicar Lane, Leeds LS2 7JF; tel 0845-4582102; fax 0113-243 0631; e-mail info-unitedkingdom@afs.org; www.afsuk.org). AFS is an international non-profit association of 54 national organisations and is one of the worlds largest voluntary organisations providing over 10,000 participants with an intercultural learning experience each year.

Volunteers for 6 month placements with AFS International Volunteer Programmes in Latin America or Africa on voluntary projects dedicated to healthcare, education, social welfare, environmental protection and other pressing human issues such as homelessness among urban poor, (with a special emphasis on meeting the needs of children). Participants live with a local volunteer host family and are provided with an excellent support structure. Applicants must be aged 18-29 and no language skills or qualifications are required. Departures from the UK are in January and July.

School Programme. A unique opportunity for young people aged 16-18 to spend an academic year studying in one of over 20 countries. Participants live with a local host family and enrol in the local school/college system. Departures from the UK are between July and September. Must be able to fundraise.

APARE/GEC: 41 Cours Jean Jaures, F-84000 Avignon, France (tel 33-(0)4-90-85-51-15; fax 33-(0)4-90-86-82-19; e-mail apare@apare-gec.org). APARE/GEC is a voluntary organisation which aims to promote participation (especially among young people) through voluntary service, in local development projects.

Volunteers (300) for short term (3-4 weeks) placements in workcamps; minimum period of work 3 weeks from July to October. To perform mostly manual tasks involving restoration, construction and conservation. Applicants need motivation.

Volunteers (60) for long term placements (6-12 months); minimum period of work 6 months in another country. To conduct study and research on environmental, heritage and sustainable development projects. Long term volunteers receive an allowance (pocket money). Ages 18-25. Applicants need to be motivated *and live in one of the countries of the EU, Central and Eastern Europe or the Mediterranean Countries.*.

Placements in Austria, Bulgaria, France (Provence), Germany, Great Britain, Greece, Ireland, Italy, Morocco, Poland, Portugal, Spain, Romania, and Tunisia. To work 6 hours a day, 5 days a week. Accommodation is provided. Knowledge of French and English required.

Applications for voluntary service (long term placements) from now onwards; applications for voluntary workcamps from March at the above address.

ATD FOURTH WORLD: 48 Addington Square, London SE5 7LB (tel; 020-77033231; fax 020-7252 4276; email atd@atd.demon.co.uk; www.atd-uk.org). ATD Fourth World is an international organisation which adopts a human rights approach to tackling extreme poverty, supporting the efforts of very disadvantaged and excluded families in fighting poverty and taking an active role in the community. As part of their work ATD organises workcamps, street workshops and family stays all over the European Union.

The workcamps are a combination of manual work in and around ATD's buildings, conversation and reflection on poverty. The street workshops take a festival atmosphere, involving artists, craftsmen, sportsmen and volunteers to underprivileged areas. The family stays allow families split by poverty with children in care and/or adults in homes to come together for a break.

The camps, street workcamps and family stays take place from July to September, and most last two weeks: participants must pay for their own travel costs, plus a contribution towards food and accommodation. For further information write, enclosing a stamped addressed envelope or International Reply Coupon, to the above address or ATD Quart Monde, 107 avenue du General Leclerc, 95480 Pierrelaye, France,

BRIDGES FOR EDUCATION INC.: 94 Lamarck Drive, Buffalo, New York 14226, USA (tel +1 716 839-0180; fax +1 716 939-9493; e-mail jbc@buffalo.edu; www.bridges4edu.org).

Volunteer English Teachers The purpose of Bridges for Education (BFE) is to promote tolerance and understanding using English as a bridge. BFE sends Canadian and American volunteer teachers, educated adults and college students to teach conversational English in the summer in Eastern and Central Europe. Since 1994, BFE has organised 66 camps in 8 countries serving 8,500 students from 33 countries.

High School students whose parents or teachers are participants may also join a BFE team. About 130 volunteers are placed each year. Those skilled in teaching English as a Second Language are preferred but teachers who are certified in any area are welcome. College professors, educated adults, and college students are trained in basic ESL prior to departure. Applicants must be in good health.

Volunteers are required during the summer for three weeks teaching and an additional week of travel within the host country. Free room and board as well as a stipend equivalent to what a local teacher is paid for three weeks, are provided.

Applications from US or Canadian citizens only should be sent to the above address or made online.

CANADIAN CROSSROADS INTERNATIONAL: 31 Madison Avenue, Toronto, Ontario, M5R 2S2, Canada (tel 416-967 1611; fax 416-967 9078; www.crossroads-carrefour.ca).
CCI is an international non-profit organisation. Each year, CCI recruits, trains and sends over 250 **Volunteers** on short-term placements, (usually four months) where they are matched to a variety of community-based organisations working in areas such as education, health-care, women's issues, agriculture, social work and the environment.

Participants must be at least 19 years of age and be Canadian citizens or landed immigrants. However, participants from partner countries to CCI's To-Canada and Interflow programs are also accepted. Those interested in participating should contact the National Office at the above address.

CONCORDIA: Heversham House, 20-22 Boundary Road, Hove, BN3 4ET (tel 01273-422218; fax 01273 421182; e-mail info@concordia-iye.org.uk; www.concordia-iye.org.uk).
Concordia is a small not-for-profit charity committed to international youth exchange. Their **International Volunteer Programme** offers 16-30 year olds the opportunity to join international teams of volunteers working on community based projects in over 30 countries world-wide. Projects are diverse ranging from nature conservation, restoration, archaeology, construction, art and culture to projects that are socially based including work with adults or children with special needs, children's playschemes and teaching. Projects last for 2-4 weeks with the main season from June to September and smaller winter/spring programme. Generally the work doesn't require specific skills or experience, though real motivation and commitment to the project are a must.

Volunteers pay a registration fee of £85-£125 depending on the country (£60 for projects in the UK) and fund their own travel. Board and accommodation is free of charge. Concordia also recruits volunteers (20+) to act as Group Co-ordinators on UK based projects, for which training is provided and all expenses are paid. Details of projects will be published in April. Early application is advised.

For further information on volunteering or co-ordinating write (enclosing a stamped addressed A5 envelope) or e-mail the International Volunteer Co-ordinator at the address above or visit our website.

Concordia can only place volunteers who are resident in the UK. Volunteers applying from abroad should contact a volunteer organisation in their own country or country in which they are based.

CORAL CAY CONSERVATION LTD.: The Tower, 13th Floor, 125 High Street, Colliers Wood, London SW19 2JG (tel 0870-7500688; fax 0870-7500667; www.coralcay.org). Coral Cay Conservation recruits paying volunteers to help alleviate poverty through research, education, training and alternative livelihood programmes worldwide. Volunteers are provided with full training; no previous experience required.

Expedition Leaders to oversee running of marine or forest expeditions. Must have proven leadership experience. Plus, for marine expeditions scuba diving qualifications and for forest expeditions a Mountain Leader qualification is preferable.

Science Officers to oversee coral reef and/or tropical forest scientific training and survey programmes. Minimum qualification: Masters Degree and/or proven field research experience.

Scuba Instructors to provide scuba training for expedition personnel and host country counterparts.

Medical Officers to oversee all aspects of expedition medical health. Minimum qualification: paramedic, registered nurse or GP.

Equipment Officers to maintain expedition equipment. Experience in the maintenance and repair of marine outboard engines an advantage.

Mountain Leaders to oversee all aspects of expedition safety in remote forested mountains. Must be qualified Mountain Leader.

The above are needed to work for Coral Cay Conservation (CCC), a non-profit organisation established in 1986 to provide support for the conservation and sustainable use of coastal and marine resources. CCC maintains full-time expedition projects in the Philippines and Honduras. No wage is paid and expedition staff are required to cover the costs of their flights and insurance. CCC covers accommodation, food and other subsistence costs. To work 12 hours per day, 6 days per week. Minimum period of work is four months in any given year. *Applications* should be sent to Alex Page at the above address.

COUNCIL: INTERNATIONAL VOLUNTEER PROJECTS: Council Exchanges (formerly known as CIEE), 20th Floor, Third Avenue, New York, NY 10017, USA (tel toll free 1-888-Council or 212-822-2600; e-mail info@councilexchanges.org; www.councilexchanges.org).

Council Exchanges is a non-profit organisation that, in affiliation with co-operative organisations in North and West Africa, Europe, North America and Japan, which sponsors 2-4 week voluntary service projects for young people in the USA and abroad. Participants on these projects work and live as part of an international group of 10-20 volunteers and have a chance to learn about the host community as well as to explore cross-cultural perspectives on global issues such as environmental protection, cultural preservation and development.

The types of work include nature conservation, construction, renovation, historical preservation, archaeology and work with children and the elderly. Participants' costs are a $300 placement fee plus transportation. Room and board are provided during the project. Current project listings can be found on the website www.ciee.org

For more information please *contact* Council: International Volunteer Projects at the above address. Please note that Council places American residents only; residents of other countries should contact a voluntary organisation in their home country.

CROSS CULTURAL SOLUTIONS: 47 Potter Avenue, New Rochelle, New York 10801, USA (tel +1-914-632 0022; fax +1-914-632 8494; e-mail info@crosscultutralsolutions.org).

Volunteers wanted all year round to take part in programmes in China, Ghana,

India, Peru and Russia. Volunteers must be over 18, and will be matched up to local communities according to their skills and interests but no special skills or training are required. A programme fee is charged which covers food and lodging and transport to and from the worksite.

For further details please *contact* Kristin Hegazy at the above address.

THE DISAWAY TRUST: 51 Sunningdale Road, Worthing, West Sussex BN13 2NQ (tel/fax 01903-830796). The Disaway Trust relies on helpers to enable them to provide holidays for adults who otherwise would not be able to have a holiday. Young helpers can apply for funding.

About 60 volunteers are required for 8-14 day periods during the summer months to help disabled people on holiday. The organisation usually arranges three holidays a year which take place in May, July and September. A 50% contribution is required toward cost of travel, accommodation, board and entertainment.

No special qualifications or experience are required. The holiday venues are in the British Isles and in the Mediterranean. For further details including information on dates and locations please *contact* Nicki Green at the above address: applicants from overseas should enclose an International Reply Coupon with enquiries. The information pack for 2002 will be available in mid January.

EARTHWATCH: 57 Woodstock Road, Oxford OX2 6HJ (tel 01865-318838; fax 01865-311383; e-mail info@.earthwatch.org; www.earthwatch.org/europe). **Volunteers** to work with scientists around the world conducting research into rain forests, endangered species, archaeology and restoration. Volunteers pay a share of the cost of the projects (from £65 to £2,500) to cover food and lodging, as well as a contribution to the research costs. Team projects last from two days to three weeks. All adults are encouraged to join; no special skills are required. For further details *contact* the above address.

ECOVOLUNTEER PROGRAM: Meyersweg 29, 7553 AX Hengelo, Netherlands (tel +31-74 250 8250; fax +31-74 250 6572; e-mail info@ecovolunteer.org; www.ecovolunteer.org or for Britons www.ecovolunteer.org.uk). The Ecovolunteer Program organises wildlife conservation projects and wildlife research projects operated by local conservation organisations worldwide.

Volunteers: (500-600) work varies from practical fieldwork to production and support jobs in wildlife rescue centres, to visitor education, maintenance work, and household duties, dependent on each individual project.

Volunteers are recruited for projects lasting from 1-4 weeks. The minimum age of volunteers is 18; participants must be in good physical health. Accommodation is provided.

Applications should be made to the national Ecovolunteer agency of the country in which the applicant is resident. A list of the national agencies can be found on the Ecovolunteer website or obtained from the above address as there are offices in Austria, Belgium, Brazil, France, Germany, Hungary, Israel, Italy, the Netherlands, Spain, Switzerland the UK and Thailand. Their latest projects include a wildlife sanctuary in Thailand and a Kiwi bird projct in New Zealand.

EMMAUS INTERNATIONAL: Boite Postale 91, F-94143 Alfortville, France (tel 1-48-93-29-50; fax 1-43-53-19-26; e-mail contact@emmaus-international.org; www.emmaus-international.org). **Volunteers** to take part in summer camps in several European countries. The work consists of rag-picking and recycling materials to raise money for the poor.

Applicants must pay for their own travelling costs but receive free food and accommodation. For further details contact the above address.

EUROPE CONSERVATION ITALIA: del Macao 9, 00185 Rome, Italy (tel 06-474 1241; fax 06-4744671; e-mail: eco.italia@agora.stm.it; www.agora.stm.it). A non-profit organisation for the conservation of natural resources and cultural heritage.
Volunteers needed to help a study project returning gibbons to the wild on a desert island in Thailand; duties include feeding gibbons, building cages, etc. Volunteers must speak English; students of biology have the possibility of staying for longer periods as assistant researchers. Volunteers needed at all times of the year.
Volunteers to help a study project on wolves in the Appennini mountains in the Florence district. During the work it could be possible to watch eagles, wolf, deers, roebuck and wild boar. Volunteers needed at all times of the year, during the first week of each month.
Volunteers needed from October to February for Project Pro Tamar in the Espirito Santo state (turtles in the Brazilian coast). To work strictly in contact with the researchers accompanying them during reconnaissance, helping them in the capture and classification of the various species of turtles.
Volunteers needed all year round for the Project Rhino Rescue in Swaziland in the Mkhaya Game reserve. Duties include daily monitoring of endangered species, support of the activities of rangers in the reserve, helping in the research about the wildlife living in the area.
All volunteers have to pay a fee for supporting the researches; they should be over 18 and of good health. Please *contact* Europe Conservation for further information on these projects or other initiatives.

EUROPEAN VOLUNTARY SERVICE: EVS Unit, EIL Cultural and Educational Travel, 287 Worcester Road, Malvern, WR14 1AB (tel 01684-562577; e-mail k.morris@eiluk.org). EIL is an approved Sending and Hosting organisation for the European Commission's new European Voluntary Service scheme.
EVS is for 18-25 year olds from the EU who want to do a 6-12 month placement in a community based project in another EU country. Travel, food, accommodation and an allowance are provided.
For more details *contact* the above address.

EXPLORATIONS IN TRAVEL: 2458 River Road, Guildford, Vermont 05301, USA (tel +1-802 257 0152; fax +1-802 257 2784; e-mail explore@sover.net; www.volunteertravel.com). Arrange volunteer placements around the world, around the year, with placements arranged individually.
Volunteers to work with wildlife and domestic animal rescue organisations, rainforest reserves, organic farms and with social services, environmental and conservation organisations and schools. Placements are in Australia, Belize, Costa Rica, Ecuador, Mexico, Nepal, New Zealand, and Thailand. Periods of work etc. by arrangement; most placements are available around the year. Volunteers must often pay a local family for room and board. Minimum age 18.
For further details *contact* John Lee, Program Director at the above address.

FRONTIER: 50-52 Rivington Street, London EC2A 3QP (tel 020-7613 2422; fax 020-7613 2992; e-mail enquiries@frontierprojects.ac.uk; www.frontierprojects. ac.uk). For a career in conservation, Frontier is an ideal starting point: 62% of

Frontier volunteers now have a career in this area.

Frontier conduct vital conservation research into some of the world's most threatened wildlife and habitats. Projects are currently focused on biodiversity conservation and management issues in forests (Madagascar) tropical forests (Vietnam and Tanzania), savanna (Tanzania), and coral reefs (Tanzania and Madagascar). Each project is operated in association with host country institutions, typically a university or natural resource management authority.

Volunteer Research Assistants are required to carry out baseline biological surveys and socio-economic research in these areas during 10 or 20 week long expeditions. Survey data is collated into reports for use by host governments in the formulation of future management plans. For individuals looking to start a career in overseas conservation and development, Frontier expeditions provide unique opportunities for tropical research training, field experience and the chance to work on official aid-funded projects overseas. No previous experience is necessary as training is provided in situ by highly qualified field scientists, leading to a BTEC qualification in Tropical Habitat Conservation. Projects are co-funded by volunteer contributions and international donor agencies including DFID (Department for International Development); FINNIDA (Finnish Aid) and JICA (Japanese Aid). Each expedition phase runs four times a year. Volunteers are expected to raise around £2,450 for 10 week expeditions or around £3,750 for 20 week expeditions, which covers local travel, food, accommodation, science equipment and vehicle maintenance. Advice is given with fund-raising. *Contact* the above address for a free information pack.

GAP ACTIVITY PROJECTS LIMITED: GAP House, 44 Queen's Road, Reading, Berkshire RG1 4BB (tel 0118-9594914; fax 0118-9576634; e-mail volunteer@gap.org.uk; www.gap.org.uk). GAP is an educational charity based in Reading which organises voluntary work opportunities for 18/19 year olds in their 'year out' between school and higher education, employment or training. Successful volunteers undertake full-time work for between four and nine months in return for which they receive food, accommodation and (usually) some pocket money.

Currently opportunities exist in Argentina, Australia, Brazil, Canada, Chile, China, (including Hong Kong and Macau)), the Czech Republic, Ecuador, the Falkland Islands, Fiji & the South Pacific, Germany, Hungary, India, Israel, Japan, Lesotho, Malaysia, Mexico, Morocco, Nepal, New Zealand, Paraguay, Poland, Romania, Russia, Slovakia, South Africa, Swaziland, Thailand, Trinidad and Tobago, the USA, Vietnam and Zambia. A wide variety of projects is on offer including teaching English as a foreign language, general duties in schools, assisting on community projects or caring for the sick and people with disabilities, outdoor activities and sports coaching,conservation work and scientific surveys.

GAP has no closing date for applications, although you stand a better chance of being placed on your first choice project the if you apply early. GAP welcomes applications at any time from year 12 onwards. Every applicant is invited to interview with interviews taking place from the middle of October onwards in Reading, Leeds, Dublin, Edinburgh, Glasgow and and other regional locations. Brochures are available each year from August onwards for placements starting a year later. To receive a copy of the GAP brochure and application form students should *contact* careers staff at their school or college, or telephone, e-mail or write to the GAP office, stating clearly for which year they will be applying.

GLOBAL CITIZENS NETWORK: 130 N. Howell Street, St Paul, Minnesota 55104, USA (tel 651-644-0960; e-mail gcn@mtn.org; www.globalcitizens.org). **Volunteers** for projects in Kenya, New Mexico, South Dakota, Arizona, Guatemala and Nepal. Volunteer trips last 1, 2, or 3 weeks and are ongoing throughout the year. Programmes involving volunteers include building a health centre, teaching in school and renovating a youth centre. Volunteers pay a programme fee of $600-$1650 (£400-£1100), which includes most in-country costs (food, lodging, transportation etc.); the airfare is extra. No special qualifications are required but volunteers should be aged at least 18. Volunteers under 18 years must be accompanied by parent or guardian.

For more information *contact* the Program Director at the above address.

GREENFORCE: 11-15 Betterton Street, Covent Garden, London WC2H 9BP (tel 020-7470 8888; fax 020-7470 8889; e-mail: greenforce@btinternet.com; www.greenforce.org). **Work on the Wild Side** with Greenforce on one of the five conservation projects around the world; Zambia, Amazon Rainforest (Peru), Fiji, Malaysia and the Bahamas. Greenforce needs volunteers to join for ten weeks to work on projects as diverse as elephant tracking in Zambia to surveying the coral reefs in the South Pacific. No experience is necessary as full training is provided, including, BSAC diver training for Marine volunteers. Distance learning packs are distributed and a training weekend is held before departure. This is followed up with lectures in-country and supervision by qualified staff. For those interested in progressing within the conservation arena, they offer a traineship placement on each expedition. Many permanent staff are chose from former trainees providing an ideal foundation for a career in conservation.

A ten week expedition costs £2550, which includes all training, food and accommodation, use of diving equipement (marine only) and medical insurance. Projects depart each January, April, July and October. Call for the lates brochure or attend one of the Monthly Open Metings to find out more, or visit the website for photos and regular updates. Greenforce is a non-profit organisation and member of the National Council for Voluntary Organisations. **WORK ON THE WILD SIDE** in the Amazon, Africa, Borneo and the South Pacific. No experience necessary. Greenforce is invited by the host country to undertake biodiversity surveys. Greenforce volunteers attend training lectures at the local university, work alongside local students in the field and contribute to the principal conservation project in the area concerned.

Greenforce offer free Traineeship places on each expedition. Greenforce offer a structured Career in Conservation for volunteers who are interested in going on to pursue a career in conservation. This programme includes salaried positions as well as free MSc funding for all qualifying Greenforce staff. Greenforce is committed to the host country and also to improving the opportunites available for Volunteers to develop meaningful careers in the conservation field.

The 10 week expeditions cost from £2,350, departing every January, April, July, and October. Fund Raising, Kit and medical advice are all included in the Distance Learning Packs as well as at the UK based Training Weekend. Free Dive Training to BSAC Sports Diver is included on Marine expeditions. Would-be volunteers can surf the website or meet the Project Leaders at one of the monthly Open Evenings in the London offices. Call for the latest Greenforce brochure.

Greenforce is a member of the National Council for Voluntary Organisations. Registered non-profit number 3321466. All senior staff are Fellows of the Royal Geographical Society.

HABITAT FOR HUMANITY GREAT BRITAIN: 11 Parsons Street, Banbury, Oxon OX16 5LW (tel 01295-264240; fax 01295-264230; e-mail MKearney@hfhgb.org; www.hfhgb.org).

Global Village Mission Teams are small groups of people (7-15) who travel to one of 40 countries to help build simple decent houses alongside local residents. Costs include a contribution towards building costs, travel expenses, food and insurance.

Trips are for 1-4 weeks for those who are interested in both travel and a Habitat for Humanity volunteer experience; the trips are designed to promote cross-cultural understanding and to raise awareness of the urgent worldwide issue of substandard housing.

Applicants should be over 18; no experience or building skills are necessary. For further information on Global Village and details of volunteering opportunities within Britain, contact Habitat for Humanity Great Britain at the above address.

INKANATURA TRAVEL: Manuel Bañón 461, San Isidro, Lima, Peru (tel 014-402022; fax 014-229225; e-mail dm-ricalde@wayna.rcp.net.pe or jmelton@chavin.rcp.net.pe). Two conservation organisations, Selva Sur and Peru Verde have formed a non-profit travel agency to promote ecotourism and assist conservation work in order to save Peru's unique biodiversity. Volunteers are also needed for projects in Bolivia and Brazil.

Resident Naturalists required for four lodges in southeastern Peru to guide tourists and take on small research projects. Possible wildlife studies include tapirs, spider monkeys (and 5 other small monkey species), peccaries, macaws, bats, deer, large macaws and the endangered Giant River Otter. Duration of stay 90 days, with an option to extend. After training and depending on experience, the applicant may be able to get a contract for guiding tourists. Free food and lodging will be provided as well as transport from Cusco. A deposit of £188/$300 will be required to cover the first month, which will be forfeited if the volunteer leaves before the end of the 90 day period without good cause. If a volunteer should abandon the project without good cause he/she will also have to pay for his/her own transport home.

Volunteers to assist research projects. Duration of stay is 4 weeks. Food and lodging costs of £12/$20 must be met by the volunteer as must insurance and the cost of travel to the project. US residents can obtain a tax break on these costs.

Some of the projects that volunteers can work on occur throughout the year, while others run from late October-January. There are also opportunities for independent research, to teach English and help train local residents/indigeneous people who are running ecotourism schemes near reserves in Manu, Tambopata, Lower Urubamba and Madidi.

Full details of these projects, costs and how to *apply* can be obtained from the above address or on the website.

INTERNATIONALE BOUWORDE (INTERNATIONAL BUILDING COMPANIONS): for addresses see below.

Recruits volunteers for construction work camps on behalf of the socially, physically and mentally underprivileged. The camps take place in Austria, Belgium, the Czech Republic, France, Germany, Hungary, Italy, Lithuania, the Netherlands, Poland, Romania, Slovakia, Switzerland and the Ukraine.

Volunteers work for 8 hours per day, 5 days per week. Free board, accommodation and liability and accident insurance are provided: travel costs and insurance (approx. £60) are the responsibility of the volunteer. Camps last for 2-3 weeks and take place between June and September; Bouworde in Belgium and Italy operates workcamps around the year. *Applications,* mentioning the country preferred, should be sent to the relevant address listed below:

Belgium (Flemish speaking): Bouworde, Tiensesteenweg 145, B-3010 Kessel-Lo (tel 016 25 91 44; fax 016 25 91 60).

France: Compagnons Batisseurs, Secrétariat International, 2 rue Claude-Bertholet, F-81100 Castres, France (tel 33 63 72 59 64; fax 33 63 72 59 81).

Germany: Internationaler Bauorden, Liebigstrasse 23, D-67551 Worms-Horchheim (tel 06241-37900; fax 06241-37902; e-mail bauorden@t-online.de; www.home.t-online.de/home/ibo-d/).

Italy: Soci Construttori I.B.O., Via Smeraldinna, 35 44044 Cassana (FE) (tel 0532-730079; fax 0532-730545; e-mail i.b.o@fe.nettuno.it).

Netherlands: Internationale Bouworde, St Annastrat 172, NL-6524 GT Nijmegen (tel 31-24-3226074; fax 31-24-3226076; e-mail info@bouworde.nl www.bouworde.nl).

Switzerland: Internationaler Bauorden, Sekretariat Schweiz, Bahnhofstr. 8, CH-9450 Altstälku (tel +41-71-755 1671; e-mail info@bayordeuich).

INTERNATIONAL CONSERVATION HOLIDAYS: BTCV, 36 St Mary's Street, Wallingford, Oxfordshire OX10 0EU (tel 01491-821600; fax 01491-839646; e-mail information@btcv.org.uk; www.btcv.org). BTCV is the UK's leading practical conservation charity. Founded in 1959, they help over 130,000 volunteers per year to take hands on action to improve urban and rural environments.

Volunteers to take part in international conservation projects in Australia, Bulgaria, Canada, France, Germany, Greece, Hungary, Iceland, Japan, Portugal, Romania, Turkey, Thailand, and the USA. Board, accommodation and insurance provided for from £190 per week. Projects take place throughout the year and last from 1-3 weeks. Minimum age 18: knowledge of languages not essential. Volunteers must pay their own travel expenses.

For full details of BTCV's Conservation Holiday programme, contact BTCV for an up-to-date brochure. Full project details are also available on the BTCV website.

INTERNATIONAL VOLUNTARY SERVICE (BRITISH BRANCH OF SERVICE CIVIL INTERNATIONAL): IVS Field Office, Old Hall, East Bergholt, Colchester C07 6TQ (e-mail ivsgbn@ivsgbn.demon.co.uk; www. ivsgbn.demon.co.uk).

International Voluntary Service sends volunteers to international workcamps and short-term projects across a choice of 25 countries in eastern and western Europe including the former Soviet Union, as well as Japan, North Africa, Turkey, the US and Australia. Volunteers work for two to four weeks in an international team of 10-20 people, sharing domestic and social life as well as the work. The projects include work with children, work with people with physical or mental disabilities, solidarity work with people of other countries, and manual work, often connected with ecology or conservation. The projects are not holidays. The work can be hard and demands commitment.

Most workcamps are between June and September. Volunteers must pay for membership of IVS, a registration fee and their own travel costs. Free board and accommodation are provided on the project. For certain countries previous experience of voluntary work is required or preferred. English is the language of most projects, but other languages are an advantage. IVS is working towards equal opportunities, and welcomes applications from women, black people, people with disabilities, people from ethnic minorities, gay men and lesbians. *IVS can only accept applications from people with an address in Britain.*

Applications should be sent with a stamped addressed envelope, for more information to the address above or to IVS North, 21 Otley Road, Headingley, Leeds LS6 3AA: £4.00 postage and packing is only necessary for the listing of summer workcamps (available from April). Enquiries from January will be put on a mailing list to receive the listing when it is ready. *The address of the American branch of Service Civil International for volunteers living in the USA, or US nationals is* 814 NE 40th Street, Seattle, WA 98105, USA; e-mail scitalk@sci-ivs.org; www.sci-ivs.org

INVOLVEMENT VOLUNTEERS ASSOCIATION INC (IVI): PO Box 218, Port Melbourne, Victoria 3207, Australia (tel +61 9646-9392; fax +61 396465504; e-mail: ivworldwide@volunteering.org.au). Involvement Volunteers Association Inc. (IVI) was established in 1988 with the aim of making voluntary work available to people who wish to assist others and to learn from their volunteer experiences.

IV volunteers participate as individuals or groups of individual volunteers in Networked International Volunteering as unpaid participants. The aim of Involvement Volunteering is to enable volunteers to assist non-profit projects related to the natural environment (at farms, national or zoological parks, animal reserves or historic places) or social service in the community (at homes, camps or schools for disadvantaged people, orphanages, villages). Placements of 2-12 weeks are currently available in Argentina, Armenia, Australia, Bangladesh, Belgium, Cambodia, China, Denmark, Ecuador, England, Fiji, Finland, Germany, Greece, India, Italy, Japan, Kenya, Korea, Lebanon, Macau, Mexico, Mongolia, Nepal, New Zealand, Philippines, Poland, Russia, Sabah (Malaysia), Samoa, South Africa, Spain, Thailand, Turkey, Ukraine, USA, Vietnam and Venezuela. Single Placement Programs or Trip Programs (as many placements as can be fitted in a 12 month period travelling the world) can provide valuable practical experience related to potential tertiary education, completed degree courses or completed careers (for early retirees). Some placements have food and accommodation provided while some can cost up to about £35 per week for food and accomodation, depending on the economy of the country and the host organisation.

Involvement Volunteers Association Inc. is a registered non-profit making organisation which charges fees to conver administration cost for a programme of any number of Networked International Volunteering; placements with suggested travel arrangements in any number of the countries in a period of up to 12 months. IV Associates support the volunteers in Australia, England, Fiji, Germany, New Zealand Sabah (Malaysia), Thailand, Korea, Nepal, South Africa and South American Countries.

Where appropriate, IV volunteers are met on arrival at the airport and provided with a communications base during their visit. Advice is given on banking, specially discounted internal travel, special trips, eco trips, discounted scuba diving courses, sea kayaking, snorkelling and sailing in suitable areas.

European applicants can *contact* Involvement Volunteers UK, 7 Bushmead Avenue, Kingkerswell, Newton Abbot, Devon, TQ12 5EN (tel 01803-872594; e-mail ivengland@volunteering.org.au) or Involvement Volunteers-Deutschland, Naturbadstr 50, D-91056 Erlangen, Germany (tel/fax 091 358075; e-mail ivgermany@volunteering.org.au).

LATITUDES INTERNATIONAL INC.: 51 First Avenue, East Haven, CT 06512, USA (tel free in USA only 800-398 4960; fax 203-468 9260; e-mail info@latitudesinternational.com; www.latitudesinternational.com). Latitudes' founders are world travellers and returned Peace Corps volunteers. All Latitudes' Group Leaders are First Aid and CPR certified.

Volunteers required for a non-profit organisation that arranges community service programmes for students interested in performing community service in an international setting. Projects planned for 2002 include working on an American Indian reservation in Pine Ridge, South Dakota, in a remote village in Botswana and on the Caribbean island of Antigua.

Projects last for 3-5 weeks; the work on each project varies but they are all concerned with community service in a developing area. Projects are open to both secondary school and university students and include opportunities to sightsee. For full details *contact* the above address.

THE MISSION TO SEAFARERS: St Michael Paternoster Royal, College Hill, London EC4R 2RL (tel 020-7248 5202; e-mail ministry@ missiontoseafarers.org). The Mission to Seafarers is a missionary society that cares for the welfare of seafarers of all nationalities and creeds in 300 ports around the world.

Volunteers to the Chaplains are required to help run centres, visit ships and to be outgoing, friendly and welcoming to visiting seafarers. Board and accommodation and pocket money are provided. Centres are in Europe, the Far East, Africa and New Zealand. Applicants should be aged between 21 and 26. Usual period of work 12 months. Fares paid. Must hold current driving licence. All applicants must be practising members of the Church (any denomination). *Applications* to the Ministry Secretary at the above address.

PEACE BRIGADES INTERNATIONAL: PBI Britain, 1b Waterlow Road, London N19 5NJ (tel/fax 020-7281 5370;e-mail pbibritain@gn.apc.org; www.peacebridges.org).

PBI is an international non-govermental-organisation working for the non-violent transformation of conflict. For the past 16 years PBI has provided physical and moral support to peace and justice activists whose lives are threatened by violence. The work is carried out by sending teams of international volunteers to provide an international presence in Colombia, Mexico, the Balkans and Indonesia/West Timor. Volunteers receive training and are required to commit for a period of one year.

For further information please send an A4 envelope with a 33p stamp on it to Susi Bacon at the above address.

THE PROJECT TRUST: The Hebridean Centre, Ballyhough, Isle of Coll, Argyll PA78 6TE (tel 01879-230-444; fax 01879-230-357; e-mail info@projecttrust.org.uk).

The Project Trust is an educational trust which sends 200 school leavers overseas every year to over twenty countries around the world. At present these are: Botswana, Brazil, Chile, China, Cuba, Dominican Republic, Egypt, Guyana, Hong Kong, Honduras, Japan, Jordan, South Korea, Malawi, Malaysia, Morocco, Namibia, Pakistan, Peru, South Africa, Sri Lanka, Thailand, Uganda and Vietnam. There are a wide variety of projects on offer, from teaching to development work, outward bound activities, and child and health care. Placements last for twelve months.

All volunteers attend a selection course on the Isle of Coll in the autumn before they go overseas. Week-long training courses take place on the Isle of Coll after final exams in the summer, and following a year overseas the volunteers assemble again on the Isle of Coll for a final farewell before dispersing to university or their future careers.

Volunteers are given pocket money, free board or a food allowance and accommodation. The cost is £3,550 for the year which includes insurance and travel; fundraising workshops are held throughout the country to help volunteers raise the necessary finance. *Apply* as early as possible to avoid disappointment.

QUAKER VOLUNTARY ACTION (QVA): Friends Meeting House, 6 Mount Street, Manchester, M2 5NS (telfax 0161-819 1634; e-mail qva@ quakervolaction.freeserve.co.uk).
QVA runs short-term (2-3) weeks volunteer projects in Britain, Northern Ireland, Europe (including Eastern Europe and Turkey), Japan, the USA and elsewhere. There are many types of projects to choose from, including building/renovation, environmental protection, archaeology, work with children, disabled people or the elderly. Most projects run in the summer and last from 1 to 4 weeks. Some medium and long-term opportunities are now being developed. Please phone or e-mail for details. There are usually between 10 and 15 volunteers per project. The aims of QVA are to promote co-operation and international understanding between people and to support community initiatives.

Food and basic accommodation is provided free of charge for the duration of the project. Volunteers pay a registration fee (2001 costs: UK projects, unwaged £140, waged £65; projects abroad, unwaged £75, waged £100) and their travel to the project and their personal insurance.

For a free brochure (available from April) send a large £0.33 s.a.e. and a covering letter to the address above.

QUEST OVERSEAS: 32 Clapham Mansions, Nightingale Lane, London SW4 9AQ (tel 020-8673 3313; fax 020-8673 7623; email emailus@questoverseas. com; www.questoverseas.com). Quest Overseas run Gap Year projects and expeditions in South America and Africa.
Volunteers are wanted for 3 month expeditions to South America and Africa. South American projects begin with a 3 week long one-to-one Spanish tuition course in Quito, Ecuador, followed by a month working on a community project such as looking after children in Peru or a conservation project, perhaps in the rainforests or cloud forests of Ecuador; the trip concludes with a stunning six-week expedition through Peru, Bolivia and Chile.

Projects in Africa need volunteers to work for 6 weeks either on game-reserves in Swaziland (ecological surveys, trail building) or in coastal villages in Tanzania (building schools, medical facilities). Both projects are followed by an adventurous six week expedition through Swaziland, Mozambique, Botswana and Zambia including a week's PADI Scuba-diving course in Mozambique.

Teams of 16 gap year students aged 18 or 19 years leave throughout the year. No qualifications are needed, except for those wishing to look after children in Peru, for which a good level of Spanish is required.

Projects cost between £3,230 and £3,510 which includes all board and accommodation as well as support on the project. Part of the cost of the project goes directly to the project, helping to finance it for the rest of the year. Flights and insurance are not included; applicants should budget approx. £700 for these. During the voluntary work section of their time abroad volunteers will work for an average of 6 hours per day, 6 days a week.

Prospective applicants should note that Quest Overseas also run 6 week summer expeditions without the voluntary work. For more information on the cost of these, contact the above address. *Applications* should be made to the above address as early as possible in order to alow you to get your first choice of project.

RALEIGH INTERNATIONAL: Raleigh House, 27 Parsons Green Lane London SW6 4HZ (tel 020-7371 8585; e-mail info@raleigh.org.uk; www. raleighinternational.org). Raleigh International is a charity that aims to inspire and develop people through challenging community, conservation and adventure projects on expeditions around the world. Opportunities available for Volunteers aged 17-25 and staff aged 25+.

Expedition destinations in 2002/2003 include Chile, Ghana, Nambiba, Mongolia, Costa Rica/Nicaragua and Borneo. Projects range forom building straw bale clinics in Mongolia, trekking across Costa Rica from the Caribbean to the Pacific, conservation work in National Parks in Namibia, school building in Ghana and bio-diversity research in glacier rich southern Chile.

Applicants must attend an introductory weekend which, through dynamic fun events realistically reflects expedition life with Raleigh International. Teamwork skills are developed and motivation is tested. Volunteers are asked to fundraise £3,200 on behalf of Raleigh International. On expedition all costs are covered and a six month return ticket is provided allowing the option of independent travel after expedition. Fund raising for Raleigh International is great fun with regional and national events provided and many years of advice and experience.

REMPART: 1 rue de Guillemites, 75004 Paris, France (tel 01-42 71 96 55; fax 01-42 71 73 00).
This is an association set up to use help from volunteers to preserve heritage sites mostly across France, but also Europe, and Canada. Volunteers pay a membership fee of approx £20, with reductions for previous participants, and registration fees for whichever project they wish to participate in. Details of projects, costs and accommodation available are listed in the annual brochure. Most stays are for two weeks only, by arrangement with the project leader at the site. Volunteers pay their own travel expenses and should bring their own sleeping bags and working clothes.

THE RIGHT HAND TRUST: Gelligason, Llanfair Caereinion, Powys SY21 9HE (tel/fax 01938-810215; e-mail RightHandTrust@compuserve.com). The Right Hand Trust is a Christian charity offering a life-enriching experience for young volunteers living and working as guests of the Christian church in rural African communities.
Volunteers to live and work with a local church in Africa. Placements are from January to August, but prior training begins in July. Duties vary according to the skills and talents of the volunteer and the local needs overseas; endless opportunities can include teaching, church and community work. No allowance is paid; volunteers live as part of the community in basic but adequate conditions.

Applicants should be Christians aged 18-30. Training and fundraising occur in connection with the Trust prior to the overseas placement. *Applications* to Mark Wright, Director, at the above address.

SCRIPTURE UNION: 207-209 Queensway, Bletchley, Milton Keynes, Bucks MK2 2EB (tel 01908-856000; fax 01908-856012; e-mail: holidays@ scriptureunion.

org.uk; www.scriptureunion.org.uk). Scripture Union activities include programmes for Bible reading, children's missions, residential holidays for children and young people, work in schools, youth work and the publishing and distribution of Christian literature.

Activity Holiday Voluntary Instructors (4,000) to work a minimum of one week throughout the summer. Volunteers are expected to help organise Christian activity holidays for young people and carry out residential work. Volunteers work on sites for up to 24 hours per day in Britain and overseas. Applicants must be in sympathy with the aims of Scripture Union, committed Christians and over 18 years old. There is always a need for those who have qualifications or interests in outdoor activities, sports, working with the disabled, first aid or life saving. *Applications from December onwards to the Holidays Administrator, at the above address.*

SERVICE CIVIL INTERNATIONAL/SCI-INTERNATIONAL: see the entry for International Voluntary Service above.

STUDENTS PARTNERSHIP WORLDWIDE (SPW): 17 Dean's Yard, London SW1P 3PB (tel 020-7222 0138; fax 020-72330008; e-mail: spwuk@ gn.apc.org; www.spw.org).

SPW is a youth development charity which offers 18-28 year olds the opportunity to work in rural communities in South Africa, Tanzania, Uganda, Zimbabwe, India and Nepal. Overseas and local volunteers work together on either educational or environmental programmes for between 4 and 9 months. Projects start between September and March.

SPW is a non-profit making charity - this means that volunteers are only asked to cover their own costs (£2,600-£2,950). *Contact* the above address for further details or visit their website.

TEACHING & PROJECTS ABROAD: Gerrard House, Rustington, West Sussex, BN16 1AW (tel +44-(0)1903-859911; fax 01903-785779; e-mail info@teaching-abroad.co.uk; www.teaching-abroad.co.uk). Recruiters of English speaking volunteers interested in adventurous foreign travel and a worthwhile job.

Voluntary Placements (1,000) mostly for teaching work, in China, Ghana, India, Mexico, Mongolia, Nepal, Peru, Russia, Romania, South Africa, Thailand, Togo and Ukraine. Dates and duration are usually flexible. Volunteers are usually 17-25, but older candidates are welcome. In selected areas there are voluntary work experience programmes in business, conservation and other professions; most popular are those for medical subjects (around 250), media/journalism and supervised dissertations for degree courses. Applications are invited from anyone with good spoken English, irrespective of nationality.

All placements are self-funded and the placement fees which vary according to location, cover insurance, supervision and support, local board and lodging; fees are from £795 for a 3 month placement. Paid staff work in all locations to vet placements, accommodation and work supervisors. They meet volunteers on arrival and remain available to deal with any queries.

Details of the projects can be found on their website, or in the full brochure available from the above address.

TEARFUND TRANSFORM INTERNATIONAL PROGRAMME: 100 Church Road, Teddington, Middlesex TW11 8QE (tel 0845 355 8355; e-mail: transform@tearfund.org; www.tearfund.org/transform). Tearfund is an evangelical Christian development charity working with local partners to bring

help and hope to communities in need. Last year Tearfund supported over 500 projects in 90 countries.
Volunteers to work for 3-7 weeks from early July to the end of August; assignments are in a number of countries and include practical work, renovation and work with children.

A contribution of around £1,300 which includes travel, food and accommodation is required. Applicants should be over 18 and committed Christians. Details are available from late September from the Enquiry Unit at the above address and *applications* should be received by 1 March.

TEJO (TUTMONDA ESPERANTISTA JUNULARA ORGANIZO): Nieuwe Binnenweg 176, 3015 BJ Rotterdam, the Netherlands (tel 31 10 436 1044: fax 31 10 436 1751).
Volunteers to join work camps in various European countries arranged by TEJO, the World Organisation of Young Esperantists. Work to be done may be on reconstruction projects. Accommodation provided. Period of work normally from 1 to 2 weeks.

Applicants should be aged between 16 and 30. No previous experience necessary: all camps include Esperanto lessons for beginners, and a few are limited to Esperanto speakers. For details *contact* the above address including an International Reply Coupon.

TREKFORCE EXPEDITIONS: 34 Buckingham Palace Road, London SW1W 0RE (tel 020-7828 2275; e-mail info@trekforce.org.uk; www.trekforce.org.uk) Trekforce offers a once in a lifetime opportunity to play your part in international conservation. 8 to 20 week expeditions run in Belize, Central America and Sarawak, South East Asia concentrating on endangered rainforests and working with the local communities. Trekforce's extended programmes of four to five months incorporate expedition work, learning new languages and teaching in rural communities such as the Kelabit of Sarawak or the Mayans of Belize. Experiences span from working as a team in demanding enviornments to working independently among different cultures.

Specialist skills are not necessary in order to take part, but applicants do need to be aged 17 or over, fit, enthusiastic, have a sense of adventure, and the ability to work as part of a team.

Find out more about these challenging adventures on Trekforce's introduction days, a chance to meet previous 'trekkers' and find out more about project work, fundraising and kit. An 8 week expedition costs £2350 plus flight; a 17 week expedition to Sarawak costs £3300 plus flight; and a 20 week expedition to Belize costs £3600 plus flight. Specialist skills are not necessary in order to take part, but applicants do need to be aged 17 or over, fit, enthusiastic, have a sense of adventure, and the ability to work as part of a team.

For more information *contact* Trekforce at the above address.

UNA EXCHANGE: Temple of Peace, Cathays Park, Cardiff CF10 3AP (tel 029-20-223088; e-mail unaexchange@btinternet.com; www.unaexchange.org).
Arranges international voluntary projects in Wales and sends volunteers to camps abroad for 2-4 weeks mostly between the months of April and September but sometimes also at other times of year. Projects include: social, environmental and manual work, and playschemes. UNA Exchange also operates a 'North-South' programme in 32 countries in Africa, Latin America and Asia, volunteers for this need to attend training weekends in Cardiff in February and October. Work is

unpaid and there is a registration fee of £50 for the Welsh camps and between £90 and £125 for the camps abroad, depending on the country.

There are also some medium-term (6-12 month) projects available, mainly in Europe, through the European Voluntary Service (EVS).

Volunteers applying from abroad should go through a workcamp organisation in their own country. Board and accommodation free. Further details from the above address: please enclose an A5 stamped addressed envelope with enquiries.

VOLUNTEERS FOR PEACE (VFP): 1034, Tiffany Road, Belmont, Vermont 05730, USA (tel 802-259-2759; fax 802-259-2922; e-mail vfp@vfp.org; www.vfp.org).

Co-ordinates international workcamps lasting 2-3 weeks in 70 countries in western and eastern Europe, North and West Africa and North, South and Central America. Work includes construction, environmental, agricultural and social work, phone write or e-mail for a free Newsletter. A full listing of VFP's programmes can be found in the VFP's *International Workcamp Directory* ($20 post-paid in the USA).

YOUTH ACTION FOR PEACE: 8 Golden Ridge, Freshwater, Isle of Wight, P040 9LE (tel 01983-752577; fax 01983-756900; e-mail yapuk@ukonline.co.uk; www.yap-uk.org).

Volunteers needed to take part in voluntary work projects organised by YAP (formerly known as Christian Movement for Peace) in the UK and its sister organisations in Belgium, France, Germany, Hungary, Italy, Latvia, Mexico, the Middle East, the Netherlands, Portugal, Romania, Spain, and Turkey and 30 other countries. The work undertaken may consist of tasks such as restoring an historic building, entertaining handicapped children or clearing a forest. Projects generally last for two to three weeks each, and take place between May and October.

Participants will usually be working for around 35 hours per week with volunteers from different countries and local people; food, accommodation and leisure activities are provided. No particular qualifications are necessary, but applicants must be aged at least 18 and there is normally an upper age limit of between 30 and 35.

A brochure with a complete list of projects is published at the beginning of April each year. For further details *contact* Rocio Medland, Co-ordinator, at the above address.

YOUTH INTERNATIONAL: 1121 Downing Street, Denver, Colorado 80218, USA (tel 303-839 5877; fax 303-839 5887; e-mail youth.international@ bigfoot.com; www.youthinternational.org). Youth International aims to give exciting and fulfilling yet educational experiences to young people. Its mission is to open doors for young people to actively explore and develop a wider perspective on the world.

Volunteer Students to undertake two separate experiential education programmes: the first is to Asia and the other is to East Africa and the Middle East. Volunteers are stay in private homes in each country, participating in community work, outdoor adventure and sight-seeing. Teams of around twelve people travel together, whilst educating themselves on the region in which they are travelling. Each member has access to the Youth International library and is given a monthly book budget to purchase books whilst travelling. The students actually live and work alongside the local people to gain first hand knowledge and experience of their customs and cultures.

The Asia programme visits the Philippines, Thailand, Nepal and India: visits to Kenya, Egypt, Israel and Jordan make up the East Africa and Middle East programme. The programmes are run twice a year in Autumn from September to mid-December and in Spring, from mid January to late May.

Selection for position on Youth International teams is made through application and interview process. Prices range from $6,500 to $8,000 depending on programme length and destinations. This covers all expenses, including deep sea diving, rafting, safaris etc., educational materials and other miscellaneous expenses.

For more information *contact* Brad Gillings at the above address.

Work with Children

VILLAGE CAMPS INC: Personnel Office Dept. 815, 14 Rue de la Morâche, 1260 Nyon, Switzerland. (tel +41 22 990 9405; fax +41 22 990 9494; e-mail personnel@villagecamps.ch; www.villagecamp.com). Village Camps has been organising educational and activity camps for children from all over the globe for over 25 years with a serious commitment to client and staff alike.

Specialists and General Counsellors required for outdoor education, orienteering, leadership training, nature/environmental studies, swimming, archery, tennis, outdoor education, soccer, arts and crafts, mountain biking, gymnastics and drama etc.

Qualified Instructors in rock climbing, canoeing, mountain leading, watersports.

Language Teachers for English, French and German classes.

Nurses/Medical Staff: must be qualified RSN or equivalent.

Kitchen and **Domestic Staff** (EU passport holders only for these domestic positions)

Drivers

Junior Staff: for the Day Camp only (No accommodation included).

The Outdoor Education Programme occurs from May to June in Switzerland and France and in the autumn, August to October in Switzerland. The Summer Residential and Day Camps occur from June to August in Switzerland, UK, Holland, France and Austria. Room and board, accident & liability insurance and a generous allowance are provided. All staff must be over 21. Much is expected of staff but the rewards are generous. Experience working with children is essential and knowledge of a second language is an advantage. Motivated staff are required for short seasonal positions.

Visit the above website for more information or contact the Personnel Department at the address above for an application pack.

Work at Sea

DOLPHIN HELLAS SHIPPING SA: 71 Akti Miaouli, 18537 Piraeus, Greece (tel 01-4512109; fax 01-41388435).

Wine Stewards/Stewardesses (5-6) to serve and help in cruise ship lounges. To work 8-10 hours per day, 7 days per week. Wages of approximately £275 per month plus insurance and free accommodation on board. Period of work at least 3 months. Must have a pleasant personality and knowledge of at least one major European language.

Trainee Wine Stewards (6) for the summer period. Requirements as above. Return ticket and insurance provided plus around £60 pocket money per month. Period of work at least 3 months.

Hostesses (6) for duties including office work, reception and accompanying passengers on land excursions. Wages £330-£500 per month plus insurance. To work 8-10 hours per day, 7 days a week. Period of work 1-7 months. Must have excellent written and spoken knowledge of at least two major European languages, energy and a pleasant personality. Experience in dealing with people essential. Knowledge of Japanese an advantage.

Trainee Hostesses (4) for the summer period. Requirements as above. Return ticket and insurance provided plus around £60 pocket money. Period of work 2-7 months.

To work on cruise ships on three, four and seven day cruises in the Mediterranean: minimum period of work 3 months days between April and November. Some winter work may also be available in the Caribbean. *Applications* from December to Dolphin Hellas Shipping at the above address or attn. Mrs Devouros, Golden Sun Cruises, Akti Miaouli 85, Piraeus, Greece.

OPENWIDE INTERNATIONAL LTD.: 7 Westmoreland House, Cumberland Park, London NW10 6RE (tel 020-8962 3400; fax 020-8962 3440; e-mail info@openwide.co.uk; www.openwideinternational.com). Europe's largest entertainment consultancy and the leaders on providing innovative entertainment to the leisure and tourism industry. Working with Openwide is an excellent way to develop professional and creative skills as an entertainer; over 150 people are recruited annually to work on cruise ships.

Cruise Staff Entertainers and performers to work on ships in the Mediterranean and Caribbean. Dancers, Vocalists, Presenters, DJs and childrens entertainers required to deliver daytime and evening entertainment programmes. Excellent PR skills essential; knowledge of a Scandinavian language desirable. Salaries from £200+ per week plus meals, accommodation and flight. Full training given.

Positions are available all year round. Contracts approx. 5 months. All applicants are invited to send a CV and photographs to the Overseas Recruitment Department at Openwide International and also to visit their website. Auditions held all year round.

Other Employment Abroad

ALLIANCES ABROAD: 702 West Avenue, Austin, TX 78701, USA (e-mail INFO@alliancesabroad.com). Organises a variety of employment including placements in both paid and voluntary positions.

Paid Internships and **Work Experience Placements** with employers in San Francisco, California, Washington DC, Denver and Boulder, Colorado. Wages paid; accommodation with families or American students.

Paid Teaching opportunities, many of which require no prior teaching experience and professional certification in Brazil, China, Taiwan, Mexico and Thailand.

Hotel/Restaurant Placements in Great Britain for 2-6 months, largely in the south of England. Wages £40 per week plus tips and full board.

Volunteer Internships with employers in or near major cities in Germany, France and Spain for 1-3 months; no wage, room and board provided with families.

Voluntary Work on social, medical, developmental and educational placements in Africa, Costa Rica, Mexico and Asia for 2-12 months.

For all the above application fees of approx. £46 are payable plus varying programme fees to cover accommodation, insurance, local back-up etc. *Contact* the above address for details.

anyworkanywhere.com e-mail info@anyworkanywhere.com; www.anywork anywhere.com.

This organisation provides a free source of information to people looking for

casual, seasonal and temporary work in the UK and worldwide through the site www.anyworkanywhere.com. It lists a variety of employment including work in 16th century pubs, white water rafting in the Austrian Alps, forestry conservation in the Caledonian mountains, hotel work, fruit and vegetable picking, jobs in activity centres, care work and childcare.

The site also provides other useful information on work and travel such as directories of hostels, cyber cafés and embassies and links to other useful and relevant sites. For those who are a little more adventurous and just want to turn up and see what jobs are available, they have a guide to the main locations and times of ski seasons and harvests worldwide.

BUNAC: 16 Bowling Green Lane, London EC1R OQH (tel 020-7251 3472; fax 020-7251 0215; e-mail enquiries@bunac.org.uk; www.bunac.org).
BUNAC, a non-profit organisation, has enabled over 250,000 Gap Year and full time students to work overseas since 1962. BUNAC is a national club whose members are able to obtain jobs, work permits and affordable flight packages. There are a great variety of programmes on offer including summer camp counselling in the USA and work and travel programmes to the USA, Canada, Australia, New Zealand, South Africa, Ghana and Argentina.

BUNAC also offers an internship programme, OPT USA, enabling students and non-students to undertake course or career-related training in the USA.

BUNAC provide help and advice on jobs, accommodation and travel as well as providing back-up services while working and travelling.

COUNCIL EXCHANGES: 20th Floor, 633 Third Avenue, New York, NY 10017, USA (tel toll free 1-888-COUNCIL; e-mail: Info@councilexchanges.org; www.us.councilexchanges.org/).
Council Exchanges (a division of the Council on International Educational Exchanges, or CIEE) in New York administers a Work Exchange programme that enables US citizens (with some exceptions for permanent residents of the US) who are college students over 18 years of age to work legally in the following countries for the following lengths of time:

Australia: for up to 4 months at any time of year;
Canada: at any time of year for up to 5 months;
France: any time of year for up to 3 months;
Germany: summer option from May 15-October 15 for up to 3 months;
      internship option any time of year for up to 6 months;

Ireland: any time of year for up to 4 months;
New Zealand: anytime from April 1-October 31.
The cost of participating in this programme varies according to destination and includes work documentation, a programme handbook, an orientation upon arrival in the country of destination and a resource office which students can make use of during their stay. Applicants must be either full time students (enrolled for at least eight credits) or within one semester of study at an accredited college or university and matriculated towards a degree (Australian participants DO NOT need to be students, they only need to be between the ages of 18 and 30). Applications must be made from inside the USA. Council also offers more than 900 International Volunteer Projects in 30 countries. Open to all team-minded individuals. Council's *Teach in China* programme enables Bachelors degree holders to spend a semester or full academic year teaching English to Chinese college students of all ages. Wages and room and board provided. US applicants contact 1-888-COUNCIL; UK contact Council on 020-7-478 2000; Australia contact 61-2-8235-7000.

INTEREXCHANGE: 161 Sixth Avenue, New York, NY 10013, USA (tel 212-924-0446; fax 212-924-0575; e-mail info@interexchange.org; www.interexchange.org). Inter-Exchange is a private non-profit organisation that can help US citizens to find short term jobs, au pair, internship, voluntary and English teaching opportunities throughout Europe. Various schemes exist in Belgium, Bulgaria, France, Germany, Italy, Netherlands, Norway, Poland, Russia, Spain, Ukraine and the UK. For further details *contact* Inter-Exchange at the above address.

i-to-i: One Cottage Road, Headingley, Leeds, LS6 4DD (tel 0870-333 2332; fax 0113-274 6923; e-mail: info@i-to-i.com; www.i-to-i.com). i-to-i is a working holiday organisation specialising in voluntary teaching, conservation and work placements in Latin America, Russia, Africa, Australia and Asia. i-to-i also offers weekend and online TEFL (Teach English as a Foreign Language) training for those who want to combine teaching as part of their travel. Around 1000 volunteers are trained and placed each year. All projects are thoroughly researched and volunteers are met and supported whilst away by paid in-country co-ordinators. All prices include pre-departure training (TEFL for teaching placements), comprehensive insurance and 24 hour support from the UK. Food and accommodation included on most projects and some also offer local language courses on arrival. i-to-i projects are suitable for anyone over the age of 18: gap year and university students, graduates, career breakers and older volunteers with a sense of adventure.

i-Ventures: Voluntary teaching, conservation, business, journalism, media and medical placements abroad. Current projects include an elephant orphanage in Sri Lanka, sea turtle conservation in Costa Rica, newscasting on a radio station in Ghana, and teaching English in a Nepalese Buddhist monastery amongst many others. Accommodation varies from homestays with local families to camping, guesthouses, and apartments. Projects are available all year round from one month to the complete year out.

Mini-Ventures: Two week projects in Ecuador, Nepal, Sri Lanka and Mongolia for those with a desire to travel with purpose but without the time for a full i-Venture. Also suitable for groups. Inclusive price for pre-departure training, 13 nights full-board, airport pickup and comprehensive insurance.

TEFL Training: i-to-i offers intensive weekend TEFL courses in 13 UK cities. There is also an optional 20 hour home-study grammar module. Fees are £195 waged or £175 unwaged. An online TEFL course is now available at www.onlineTEFL.com allowing study from any location worldwide. Both courses are designed for travellers and include a module on finding work abroad.

TRAVEL ACTIVE: PO Box 107, N-5800 AC Venray, The Netherlands (tel +31-478 551900; fax +31-478 551911; e-mail info@travelactive.nl; www. travelactive.nl). Travel Active is Holland's largest youth exchange organisation, offering work exchange, au pair and high school programmes on a global scale.

Travel Active also receives students from all over the world on its incoming high school, au pair and work exchange programmes. For these programmes Travel Active also offers its own, tailor-made insurance. Dutch and Belgian youngsters may choose from a variety of work programmes, with or without job placement. Internships are also available. Several programmes combine a language course with a job placement. Travel Active is member of FIYTO, ALTO, IAEWEP and a founding member of IAPA.

WORLDNETUK: Southern Office, Avondale House, Sydney Road, Haywards Heath, West Sussex; Central Office, Emberton House, 26 Shakespeare Road, Bedford MK40 2ED (tel 07002 287 247; fax 01234 351070; e-mail info@worldnetuk.com; www.worldnetuk.com). Leading work and travel specialists offering the following programmes: Camp USA; Nanny/Childcare Programmes to USA;

Ski/Summer Resort Nannies; Work and Travel USA; Study Programmes USA – Educare and Academic Year Abroad. Destinations include 180 clusters throughout the USA, France, Corsica, Spain, Belearics, Turkey, Italy, Sardinia, Greece, Austria and Switzerland..

Nanny/Childcare Programme USA for 18-26 year olds with childcare training, NNEB, Btec National Diploma in Nursery Nursing or NVQ level III. Full clean driving licence required. Departures every month. Opportunity to travel at end of year.

Au Pair Programme USA: for 18-26year olds with 200 hours childcare/babysitting. Full clean driving licence. Departures every month. Opportunity to travel at end of year.

Camp USA: 19-28 year olds needed to take up posts as Counsellors or Support Staff for min 8-10 weeks during summer months. All departures in June. Opportunity to travel at end of stay.

Ski/Summer Resort Nannies for work with all major travel companies; applicants must be qualified /experienced in childcare to work either in activity clubs, creche or with individual families and available for either the full summer or ski season. No age limit. Applicants must be available for either the full summer or ski season (some shorter term placements sometimes available)

Work & Travel USA: exciting opportunity to work in US for between 2.5 and 4 months. Summer jobs in hotels, restaurants, theme parks, county fairs, camping centres and national parks. Winter jobs in ski and recreation areas and warm weather tourist destinations.. Summer programme begins May - August and winter programme begins in December.

Study Programmes offered by Worldnetuk include:

Educare: a chance for 18-26 year olds to study part-time at college or University whilst working with
school age children and living with an American family.

Academic Year America: opportunity for 15- 8 year olds to spend either one term or a full academic year with an American family and attending a US High School. Departures August and January. Programme sponsored by the American Institute for Foreign Study

For a full brochure call 07002-287247, fax 01234 351070, email info@worldnetuk.com or visit www.worldnetuk.com.

Au Pairs, Nannies, Family Helps and Exchanges

A-ONE AU-PAIRS and NANNIES: Suite 216, The Commercial Centre, Picket Piece, Andover, SP11 6RU (tel 01264-332500; fax 01264-362050; e-mail info@aupairsetc.co.uk).

Au Pairs/Au Pairs Plus required for light housework and childcare 5 days per week in a variety of countries. Wages, board and accommodation vary according to country of placement. Applicants should be 17-27 years old.

Contact Karen Hopwood, Proprietor, for details.

ACADEMY AU PAIR AND NANNY AGENCY: 42 Milsted Road, Rainham, Kent ME8 6SU (tel 01634-310808; e-mail academy4aupairs@hotmail.com; website www.academyagency.co.uk).

Au Pairs: pocket money around £45 per week for 25 hours work. Should be aged 18-27.

Au Pairs Plus: pocket money £60 per week. Should be aged 18-27.

Nannies: wages £200 or more per week. Minimum age 18; must have NNEB or

B-Tech qualifications and be able to produce references.
Mothers' Helps: wages £150 or more per week. Need not be qualified, but previous experience and references are essential.

All the above are needed for positions in Europe, including Britain; au pair positions can also be arranged in Australia. Positions are available throughout the year. Applicants should have some knowledge of the language of the country chosen. *Applications* for summer placements should be made before March. For further details send a stamped addressed envelope or International Reply Coupon to the above address, stating which type of work is of interest.

A.C. LINK: via F. Ugoni 7/B, I-25100 Brescia, Italy (tel 30-375 4471).
Au Pairs and **Mothers' Helps:** placed all over Italy. 6-12 month placements and summer placements of 2-3 months available. Minimum age 18 years. Applicants must be well educated and mature with proven child-care experience. Knowledge of Italian not usually essential. For further information *contact* the above address.

AMICIZIA di Maria De Angelis: Via XX Settembre 21/7 - 16121 Genova, Italy (tel 010-533-1096; fax; 010-553-1152; e-mail insedit@libero.it; www.mamicizia.it).
Au Pairs, Mothers' Helps, Domestic Nannies to stay with children and help with household duties. Wages from approx. £170/200-£400/460 per month depending on position plus board and lodging. Minimum period of work 3 months in the summer or longer over the winter season. Knowledge of Italian and English is strongly preferred, but is not essential if with families who know English and/or other languages. Applicants must be experienced with children and household duties. Placements available in Italy and across Europe, through Amicizia or through Amicizia correspondent agencies, and in Canada. Please Note: *under Italian law, Amicizia can only accept EU females for stays in Italy.* *Applications* to Mrs Maria de Angelis at the above address.

ANGLO CONTINENTAL NANNY AU PAIRS PLACEMENT AGENCY: Dial Post-House, Dial Post, Nr. Horsham, West Sussex RH13 8NQ (tel 01403 713344/55; fax 01403 713366; e-mail sharon@anglocontinental.fsnet.co.uk; www.anglocontinentalplacements.com/www.anglocontinentalplacements.co.uk). Established 1985.
Au Pairs recruited for Austria, Croatia, Czech Republic, Finland, France, Germany, Holland, Hungary, Iceland, Italy, Norway, Slovakia, Spain, Sweden, Switzerland and Turkey. Pocket money between £40 and £55 per week, plus board and lodging in own room, in exchange for around 5 hours' work a day. 12 months' long term stays for applicants from abroad can be arranged in the UK; pocket money £40-£55 per week.
Chefs, Receptionists, Waiters, Waitresses, Chambermaids, Kitchen Porters for hotel work UK and Spain. Applicants must be EU nationals, or must have a Visa for the appropriate country. *Applications* enclosing 4 International Reply Coupons to Mrs Sharon Wolfe at the above address.
Anglo Continental Placements are also advertising for **Chefs, Sous Chefs, Chefs de Partie, Commis Chefs, Wine Waiters, Receptionists, Waiters, Waitresses, Chambermaids, kitchen Porters, Porters, Jobs available in 2, 3, 4 and 5 star hotels. Accommodation provided for all jobs.** *EU nationals, Austrians, and South Afrians may apply.*

L'AQUILONE AU PAIR BUREAU: Via Giovanni Pascoli 15, I-20129 Milan, Italy (tel 0039-2-29 52 96 39; fax 0039-2-29 52 21 75; e-mail: aquilone@

azienda.net; www.s.snf.it/aquilone).
Au Pairs to work 30 hours a week. Salary £35 per week.
Au Pair Plus to work 36 hours a week. Salary £45 per week.
Mother's Help to work 48 hours a week. Salary £73 per week.

Italian applicants are placed in the following countries: Austria, Belgium, Denmark, France, Germany, Great Britain, Greece, Holland, Norway, Spain and Switzerland. Non-Italian applicants placed in Italy, Australia and New Zealand. Period of work varies from country to country but is usually 8-9 months during the academic year and 2-3 months during the summer. Applicants must have childcare experience and be aged between 18 and 28.

For more information about agency fees and details *contact* the above address.

THE AU PAIR AGENCY: 231 Hale Lane, Edgware, Middlesex HA8 9QF (tel 020-8-958 1750; fax 020-8-958 5261; e-mail: elaine@aupairagency.com; www.aupairagency.com).
Au Pairs from Britain mainly placed in France, Spain, Italy and Germany.
Mothers' Helps placed in France.

Applicants should be aged between 18 and 25. Non-smokers preferred; drivers always welcomed. Summer stays of 12 weeks possible – early applicants receive priority. At all other times, a minimum commitment of 9-12 months is required. A reasonable knowledge of the language of the chosen country is needed. European au pairs and nationals of participating non-EU countries also placed in Britain. The Au-Pair agency does not place au-pairs in the USA. Although the agency works wth all the British government approved participating countries, it cannot place applicants from one country, via London, into another country. e.g. it cannot place au-pairs from Spain with families in Turkey.

All applicants receive pocket money plus full board and lodging. For further details *contact* Mrs Newman on the above number at least 12 weeks before preferred starting date.

AU PAIR CONNECTIONS: 39 Tamarisk Road, Wildern Gate, Hedge End, Hants SO30 4TN (tel 01489-780438; fax 01489-692656; e-mail Aupairconnect@ aol.com; www.aupair-connections.co.uk).
Au Pairs, Mothers' Helps placed in France, Spain, the Balearic Islands, Italy, Austria and elsewhere in Europe; applicants from overseas also placed in the UK. Pocket money approx. £40-£45 per week. Minimum stays normally 6 months, but some summer stays of 10 weeks. Applicants must have experience of childcare, babysitting etc.; a good knowledge of English is also useful as some families want their children tutored in English. The Agency also have 'homestay' for students. For further details contact Ms Denise Blighe at the above address. All *applications* should be in writing enclosing a s.a.e.

AU PAIR IN EUROPE: P.O. Box 68056 Blakely Postal Outlet, Hamilton, Ontario, Canada L8M 3M7 (tel 1-905 545 6305; fax 1 905-544 4121; e-mail aupair@princeent.com; www.princeent.com).
Au Pairs placed with families around the world. Au Pair in Europe helps applicants step by step through the whole process, including visa, medical insurance and travel arrangements. Countries available: Australia, Austria, Belgium, Bermuda, Denmark, England, Finland, France, Germany, Greece, Holland, Iceland, Italy, Japan, Monaco, New Zealand, Norway, Spain, Russia, Sweden, and Switzerland. Contracts range from 3 months to one year. Salary

approximately $75-$120 per week plus room and board.

Applicants should be aged 18-30. Childcare experience necessary. To work approximately 30 hours per week, plus some babysitting. Registration fee charged. *Contact* the above address for a free brochure; please include your complete mailing address or see the organisation's web page for further information.

AU PAIR INTERNATIONAL: 115 High Street, Uckfield, East Sussex TN22 1RN (tel 01825-761420; fax 01825-769050; e-mail aupairinternat@onetel.net.uk; www.aupairinternational.co.uk). In business since 1981 Au Pair International is a member of REC. Friendly and thoroughly experienced.

Au Pairs recruited throughout the year for the UK and Europe. Live-in, £50 per week minimum pocket money or equivalent. 25 hours work per week, 2 days off. Unlimited number of posts available for 6-24 months stay , but some 10 weeks summer placements. Their families in the UK are mostly in London, London suburbs and the southern counties and south coast. Vacancies in Europe are mainly in Cities and Coastal Towns.

Mothers' Helps/Nannies recruited for the UK throughout the year. Live-in salary between £75-£214 net plus per week depending on age, experience and location. Applicants from Australia, South Africa and Canada, can work as Mother's Help/Nannies and obtain a 24 months working holiday before they come to the UK.

Other Services: advice on Language courses, introduction to other au pairs, mothers helps and nannies, basic counselling, help to establish friendly working relationship between applicants and families, social events holiday pay or return ticket, and a Certificate of Achievement on completion of stay. *Applications* to the above address in writing, by fax or e-mail.

BLOOMSBURY BUREAU: PO Box 12749, 37 Store Street, London WC1E 7BH (tel 020-7-813 4061; fax 020-7-813 4038; e-mail bloomsburo@aol.com).

Au Pairs (300) for placements in EU countries throughout the year. Also unlimited number of posts for long stays 6-12 months, especially in Austria, France, Germany, Italy, Spain, Switzerland and throughout the UK. Pocket money £50 per week, in return for 30 hours help with childcare and light housework and helping with English.

There are also some hotel posts in Bavaria (20/30) for *EU nationals only* for the summer season May-October, approx. £400 per month live-in. Applicants should be aged at least 18 and supply a c.v. and one refernece. *Applications* to Marianne Dix, Principal, at the above address. Personal interviews are encouraged.

BUNTERS AU PAIR AGENCY: The Old Malt House, 6 Church Street, Pattishall, Towcester, Northants, NN12 8NB (tel 01327-831144; fax 01327-831155; e-mail office@aupairnannies.com; www.aupairnannies.com).

Au Pair Jobs in Spain, France, Belgium, Austria, Italy, Holland and the UK; duties consist of light housework and assisting with children. Minimum stay 6-12 months; 10 week summer stays also arranged in Spain and France, but these must be applied for before May. Pocket money is a minimum of £45 per week depending on hours worked and location of placement.

Applicants should be aged 18-27, preferably be non-smokers, and should have experience with children (babysitting etc.), be able to provide references, and have some knowledge of the language of the country of placement. For further information send a stamped addressed envelope to Caroline Jones at the above address.

AMERICA * AUSTRALIA
CANADA * EUROPE * SOUTH AFRICA
NANNY - MOTHER'S HELP - AU PAIR

An opportunity to live abroad in a secure family environment, caring for children and helping in the home. Continuous support while overseas. For further information please contact:

CHILDCARE INTERNATIONAL LTD.
Trafalgar House, Grenville Place, London NW7 3SA
Tel: 020 8906 3116
Fax: 020 8906 3461
Email: office@childint.co.uk
Web: http://www.childint.co.uk

CHILDCARE INTERNATIONAL: Childcare International Ltd., Trafalgar House, Grenville Place, London NW7 3SA (tel 020-8-906 3116; fax 020-8-906 3461; e-mail: office@childint.co.uk; www.childint.co.uk).
CHILDCARE EUROPE, CHILDCARE CANADA, CHILDCARE SOUTH AFRICA, and CHILDCARE AUSTRALIA off au pair/au pair plus, mother's help and nanny positions with associate agencies overseas: provides the opportunity to live abroad in a secure family environment caring for children and helping in the home. Opportunities to learn a language and experience different cultures through both study and everday life. Salary provided according to age and experience. Full support available from a local representative to assist with language course and meeting friends. Placements in Canada require a nanny qualification. *Applications* to the above address.

EDGWARE AU PAIR AGENCY: 1565 Stratford Road, Hall Green, Birmingham, B28 9JA (tel 0121-745 6777; fax 0121-243 4200/0121-733 6555; e-mail edgware@100s-aupairs.co.uk; www.100s-aupairs.co.uk).
Au Pairs needed for families all over Europe and the UK, placed in all the capital cities, e.g. London, Paris, Rome, Barcelona. Au pairs need a working knowledge of the country in which they wish to be placed. Good child-care experience and character references are essential. For more information visit the website or *write* to the above address enclosing 2 Internatonal Reply Coupons.

EN FAMILLE OVERSEAS: The Old Stables, 60b Maltravers Street, Arundel, West Sussex BN18 9BG (tel 01903-883266; fax 01903-883582; e-mail enfamilleoverseas@aol.com).
Paying Guest Stays Arranged in France, Germany and Spain. Also language courses with homestays arranged in France and Spain. Contact above address.

EUROYOUTH ABROAD LTD: 301 Westborough Road, Westcliff, Southend-on-Sea, Essex SS0 9PT (tel 01702-341434; fax 01702-330104). Established in 1961.
Paying Guest Holidays with or without language courses arranged around the year in Austria, France, Germany, Greece, Italy, Hungary, Portugal, Spain and Turkey for groups and individuals.
Holiday Guest Stays also arranged in Austria, France, Germany, Hungary, Italy, Spain and Turkey, mostly during the summer holiday period. Accommodation

and food are provided in exchange for English conversation. Those interested must apply very early or consider a paying guest stay as an alternative.

Ages rro both programmes 18-25 and in some cases for those over 25. Please send a stamped addressed envelope to the above address for details. Early application is essential for both programmes.

INTER-SEJOURS: 179 Rue de Courcelles, F-75017 Paris, France (tel 01-47 63 06 81; fax 01-40 54 89 41; e-mail marie.inter-sejours@libertysurf.fr; www.multimania.com/intersejours/index/html).

Inter-Sejours is a non-profit making organisation with 33 year's experience. An immediate start is possible.

Au Pairs placed in Australia, Austria, Balearics, Canada, Denmark, France, Germany, Ireland, Italy, the Netherlands, New Zealand, Spain, Sweden the USA and the UK. Working hours 15 to 45 hours a week depending on country. Pocket money minimum £160 per month. Some summer stays of 2-3 months available, but normal minimum stay 6 months; applicants who can stay for the whole school year preferred. Applicants should be aged 18-27; previous childcare experience an advantage.

Paying Guest stays also arranged all over the world, around the year. Inter-Sejours also organise work placements in hotels and restaurants throughout England.

For further details *contact* the above address

JOLAINE AU PAIR AND DOMESTIC AGENCY: 18 Escot Way, Barnet, Herts. EN5 3AN (tel 020-8449 1334; fax 020-8449 9183; e-mail aupair@jolaine.prestel.co.uk; www.jolaine.com).

Au Pair/Mother's Help stays: Jolaine can arrange for applicants to be placed as au pairs/mother's helps with families in Europe. 6-12 month stays preferred (summer stays minimum 2 months). Paying guest stays also arranged in France, Belgium and Spain; minimum stay 1 week. For further details, please *write* enclosing a large stamped addressed envelope.

LANGTRAIN INTERNATIONAL: Torquay Road, Foxrock, Dublin 18, Ireland (tel +353-1-289-38-76; fax 1-289-25-86).

Au Pairs from abroad placed in Dublin and provincial towns throughout Ireland for a minimum of 3 months in the summer and a minimum of 9 months from September and 6 months from January. Pocket money of £30 per week is paid, and English classes are also arranged. Au pairs are placed in France, Germany, Italy, Spain, Luxembourg, Switzerland, Austria, Canada, Belgium and Holland. Minimum age 18 years. Paying guest stays also arranged. *Applications* to the above address at any time.

LAURENCE CHERIFAT PROGRAMMES AU PAIR: 95 Avenue Général Leclerc, Bat. B, F-94700 Maisons Alfort, France (tel/fax +33-(0)1-43-76-48-61).

Au Pairs aged 18-27 placed in England, Ireland, Spain, Greece and one year stays in the USA. Free board and lodging, medical insurance and pocket money £30-60 per week in exchange for 25-40 hours of help (childcare, light housework and language tuition). Minimum stay normally 6 months, except for Greece (12-18 months) but there are some summer stays in England and Spain.

Basic knowlededge of the destination language not compulsory for Spain and Greece, applicants do not need any special qualifications apart from babysitting/childcare experience. Good back-up service and social programmes in each country.

Mother's Help/Nanny positions for native speakers of English, French or German, in Greece. Monthly salary £300-£500 with free board and lodging, medical/accident insurance and return airfare. *Applications* to Miss Laurence Chérifat, at the above address.

LUCY LOCKETTS & VANESSA BANCROFT DOMESTIC AGENCY: 400 Beacon Road, Wibsey, Bradford, BD6 3DJ (tel/fax 01274-402822; e-mail lucylocketts@blueyonder.co.uk). Est. 1984.

Au Pairs and **Au Pairs Plus** (20-30) from June to September. Child care and light housework. Age limits 17-28. Working hours: au pairs 30 hours, Monday to Friday, au pairs plus 40-45 hours weekly, Monday to Friday. Weekly wages £30-£35 for au pairs and £45-£50 au pairs plus. Jobs in France, Spain, Italy, Greece, Austria etc.

Nannies (5-15) in Greece, from June to September. must be qualified and have 1/2 year's experience and be aged 19-35. £100 plus per week. Long hours, some evenings free and one day off per week.

MONDIAL AGENCY: The Old Barn, Shoreham Lane, Halstead, Sevenoaks, Kent TN14 7BY (tel 01959 533664; fax 01959 533504; e-mail mondialaupairs@aol.com; www.mondialaupairs.co.uk).

Au Pair posts (for females only) arranged in Austria, Germany and Spain. Pocket money paid in return for about 5 hours work per day, $5^1/2$ days per week. Minimum period of work normally 6 months, but shorter stays are possible in the summer. Agency fee £40.

Write or e-mail to the above address about 8 weeks before a position is desired.

MORTON AND DAIS: The Stores Cottage, Warings Green Road, Solihull, West Midlands, B94 6BT (tel 01564-702-870; fax 01564-700-006).

Nannies, Nursery Nurses, Mothers' Helps. Up to 400 placed per year in Belgium, France, Germany, Italy, Spain and Turkey. Placements last for 6-12 months and summer nannies are placed from May onwards. Applicants should provide two or three childcare references, two character references, 3 photos and a 'Dear Family' letter. Nannies must hold the relevant qualifications. Wages of up to £400 per week for nannies.

Nannies: Temporary placements available in Turkey, Corsica and Sardinia in exclusive holiday resorts during the summer. Accommodation provided. Full use of sports facilities and salary. Airfare paid by the resort.

For an application form *send* a SAE to the above address or telephone for further details.

MUM'S ARMY: The Torrs, Torrs Close, Redditch, B97 4JR (tel 01527-402266; fax 01527-403990; e-mail marion@mumsarmy.u-net.com; www.mumsarmy.u-net.com).

Au Pairs placed in France, Germany, Italy, Spain, Western Europe, the USA and the United Kingdom. Minimum stay 2-3 months in the summer or 9 months plus at any other time of year. Applicants must be over 18 years old. For further details *contact* Marion Farr at the above address.

NEILSON: 120 St George's Road, Brighton, East Sussex BN2 1EA (tel 01273-626281; fax 01273-626285; e-mail recruitment@neilson.com). Neilson is a holiday company committed to providing excellent quality activity holidays. They pride themsleves on having a high staff/client ratio and the exceptional calibre of their overseas staff.

Child Minders (NNEB, BTEC or equivalent) (10) to care for 0-5 year olds in resorts in the Mediterranean and Caribbean. Summer and winter work is available, working 6 days a week plus the possibility of some unpaid overtime. Pay from £95 per week in local currency. Flights paid to and from the resort, accommodation and uniform provided. Applicants should be at least 18 years old with experience of working with children and be fun, creative and a good team player. *Contact* recruitment@neilson.com or Overseas Recruitment at the above address.

RICHMOND & TWICKENHAM AU PAIRS & NANNIES: The Old Parsonage, Main Street, Barton-under-Needwood, Staffs. DE13 8AA (tel 01283-716611; fax 01283-712299; www.aupairsnationwide.co.uk).
Placements available in Denmark, Spain, Italy and France. Minimum age 18, non-smokers preferred, wages vary from country to country.

SOLIHULL AU PAIR & NANNY AGENCY: 1565 Stratford Road, Hall Green, Birmingham B28 9JA (tel 0121-733 6444; fax 0121-733 6555; e-mail solihull@100s-aupairs.co.uk; www.100s-aupairs.co.uk).
Nannies: Wages £650-£1,050 net per month.
Starter Nannies: Wages £600-£700 per month.
Mothers' Helps: Wages £550-£650 per month.
Au Pairs: Pocket money: £160-£200 per month placed all over Europe and the UK. The agency place au pairs in France, Italy, Spain, Germany, Sweden and many other countries.
Au PairCare: Au Pairs and Nannies recruited for 12 month stays with carefully selected host families in America. £90 per week. For AuPairCare, round-trip airfare from your home country to the USA. 5 day/4 night training session in central New York City. Medical insurance. Private room and board with pre-screened host family. A local Area Director living nearby. Regularly scheduled social and cultural activities with other au pairs. Approximately £325 educational fund to pay for local classes. Two weeks paid vacation. 24 hour telephone helpline. Opportunity to travel in the 13th month. Comprehensive training and support.

The Solihull Au Pair & Nanny Agency will deal with all visa requirements. You must be able to drive, be aged 18-26, have a good knowledge of English, and be able to commit to a 12 month stay. Nannies working in the UK for American families who are re-lcoating to the USA can get help from the agency with their visa if they plan to travel to the States with their host family. If a pre-matched au pair, the agency can help to arrange the visa.

Camp USA Programme. Summer programme in the USA open to male and female applicants. Applicants must have some specialist skills, e.g. horse-riding, sports, tennis, football, handicrafts, painting. Minimum age is 19 and there is no maximum age. Free return fares, orientation in New York on arrival, board and lodging and remuneration of approximately £270. Visas and paper-work arranged by the Solihull Au Pair and Nanny Agency. Applicants must have a keen interest in working with children and have an appreciation of outdoor living.

For further details *send* a stamped addressed envelope or two international reply coupons to the above address stating clearly the vacancy you wish to apply for.

SOUTH EASTERN AU PAIR BUREAU: 39 Rutland Avenue, Thorpe Bay, Essex, SS1 2XJ (tel/fax 01702-601911; e-mail sandra_c@madasafish.com).
Au Pairs, Demi Pairs, Au Pairs Plus, Mothers' Helps and Nannies for placements in the UK and Europe. Pocket money/wages from £140-£600 or more per month. Au pairs work 5 hours daily and 2 evenings babysitting with 2 free days a week and are expected both to assist with general housework and children. **Au Pairs Plus** perform similar duties, but work increased hours and receive more pocket money. Both of these posts allow free time for language study. Not all nationals are free to take up these opportunities.

Applicants should be aged at least 17 and have some basic childcare experience. For placements abroad some knowlege of the relevant language would be useful. Minimum period of work 6 months, except for limited vacancies in the summer when a minimum of 2 months is accepted. Board and accommodation provided free of charge. *Applications* to the address above at any time.

TRAVEL ACTIVE: PO Box 107, 5800 AC Venray, The Netherlands (tel 478-551900; fax 478-551911; e-mail info@travelactive.nl).
Au Pairs for placements in Europe and the USA. Wages of approx. £70 per week in the USA and Switzerland, £120 per month elsewhere. To work minimum 30 hours per week and maximum 45 hours per week. Minimum length of stay 6-12 months or 2 months as a summer au pair. Applicants need a basic knowledge of the language of the country of placement and/or of English. For further information *contact* the above address. Applicants must be Dutch or Belgian.

UK AND OVERSEAS AGENCY LTD: Suite 21-23 (Kent House), 87 Regent Street, London W1R 7HF (tel 0207-494-2929; fax 0207-494-2922; e-mail enquiries@nannys.co.uk; www.nannys.co.uk). This agency was established over thirty years ago, and places live-in nannies, and au pair in locations worldwide.
Au Pairs, Nannies, Mothers' Helps, Domestics: the Agency offer jobs throughout the UK, Europe and in the Middle East, Australia, Japan, Singapore and the USA, as well as many other countries. Currently available jobs are listed on the agency's website.

Applicants must speak English. The agency employs both experienced and inexperienced staff. Pay and conditions vary, as do hours of work. The minimum period of work for any position is three months. All positions provide board and lodging free of charge.

Recruitment is ongoing. It will normally take between two and ten weeks to find a suitable overseas placement. *Apply* through the website.

Western Europe

Andorra

Only limited opportunities for finding temporary employment exist in Andorra, chiefly because of its small size. Opportunities are best in the tourist industry – particularly in the winter ski season: there is a chapter on Andorra in *Working in Ski Resorts – Europe & North America* (see the *Useful Publications* chapter). Once governed jointly by France and Spain, Andorra has been a sovereign country in its own right since 1993, and while it straddles the borders of France and Spain, Andorra is not itself a member of the European Union. This means that all foreigners, including nationals of EEA countries, need work permits before they can take up employment. These must be obtained by the employer once a job has been pre-arranged.

Hotel Work and Catering

HOTEL ROC BLANC: Placa des Coprinceps, 5, Escaldes, Andorra (tel +376-871400; fax +376-860 244; e-mail hotelrocblanc@gruprocblanc.com).
Receptionist/Restaurant Assistant (1) to work 6 days a week. Required all year. Applicants must have a knowledge of French, English and Spanish. Board and lodging provided. *Applications* from April to the above address.

Teaching and Language Schools

CENTRE ANDORRA DE LLENGUES: 15 Carrer del Fener, Andorra la Vella, Andorra (tel +376-804030; fax +376-822472; e-mail centrandorra.lang@ andorra.ad; www.call.ad). A small language school established in 1976 in the very centre of Andorra La Vella. Students range from six year old children to professional adult employees.
Teachers (1/2) of English as a foreign language. £750, approximately, per month. To work 27 hours per 5 day week. Board and lodging available from £150 per month. Minimum period of work 9 months between October and June.

TEFL qualifications or two years' experience of teaching English essential. Applicants should be between 22 and 35 and willing to work between 4pm and 9.30pm. Non-smokers preferred: reasonable knowledge of French or Spanish is important. *Applications* should be sent with a recent photograph to Claude Benet at the above address in May or June.

Austria

For many years Austria has offered the seasonal worker jobs in its summer and winter tourist industries. Prospects for finding work are helped by the fact that at around 3.2%, unemployment in Austria is well below the EU average. Jobs in the tourist industry can also be found in the *Worldwide* chapter. Some knowledge of German will normally be necessary unless you are working for a foreign tour operator with English-speaking clients. The Austrian Embassy in Britain (www.austria.org.uk) produces a handy booklet *Living and Working in Austria* which contains details of immigration, work and residence permits and social security procedures as well as information for the job seeker about Austrian Employment offices.

During the summer, fruit is grown along the banks of the Danube, and in the early Autumn chances of finding a job grape-picking are best in the Wachau area around Durnstein west of Vienna, or Burgenland on the Hungarian border around the Neusiedler See.

The public employment service of Austria, the *Arbeitsmarktservice*, publishes its vacancies on its website: www.ams.or.at. For hotel and catering vacancies in the South Tyrol try AMS Euro Biz/JobCenter International, Südtiroler Platz 14-16, 6020 Innsbruck (512-58 63 00/fax 512-58 63 00-20). Private employment agencies operate in Austria, but most of these specialise in executive positions or seasonal positions in the tourist industry for German speakers. It is worth checking for leads on the website of Oscar's Agency (Gymnasiumgasse 2, A-6800 Feldkirch; tel +43-5522 76563; fax +43-5522 82134; e-mail oscars@cable.vol.at; www.oscars.at).

It may be possible to find employment by placing an advertisement in daily newspapers: try *Salzburger Nachrichten* (Karolingerstrasse 40, 5021 Salzburg; tel +43-662-83730; www.salzburg.com), *Kurier* (Seidengasse 11, A-1070 Vienna; tel +43-(0)1-52100; fax 01-5210 02263; www.kurier.at) and *Die Presse* (Parkring 12a. 1015 Vienna; tel 0043-(0)1-51414; fax 01-5141 4400; www.diepresse.at). *Die Presse* also organises an annual initiative to get leading Austrian companies to take on students for summer traineeships. These papers advertise job vacancies as well on Fridays, Saturdays and Sundays. See also *Der Standard*, (www.DerStandard.at) one of the biggest newspapers concerning job vacancies. There is also an English language magazine for Austria on the internet *Austria Today* (www.austriatoday.at).

The Austrian Embassy in London has pointed out that temporary workers may not be covered by the Austrian Social Security and Health Scheme, in which case they should join a private insurance scheme or if from an EU state, ensure that they carry the form E111 or E128.

There are opportunities for voluntary work in Austria arranged by UNA Exchange.

RED TAPE

Visa Requirements: visa requirement depends upon the nationality of the visitor. Certain nationals do not require a visa providing their stay in Austria does not exceed 3 months. EU citizens who intend to work and stay for longer than 3 months should register with the nearest Aliens Administration Office (*Polizei* or *Gendarmerie-Wachzimmer*) within 3 days of arrival.

Residence Permits: *Lichtbildausweis für Fremde* is an ID card which EU/EEA nationals can apply for within 3 months of arrival, though it is not compulsory. Non-EU/EEA nationals wishing to work or live in Austria must apply for a residence permit (*Aufenthaltsgesetz*). These will be granted only to people who have already been granted a work permit and who apply from outside the Schengen area, preferably in the country of nationality. It will normally be valid for 6 months.

Work Permits: British and Irish citizens and nationals of other EU/EEA countries (and Liechtenstein) do not need work permits. If you are from a non-EEA country your prospective employer in Austria must obtain a permit (*Sicherungs bescheinigung*) from the local labour exchange and send it to you. With this work permit you must ask for a residence permit (*Aufenthaltstitel*) at an Austrian embassy before leaving for Austria. Work permits will not normally be granted to applicants who are already in the country. When in Austria work permits must be accompanied by a residence permit.

Au Pair: au pairs from outside the EU/EEA must obtain work and residence permits as above with the assistance of the mediating agency and/or the au-pair family in Austria who must inform the local employment office (*Arbeitsmarktservice*).

Voluntary Work: work permits are also required by non-EEA nationals for work with recognised voluntary organisations.

Agricultural Work

WWOOF AUSTRIA: Langegg 155, A-8511 St Stefan ob Stainz (tel/fax 03463-82270; e-mail wwoof.welcome@telering.at; http://members.telering.at/wwoof.welcome).

Volunteers required to take part in a form of cultural exchange where you live and help a farming family, learning about organic farming methods in the process (see WWOOF entry in *Worldwide*). Work is available on more than 100 farms. Movement between farms is possible. Board and accommodation will be provided, however a separate wage will not. Applicants from outside the European Union must secure their own travel insurance and pay for their own travel. In Austria they are covered by an insurance against accidents. A year's membership for WWOOF Austria costs approx. £13 and two International Reply Coupons. Membership includes a list of Austrian organic farmers looking for work-for-keep volunteer helpers. Lists of all such farmers in Austria and Switzerland, or in Austria, Switzerland and Germany, are also available for approx. £18 and £25 respectively. For more information *contact* Hildegard Gottlieb at the above address.

Hotel Work and Catering

HOTEL BRISTOL: Markatplatz 4, A-5020 Salzburg, Austria.
Housemaid: around £450 per month.
Waiting Staff: around £400 per month.
To work 8 hours per day, 6 days per week. Minimum period of work 8 weeks. Please note that no accommodation is available at the hotel. Applicants must speak German. *Applications* to the above address.

HOTEL HOCHSFIRST: A-6456 Obergurgl Nr 37, Austria (tel 05256-231/232).
Housemaids (2), **Waiters/Waitresses** (2), **Kitchen Assistants** (2). £125-£157 per month. Knowledge of German and experience in the hotel and catering industry required. 10-11 hour days, 6-7 day week. Working shifts between 7am and 10pm. Board and lodging provided free. Minimum work period 2 months. *Applications* in January/February to Franz Gstrein at the above address.

HOTEL MARIAHILF: A-8020 Graz, Mariahilfstrasse 9, Austria.
Kitchen Assistants (females), **Bar Waitresses** Wage by arrangement. Hours 7-10am, 6 days per week. Free board and accommodation. Must have previous

experience or some knowledge of German. Period of work May to October. *Applications* to Irmgard Kossar.

PENSION BERGKRISTALL: A-9844 Heiligenbut, Austria.
Assistant to wait at table and clean rooms. £255, approximately per month. To work around 4 hours per day, 7 days per week. In winter it is possible to ski daily from 1pm. Free board and lodging provided. Periods of work from July to September or December to March: minimum period of work two months. Applicants should be able to speak English and German. *Applications* to Herr H. Fleissner at the above address in April in the summer season or October for the winter season.

HOTEL POST KG: Fam Hofer, A-5672 Fusch/Glstr, Land Salzburg, Austria.
Waiting Assistant (1) and Receptionist (1). Wages approximately £400 per month. To work 8-10 hours per day, 6 days per week. Minimum period of work is 2 months. Free board and lodging are provided. Knowledge of German and French are required. *Applications* to the above address between April and June.

SPORTHOTEL GUNTER SINGER: A-6622 Berwang, Tirol, Austria (tel+43-5674-8181; fax +43-5674-818183). The hotel is a member of Relais & Châteaux hotels and is situated in a small village in the mountains. It caters for international guests.
Assistants (2) to serve and clean in a restaurant.
Housemaid to clean the rooms of guests, the lounge, reception, etc.
Wages from £400 to £500 per month. Around 8 hours per day, 5¹/2 days per week. Free board and accommodation provided. Minimum period of work from 1 July to 10 September. Knowledge of some German required, plus some French if possible. *Applicants must be EU nationals.* Applications to the above address from January-March.

TRAUM-HOTEL CLUB MONTANARA: Seestrasse 5, A-6673 Haldensee/ Gran, Austria (tel +43-5675-6431; fax +43-5675-6436).
Lifeguards, Open Air Swimming Pool Attendants, Buffet Assistants, Wages and period of work by arrangement. To work 9¹/2 hours per day, 47¹/2 hours per week. Board and accommodation provided. Applicants must speak German. *Applications* to Frau Sonja Huber at the above address at any time.

Sports, Couriers and Camping

CANVAS HOLIDAYS: East Port House, 12 East Port, Dunfermline, Fife KY12 7JG (tel 01383-629018; fax 01383-629071; www.canvasholidayscom). Canvas Holidays are looking for enthusiastic, resourceful people who enjoy a challenge and love the outdoor life. Main positions for 2002 include:
Campsite Courier. Varied responsibilities. Involves cleaning and preparation of customer accommodation, welcoming and looking after customers during their holiday and ensuring that they have the best holiday ever. As a campsite courier you will have new challenges every day which can lead to one of the most enjoyable summers you will ever have. Variable working hours.
Children's Courier. As a Canvas Holidays Children's Courier you will have had formal experience of working with children. You will organise and carry out a six day programme which involves four hours a day of Children's Club for children between the ages of 4 and 11. You will be prepared to help out with courier duties as and when requried. For many customers, the Children's Club is one of the main

parts of the holiday. You will need to have the energy of a seven year old and the imagination of an eleven year old to succeed.

Package includes tented accommodation, medical insurance, full uniform and return travel to and from a UK port of entry. Positions are available from March until October. *Applications* are invited from individuals and couples. Contact Sandy, Karen or Michele at the above contact details for an application pack.

EUROCAMP: Overseas Recruitment Department (Ref SJ/02) (tel 01606-787522). Eurocamp is a leading tour operator in quality self-drive camping and mobile home holidays in Europe. Each year the company seeks to recruit up to 1,500 enthusiastic people for the following positions:

Courier: job involves cleaning and preparing customer accommodation, providing assistance, acting as an information service and an interpreter and performing some administrative duties. Couriers need to be flexible to meet the needs of the customer to provide them with excellent service. Minimum age 18 years. Applicants should be independent with plenty of initiative and relish a challenging and rewarding position. They should also possess a friendly and helpful personality. Some working knowledge of another European language is required and previous customer service experience would be an advantage. Applicants should be available to work from April/May to September.

Children's Couriers: work involves organising a wide range of exciting activities for children aged 4-13. Applicants should possess initiative, imagination and enthusiasm along with good safety awarenmess. Previous childcare experience is essential. Minimum age is 18 years and applicants should be available from April/May to September. Languages are not a requirement but would be an advantage (in particular German).

Senior Couriers: required to work alongside a team of Campsite Couriers and organise their daily workload, as well as carrying out the normal day to day duties of a Campsite Courier. Applicants should have good language skills and experience of leading a team.

Site Managers: required to lead a large team of Campsite Couriers, organising their daily workloads and ensuring they provide the very best customer service. Applicants should be 21 or over, have proven managerial experience, excellent communication skills and language ability.

In all the above positions you should be be available for the full season commencing in April/May through to September. Comprehensive training is provided together with a competitive salary, insurance and return travel. *applications* are accepted from September/October and *can only be accepted from UK/EU passport holders.* Interviews will be conducted in Hartford, Cheshire between October and April.

Teaching and Language Schools

ENGLISH FOR KIDS: A. Baumgartnerstr. 44/A 7042, 1230 Vienna, Austria (tel +43-(0)1-667 45 79; fax 01-667 51 63; e-mail office@e4kids.co.at; www.e4kids.co.at).

TEFL Teachers: (6-8) required for residential summer camp. Applicants for teaching posts should have CELTA or Trinity Certificate (minimum grade B) and some formal teaching experience is preferred. Period of work 6-8 weeks in July and August, the teaching style is full-immersion courses with in-house methods following carefully planned syllabus and teachers' manual, supplemented with CD-Roms, etc. Pupils range in age from kindergarten to age 8 at level one and from 9 to 15 at level two. The salary varies depending on qualifications, ranging from £895 plus full board and accommodation for 6 weeks. *Applications from EU or others with work permit for Austria,* personal interviews essential, (these are sometimes held in UK). Apply to Irena Küstenbauer, Principal at the above address.

Work with Children

AUSLANDS SOZIALDIENST: A-1010 Wien, Johannesgasse 16, Austria (tel 1-512-7941; fax 513-9460; e-mail aupair-asd@kath-jugend.at).
Au Pairs placed in Vienna and in other parts of Austria for periods of 8 weeks in the summer or 6 months to 1 year at other times of the year.

The au pair gets free board and lodging, a room of her own and pocket money of £35 per week. The au pair has to work about 25 hours per week, must have one entirely free day per week and has the possibility of attending language classes. A basic knowledge of German, plus some experience with children and domestic work is required. *Applications* to the above address 2-3 months before the desired starting date.

ENGLISH FOR CHILDREN/ENGLISH LANGUAGE DAY CAMP: P.O. Box 160, Kanalstrasse 44, A-1220 Vienna, Austria (tel +43-1-282 7717; fax +43-1-282 77177; e-mail english.for.children@eunet.at).
Camp Counsellors: to instruct Sports (2-4), Arts & Crafts (2-3), Music (1-2), English (2-4). To work in a total immersion summer camp, motivating children to speak English through different activities: sports, English language classes, arts & crafts, music, and to acquaint children with the different cultures of the English speaking world through games and songs etc.

Applicants must have experience of working with children aged 5-15, and of camps, be versatile, conscientious, oriented towards children and safety and have an outgoing personality. Experience in more than one subject area preferable.

To work 8 hours per 5 day week, for 4 weeks in July. Help with finding accommodation is available and lunch is included in the working day. Wages Junior Counsellors c. £190-£290, Subject Counsellors c. £380-£575 and Head Counsellors c. £670-£860.

Applications from native English speakers invited from January to the above address.

YOUNG AUSTRIA: Alpenstrasse 108a, A-5020 Salzburg, Austria (tel 0662-6257580; fax 0662-6257582).
Monitors to be responsible for the daily welfare of a group of approximately 15-20 children. The job includes organising indoor and outdoor activities, including sports, music and crafts, excursions and helping the children with their English conversation. Wages of around £275 for a three week session. Minimum age 21.
Teachers are responsible for the children's English tuition for 3½ hours per day, but they also have to act as monitors. Payment of around £335 for a 3 week session. Applicants should be aged at least 21: those with TEFL qualifications are preferred.

The camps take place around Salzburg and are for Austrian and German children aged from 10 to 17 who wish to improve their knowledge of English and the British way of life. Around 30 staff are needed in all. 7 days per week: period of work either 3 or 6 weeks from the end of June to the beginning of September. Full board, lodging and a lump sum of around £115 for travel expenses provided. Applicants should be native English speakers (UK and Eire residents preferred) with experience of teaching or working with children. A knowledge of German is not necessary. Information from Miss Andrea Brunnbauer at the above address from December to the beginning of March.

Belgium

With an unemployment rate of 6.8% Belgium may not seem to offer the best of prospects for seasonal work, though at least inflation is predicted to fall to 1.5% in 2002 so the economy looks a little more stable than it did.

Although small in area Belgium is densely populated and can seem complicated to the outsider, as three languages are spoken within the country's federal states. These languages are Dutch or Flemish, French and German. In broad terms Dutch is spoken in the north (Flanders) and French in the south (Wallonia), with both being spoken in Brussels in the centre of the country; German is spoken mainly in the Eastern Cantons. With its coastal resorts Belgium has an active hotel and tourism industry in the north which makes seasonal work in Belgium a viable prospect.

EU nationals looking for work can get help from the Belgian employment services, which are organised on a regional basis. They cover three main areas: in the Flemish region the services are known as the *Vlaamse Dienst voor Arbeidsbemiddeling en Beroepsopleiding* (VDAB) – headquarters at Keizerslaan 11, B-1000 Brussels (tel +32-2-506-15-11; e-mail info@vdab.be; www.vdab.be); in the French region they are *Office Wallon de la Formation Professionnelle et de l'Emploi* at Boulevard J. Tirou 104, B-6000 Charleroi (tel +32-71-20-61-74; e-mail communic@forem.be; wwwhotjob.be); and in the Brussels Region they are known as *Office Régional Bruxellois de l'Emploi (ORBEM)/Brusselse Gewestelijke Dienst voor Arbeidsbemiddeling (BGDA)* based at Boulevard Anspach 65, B-1000 Brussels (tel +32-2-505-14-11; e-mail info@orbem.be or info@bgda.be; www.orbem.be or www.bgda.be). There are local employment offices in most towns.

There are also some employment offices specialising in temporary work, known as the *T-Interim,* which are operated as Dutch and French speaking offices under the aegis of VDAB and FOREM; as may be expected the VDAB T-Interim offices are in Flanders and the French T-Interim offices are found in Wallonia, with ORBEM/BGDA running the T-Interim offices for Brussels. These offices can only help people who visit them in person, and the staff are multi-lingual in most cases. They can assist in finding secretarial work, especially in Brussels where there are a large number of multinational companies needing bilingual staff. Other opportunities they may have available consist of manual work in supermarkets and warehouses or engineering and computing. They are most likely to be able to help you during the summer, when companies need to replace their permanent staff who are away on holiday. Below are addresses of these offices in some of the larger towns:

T-Interim: Sint Jacobsmarkt 66, B-2000 Antwerp (tel 03-232-98-60).

T-Interim: 24 Rue Général Molitz, B-6700 Arlon (tel 063-22-66-45; fax 063-21-96-48; e-mail mh.pivetta@tinterim.com).

T-Interim: Smedenstraat 4, B-8000 Brugge (tel 050-44-20-44; fax 050-34-20-84).

T-Service Interim: Anspachlaan 69, 1000 Brussels (tel 02 511.23.85).

T-Interim: Rue de Montigny 36B, B-6000, Charleroi (tel 071-20-20-80; fax 071-20-20-80).

T-Interim: Neuestrasse 3, B-4700 Eupen (tel 087-74-34-75; fax 087/55 22 64; e-mail n.lancel@tinterim.com).

T-Interim: Kortrijksesteenweg 130 B-9000, Ghent (tel; 09-243-88-50).

T-Interim: Lippensplein 22, B-9000, Ghent (tel; 09-269-89-50; fax 09-269-89-59).

T-Interim: Thonissenlaan 18/1 3500 Hasselt (tel 011-26-49-90; fax 011-26-49-99).

T-Interim: 2 Kloosterstraat 2 B-2200 Herentals (tel 014-23-39-43; fax 014-21-44-20).

T-Interim: Reepkaai 3 bus 19, B-8500 Kortrijk (tel 056-25-36-90; fax 056-20-29-56).

T-Interim: Boulevard de la Sauvenière 60, B-4000 Liege (tel 04-230-30-80; fax 04/232 03 71; e-mail l.dechany@tinterim.com).

T-Interim: Schuttersvest 75, B-2800 Mechelen (tel 015-27-81-37; fax 015-27-81-36).

T-Interim: H. Serruyslaan 66, B-8400 Oostende (fax 059-80-75-99).

T-Interim: 86 de Merodelei, B-2300 Turnhout (tel 014-42-27-31; fax 014-42-09-15).

T-Interim: Witherenstraat 19, B-1800 Vilvoorde (tel 02-253-98-63; fax 02-252-23-99).

T-Interim can also be found on the internet at www.tinterim.com.

You could also try advertising yourself as being available for work. One of the main newspapers published in Belgium is *Le Soir* (French) at Rue Royale 120, B-1000 Brussels (tel 02-225-55-00/54-32; e-mail journal@lesoir.be). The daily newspaper *De Standaard* is published by VUM, Gossetlaan 30a, B-1702 Groot-Bijgaarden (Brussels) (tel 32-2-467-22-11). There is a weekly English language magazine called *The Bulletin*; it comes out on Thursdays and is available from news-stands. *The Bulletin* can be contacted at 1038, Chaussée de Waterloo, B-1180 Brussels (tel 02-373-99-09; e-mail ackroyd@innet.be) and offers of work are listed on their website www.xPATS.com. Twice a year they publish a very useful supplement called *Newcomer* aimed at new arrivals in Belgium.

Americans can apply through Interexchange in New York (see entry in *Worldwide* chapter) to be placed in a summer job, internship or teaching position in Belgium. Applicants over 18 with a working knowledge of French (or Dutch) can be placed in companies or organisations for between one and three months. The programme fee is $700 and the application deadline is late April; full details on the website (www.interexchange.org).

Voluntary work in Belgium can be arranged for UK nationals by Concordia, International Voluntary Service, Youth Action For Peace or UNA Exchange. Council: International Volunteer Projects in New York helps to place Americans in short term voluntary positions in this country, as does Service Civil International (see the International Voluntary Service entry). Entries for these organisations can be found in the *Worldwide* chapter at the beginning of the book.

Those looking for work on Belgian farms should be warned that most conventional Belgian farms are highly mechanised and thus offer little scope for casual work.

The *Federation Infor Jeunes Wallonie-Bruxelles* is a non-profit organisation which co-ordinates 12 youth information offices in French-speaking Belgium. These can give advice on work as well as leisure, youth rights, accommodation, etc. A leaflet listing the addresses is available from the *Federation Infor Jeuenes* at Henri Lemaitre 25, B-5000 Namur (tel 081-8-22 08 72; e-mail federation@ inforjeunes.be; www.inforjeunes.be). Among Infor Jeune's services, they operate holiday job placement offices (*Service Job Vacances*) between March and September.

For yet further information consult the free booklet *Working in Belgium* published by the Employment Service (see the *Useful Publications* chapter towards the end of this book) or for jobs abroad you can contact the European Employment Service (EURES; http://europa.eu.int/jobs/eures): EURES VDAB (tel 09-265-47-32), EURES BGDA/ORBEM (tel 02-505-14-20), or EURES FOREM (tel 087-30-71-10).

RED TAPE

Visa Requirements: Visas are not required by EU/EEA citizens, or those of the USA, Japan, Australia, Canada or New Zealand provided they have a valid passport and that the visit is for less than three months. Other nationalities will have to obtain an entry permit which should be applied for at a Belgian Embassy or Consulate in advance of travel in the applicant's country of residence.

Residence Permits: All non-Belgians must register at the local Town Hall within eight days of arrival to obtain a residence permit. EU nationals should take documents proving that they have sufficient funds and a valid passport.

Work Permits: These are not required by EU/EEA nationals; others must first arrange a job, then the prospective employer should apply for a work permit at the regional ministry of employment. There are some exceptions to work permit requirements according to the employment to be taken up; consult embassies and consulates for details.

Au Pair: permitted subject to the regulations outlined above.

Voluntary Work: it is not normally necessary to obtain permits for short term voluntary work with recognised organisations.

Hotel Work and Catering

ARDEN HOTELS – BELGIUM: rue du Collège 44, B-6830 Bouillon, Belgium (tel +32-61-46 60 27; fax +32-61-46 81 92; e-mail a.borguet@skynet.be). A young company in the tourism industry located in the 'green' part of Belgium. The two family hotels are run by a dynamic young couple.

Bartender to help with room service and barwork. Wages about £450 per month. Must have previous experience of hotel work and knowledge of French.

Chambermaids (1-2) to clean rooms, etc. Wages about £450 per month. Knowledge of French is essential.

To work variable hours, 6 days per week. Work is available throughout the year. Free board and lodging are provided. Knowledge of English and/or Dutch is desirable.

Girl to take care of a five year-old girl and to clean, cook and serve in a private house. For 6 months minimum. French is essential.

Applications should be sent in French to Monsieur Alain Borguet as soon as possible at the above address.

HOTEL DE LA POSTE: Place St. Arnould 1, B-6830 Bouillon, Belgium (tel 061-46 65 06).

Assistants for bar, restaurant, room service, kitchen, etc. Official Belgian salary rates; 7 hours per day, 6 day week. Board and lodging available starting from £50 per month. Knowledge of languages an advantage. Minimum period of work 1 month between May and September. *Applications* as soon as possible to the above address enclosing a c.v. and a recent photograph.

HOTEL LIDO: Zwaluwenlaan, 18 Albert Plage, B-8300 Knokke-Heist, Belgium (tel 050-60 19 25; fax 050-61 04 57; e-mail lido@hotlknokke.isabel.be or lido.hotel.knokke@vt4.net)

Waitresses (2), basic French required, **Kitchen Assistants** (2) to work from 9-12am, 1-3pm and 6-9.30pm. Wages £550 net per month with board and lodging provided free. Minimum period of work one or two months between June and September. *Applications* with a recent photograph to A. Simoens at the above address.

HOSTELLERIE 'LE RY D'AVE': Sourd d'Ave 5, B-5580 Ave-ee-Auffe, Rochefort, Belgium (tel +32-(0)84-388820; fax 084-389550; e-mail ry.d.ave@skynet.be; www.rydave.be). A small family run rustic style hotel-restaurant, owned by M & Mme Marot-Champion. M. Marot-Champion runs the kitchen while Mme Marot-Champion is in charge of the restaurant.
Receptionist, Waiter/Waitress required to work a 40 hour week, of 8 hours per day over 5 days, wages around £650 per month. Outgoing friendly personality, with a hotel diploma or relevant experience necessary and preferably knowledge of English, Dutch, French or German. Board and lodging are free. Period of work between mid-May and mid-September. *Applications* should be sent between February and May to M. & Mme Marot-Champion.

JULES RICAIL: 5 rue de la Gendarmerie, B-5570 Beauraing, Belgium.
Waitress: £500 per month plus tips. To serve, lay tables and wash up. 8 hours work a day, 6 days a week. Applicant should be efficient, good humoured and able to speak French. Board and lodging free. Minimum period of work 2 months between May and July. *Applications* to M Jules Ricail at the above address.

HOTEL ROYAL: Avenue de la Mer 180, B-8470 Le Panne, Belgium.
Assistant Cook. £150.34 per month. Must be catering student or qualified.
Waitresses (2). £150.34 per month.
  10 hours per day. 6 day week. Free board and accommodation. Knowledge of Dutch and French required. Minimum period of work 2 months between 1st June and 30th September. *Applications* in January to the above address.

Sports, Couriers and Camping

3D EDUCATION AND ADVENTURE LTD: Business Support, Osmington Bay, Weymouth, Dorset DT3 6EG (tel 01305-836226; fax 01305-834070; e-mail darren@3d-education.co.uk). 3D is a specialist provider of activity and educational experiences for young people. Owned by Center Parcs, 3D has been operating since 1991 and gone from strength to strength year on year.
Activity Instructors (500) Employed and trained as either multi-activity instructor, field studies instructor, specialist watersports instructor or IT instructor, staff will work with children at specialist holiday centres across the south of England as well as across the UK and Europe with Pontins and Center Parcs.
  Field studies instructors must hold or at least be gaining a relevant degree. IT instructors need to have a broad range of IT skills. Any sports coaching awards or national governing body awards are advantageous, if applying for Activity Instructor and Watersports Instructor postitions, although those with relevant experience will be considered. Training courses are held from late January through to July, so there is plenty of opportunity to develop your skills and qualifications.
  Most important is an applicant's enthusiasm, personality and energy, coupled with a true desire to work in the outdoor leisure industry. Excellent accommodation and catering packages are offered with payment and working hours as covered by minimum wage and working time legislation. Minimum period of work 14 weeks.
  Applicants should telephone 01305-836226 for a recruitment pack between September and June. Before employment all applicants must complete a residential training programme in the UK.

EUROCAMP: Overseas Recruitment Department (Ref SJ/02) (tel 01606-787522). Eurocamp is a leading tour operator in quality self-drive camping and mobile home holidays in Europe. Each year the company seeks to recruit up to 1,500 enthusiastic people for the following positions:

Site Managers: required to lead a large team of Campsite Couriers, organising their daily workloads and ensuring they provide the very best customer service. Applicants should be 21 or over, have proven managerial experience, excellent communication skills and language ability.

Campsite Courier: job involves cleaning and preparing customer accommodation, providing assistance, acting as an information service and an interpreter and performing some administrative duties. Couriers need to be flexible to meet the needs of the customer to provide them with excellent service. Minimum age 18 years. Applicants should be independent with plenty of initiative and relish a challenging and rewarding position. They should also possess a friendly and helpful personality. Some working knowledge of another European language is required and previous customer service experience would be an advantage. Applicants should be available to work from April/May to September.

Children's Couriers: work involves organising a wide range of exciting activities for children aged 4-13. Applicants should possess initiative, imagination and enthusiasm along with good safety awareness. Previous childcare experience is essential. Minimum age is 18 years and applicants should be available from April/May to September. Languages are not required but would be an advantage.

Senior Couriers: required to work alongside a team of Campsite Couriers and organise their daily workload, as well as carrying out the normal day to day duties of a Campsite Courier. Applicants should have good language skills and experience of leading a team.

In all the above positions you should be be available for the full season commencing in April/May through to September. Comprehensive training is provided together with a competitive salary, insurance and return travel. Applications are accepted from September/October and *can only be accepted from UK/EU passport holders.* Interviews will be conducted in Hartford, Cheshire between October and April.

Teaching and Language Schools

SKI TEN INTERNATIONAL: Chateau d'Emines B-5080 Emines, Belgium (tel +32-81-21 30 51; fax 81-20 02 63; e-mail ski-ten.goffinet@skynet.be; www.ski-ten.be)

English Teacher required to work and live in a summer camp in July and August. The successful candidate will work for six hours a day; duties will include looking after, eating with and arranging games for the children in their care. In return for this, a salary of £600 approx and accommodation will be provided. Some knowledge of French and previous experience working with children would be useful.

Applications should be sent in writing, with a photograph, to the above address.

Denmark

Despite the low level of unemployment (below 5%) in Denmark, would-be job seekers there have a hard time of it, especially if they don't have some notion of the Danish language. Non-EU/EEA citizens will find it hard to obtain a job in Denmark, as work permits are only issued where an employer can prove that there is no EU citizen who can do that job.

Anyone serious about wanting to work in Denmark should obtain a copy of the free booklet *Working in Denmark* published by the Employment Service in Britain (see the *Useful Publications* chapter towards the end of this book). There is also a useful leaflet called *Working and Studying in Denmark* which is available from UseIt Touristinformation, part of the Youth Information (UI) at Radhusstraede 13, 1466 Copenhagen K, Denmark (tel +45-33-730620; fax +45 33 73 06 49; e-mail useit@ui.dk; www.useit.dk). Please note that *Use It* is not an employment agency but an information centre for low budget travellers.

Despite the increasing mechanisation of farming there is still a need for fruit pickers during the summer; up to 1,000 people are needed each year for the strawberry harvest. Be warned, however, that the hours can be very long when you are paid by the kilo with picking taking place between 6am and noon. The main harvests are strawberries in June/July, cherries in July/August, apples in September/October and tomatoes throughout the summer. Fruit producing areas are scattered around the country: some of the most important are to be found to the north of Copenhagen, around Arhus, and to the east and west of Odense.

You may be able to obtain a job on a farm by contacting the pan-European agency EURES through your local job centre; vacancies for the fruit harvest are announced in the spring on the Danish EURES website www.eures.dk.

Another method is to advertise in the farming magazine *Landsbladet* (Vester Farimagsgade 6, 2 sal, DK-1606 Copenhagen V; tel +45-33-38-2222; fax +45-33-11-31-48). It is also possible to arrange unpaid work on an organic farm. Another possibility is to contact VHH (the Danish WWOOF) to obtain a list of their 25-30 member farmers, most of whom speak English. In return for three or four hours of work per day, you get free food and lodging. Always phone or write before arriving. The list can be obtained only after sending £5/US$10/kr50 to Inga Nielsen, Asenvej 35, 9881 Bindslev.

The Danish state employment service is obliged to help Britons and other EU nationals who call at their offices to find a job. The administrative headquarters of the employment service – the Directorate General for Employment, Placement and Vocational Training (*Arbejdsmarkedsstyrelsen*) – is at Blegdamsvej 56, Postboks 2722, DK-2100 Copenhagen (tel 45-3528-8100; e-mail ams@ams.dk; www.ams.dk). When you are actually in Denmark, you can find the address of your nearest employment office under *Arbejdsformidlingen* in the local telephone directory.

There are also opportunities for voluntary work in Denmark, arranged by International Voluntary Service, UNA Exchange, Youth Action for Peace and Concordia for British applicants and Council: International Volunteer Projects and Service Civil International for Americans. See the *Worldwide* chapter for details.

There are a number of private employment agencies in Denmark, but most are looking for trained secretarial staff who speak fluent Danish.

An advertisement in a Danish paper may bring an offer of employment. Crane Media Partners Ltd, 20-28 Dalling Road, Hammersmith, W6 OJB (tel 020-8237 8601; fax 020-8735 9941) are advertising agents for *Berlingske Tidende*. *Morgenavisen-Jyllandss-Posten*, one of the more important papers for job advertisements, is published at Grondalsvej 3, DK-8260 Viby J, Denmark (tel +45-87-38-38-38).

RED TAPE

Visa Requirements: a visa is not required by citizens of EU countries.
Residence Permits: Residence permits should be applied for through Kobenhavns Overpraesidium at Hammerensgade 1, 1267 Copenhagen K, Denmark, (tel 33 12 23 80). EU nationals wishing to stay in Denmark for longer than 3 months and all visitors from non-EU countries must gain a residence permit.
Work Permits: The Royal Danish Embassy has indicated that nationals of countries not in the EU or Scandinavia will not be granted work permits except where the employer can prove that the applicant has a unique skill. EU nationals who wish to take up employment in Denmark may stay there for a period not exceeding 3 months from the date of arrival in order to seek employment provided they have sufficient funds to support themselves. As soon as possible after arrival, they should ask about the need for a residence permit and the procedure for obtaining one.
Au Pair: allowed, but subject to the regulations outlined above. Prospective au pairs will need an au pair contract.
Voluntary Work: all work, paid and unpaid, is subject to the above regulations.

Agricultural Work

ALSTRUP FRUGTPLANTAGE: Alstrupvej 1, Alstrup, DK-8305 Samsø, Denmark (tel 86591338; fax 86593138, e-mail elicc@samso.com; www.alstrupfrugt.subnet.dk). Samsø is an island with lovely beaches and beautiful scenery. In addition to strawberries the farm has an apple orchard, and around 60 fruitpickers work here each year from across the EU.
Strawberry Pickers: Wages at piece work rates of approximately £0.50 per kilo. To work from 6am to 1pm with one day off a week. The season normally runs from around the 15 June until 20 July, but may be earlier or later. *Applicants must be EU nationals aged at least 19.* Those accepted will need their own camping equipment. *Applications* should be sent before 1 May, and confirmation before 15 May to Carl Christian B. Jensen at the above address.

BIRKHOLM FRUGT & BAER: V/Bjarne Knutsen, Hornelandevej 2 D, DK-5600 Faaborg, Denmark (tel/fax 62602262; e-mail birkholm@ strawberrypicking.dk; www.strawberrypicking.dk).
Strawberry Pickers: for the season which lasts for around six weeks from 1st June, approximately. Payment at piece work rates of around £0.50 per kilo. Workers are given space to put up their own tents and have the use of a bathroom and basic cooking facilities. Minimum period of work two weeks. *Applicants must be EEA nationals. Contact* the above address or check the website for further information.

EARTH WORK LTD: 8 Beauchamp Meadow, Redruth, Cornwall TR15 2DG (tel 01209 219934)
Strawberry Pickers (200) to work an island in Denmark. Applicants to work between 6 to 4 weeks starting around 12 or 26 June respectively. Work will be for 6-7 hours each morning, 6 days a week. No experience is required, but all applicants must be 18 or over. Workers will have access to camping facilities on Danish farms, located close to beaches. Workers will be paid approxmately 50p per kilo, there is no limit on how much you may pick. *Applications* invited *from EU nationals only* before 1 June.

Sports, Couriers and Camping

EUROCAMP: Overseas Recruitment Department (Ref SJ/02) (tel 01606-787522). Eurocamp is a leading tour operator in quality self-drive camping and mobile home holidays in Europe. Each year the company seeks to recruit up to 1,500 enthusiastic people for the following positions:

Courier: job involves cleaning and preparing customer accommodation, providing assistance, acting as an information service and an interpreter and performing some administrative duties. Couriers need to be flexible to meet the needs of the customer to provide them with excellent service. Minimum age 18 years. Applicants should be independent with plenty of initiative and relish a challenging and rewarding position. They should also possess a friendly and helpful personality. Some working knowledge of another European language is required and previous customer service experience would be an advantage. Applicants should be available to work from April/May to September.

Children's Couriers: work involves organising a wide range of exciting activities for children aged 4-13. Applicants should possess initiative, imagination and enthusiasm along with good safety awareness. Previous childcare experience is essential. Minimum age is 18 years and applicants should be available from April/May to September. Languages are not a requirement but would be an advantage (in particular German).

Senior Couriers: required to work alongside a team of Campsite Couriers and organise their daily workload, as well as carrying out the normal day to day duties of a Campsite Courier. Applicants should have good language skills and experience of leading a team.

Site Managers: required to lead a large team of Campsite Couriers, organising their daily workloads and ensuring they provide the very best customer service. Applicants should be 21 or over, have proven managerial experience, excellent communication skills and language ability.

In all the above positions you should be be available for the full season commencing in April/May through to September. Comprehensive training is provided together with a competitive salary, insurance and return travel. *Applications* are accepted from September/October and *can only be accepted from UK/EU passport holders.* Interviews will be conducted in Hartford, Cheshire between October and April.

Voluntary Work and Archaeology

MELLEMFOLKELIGT SAMVIRKE (MS): Stuosgade 20, DK-8000 Arhus C, Denmark (tel 8619-7766).

Volunteers to work in international work camps in Denmark and Greenland. The camps normally involve community projects such as conservation of playgrounds, renovation, conservation, archaeological work, nature protection, reconditioning of used tools to be later sent to Africa, etc. Board and accommodation are provided but the participants must provide their own travelling expenses.

The camps last from 2 to 3 weeks between July and September. Applicants should be aged over 18. British applicants should apply through IVS, IVS Field Office, Old Hall, East Bergholt, Colchester CO7 6TQ. The work is hard and demands commitment: the traditional IVS slogan is 'Holiday makers need not apply'. IVS welcomes applications from people of all racial, cultural and social backgrounds.

U-LANDSFORENINGEN SVALERNE: Oesterbrogade 49, DK-2100 Copenhagen 0, Denmark (tel 35-26-17-47; fax 31-38-17-46).
Volunteers to help U-lansforeningen Svalerne (Swallows in Denmark) with rag-picking work for raising funds for grassroot movements among the poor landless people in South India and Bangladesh. Funds are raised by the sale at second-hand marketsof the items collected by volunteers. The camp lasts for four weeks in July. Period of work is two weeks. 6-8 hours work per day. One day (Sunday) and two afternoons off a week. Accommodation and food provided free of charge. Volunteers provide their own travel costs and pocket money. Knowledge of English preferred. *Applications* to the above address from January.

Finland

Finland offers short-term paid training opportunities. The International Trainee Exchange programme in Finland is administered by CIMO, the Centre for International Mobility (PO Box 343, 00531 Helsinki, Finland; 09-7747 7033/fax 09-7747 7064; cimoinfo@cimo.fi/ www.cimo.fi or http://finland.cimo.fi); their website is in English. British students and graduates who want on-the-job training in their field (agriculture, tourism, teaching, etc.) lasting between one and 18 months should apply directly to CIMO. Short-term training takes place between May and September, while long-term training is available year round. Applications for summer positions must be in to CIMO by the end of January.

Voluntary work in Finland can be arranged for British applicants by International Voluntary Service, Concordia and UNA Exchange as well as Service Civil International (see the IVS entry) and Council: International Volunteer Projects for Americans; see the *Worldwide* chapter for details. You may be able to find a job by advertising in a Finnish newspaper. Crane Media Partners Ltd, of 20-28 Dlling Road, Hammersmith, London W6 OJB represent *Helsingin Sanomat*, the largest circulation paper in Finland as well as *Turun Sanomat* and *Aamulehti*.

RED TAPE

Visa Requirements: citizens of most countries, including the United Kingdom, the United States of America, Australia and New Zealand and all Western European countries do not normally require a visa for a visit of less than three months unless they are taking up employment.
Residence Permits: EU nationals are allowed to enter and work in Finland for up to three months, if they wish to stay longer then a residence permit must be obtained from the local police station. Non-EU/EEA nationals must obtain work and residence permits.
Work Permits: British and Irish citizens and nationals of other EEA countries do not need work permits in order to work in Finland. If you are from a non-EEA country your application for such permits may be made at a Finnish Embassy and for this you will need a letter and permission to work (obtained by the employer from their local employment office) from your prospective employer in Finland. The application is then taken to your nearest embassy where work and residence permits must be obtained. Anyone intending to work in Finland should not enter the country before all formalities have been completed.
Au Pair: in Finland this type of arrangement is popular and can be made for male as well as female students.

Hotel Work and Catering

HOTEL RUOTSINSALMI: Kirkkokatu 14, Kotka 10, Finland
Waiter and **Waitress:** wages by arrangement. Preferably with experience.
Kitchen Assistants/Dish Washers (2). Wages on application.
An 8 hour day, 5 day week is worked. Board and accommodation available at approximately £35 per month. Must have some knowledge of Swedish, and if possible Finnish. Minimum period of work 2/3 months between 1 May and 31 August. *Applications* until the end of March to the above address.

France

France has long been one of the most popular destinations for British and Irish people looking for summer work. This is due to its physical proximity: the fact that French is the first (and often only) foreign language learned; and, possibly most important of all, because during the summer France still needs many extra temporary workers for both its vibrant tourist trade and farm work. Theme parks like Disneyland Paris or Parc Asterix need extra staff even though there is currently fairly high unemployment.

Although Disneyland Paris alone employs many thousands of seasonal workers to supplement their permanent staff, this chapter contains details of many jobs in the tourist industry: you can find others in the *Worldwide* chapter at the beginning of the book and in the weekly trade magazine *L'Hotellerie* published at 5, rue Antoine Bourdelle, 75015 Paris.

British and Irish citizens, along with other EU nationals, are allowed to use the French national employment service (*Agence Nationale pour l'Emploi*), the headquarters of which is at Le Galilee, 4 rue Galilee, 93198 Noisy-le-Grand (tel 149-31-74-00), although the offices in towns throughout France will know more about vacancies in their region. There is also a comprehensive website detailing the services provided by ANPE in both French and English: www.anpe.fr. British citizens can apply for work through the service by visiting any of the over 860 *Agences Nationales pour l'Emploi* (ANPE) around the country. The ANPE for Narbonne (ANPE, BP 802, 29 rue Mazzini, 11008 Narbonne Cedex) has seasonal hotel vacancies from May to September, and others can provide details of when agricultural work is available.

There are also a number of private employment agencies such as *Manpower, Kelly, Bis, Select France*, and *Ecco* in large cities which can help people who speak reasonable French to find temporary jobs in offices, private houses, warehouses, etc. They can be found in the Yellow Pages (*Les Pages Jaunes*) under *Agences de Travail Temporaire*. These can normally only find jobs for people who visit in person.

For further information relevant to British citizens consult the free booklet *Working in France* published by the Employment Service (see the *Useful Publications* chapter towards the end of this book).

Council Exchanges in New York administers a *Work in France Programme* for American citizens, see the Council entry in the *Worldwide* chapter.

Seasonal farm work can be difficult to obtain from outside France. If you cannot arrange a job in advance using the information in this chapter it is best to be on the spot and approach farmers in person, or ask at the local employment offices, town halls (*mairies*) or youth hostels. A word of warning: if you arrange to go grape picking with an organisation not mentioned in this chapter read the small print carefully: you may be buying just a journey out to France, with no guarantee of a job at the end.

For help in finding temporary work during the grape picking season, you could contact ANPE. ANPE have offices in most large towns in France's main agricultural regions. Each office can offer around 1000 jobs to those who wish to work on farms up to 50km from the town, apple-picking and grape-picking being the most prevalent jobs available.

The addresses and dates for the ANPE below are provided only as a guide: there is no guarantee either that they will have definite vacancies to offer, and the exact dates of harvests can vary considerably from year to year and from region to region. The work period also varies. The ANPE office in Castelnaudry asked to be removed from this edition as the maize-topping work in their region only lasts 4 days.

For temporary agricultural work (July-September):
ANPE, 2 avenue Henri Farbos, F-40000 Mont de Marsan (tel 5-58-46-15-02).
For grape picking (by region):
Alsace – 15th October
ANPE, 54, Avenue de la Republique, BP 50868021, Colmar (tel 3-89-20-80-70;
   fax 0389-20-80-78)
Beaujolais – 10th September
ANPE, 169 rue Paul Bert, F-69665 Villefranche Cedex (tel 4-74-60-30-03)
Bordeaux – 25th September
ANPE, 34, avenue du General Leclerc, F-33210 Langon (tel 2-54-98-02-60)
ANPE, 35 rue JJ Rousseau, F-33504 Libourne (tel 5-57-55-32-20).
ANPE, 19, rue Adrien Chauvet, BP 108, 33250 Pauillac (tel 5-56-73-20-50; fax
   5-56-59-62-49)
Burgundy – 10th September
ANPE, 6 boulevard St. Jacques, B.P. 115, F-21203 Beaune (tel 3-80-25-07-06)
ANPE, 71 rue Jean-Macé, F-71031 Macon Cedex (tel 3-85-21-93-20; fax 03-85-
   38-46-88)
Languedoc-Roussilon – 15th September
ANPE, BP 65, 29 av. Léon Blum, 30205 Bagnols sur Ceze
ANPE, BP 4236, 13 Alphonse Mas, 34544 Beziers Cedex
ANPE, 90 Avenue Pierre Sémard, BP 586 Iéna,11009 Carcassonne Iéna Cedex
ANPE, BP 3054, 60 rue Siegfried, 30002 Nimes Cedex
Indre et Loire – early September to Mid-October (Apple-picking also available).
ANPE Joue Les Tours, Champ Girault, 57 rue Chantepie, B.P. 304, 37303 Joue
   Les Tours CEDEX (tel 2-47-60-58-58)

Workers are also needed to help harvest the following fruits, especially in the valleys of the Loire and the Rhone and the south east and south west of the country. The dates given are only approximate: bear in mind that harvests tend to begin first in the south of the country.

Strawberries: May to mid-June
Cherries: mid-May to early July
Peaches: June to September
Pears: mid-July to mid-November
Apples: mid-August (but chiefly from mid-September) to mid-October.

French farmers employ over 100,000 foreigners for seasonal work during the summer. Many of these are skilled 'professional' seasonal workers from Spain, Portugal and Morocco who return to the same regions every year: if there is a choice of applicants for a job, a farmer will prefer an experienced worker to a total

KEY JOBS for KEY PEOPLE at KEYCAMP

KEYCAMP *Holidays*

Campsite Couriers in Europe

if you . . .

- ✓ are over 18 years of age
- ✓ are self motivated
- ✓ have a positive attitude
- ✓ enjoy working in a fun atmosphere
- ✓ could meet our high standards
- ✓ would like us to bring out the best in YOU

... and you really know what "makes" someone's holiday

The write quoting reference SJ/02 to Overseas Recruitment Department, Keycamp Holidays, Hartford Manor, Greenbank Lane, Northwich CW8 1HW Telephone 01606 787522

"YOUR KEY TO AN UNFORGETTABLE SUMMER"

beginner. In recent years there has also been an influx of people from Eastern Europe who are desperate for work and prepared to work for less than the minimum wage *(le SMIC)* for any farmer who will employ them illegally. Anyone going to France to look for farm work should be prepared to move from area to area in the search for a job: it would also be wise to take enough money to cover the cost of returning home in case of failure. Also be warned that payment is generally by piece work, so there are no wages if picking is suspended because of bad weather.

The publishers Mitchell Beazley produce a series of useful guides to wine regions (Alsace, Bordeaux, Provence, Rhone and Loire) under the title *Touring in Wine Country* which cost £12.99 each. You can remove some of the uncertainty of the job-hunt by visiting farmers to arrange a job before their harvests start: by doing so you should also be given an informed estimate of when the harvest will start. Note that although vineyard owners normally provide accommodation for grape pickers, workers on other harvests will normally need camping equipment.

The increasing sophistication of grape-picking technology is beginning to work against the prospective picker: the ANPE in Blaye asked not be included in this book any more because the local grapes are picked by machine – except when it is wet and the machine isn't allowed out. In recent years other ANPE offices including those in Epernay, Angers, Reims, Perpignan and Bordeaux have also asked to have their addresses removed from this book principally because the numbers of those looking for work exceeded jobs available and they do not wish to encourage too many.

France sets a national minimum wage and has regulated the number of hours which can be worked in one week. Currently the minimum wage is worth 43 francs an hour, while the working week can be from 35 to 39 hours according to the size of the company; as a result of efforts by the French government to stimulate the economy by giving tax breaks to firms that cut their working week and took on extra staff to maintain productivity. In the past a blind eye has been turned to foreign-based tour operators who employ foreign workers for the tourist season and pay far less than that figure, but there have been hints in recent years that in future they might be forced to pay the statutory minimum wage. The tour operators in turn claim that in order to afford these wages they would have to increase the costs of their holidays and would end up employing fewer people.

France is rich in opportunities for voluntary work, as the entries at the end of this chapter will testify. Council: International Volunteer Projects in New York and Service Civil International (see the IVS entry) can assist Americans. International Voluntary Service (IVS), UNA Exchange, Youth Action for Peace and Concordia can help can UK residents to find short term voluntary work; their entries can be found in the *Worldwide* chapter at the beginning of the book.

A great many archaeological digs and building restoration projects are carried out each year. The French Ministry of Culture has two departments dealing with antiquities, one focuses on archaeology and the other on the restoration of monuments (Ministère de la Culture, *Direction de l'Architecture et du Patrimoine, Sous-Direction de l'Archeologie,* 4 rue d'Aboukir, 75002 Paris (tel 1-40-15-77-81) and Ministère de la Culture, *Direction du Patrimoine, Sous-Direction des Monuments Historiques* at the same address (tel 1-40-15-76-81). Each year the ministry publishes in a brochure and on the internet (www.culture.gouv.fr/fouilles) a list of these archaeological fieldwork projects throughout France requiring up to 5,000 volunteers. Another brochure, *Chantiers de benevoles* published by Rempart (see entry under Voluntary Work), lists projects relating to building restoration. It has pages in English or can be found at www.rempart.com.

Advertising for a job in France can be arranged in the Paris edition of the *International Herald Tribune* contact the London office, 40, Marsh Wall, London E14 9TP (tel 020-7836 4802; e-mail ukadv@iht.com), or New York Office, 850 Third Avenue, New York, NY 10022 (tel 212-752 3890; e-mail usadv@iht.com), or on the internet www.iht.com.

RED TAPE

Visa Requirements: visas are not required for visits to France by EU, American, Canadian, Australian or New Zealand nationals. Others should check with their nearest French Consulate.

Residence Permits: such permits (*cartes de séjour*) are necessary for foreigners staying for more than 3 months in France. Application for this permit should be made on a special form available from the *Prefecture de Police* in Paris, or the local *Prefecture* or *Mairie* (town hall) elsewhere. Non-EU nationals need to possess a long stay visa before applying for a *carte de séjour*. Application for a long stay visa should be lodged with a French consulate in the applicant's country of residence.

Work Permits: the standard procedure for non-EEA nationals is that the prospective employer in France must apply to the *Office des Migrations Internationales* in Paris (www.omi.social.fr) only after receiving permission from the DDTEFP which oversees the employment of foreign professionals. Like other nationals of the EU Member States, Swiss nationals and citizens of the United Kingdom do not need work permits to work in France.

Au Pair: the family with which you are to stay should apply to the Direction Departmentale de Travail for the necessary *Accord de Placement au pair d'un stagiaire aide-familial.*

Voluntary Work: a work permit is necessary for non-EEA nationals.

Agricultural Work

BERNARD LACOMBE: Les Crouzets, F-12160 Baraqueuille, France (tel 05-65-69-01-46).

Farm Helper to milk cows and feed animals on a farm in the South of France. To work 4 hours a day, 6 days a week. Pocket money and board and lodging provided. Some knowledge of French required. Minimum period of work 1 month at any time of the year. Applicants must be hard-working and like nature and animals. There is also the possibility of some supplementary Bed & Breakfast related work. *Applications* to M. Lacombe at the above address.

G. ESPINASSE: Sevignac, Druelle F-12510, Olemps, France.

Farm Helper to carry out all types of work in the field and assist with breeding (mainly sheep), also to study and practise bio-organic farming. No salary but about £30 per month pocket money and the opportunity to learn about herbal medicines and the occult sciences. Board and lodging provided. Some knowledge of French useful. Minimum period of work 2-3 months all year round. *Applications*, in French, as soon as possible to the above address.

FERME DES BERTTRANGES: Murlin, 58700 Premery, France (tel 386-38-17-58).

General Assistant to work on a 40 hectare farm with goats, pigs, cows etc; duties to consist of general farm work including cheese production, looking after animals, erecting fences etc. Wages of around £115 per month. To work for around ten hours per day, 6 days per week. Period of work by arrangement around the year. Applicants should speak English and French and love animals and nature. *Applications* should be sent to Chantal Villain at the above address at any time.

M. MICHEL GARRIC: Cesars, le Pas, F-12510 Druelle, France (tel 565-69-33-15).
Student required to assist on a French dairy farm. No salary is paid, but full board and lodging with family, laundry and insurance are provided. It is essential that applicants speak French; they must also be prepared to work hard, face very long hours, improve their spoken French and learn something about agriculture and French family life. Male applicants preferred.
Applications should be sent to M. Garric at the above address.

S.C.A. SOLDIVE: BP 72 - Brie, F-79102 THOUARS Cedex, FRANCE (tel 05-49-67-41-61; fax 05-49-67-43-56; e-mail SOLDIVE@wanadoo.fr).
Farm Labourers (1,000) to harvest melons.
Workers (30) to pack the fruit in factories.
Mechanics (30) to repair and maintain farm machinery, must speak French.
Wages are French SMIC (43,72 Francs). To work 6 days per week and 6 hours per day. Minimum period of work 2 months between August and October. EU nationals must be in possession of a temporary residence permit or student card.

Boats

CONTINENTAL WATERWAYS: PO Box 31, Godalming, Surrey GU8 6JH (tel 01252-703577; fax: 01252-702860; e-mail di-mathisen@continentalwaterways. co.uk). French Office: Continentale de Croisières SA, 1 Promenade du Rhin, BP 41748, F-21017 Dijon, France (fax +33 380-41-6773). Continental Waterways have operated a fleet of luxury floating hotel barges on the waterways of France for the last 30 years.
Crew Members required to work from March to November in a fleet of 15 luxury hotel barges, including 3 large river boats, crewed by French, British and other EU nationalities. Young dynamic teams crew for mainly American passengers, this is an ideal job for those who wish to improve their language skills, appreciate gourmet food, wine and cheese and who wish to immerse themselves in French culture for 7 months.
Continental Waterways demand the highest standards and are looking for highly committed team players, who will work hard to provide memorable cruises for customers. Salaries, gratuities and paid holidays are generous. *Applicants must have a valid National Insurance number.*
For details of the company and jobs on offer visit www.continentalwaterways. co.uk, where you can download an *application form* or apply to Diana Mathisen, Crew Recruitment at the UK address (above).

EUROPEAN WATERWAYS: 35 Wharf Road, Wraysbury, Staines, Middlesex TW19 5JQ (fax 01784-483072; e-mail sales@GoBarging.com; www.GoBarging. com).
European Waterways are in their 27th year of designing, building and operating a fleet of fully crewed luxury hotel barges in England, France, Germany, Ireland and Scotland.
Cordon Bleu Chefs (4). Wages £1,000-£1,200 per month. Must have training to

Cordon Bleu standard, speak French, hold a driving licence and be at least 25 years old.

Skippers (2). £1200-£1400 per month. Applicants must be over 25, speak French, have a driving licence and have some mechanical experience.

Deckhand Mechanics (4). £600 per month. Must have suitable experience, a driving licence, and speak French.

Stewards/Stewardesses (4). £500 per month. Cleaning, ironing waitressing etc. Must be hard workers.

Period of work from April to October for work on 12 hotel barges. Applications from *EEA nationals only*. Application forms to Mrs A Green at the above address.

FRENCH COUNTRY WATERWAYS: Croisières Touristiques Francaises, 2 Route de Semur, F-21150 Venarey-les-Laumes, France (tel 3-80-96-17-10; fax 3-80-96-19-18; e-mail ctf.bateau@wanadoo.fr). French Country Waterways owns and operates five ultra-deluxe hotel barges, offering six-night cruises in five regions of central France The clientele is principally North American. **Chefs:** gross salary from £1.300 per month. Required to plan menus and prepare gourmet cuisine. Professional training and experience in haute cuisine establishments essential. Some knowledge of French useful.

Drivers/Guides: Gross salary from £1,100 per month. Applicants must have a P.S.V. licence, should speak fluent French and have a full knowledge of French heritage and culture.

Pilots: Gross salary from £1,300 per month. Must have French Inland Waterways Permit to drive 38m Hotel Barge and have mechanical experience. Some knowledge of French useful

Stewardesses: Gross salary from £900 per month. Work involves cleaning cabins, general housekeeping, food/bar service and care of passengers. Knowledge of French useful, but not essential.

Deckhands: Gross salary from £900 per month. To assist the Pilot during navigation and mooring and to carry out exterior maintenance of the barge. Some knowledge of French useful.

Crew Members must be EU nationals, or possess appropriate visas permitting work in France and be available for work from April to early November. Salaries quoted are for inexperienced crew members and include accommodation, full board and uniform. Social Security coverage is taken care of by the Company. Gratuities are divided equally amongst crew members. Minimum age 21. For all positions the hours of work are long, over a five to six day week. Applicants must be energetic, personable, and able to provide a consistently high standard of service.'

Apply with CV, contact telephone number and recent photo to Mr. Thierry Bresson at the above address.

Holiday Centres

DISNEYLAND PARIS: Casting, BP110, F-77777 Marne La Vallée cedex 4, France. Disneyland Paris will see many exciting developments in 2002 including the opening of Walt Disney Studios in Spring and its own 10th anniversary.

Permanent or Seasonal Staff to work in the Disneyland Paris Resort situated 30 km east of Paris, consisting of 5,800 hotel rooms, and Entertainment Centre and the Theme Park, with restaurants, shops and attractions. Open ended contracts start from October; most seasonal positions start between March and May 2002 to September 2002, however there are also positions from 15 June 2002 to 31

August 2002 (minimum length) available for those who only want to work during the summer period. Opportunities exist in the Attractions, Merchandise Food and Beverage, Reception and Cleaning departments.

Monthly gross wage is Euros 1,082.39 for a 35 hour week; staff contribute towards and are covered by French social security during their contract. Assistance is provided to help find accommodations and travel expenses will be reimbursed providing the contract is successfully completed.

Applicants must be aged over 18, be of European nationality or have a valid work permit to work in France, and be friendly and cheerful and outgoing as the work involves a good deal of contact with visitors. It is also necessary to be able to communicate well in French and English and knowledge of a third European language is an asset. *Applicants* should write to the above address.

Hotel Work and Catering

ALPINE TRACKS: 40 High Street, Menai Bridge, Anglesey LL59 5EF (tel 01248-717440; fax 01248-717816; e-mail alpinetrac@cs.com; www.alpinetracks. com). Alpine Tracks are a friendly and informal small professional holiday company operating chalets with a high level of personal service in the French Alps for skiers and mountain bikers.
Chef, Cleaners (3), Minibus Driver, Bar person, Mountain Bike and Ski Guides to earn between £350-£500 for dining and bar work, catering for up to 30 people. Applicants should be friendly, outgoing, preferably French speakers and hold relevant qualifications. Hours of work are 7am to 10am and 5pm to 9pm 7 days per week, between 1 July and 30 September; minimum period of work 2 months. Board and lodging are provided at no cost.
Applications are invited from September onwards.

L'ALAMBIC ROCK CAFÉ: 48 Avenue de la Mer, F-85160 St Jean de Monts, France (tel 00 33 25158 06 83). A lively and very busy Tex Mex restaurant and Rock Café situated in the main tourist area of St Jean. The friendly French owner employs a staff of 10 for the season.
Barman/Woman, Waiter/Waitress: Dynamic, fun loving and fit young people sought to work in June, July and August. Must speak good French and have previous experience in fast-moving bar/restaurant.
Wage £170 per week and free accommodation.
To *apply* send a c.v. and photo to Bertrand Boissinot at the above address.

HOTEL RESTAURANT ALTAIR: 18 Boulevard Féart, F-35800 Dinard, France (tel 02-99 46 13 58; fax 02-99 88 20 49). Pleasant two-star hotel-restaurant with terrace, near St Malo.
Chef, Waiter/Waitress, Chambermaid required to work hours as required by the job over a 5¹/2 day week, minimum of 4 hours work per day. Waiting staff will be serving meals in the restaurant and on the terrace. Wages and period of work by arrangement. Applicants should speak French and English or German, and have some previous experience of hotel work.
Places are *available* all year round and *applications* should be sent to the above address.

MOTELARCADE: 60, Quai de Bosc, F-34200 Sete, France (tel 467-74-95-90).
Receptionist: work includes reception duties, setting breakfast and putting away washing up. Wages by arrangement. To work 45 hours per 5¹/2 day week. Free

More than an experience

- **Restaurants**
- **Fast-food outlets**
- **Reception sales**
- **Amusements**
- **Sport and leisure activities**

With 12 million visitors a year, Disneyland® Paris is the top amusement park in Europe.

To make sure our customers have an unforgettable experience, we are looking for people who are very good at customer services to work in a dynamic and international environment.

You are at least 18 years old and you speak good French - whether you are a complete beginner or already have some experience, you are welcome to apply ! Supervisor positions are also available.

You can join us on a permanent contract starting from now (35 hours a week) or on a temporary contract from 2 to 7 months starting March 2002 (including July and August). Come join the team to take part in exciting events like the opening of the Walt Disney Studios Park® and help us blow out the candles for the 10th anniversary of Disneyland Paris !

© Disney

Interested ? Send us your application, quoting the reference SJA/02, to Disneyland Paris, Recruitment Department, BP 110, 77777 Marne-la-Vallée Cedex 4, France.

See you soon !

board and lodging provided.

To work either in the Easter holidays or for at least one month between 1 June and 30 October. Applicants must be adaptable, fit in with a team and speak French and some English and German. Applications to the above address from January.

HOTEL ARVERNE: Ave Antoine Fayets, F-15800 Vic sur Cere, France (tel 471-49-60-54; fax 471-49-63-82).
Barman (1), Waitresses (2), Kitchen Porter (1). Wages approx. £180 per month plus tips, food, accommodation and free ski pass. To work 5 days per week during the summer from June to August and in winter from January (or possibly late December) to March. Must have catering experience.

Applications should be sent to Mr Michel at the above address with a curriculum vitae in French and a recent photo, stating when available to work.

L'AUBERGE DU CHOUCAS: F-05220 Monetier le Bains, Serre-Chevalier 1500, Hautes-Alpes, France (tel 492-24-42-73; fax 492-24-51-60). The hotel is a converted old farm, and prides itself on its attentive service and its gastronomic food. It is located in a charming and lively village in one of the most important ski resorts in France. The area is a popular tourist destination throughout the year.
Hotel Staff (2); wages and duties by arrangement. To work 5 days per week. Board and accommodation provided. Minimum period of work 12 weeks in the summer or winter, or any other period.

There is a family atmosphere, but diligent work is demanded,
Applicants should be discreet and well-educated, have a pleasant disposition, speak adequate French and have previous hotel or restaurant work. The manageress attaches great importance to language ability and sensitivity to the culture. Some knowledge of German would also be an advantage. *Applications* should be sent to Nicole Sanchez-Ventura at the above address.

AUBERGE SUR LA MONTAGNE: La Thuile, F-73640 Sainte Foy Tarentaise, France (tel 4-79 06 95 83; fax 4-79 06 95 96; e-mail sue&andymac@auberge-montagne.co.uk; www.auberge-montagne.co.uk). This private 8-bed hotel is situated in the French alps between Val D'Isere an Bourg Saint Maurice. Apart from the obvious winter sport, walking, cycling and watersport opportunities in the area there is glacier skiing in summer.
Waitress/Chambermaid required to clean rooms, public areas (bar, lounge and restaurant), wash up and help serve breakfasts and dinner. Hours of work 7.30-11.30am and 7-10pm 4 days per week. Period of work June 29th-September 21st, minimum period of work 8 weeks. Wages are £400 per month with free board and lodging. Applicants should have previous experience and speak English and French.

To *apply* contact Sue & Andy Macinnes from May onwards.

AUDE HOTEL: aire de Narbonne, Vinasson, Autoroute A9, 11110 Vinasson, France (tel 468-45-25-00; fax 468-45-25-20).
Hotel Staff to work in reception, serve in the restaurant, clean, take messages, various other duties as necessary. Wages at the usual national rate. To work 8 hours per day, with one day off per 48 hour week. Period of work by arrangement. Accommodation can be provided at the usual national rate.

Applicants should have a good sense of service and a desire to work well; they should also, if possible, speak French, English, German and Italian. *Applications* should be sent to the Manager at the above address between March and April.

HOTEL DU BAS-BREAU: 22 Rue Grande, F-77630 Barbizon, France (01-60-66-40-05; fax 01-60-69-22-89; e-mail basbreau@wanadoo.fr; www.bas_breau.com).
Waiting Assistant, Washer up. Wages according to qualifications and experience. To work 5 days per week. Board and accommodation provided. Minimum period of work 2 months. Knowledge of French and English necessary.
Chambermaid to clean rooms and bathroom. 39 hours per week; 2 months minimum. Approx. £375 per month, with board and lodging provided. A little French speaking necessary. *Applications* to M Jean Pierre Fava at the above address from the beginning of the year.

HOSTELLERIE LE BEFFROI: BP 85, F-84110 Vaison la Romaine, Provence, France (tel 490-36-04-71; fax 490-36-24-78; www.le-beffroi.com).
Reception Assistant, Bar, Kitchen and Restaurant Staff. Duties by arrangement. To work 8 hours per day, 5 days per week. Wages of c. £495 (Euros 800) per month, board and accommodation provided. Minimum period of work 3 months between April and the end of September. Applicants should speak French (and German if possible) and must have experience of hotel or restaurant work. *Applications* to Yann Christiansen at the above address.

HOTEL LA BELLE ETOILE: Le Bettex, St. Gervais, F-74170 France (tel +33-450 93 11 83; fax; +33-450 93 14 91; e-mail kieron@belletoile.com; www.belletoile.com). Small, friendly chalet style hotel run by an English owner. Clients are mainly British adults on organised walking holidays with some school groups on Field Study Tours.
Chambermaid/Waitress (3) to carry out hotel work including cleaning rooms and public areas, waiting tables and performing a small amount of bar work in Le Bettex, St. Gervais. Clients are normally Britons on walking or skiing holidays. To work split shifts approx. 9 hours per day, 6 days a week. Wages £60 per week plus board and lodging. Minimum period of work 3¹/2 months from early June to mid September. Knowledge of French an advantage but not essential. Applicants must have common sense, a mature outlook and take pride in their work. The positions would suit people who enjoy an outdoors/mountain environment. Travel from the UK and medical insurance provided and training is given. *Applications* from December onwards to the above address.

HOTEL BELLE ISLE SUR RISLE: 112 Route de Rouen, F-27500 Pont-Audemer, France (tel 232-56-96-22; fax 232-42-88-96).
Waiter (1); Receptionist (1) to work at reception and switchboard.
Salary according to qualifications and competence. 169 hours work a month. Minimum period of work 1-2 months during the summer vacation: July and August. Accommodation available in the local town at a maximum of £99 per month. Applicants must be male with excellent presentation. English and/or German languages required. *Applications* at any time at the above address.

HOTEL MANOIR DE BELLERIVE: F-24480 Le Buisson de Caudouin, France (tel 0553-221616; fax 0553-220905; e-mail manoir.Bellerive@wanadoo.fr; www.bellerivehotel.com). A typical French chateau, this hotel is situated near the River Dordogne in the heart of superb and serene grounds.
Dining/Breakfast Assistant, Kitchen Pastry Helper, General Assistant. Wages of approx. £625 per month net (Pastry chef: £645 net per month).
Receptionist: for reception and administrative work. Wages of £645 net per

month. Must speak two European languages.

Employees will work split shifts five days per week. Minimum period of work eight weeks between April and October.

Board and accommodation provided. Applicants should speak French, and possess the relevant qualifications for hotel work. *Applications* from April onwards to the above address.

HOTEL BELLEVUE: F-63790 Chambon-sur-Lac, France (tel 473-88-61-06; fax 473-88-63-53).

General Assistant. Wages by arrangement. Period of work June-September. Applicants must be keen workers, non smokers, well-educated, and speak French. Knowledge of German and English an advantage. *Applications* to Madame Jury at the above address from April enclosing an photograph and an International Reply Coupon.

RELAIS DU BOIS SAINT GEORGES: Parc Atlantique, Cours Genet, F-17100 Saintes, France (tel 5-46-93-50-99; fax 5-46-93-34-93; e-mail info@relaisdubois. com; www.relaisdubois.com). This charming establishment is featured in *The Good Hotel Guide.*

Bell-boys (1 or 2) to welcome clients and show them and carry their luggage to their rooms.

Kitchen Assistants to help in the kitchens and assist the chambermaids each morning.

Applicants for both positions should be well-presented, motivated and good team workers. The period of work is from July to September; minimum period of work one month, working eight hours per day, five days a week. Board and accommodation is available if needed and is provided free of charge. Applicants should speak English and French. *Applications* invited from January 2002.

HOTEL CHATEAURENARD: F-05350 Saint Veran, France (tel 492-45-85-43; fax 492-45-84-20; e-mail chateaurenard@wanadoo.fr; www.chateaurenard-stveran.com). This 20 room chalet style hotel, run by a French speaking Australian with her French chef husband is located at the foot of the ski slopes (2080m). It has spectacular views overlooking the 18th Century village of Saint Veran, the Hautes Alpes, and the border with the Italian Piedmont.

General Assistants (4) to clean rooms, work in the restaurant and the laundry. To work 43 hours a week, 5 days a week. Wages at the usual national rate for hotel work. Board and accommodation provided. To work minimum period of 1 week over Christmas/New Year, 4 weeks in February/March or 4-6 weeks during July to August/September. No special qualifications required except a happy nature and the ability to work with people and to work hard. Knowledge of French is essential.

Applications to the Director at the above address.

HOTEL-RESTAURANT CHEVAL-BLANC: F-67510 Niedersteinbach, France (tel 388-09-55-31; fax 388-09-50-24; e-mail contact@hotel-cheval-blanc.fr; www.hotel-cheval-blanc.fr). A 26 room hotel combined with a 120 place restaurant located in a small village in a natural park. Facilities include a tennis court and a swimming pool

Assistant Waitress: £520-£550 per month plus tips.

Kitchen Assistant: £520-£550 per month.

$5^1/2$ day week. Board and lodging provided free. Must have previous experience and knowledge of French and German. Period of work 3 months minimum from July to November. *Applications* to May to M Michel Zinck at the above address.

HOSTELLERIE ST. CLEMENT: Curebourse, F-15800 Vic-Sur-Cere, France (tel 471-47-51-71; fax 471-49-63-02).
Waiter, Bar Person, Chamber Person: Wage £150 per month approximately. 45 hours per week, 5^1/2 days per week. Board and accommodation provided free of charge. Minimum period of work 2 months from July to August. Season runs from 1 June to 15 September. A knowledge of French and English is required. *Applications* should be sent to the above address from February/March onwards.

CLUB CANTABRICA HOLIDAYS LTD: 146/148 London Road, St. Albans, Herts AL1 1PQ (tel 01727-833141; fax 01727-843766). A leading coach and camping operator to France and the Mediterranean, they also run three hotels in France in the Savoix and Chamonix valleys, with the latter being open all year.
Hotel Managers required to run hotels at St Gervais in the French Alps. Approximately 40 hours work per 6 day week, applicants should have French language skills and previous hotel experience. Wages approx. £130 per week.
Chefs to cook for up to 80 guests. Must have previous experience of working at this level. Wages approx. £130 per week.
Free accommodation provided. Period of work from April to October.
General Duty Reps required to help in bar, kitchen cleaning of hotel and reception work, wages approximately £70 per week
Applications with curriculum vitae and stamped addressed envelope to the above address from December.

CLUB TELI: 7 rue Blaise Pascal, F-74600 Seynod, France (tel 4-5052-2658; fax 4-5052-1016; e-mail clubteli@wanadoo.fr; www.aussieworld.com/teli/). The Club TELI offers an interesting alternative for any person wishing to go abroad whether for a training course, a summer job or a career job. Club TELI is a non-profit organisation.
Secretary: Club TELI seeks an intern from March-November who has a good knowledge of French. Age 20-30, good telephone manner. Seynod is a small town near Annecy (90 km to Chamonix-Mont Blanc, 45 km to Geneva). *Apply* by e-mail to Dominique Girerd.

RESTAURANT CRUAUD: 8, rue du Pardon, F-56800 Ploërmel, France (tel/fax 02-97742781).
Summer Staff to work in a hotel and restaurant; wages and details of work by arrangement. To work 186 hours per month, 5 days per week. Board and lodging provided. To work from April to October.
Applicants must speak French and English. *Applications* should be sent to Mr and Mrs Cruaud at the above address from January.

HOTEL-RESTAURANT LES 3 COLOMBES: 148 avenue des Garrigues, 84210 Saint Didier, Provence, France (tel 04-90-66-07-01; fax 04-90-66-11-54). A three-star hotel restaurant in the heart of scenic Provence.
Restaurant Staff (2) for waiting service, place-setting, taking orders and washing up, preferably with 2/3 years experience in restaurant work. Hours of work are based around mealtimes over a 5^1/2 day week, totalling 195 hours per month, board and lodging are provided for approx. £45 per month. Applicants must be smartly dressed, well-groomed non-smokers, and preferably English

speakers. *Applications* are invited between April and May, with the working period being between 1 May and 30 September.

LE DOMAINE DE LA TORTINIERE: F-37250 Montbazon-en-Touraine, France (tel 247-34-35-00; fax 247-65-95-70; e-mail domaine.tortiniere@wanadoo.fr). A graceful second-empire turreted chateau converted into a hotel in 1954 and managed by the same family since then; guests are from France and the rest of the world.
Barman/Bellboy (1/2) to serve drinks from 3pm to midnight and to help staff at front desk, carry suitcases and show guests to their rooms. No wage, but free board and lodging. Minimum period of work 1 month between 1 March and 25 December.

Applicants should be well presented and speak French and English. *Applications* to M.X. Olivereau at the above address.

DOMAINE VALLEE HEUREUSE: Route de Geneve, F-39800 Poligny, France.
Waiter. Hours: 9am-3pm and 7-10.30pm. Cleanliness, cheerfulness and good appearance essential. Waiting experience preferred. £300 plus tips per month.
Chambermaid. Hours: 8am-noon and 1-5pm. Must be of good appearance. Wages: £300 per month.

Free board provided. Some knowledge of French is required for both positions. Minimum age 18 years. Minimum period of work 1st April to 30th September. *Applications* during April to the above address.

EVOLUTION 2/HARRI'S BAR: Le Lavachet, F-73320 Tignes, France (tel +33 4 79 06 48 11; fax +33 4 79 06 57 13; e-mail evolution2hotel@wanadoo.fr).
Bartenders (2) to work in Harri's bar. Shift work, with hours for the summer season being either from midday to 6pm or 6pm to midnight, with at least one day off per week. Knowledge of Italian and/or French an advantage.
Swimming Pool Supervisor; duties to include pool maintenance and general supervision. Must hold a lifesaving qualification.
Chamber/Waiting Staff (4). Knowledge of Italian and/or French helpful.

To work for a hotel/bar complex that is run by the owners from May to November and rented to a tour operator for the winter season. Wages approx. £315 per month plus board and accommodation and fringe benefits including access to an activity centre and ski hire and passes during the winter season. Minimum period of work from mid June to mid September, but work is available around the year; there will be around 10 vacancies for the winter season from September.
Applications to Jeremy Goodall at the above address.

EXODUS TRAVELS: 9 Weir Road, London, SW12 OLT (tel 020-8675 5550; fax 020-8673 0779).
House Staff (2) required for work in the French Pyrenees. Work is available throughout the year. Job involves cooking, cleaning, shopping, running the bar. 6 days/around 40 hrs work a week, no overtime. A driving licence, some French and cooking experience are all useful, but not essential. Board, lodging and transport are paid for, and on top of this there is a wage of £75 per week.
Applications throughout the year should be sent to the above address, quoting 'Ref: La Feniere.

HOTEL-RESTAURANT LE FLEURAY: F-37530 Cangey, Amboise, France (tel 02-47-56-09-25; fax 02-47-56-93-97; e-mail LEFLEURAYHOTEL@ wanadoo.fr; www.lefleurayhotel.com). This highly acclaimed English-run, country house hotel is situated in a peaceful location in the Loire valley, only 55 minutes from Paris by TGV, and listed in many *Best Hotel* guidebooks worldwide. **Staff** required for all aspects of work in the hotel (including restaurant service, housekeeping, kitchen work and gardening). Male and female staff required. Candidates must be outgoing, friendly, keen to work closely with a sophisticated international clientele and not be afraid of hard work. Knowledge of French is useful but not essential. Applicants will ideally be students, although those taking time off or who have graduated will be considered. To work ten hours per day (mornings and all afternoons free) six days per week. Minimum period of work, four months, between March and October. Attractive weekly wage, and full board and accommodation provided. *Applications* from November onwards to Peter or Hazel Newington at the above address.

GARDEN BEACH HOTEL: 15-17 Bd. Baudoin, F-06160 Juan les Pins, France (tel 493-67-25-25).
Chamber Staff (2-4). Wage by arrangement; accommodation available. To work 8 hours per day, 5¹/₂ days per week. Period of work from May to October. *Applications* should be sent to the Personnel Manager at the above address.

HOTEL IMPERIAL GAROUPE: 770 Chemin de la Garoupe, 06600 Le Cap d'Antibes (tel 04 92 93 31 61; fax 04 92 93 31 62; e-mail hotel-imp@webstore.fr; www.imperial-garoupe.com).
Chef de Rang (3), Commis Chef (1) to prepare food in the restaurant.
Chambermaids (3) required to clean and prepare bedrooms for guests.
    All staff will work 8 hours a day, 5 days a week for at least 4 months between April and October. Board and accommodation are provided free, along with a wage of approx. £750. Applicants should be able to speak both French and English confidently.
    Applications should be sent to Mr Gilbert Irondelle at the above address from January.

L'AUBERGE LIMOUSINE: F-19320 La Roche-Canillac, France (tel 05-55-29-12-06).
Waiter, Barman, Chambermaid, Dishwasher required for small hotel. Wages approx. £150 net per month for working a 45 hour week over 5¹/₂ days. Period of work April to end of September. Knowledge of English and French essential. *Applications* should be made between February and March; contact Michele Coudert at the above address.

HOTEL RESTAURANT 'AU LION BLEU': 176 Rue Koeberlé, Lutzelbourg, Moselle 57820, France (tel 0033-387 25 31 88; fax 0033-387 25 42 98; e-mail lion.bleu.ltz@wanadoo.fr; www.hotelaulionbleu.com). Small family business. Lutzelbourg is 45km from Strasbourg. Areas within 2 hours drive or day outings by train include the Black Forest, Baden-baden/Stuttgart, Frankfurt, Basel (Switzerland), Luxembourg, Leige (Belgium).
Kitchen Helps/Housekeepers (2), Waiters/Waitresses (2) required from May until October, candidates can have July to travel around neighbouring countries and resume work in August. Wages are negotiable with full board and lodging plus a share of weekly tips. Hours by arrangement (5¹/₂ day week).
    Experience is not essential, some training can be given, but spoken German is

an advantage as 70 per cent of clients are German/German Swiss.

Applications to Mr & Mrs Jaques Balinski, Owners, at the above address.

LE RELAIS DU LYON D'OR: 4 Rue d'Enfer, 86260 Angles sur L'Anglin, France (tel 05494-83253; fax 054984-0228; e-mail thoreau@lyondor.com; www.lyondor.com). The Lyon D'or is a three star hotel and restaurant in Angles sur l'Anglin, near Poitiers. The hotel is listed in all leading guides and is run by Anglo-French owners.

Cleaners/Waiters/Waitresses: (3) For general help in the hotel and restaurant. Applicants should have a positive attitude, a sense of humour. English and at least conversational French are essential, and Dutch would be an advantage. To work 10 hours a day, 5^1/2 days per week. Positions available between May and end of October; minumum period two months. The village is very isolated, so own transport is an advantage. Wages of £470 per month, plus bonus, and board and lodging. Applicants must be EU nationals or have the correct permits to work in France. *Applications* to Heather Thoreau from December onwards at the above address.

HOSTELLERIE DE LA MARONNE: Le Theil, F-15140 St Martin-Valmeroux, France (tel +33-(0)4-71-69-20-33; fax 04-71-69-28-22; e-mail hotelmaronne@cfi15.fr; www.cfi15.fr/hotelmaronne). A hotel-restaurant in the countryside near Clermont-Ferrand with heated pool, tennis courts and sauna, attracting customers from all over the world.

Receptionist, Waitress gross wages approx. £600 per month.

Second/Assistant Chefs gross wages may be between £600-£800.

Experience of working in 3 or 4 star hotels necessary; knowledge of French is preferred but not essential. To work 42^1/2 hours per 5 day week, for a minimum of two weeks between 1 May and 15 September. Board and lodging provided free. *Apply* from January to June to Alain Decock at the above address.

HOTEL MIREILLE: 2 Place St. Pierre, F-13200 Arles en Provence, France (tel +33-(0)4-90-70-74; fax 04-90-93-87-28; e-mail contact@hotelmireille.com; www.hotelmireille.com). This hotel is a hideaway nestled in the countryside of the Camargue, not far from the old town of Arles.

Waitress, Chambermaid, Receptionist: wages of £325 per month, with board and lodging included. Receptionists and waitresses must speak very good French and English, preferably with some experience of reception and food service work. Minimum period of work 5 months between March and early October. *Applications* to the above address.

CHATEAU DE MONTREUIL: 4 Chaussee Des Capucins, 62170 Montreuil-sur-Mer, France (tel 3-21-81-53-04; fax 3-21-81-36-43; e-mail chateau.de.montreuil@ wanadoo.fr; www.relaischateau.fr/montreuil). This family run, four star hotel has 14 bedrooms and a gourmet 45-seater restaurant.

Gardener's Aide. (2) For weeding, watering, mowing lawns etc.

Glass Washer/Suitcase Carrier.

Chambermaid Helper For cleaning, ironing, turndown and general service.

Vegetable Preparer. General vegetable preparation and other small kitchen tasks.

Applicants for all positions must be willing workers, pleasant and have a sense of humour, a little French is advantageous. Wages for all positions £190 per month, board and accommodation is provdided free of charge. To work 39 hours per week, 5^1/2 hours per day, period of work June to September. *Applications* to

Mrs Germain at the above address. Applicants must send a c.v. with a reference and a colour identity photo.

HOTEL MOULIN DES POMMERATS: F-89210 Venisy-St-Lorentin, France (tel 86-35-08-04).
Hotel Staff: Wages and duties by arrangement. Board and lodging provided. Minimum period of work 1 month between July and September. Knowledge of languages not required. *Applications* to the above address.

HOTEL RESTAURANT LE MOULIN DU ROC: 24530 Champagnac de Belair, France (tel 05 53 02 86 00; fax 05 53 54 21 31; e-mail moulinroc@ aol.com; www.moulin-du-roc.com). Run by a young and dynamic team (the directors are only 30 years old). The Hotel-Restaraunt is situated in Perigord, a popular region with tourists. The village in which it is situated contains facilities for playing tennis, fishing and many other pursuits.
Chefs (2), Waiters/Waitresses (2), Assistant Chefs (2): required in a gastronomic restaurant serving high quality food with excellent service. Previous experence in similar restaurants required. Wages range from approx £750 to £1,000 per month depending on position.
Hotel Manager (1) Previous experience in the hopitality industry required. Wage £1,000 per month approx.
   Work is available between April and November, May and October or June and September. Waiters and Hotel Manager must be able to speak English and French confidently. All staff need a passion for their work.
   Applications are invited as early as possible to the the the above address.

HOTEL-RESTAURANT L'OCEAN: 172, rue de St Martin, F-17580 Bois - Plage en Ré (tel 05-46-09-23-07; fax 05-46-09-05-40; e-mail ocean@ledeu.com; www.le-hotel-ocean.com). This hotel and restaurant are in a peaceful location with a unique and pleasant ambience, by a small and picturesque port.
Waitresses (2) to work during July and August, and possibly longer. Wages £670 approx in July and August; £650 approx during other months. To work split shifts, with two days free per week. Accommodation costs approx. £190 per month; Board is provided free of charge. Applicants should speak English and French. *Applications* to the above address.

HOTEL DE LA POSTE: F-29950 Benodet, France.
Barmaid, Waiting Assistants, Chambermaid, Receptionist: Wages by arrangement. To work around 8 hours per day, 5½ days per week. No accommodation available. Minimum period of work 2 months between April and September. Applicants must speak French and English. *Applications*, with photographs, to the above address from March.

HOTEL DU PONT NEUF: F-03320 Le Veurdre, France (tel 470-66-40-12; fax 470-66-44-15; e-mail HOTEL.LE.PONTNEUF@wanadoo.fr; www.hotel-lepontneuf.com). This pleasant 46 room hotel is run by an American and her husband so French is not essential, although the chambermaids will be working with French staff.
Chambermaids to clean rooms, wash dishes and possibly some serving at the bar. Wage approx. £250 per month; board and lodging provided. To work a 5 day week; minimum period of work 10 weeks between 15 May to 31 July and 1 August to 15 October.

General Worker to prepare garden, pool, tennis court, and terrace for summer season and help with dish washing. To work a 5 day week for approx £250 per month, period of work 15 April to 15 September, minimum period of work 2¹/2 months.

Apprentice Cook for a two year period. 1st six months at £250 per month, then £500 per month depending on ability. Working long hours over a five day week. Expect to learn a good trade.

Applicants should be hardworking, pleasant and hoping to improve their French. Board and lodging included.

Applications *from EU residents only*, to Mrs Denise Ducroix at the above address from January.

HOTEL LE RIVET: F-06450 Lantosque, France.
Chambermaids to serve breakfasts, make beds and do the laundry.
Kitchen Assistants, Waitresses, Handyman, Washer Up.

To work in a small three star hotel. Wages by arrangement: board and lodging provided. To work 8 hours per day, 6 days per week. Minimum period of work 8 weeks between 1 April and 15 October. Applicants should be serious, well behaved and dress in a suitable manner for exclusive hotelwork. *Applications* to M Henrik Winther at the above address from 1st March.

HOTEL DE LA TONNELLERIE: 12 rue des Eaue Bleue, F-45190 Tavers, France (tel +33-2-38 44 68 15; fax +33-2-38 44 10 01; e-mail tonelri@club-internet.fr; www.chateaux-france.com/-latonnellerie). A four star hotel-restaurant with a young staff team, catering to upper class clients; located in the Loire valley.
Chef (2-3) to cook for a clientele of gourmands. Must have experience.
Waiter (3) to wait on tables in the restaurant, on the terrace and by the swimming pool. Must have experience of 4-star service.
General Help (2-3) to wash dishes, help serve breakfasts and clean rooms. No experience necessary, just a calm and good natured outlook.

Hours of work are shifts between 7am and midnight, over a 5-5¹/2 day week. Period of work May to September, with a minimum period of work of two months. Wages £520 per month. Some free board and lodging is available. Ideally candidates should speak French and English.

Applications from 1 March to the above address.

CHATEAU DE TRIGANCE: F-83840, Trigance, France (tel 04-94-76-91-18; fax 04-94-85-68-99; e-mail trigance@relaischateau.fr; www.relaischateax. fr/trigance). This beautiful medieval castle-hotel in Provence, has ten rooms, a twenty-five seater gourmet restaurant and a team of 15 staff.
Waiters and Kitchen Helps (2) to wait at tables in the gourmet restuarant and to welcome clients. also to be in charge of service from midday until evening. Applicants must have relevant experince, be well-presented and have good initiative skills. Applicants should also be organised with a team spirit. Wages £575 (beginning) to £700 approx.
Culinary Staff (2) to set places, change produce and dispatch plates. Applicants should have a good basic knowledge of cooking, and be very organised, motivated and have a team spirit.

All applicants will work 39 hours per five day week. Minimum period of work is two months between beginning April to end October. Board and accommodation is provided. Applicants should speak English and French. *Applications* invited from 1st April, to Thomas Guillaume at the above address.

UK OVERSEAS HANDLING (UKOH) INTERNATIONAL RECRUITMENT: U.K.O.H., P.O. Box 2791, London, W1A 5JU (tel 020-7629 3064; fax 020-7495 0411; e-mail personnel@nbultduk.freeserve.co.uk). In business since 1989, UKOH is a UK recruitment company for French-owned tour operators and accommodation management companies including rapidly expanding company, Eurogroup.

Waiting, Bar, Night Auditor, Kitchen, Reception, Housekeeping, Grounds and Maintenance/Handy Staff Succesful candidates should be over 18 years of age and EU passport holders. Must be bright, flexible, keen and prepared for hard work. Experience and very good French preferred for most positions. Gap Year students and those looking for a career in tourism welcomed, Student Placements available. Package includes full board and shared accommodation. One day off a week except at peak times.

Staff required from May to October for hotels and tourist residences located in coastal resorts on the south and west coasts of France during the summer, as well as in the French Alps where the Head Office and mountain resort operations are based.

HOTEL RESTAURANT LE VEYMONT: F-26420 St Agnan-en-Vercore, France (tel 475-48-20-19; fax 475-48-10-34).

Chambermaid, Waitress: Wage of £300 per month with accommodation provided. Period of work by arrangement; staff needed around the year. Applicants should speak some French.

Applications should be sent to the Manager at the above address.

Industrial and Office Work

THE AUTOMOBILE ASSOCIATION

The AA is part shareholder of a 24-hour multi-lingual European Call Centre situated in Limonest, just north of Lyon. Each year we employ up to 80 individuals to assist with our ever-increasing summer workload. Minimum age for applicants is 18 years so if you want to gain unique work experience with us, we are seeking English mother-tongue speakers with fluency in French, plus another European language, to be available to work from March through to September 2002 (minimum work duration 8 weeks). Full training induction courses will be phased in at intervals.

The job involves working to a shift pattern, 35 hrs per week, as a Call Handler providing a high standard of customer care and incident management for AA customers who have broken-down or have been involved in a road traffic accident in Europe. Your language skills are essential for liaising with garages and other suppliers.

You will need to be efficient, responsible, and compassionate when dealing with customers in what can sometimes be stressful circumstances. The ability to work professionally in a high-pressure environment is essential.

Local subsidised basic accommodation can be arranged within walking distance of the Call Centre.

For more information please contact me at elaine.badham@theaa.com or telephone me at AA European Operations on 01256 492398.

The AA is part of Centrica PLC

THE AUTOMOBILE ASSOCIATION: European Operations, 2nd Floor, Fanum House, Basing View, Basingstoke RG21 4EA (tel 01256-492398; e-mail elaine.badham@theaa.com).

Call Handlers (up to 80) to assist the AA's multi-lingual European Call Centre in Limonest, north of Lyon: the Centre provides 24-hour assistance to AA customers who have broken down or become involved in a road traffic accident in Europe. Wages by arrangement. To work 35 hours per week on shifts. Minimum period of work 8 weeks between March and September. Local accommodation can be arranged. Applicants must speak English (mother-tongue), be fluent in French and preferably one other European language; you will need to be efficient, responsible, compassionate and able to work under pressure.

Please send your c.v. to Elaine Badham by e-mail or to the above address.

HORIZON HPL: Signet house, 49/51 Farringdon road, London EC1M 3JB (tel 020-7404-9192/93; fax 020-7404-9194; e-mail horizonhpl.london@ btinternet.com). Horizon HPL is a training centre established in 1991 which organises paid work placements in hotels and companies in the UK and in France for EU citizens. This includes English and French tuition and preparation to sit British and French examinations.

Hotel Work/Company Staff: placements are available all year round (in a variety of fields) from three months up to one year. Staff receive a trainee wage and free accommodation if working in a hotel. Applicants accepted between 17-50 years old.

Applicants should contact the agency two months in advance of intended work date, as an interview is necessary.

Other contacts: Paris (tel 0033-1-40-01-07-07; e-mail horizon1@club-internet.fr), Aix-en-Provence (tel 0033-4-42-26-50-85; e-mail hplaix@clubinternet.fr) and Dublin (tel 00353-1874-5002; e-mail horizonhpl@eircom.net).

SOLTOURS: 46 rue de Rivoli, F-75004 Paris, France.
Sales Assistant to work for a travel agent. Wages of approximately £700 per month. To work 8 hours per day, 5 days per week. No board or accommodation available. Minimum period of work 3 months between March and June. Applicants should be efficient, responsible and speak English. Applications to the above address from February.

Sports, Couriers and Camping

ACORN ADVENTURE: 22 Worcester Street, Stourbridge, DY8 1AN. (tel 01384-446057; fax 01384-378866; e-mail topstaff@acornadventure.co.uk). Adventure Activity Holiday company offering groups multi-activity camping holidays in North Wales, the Lake District, Spain and Italy as well as France.

300 seasonal opportunities: **instructors, maintenance staff, administrators, catering staff and nurses** needed mid-April to September (some shorter contracts). Activities include sailing, canoeing, kayaking, climbing, abseiling and caving. Living allowance of approximately £50 plus supplement/bonus subject to centre and position. Please send an application letter for the attention of Recruitment and a full information pack will be sent to you.

BALLOON FLIGHTS – FRANCE MONTGOLFIERES: La Ribouliere, F-41400 Monthou Sur Cher, France (tel 02-54-71-75-40; fax 02-54-71-75-78; e-mail jane@franceballoons.com).

Ballon Crew required April-November to work for passenger-carrying operation with bases in the Burgundy and Loire Valley regions. Duties include maintaining and cleaning of vehicles and balloon equipment, driving and navigation of balloon chase vans, helping out in a balloon repair workshop, passenger liaison, etc. Knowledge of French preferred. *Applicants should be EU nationals or possess correct working papers.* Minimum age 21, with clean driving licence. No fixed days off; hours can be very long. Wages £500-£600 per month. Please send a cv, a photo, and a copy of your driving licence.

BELLE FRANCE: 15 East Street, Rye, East Sussex TN31 7JY (tel 01797-223777; fax 01797-223666;).
Bike Representatives (10) to work for a tour operator offering cycling holidays in France. The job includes maintaining bikes, transporting luggage, collecting customers from station, etc. Wage from £300 per month. Also provided are gas, electricity, insurance, travel (by Belle France car) and accommodation in a caravan including site fees. To work 20-30 hours per week. Period of work from May to September, which includes a 5 day training period. Applicants should be well organised, capable of working on their own and like working in the country. *Applications* to the above address around Christmas.

BOOTS & BIKES: Hunter Kingston Holidays Ltd, 15 Husseywell Crescent, Bromley BR2 7LN (tel/fax 020-8462-6522; e-mail julia-kingston@ bootsandbikes.co.uk; www.bootsandbikes.co.uk). Hunter Kingston organises independent walking and cycling holidays in France. They offer tours lasting 6-10 days, between small hotels and guesthoses in rural France.
Holiday Representatives: (5) to meet clients on arrival, give tour briefings, move bags between hotels, carry out cycle maintenance, deal with hoteliers, keep accounts and carry out other duties as necessary. Representatives should be fit, active young people, with an interest in outdoor activities, especially cycling and walking.

Boots & Bikes require adaptable, resourceful people who can think on their feet in a variety of situations. Minuimum age 21 years. English and French language skills and a full, clean driving licence a must. Hours/days of work are flexible but the minimum period of work is two months between April and October. Wages £480 per month, with board and accommodation provided. *Applications* invited from January 2002, interviews will be held in London in early 2002.

CANVAS HOLIDAYS: East Port House, 12 East Port, Dunfermline, Fife KY12 7JG (tel 01383-629018; fax 01383-629071; www.canvas holidayscom). Canvas Holidays are looking for enthusiastic, resourceful people who enjoy a challenge and love the outdoor life. Main positions for 2002 include:
Campsite Courier. Varied responsibilities. Involves cleaning and preparation of customer accommodation, welcoming and looking after customers during their holiday and ensuring that they have the best holiday ever. As a campsite courier you will have new challenges every day which can lead to one of the most enjoyable summers you will ever have. Variable working hours.
Children's Courier. As a Canvas Holidays Children's Courier you will have had formal experience of working with children. You will organise and carry out a six day programme which involves four hours a day of Children's Club for children between the ages of 4 and 11. You will be prepared to help out with courier duties as and when requried. For many customers, the Children's Club is one of the main parts of the holiday. You will need to have the energy of a seven year old and the imagination of an eleven year old to succeed.

Package includes tented accommodation, medical insurance, full uniform and return travel to and from a UK port of entry. Positions are available from March until October. *Applications* are invited from individuals and couples. Contact Sandy, Karen or Michele at the above contact details for an application pack.

CARISMA HOLIDAYS: Bethel House, Heronsgate, Chorleywood WD3 5BB (tel 01923-284235; e-mail personnel@carisma.co.uk).
Carisma specialises in self-drive, family holidays in mobile homes on private sandy beaches in the sunny south-west of France.
Site Managers. Up to £100 per week plus tips and accommodation. To work from 12 May to 24 September. French speakers preferred.
Full Season Couriers: £80-£85 per week plus tips and accommodation. To work from May 12th to September 24th. French speakers preferred.
High Season Couriers: £70-£80 per week plus tips and accommodation. To work from 1 July to 13 September. French speakers preferred.
To work on beach sites in France. To be responsible for client families, with duties involving welcoming families, providing information and advice, cleaning and maintaining mobile homes and babysitting. Self-catering accommodation is provided in tents or mobile homes.
Applicants should have a helpful and friendly disposition and experience of dealing with people. Travel costs are paid and full training is given on site. *Applicants should be EU nationals.* Applications to Mr R. Beare at the above address.

CENTRE DE VOILE L'ABER-WRAC'H: B.P. 4, F-29870 Landeda, France (tel 298-04-90-64; fax 298-04-97-22).
Sailing Instructors (2), **Sailing Camp Leaders** (2) to work in Brittany. Period of work is July and August. Pay is around £105 weekly plus free board and lodging. Instructors work six and a half hours a day, six days a week and leaders six days a week all day and evenings. The minimum age is 18 and sailing instructors should be qualified. *Applications* to the address above.

CENTRE D'ECHANGES INTERNATIONAUX: 1 rue Gozlin, F-75006 Paris, France.
Youth Leaders to teach one of the following activities; sports, dancing, music, crafts. Around £200 per month. To work in international holiday centres. Hours can be long; one day off per week. Free board and lodging provided.
Period of work covers July and August. Applicants must speak French: some knowledge of German an advantage. Applicants must have previous experience as an instructor in holiday camps. *Apply* to the Director at the above address between March and May.

CHATEAU DE L'EPERVIERE: F-71240 Gigny sur Saone, Bourgogne Sud, France (tel 385-44-83-23; fax 385-44-74-20). A four star castle/campsite situated in the heart of Burgundy with indoor and outdoor pools, a jaccuzi and sauna. The campsite's key-words are conviviality and family atmosphere.
Staff, ideally students, to work on a campsite. Wages by arrangement. Minimum period of work two months between March and September; those available from early in April or until late September would be at an advantage. Applicants should have some qualifications or experience in waitressing, bartending or reception work.
Applicants must speak French, be aged 20-30, hard working, and be flexible, prepared to work long hours and friendly with clients; send a c.v. and picture to Gert-Jan Engel at the above address.

CLUB CANTABRICA HOLIDAYS LTD: 146/148 London Road, St. Albans, Herts AL1 1PQ (tel 01727-833141; fax 01727-843766). A leading coach and camping operator to France and the Mediterranean, they also run two hotels in France. These are in the Savoix and Chamonix valleys, the latter being open all year.
Hotel Managers required to run hotels at Val Cenis and St Gervais in the French Alps. Approximately 40 hours work per 6 day week. Applicants should have fluent French for both hotels, and also Italian for Val Cenis.
Must have previous hotel experience. Wages approx. £130 per week.
Chefs to cook for up to 80 guests. Must have previous experience at this level. Wages approx. £130 per week.
Free accommodation provided. Period of work from April to October, except for the hotel near St Gervais, which is open all year. Applicants should be over 21 years old.
Applications with curriculum vitae and stamped addressed envelope to the above address from December.

DETENTE LTD.: 9 Hangsman Lane, Dinnington, Sheffield S25 3PF (tel 01909-550959; fax 01909-518605; e-mail mike@www.detente.co.uk; www.detente.co.uk).
Campsite Reps (3) needed to work at campsite reception, and to look after the clients. Approximately 2 hours of work a day, 7 days a week. Applicants must be

prepared to work for the full season from June to September. Board and accomodation is provided free of charge along with a salary of £320 per month.
Applications to the above address.

DISCOVER LIMITED: Timbers, Oxted Road, Godstone, Surrey RH9 8AD (tel 01883-744392; fax 01883-744913). Discover Ltd have centres in France and Morocco. They provide a relaxed and friendly environment for visiting parties.
General Assistants/Housekeepers (2) for general cleaning and kitchen duties. Wage £300 per month plus full board.
Cooks/Assistant Cooks (2) to cook for up to 90 people; good wholesome cooking required. Wage approx. £350 per month plus full board. Should have cooking qualifications/experience.
To work from approx 7.30am-noon and 5.30-9.00pm, 6 days per week. Full board and lodging provided. To work in a field study/activity centre in the South of France. Period of work from 1 April to 1 October; full season preferred. Applicants must be able to be part of a team. Knowledge of French and a driving licence would be useful but are not essential. Non-smokers preferred.
Applications to the above address from December.

EUROCAMP: Overseas Recruitment Department (Ref SJ/02) (tel 01606-787522). Eurocamp is a leading tour operator in quality self-drive camping and mobile home holidays in Europe. Each year the company seeks to recruit up to 1,500 enthusiastic people for the following positions:
Site Managers: required to lead a large team of Campsite Couriers, organising their daily workloads and ensuring they provide the very best customer service. Applicants should be 21 or over, have proven managerial experience, excellent communication skills and language ability.
Couriers: job involves cleaning and preparing customer accommodation, providing assistance, acting as an information service and an interpreter and performing some administrative duties. Couriers need to be flexible to meet the needs of the customer to provide them with excellent service. Minimum age 18 years. Applicants should be independent with plenty of initiative and relish a challenging and rewarding position. They should also possess a friendly and helpful personality. Some working knowledge of another European language is required and previous customer service experience would be an advantage. Applicants should be available to work from April/May to September.
Children's Couriers: work involves organising a wide range of exciting activities for children aged 4-13. Applicants should possess initiative, imagination and enthusiasm along with good safety awareness. Previous childcare experience is essential. Minimum age is 18 years and applicants should be available from April/May to September. Languages are not a requirement but would be an advantage (in particular German).
Senior Couriers: required to work alongside a team of Campsite Couriers and organise their daily workload, as well as carrying out the normal day to day duties of a Campsite Courier. Applicants should have good language skills and experience of leading a team.
In all the above positions you should be be available for the full season commencing in April/May through to September. Comprehensive training is provided together with a competitive salary, insurance and return travel. Applications are accepted from September/October and *can only be accepted from UK/EU passport holders*. Interviews will be conducted in Hartford, Cheshire between October and April.

Eurocamp

Eurocamp are the leading tour operator in quality self-drive camping and mobile home holidays in Europe

Summer Jobs in Europe

We operate on over 200 campsites in Europe and every year we look for enthusiastic, motivated people to be the face of the company. Are you interested in spending the summer months working in a varied, challenging but ultimately highly rewarding job overseas? If the answer is yes, then apply now for one of the following positions

CAMPSITE COURIER: You must be over 18 with previous customer service experience. A good working knowledge of a second European Language (preferably French. Italian, German or Dutch) would be a distinct advantage.

• CHILDREN'S COURIER: You must be over 18 with the enthusiasm and ability to organise a wide range of safe but stimulating activities for groups of multi-national children aged 4-13. Language ability is not essential but an experience of working with children is.

• SENIOR COURIER: Do you have the ability to organise the daily workload and work alongside a small team of Campsite Couriers? You must have good language skills and experience of leading a team.

• SITE MANAGER: You must have proven managerial experience, be 21 or over with excellent communication skills and language ability. You will lead a large team of Campsite Couriers, ensuring that they provide the very best service to our customers at all times.

For the above positions you should ideally be available from April to September. We will provide full training, a competitive salary and accommodation.

• MONTAGE/DEMONTAGE ASSISTANTS: No languages are required for these positions. You will work as part of a team either preparing accommodation at the start of the season or dismantling equipment at its end. You must be aged over 18 and be motivated, self- disciplined and physically fit. Montage Assistants should be available from March. Demontage Assistants from the end of August for a period of 5-6 weeks.

Please telephone the Overseas Recruitment Department for further details on

01606 787522
quoting reference SJ/02

We also welcome applicants from other EC nationals particularly German and Dutch speakers. For further information please phone 0031 (0) 334465 1932.

FLEUR HOLIDAYS: 4 All Hallows Road, Bispham, Blackpool, Lancs FY2 0AS (tel 01253-593333; fax 01253-595151; e-mail employment@fleur holidays.com; www.fleur-holidays.com). A company which offers mobile home and tent holidays on quality sites in France, chosen for the ambience.

Area Supervisors required to cover groups of campsites to ensure couriers are performing to the required standards. Previous courier expereince is essential. Pay in the region of £150 per week dependent on service. Vehicle provided or mileage allowance given. Accomodation provided.

Representatives/Couriers (15) required to meet clients at reception, clean mobile homes and tents, organise social events and children's clubs, and for basic maintenance of equipment. Staff work flexible hours, six days a week for £110-130. Each vacancy is an all round position with responsibility of the campsite and clients. Maximum period of work 6 months between March/May and September. Accommodation available in tents.

Applicants should be 18+, have at least basic French language skills, and preferably have experience in the service industry as customer care is of the greatest importance to this organisation. Experience of working with children is also an advantage. Fleur Holidays are also able to offer half-season contracts i.e. May to early June, and July to September. There are also positions for staff involved purely in erecting tents in April and May and dismantling them in September.

For all positions, please request an application form from the Personnel Manager.

MARK HAMMERTON TRAVEL: 90-94 High St, Tunbridge Wells, Kent, TN1 1YF (tel 01892-525456; fax 01892-510055; e-mail enquiries@ markhammerton.co.uk). Mark Hammerton Travel is a young, dynamic tour operator based in Kent and offering top quality tent and mobile home holidays throughout France.

Operations Team Managers (10) required to prepare and/or dismantle campsite accommodation in France. Staff are needed for the first twenty days of May and September. Irregular hours according to weather. Applicants should be at least 18 years old and must be prepared for heavy, physical work. A driving licence is advantageous. Full board and accommodation, insurance and travel expenses are provided. A wage of £95 per week will also be paid.

Applications for the above positions or for team leader/driver positions should be made to the above address.

HAVEN EUROPE: 1 Park Lane, Hemel Hempstead HP2 4YL (tel 01442-203287; fax 01442-241473; www.haveneurope.com). Haven Europe, a leading self-drive, mobile home and camping company, provide seasonal job opportunities in France, Spain and Italy.

Courier Staff to work on campsites in France. Staff receive free accommodation, a competitive salary, uniform and insurance. Duties include preparation of guest accommodation, reception and problem solving. The hours are long and variable. Applicants should be available from the March to the end of September. Previous customer service experience is essential. Mature and sensible couples are invited to reply.

Children's Courier Staff to work on the same parks, organising and implementing children's activity programmes. Experience with children an advantage and a genuine liking of working with children essential. Applicants should be available from March to early September. French an advantage but not essential. You must be at least 19 years old to apply. Please write to the above address requesting an application form.

HEADWATER HOLIDAYS: 146 London Road, Northwich, Cheshire CW9 5HH (tel 01606-813333; fax 01606-813334; www.headwater-holidays.co.uk). Headwater offers relaxed discovery and adventure holidays; their hallmarks are personal service, warm friendly hotels and good regional cuisine. Headwater guides and information packs help clients make their own discoveries off the beaten track.

Overseas Representatives to work for an activity holiday company in France. Duties include meeting clients at airports and stations, supervising local transportation for them and their luggage, hotel and client liaison, bike maintenance and on the spot problem solving. Good, working French, and full, clean driving licence required. Organisational skills, resourcefulness and cheerfulness essential. Minimum age 21 years.

Canoeing Instructors: duties etc. as for Overseas Representatives but also include giving canoe instruction.

Wages from £100 to £150 per week; accommodation provided. To work hours as required. Staff required for full season from April to October. Further information and an on-line application form can be found on their website, or an application form can be requested from the above address.

Quality self-drive camping and mobile-home holidays in France

IAN MEARNS
Holidays
CAMPSITE REPRESENTATIVES

The job involves welcoming customers, providing general assistance and information, cleaning and maintaining tents and mobile homes and associated administrative tasks. We provide your accommodation and transport and wages of £400 per month plus bonuses.
If you have a confident and outgoing personality and you are good at solving problems, we have positions for the following dates:

❖ Early-season representatives   Easter-July
❖ Mid-season representatives   May-July
❖ High-season representatives   July- September

Please send your full CV with a covering letter giving the exact dates you are available to:
Ian Mearns Holidays
Tannery Yard • Witney Street • Burford • Oxon • OX18 4DP • Tel: (01993) 822655

IAN MEARNS HOLIDAYS: Tannery Yard, Witney Street, Burford, Oxon OX18 4DP (tel 01993-822655; fax 01993 822650; e-mail karen@ ianmearnsholidays.co.uk). Tour operator offering self-drive camping and mobile home holidays to families on 4-star campsites in France.

Area Supervisors (2) to supervise montage/demontage teams and campsite reps, and to ensure that high standards of accommodation, customer service and staff morale are achieved. To work a 5¹/2 day week with wages of £600 per month plus £15 per week bonus on completion of contract. Accommodation and travel provided, plus generous mileage allowance if own car used. A-level French and a full clean driving licence required. Applicants must be fit as some heavy lifting is involved. The period of work is April to October.

Campsite Representatives (31) to welcome clients, provide general assistance and information, and clean and maintain tents and mobile homes. Wages approx. £400 per month plus up to £15 per week bonus payable on completion of contract. To work a 5¹/2 day week on average. Accommodation is provided free of charge.

Minimum period of work is 10 weeks between March and October. Applicants must be healthy and able to work without supervision.

Montage/Demontage Assistants (14) to assist in erecting tents and preparing mobile homes at the beginning of the season and/or dismantling tents and closing down at the end of the season. Some heavy lifting is involved. The period of work is 6 weeks from March to May and 6 weeks from September to October.

Applications, with a curriculum vitae, to the above address from 1st October, giving exact dates of availability for work. Interviews are held for these positions in Burford; only those applicants invited for interview will be contacted.

INTERNATIONAL LIFE LEISURE: Kerry House, Kerry Street, Leeds, LS18 4AW (tel 0113-2050292; fax 0113 2584211; e-mail overseasemployment@ frenchlife.co.uk; www.frenchlife.co.uk). International Life Leisure run campsites and holidays throughout France. A branch of their organisation is French Life Holidays, who have tents and mobile homes on over 16 campsites in France.

Couriers to greet clients on arrival, prepare accommodation and carry out general duties whilst clients are on the campsite. Wage £105 per week. Good customer relations skills are important and experience is an advantage.

Children's Couriers required to organise kid's club, entertain children and carry out general cleaning duties. Wage £95 per week. Experience of working with children is preferable.

No qualifications are required, but knowledge of French would be beneficial and a hard-working, flexible attitude is required. Period of work at least 3 months between early March and September, 6 days, $37^{1}/2$ hours per week. Free accommodation is available.

Applications to the above address from December.

KEYCAMP HOLIDAYS: Overseas Recruitment Department, Hartford Manor, Greenbank Lane, Nothwich CW8 1H (tel 01606-787522)..

Campsite Couriers: to look after British, Dutch and Scandinavian customers on campsites in France. Duties include welcoming customers, providing local information, organising social activities on site and ensuring that all accommodation is prepared prior to arrival.

Chidren's Courier: to organise and provide up to 24 hours of activities per week for children aged 4-13 years, to advertise the club activities and visit families on arrival.

Senior Courier: incorporating the role of campsite courier with the additional responsibility of organising and managing the team and ensuring the smooth running of the Keycamp operation on site.

Montage/Demontage: for a period of approximately 6 weeks at the beginning/end of season to erect/dismantle equipment.

Minimum age 18 years. Accommodation, uniform and training provided. A working knowledge of French would be an advantage. Period of employment between March and July/October.

Applicants should write to the Overseas Recruitment Department, Keycamp Holidays, quoting reference SJ/02.

MARK WARNER. Telephone 020-7761-7300 (24 hour).

Club Managers, Accountants, Receptionists, Watersports Instructors, Tennis and Aerobics Instructors, Chefs, Kitchen Porters, Waiting and Bar Staff, Nannies, Handymen and Nightwatchmen are required to work in Beachclub Hotels in Corsica during the summer from April to October. Wages from £50-

£230 per week plus full board, medical insurance, travel expenses and free use of watersport and activity facilities. Some reserve staff also needed throughout the season. Requirements for languages, age, experience, qualifications etc. vary according to the job applied for. For further details, please call the Resorts Recruitment Department on the above number.

MATTHEWS HOLIDAYS: 8 Bishopsmead Parade, East Horsley, Surrey KT24 6RP.
Couriers/Campsite Representatives to receive clients and maintain and clean caravans in western France. £120 per week. 35 hour, 6 day week. Accommodation provided. Knowledge of French necessary. Applicants should be at least 20 years of age and available to commence work during April or May and work until mid/late September. A few vacancies available for the period July-September. *Applications* to the above address enclosing an sae and giving details of age, present occupation and other relevant experience, and date available to commence work.

NSS RIVIERA HOLIDAYS: 288, Chemin du Caladou, F-06560 Valbonne, France. (tel/fax +33-4 93 12 95 81; e-mail nss@wanadoo.fr). NSS has a number of agents working in several European countries. Customers come from the UK, Holland, Belgium, Germany, Switzerland and Denmark. Working language is English.
Small British, privately-owned holiday operation in the South of France, seeks short-term help - ACTIVE couples aged 45 or older - to work in a complex of 27 chalets, cottages and mobile homes on a 4 star holiday village complex at Frejus, between St. Tropez and Cannes. Maintenance duties require people with some of the following DIY skills to a good standard: joinery, plumbing, electrics, building, painting & decorating, gardening and cleaning. In exchange for 3 days' work per week couples will receive free self-contained, furnished accommodation with own patio and private parking plus free electricity, gas, water, local rates, local taxes and site fees.
   Helpers are needed for periods ranging from 3-6 weeks in the Spring and Autumn. In addition we have one couple working full-time as our Representatives on site from March to October. Applicants should be enthusiastic, self-motivated, self-taught and disciplined adults, preferably non-smokers, who own a reliable car. *Applications* should be sent to Don Nimmo at the above address and provide information on each person, a recent photograph, a summary of the relevant skills for each person and stating preferred dates.

NST TRAVEL GROUP: Recruitment, Chiltern House, Bristol Avenue, Blackpool, Lancashire FY2 OFA (tel 01253-503011; fax 01253-356955; e-mail info@nstjobs.co.uk; www.nstjobs.co.uk). NST Travel have two residential centres in France. Le Chateau, offering educational and French language courses for secondary school groups and Lou Valagran which offers adventurous activity holidays for secondary school groups.
Group Co-ordinators (3) for Le Chateau to accompany guests on excursions around the French countryside. Excellent working knowledge of French required.
Evening Entertainment Organisers (3) for Le Chateau to assist in the smooth running of the dining room, including ensuring its cleanliness and to assist in running evening entertainments.
Activity Instructors (20) for Lou Valagran to instruct a range of outdoor activities and to assist with the evening entertainment programme. Qualifications in canoeing, kayaking, archery, or climbing adavantageous.

Catering Assistants (5) for Lou Valagran to assist the Catering Manager and be involved in all aspects of kitchen work. No previous experience required.
Support Staff (6) for both centres), including positions for drivers, boat loaders, bar, shop, support, cleaning and maintenance staff. No experience required though a full driving licence is needed for driving positions.

Staff required from January through to November. All positions are residential. Minimum period of work 2 months: average working week 42 hours over 6 days.

For more information and an application form please *contact* the above address.

PGL TRAVEL: Alton Court, Penyard Lane (874), Ross on Wye, Herefordshire HR9 5GL (tel 01989-767833; www.pgl.co.uk/personnel).
Staff to assist in the running of activity centres throughout France. Vacancies exist for qualified sailing, canoeing, windsurfing and climbing instructors and other activity specialists, experienced youth leaders and teachers, cooks, caterers, nurses, drivers and assistants to work in kitchens, bars and stores.

Pocket money between £50 and £100 per week plus board and accommodation provided. Vacancies for long or short periods between March and September. Further information from the Personnel Department at the above address.

ROCKLEY WATERSPORTS: Poole, Dorset BH15 4LZ (tel 01202-677272; fax 01202-668268; e-mail info@rockleywatersports.com). Based in beautiful Poole harbour and South-West France, Rockley teach watersports to all abilities and ages; and are one of Europe's most highly regarded watersports centres.
Watersports Instructors (50); experienced instructors, senior instructors and sailing managers are required to work in South West France at two of the largest RYA recognised watersports centres in Europe.
Couriers (10) for duties including assisting in the kitchens, cleaning and general site duties. The jobs offer the opportunity to gain watersports experience and use all the facilities of the centres.

The above are needed to work for the summer season which runs from March until October. Those interested should contact Rob Grimm for an application form.

SANDPIPER HOLIDAYS LTD: Walnut Cottage, Kenley, Shrewsbury, SY5 6NS (tel 01746-785123; fax 01746-785100; e-mail sandpiperhols@hotmail.com). Small friendly holiday tour operator specialising in self-drive camping holidays to France. Reps are chosen for their enthusiasm; they work hard, have a lot of fun and definitely improve their French.
Representatives (8) to look after clients, clean and maintain tents and mobile homes and organise children's activities on camp sites in France. Wages by arrangement (c.£400 per month). Period of work from mid May to mid September: applicants must be prepared to work for at least half the season.

Applicants must speak good French, be over 19, and have a sense of humour. Accommodation is provided in tents. Telephone above number for an application form before the end of January.

SELECT FRANCE: Murcott, Kidlington, Oxford OX5 2RE (tel 01865-331350; e-mail selectfrance@sol.co.uk; www.selectfrance.co.uk). Select France is a family company with a reputation for personal service. They use campsites in Brittany, Vendee, Charente and the Western Mediterranean.

Campsite Representative: Successful applicants will be responsible for ensuring that the accommodation provided for clients is kept clean and well maintained. They will also be expected to keep up to date with a small amount of paperwork and organise some activities for children and adults. Some sites require couples.

Applicants, preferably over 21, must be cheerful, pragmatic, responsible, self-reliant and above all, honest. Knowledge of French and a clean driving licence is an advantage. Free accommodation and casual uniform provided. Period of work is from mid-May to end of September. Wages of around £400 per month, with the opportunity to earn more.

SIMPLY CORSICA: Simply Travel, King's House, 12-42 Wood Street, Kingston-upon-Thames, Surrey, KT1 1SG (tel 020-8541 2227; fax 020-8541 2278; e-mail personnel@simply-travel.com; www.simply-travel.com). Simply Travel is part of the Specialist Holidays Group, providing holidays for the discerning travellr. Offering a selection of top Mediterranean destination as well as a winter ski programme in the top ski destinations.

Resort Representatives: seasonal and year-round. Working to very high company expectations, applicants should be hard working, self-motivated and have initiative. Simply Travel look for staff with excellent customer service and problem solving skills. A second European language and full clean driving licence are essential for all customer-facing positions. The representative's job is to ensure that customers have an enjoyable holiday exceeding their expectations.

A competitive package including salary, accommodation, transport to and from resort and insurance is offered.

Other roles available: **Chamber Persons, Drivers, Chefs, Watersports Instructors**.

For more information on the above please contact the Overseas Recruitment Department on 0870-888 0028.

SOLAIRE HOLIDAYS: 1158 Stratford Road, Hall Green, Birmingham, B28 8AF (tel 0121-778 5061; fax 0121-778 5065; e-mail holiday@solaire.co.uk; www.solaire.co.uk). Solaire Holidays provides self-drive self-catering holidays to France and Spain. They also have their own holiday park in Southern Brittany.

Site Couriers (20) to look after clients and prepare accommodation. Knowledge of French preferred. Wage £280-£400 per month.

Children's Couriers (4) to run a children's club. Previous experience of working with children is required. Wage £280-£400 per month.

Cleaners (4) to clean site facilities. No experience or qualifications required. Wage £280-£340 per month.

Bar Staff (2) to work in site bar. Previous bar work experience required. Wage £280-£340 per month.

Receptionists (2) with fluency in French required. Wage £360-£400 per month.

General Site Managers (4) required to keep site and facilities tidy. Wage £280-£340.

Maintenance Staff (2) required to carry out on-going site and accommodation maintenance. Previous experience in maintenance work required. Wage £400-£600 per month.

Applicants can apply for work between April and October, May and September or July and August. Hours of work vary according to demand, but applicants can expect to work for six days a week, on a rota system. Accommodation is provided as part of contract. Food is not provided. *Applications* are invited from late 2001 onwards to the above address.

SUN ESPRIT: 185 Fleet Road, Fleet, Hants GU51 3BL (tel 01252-618318; fax 01252-618328; e-mail recruitment@esprit-holidays.co.uk; www.esprit-holidays.co.uk) Sun Esprit run Alpine holidays (France) for families in catered chalets and provide childcare in nurseries and Alpine adventure clubs for children aged 4 months to 12 years old.

Resort Managers. Minimum age 23: should be French speakers, with some management, customer care and accountancy experience.

Chalet Hosts for various grades of responsibilities: minimum age 18, Cordon Bleu/City and Guilds 706/HND/OND or equivalent or experience in cooking professionally required.

Nannies: should be aged 18 or over with NNEB, NVQ3, BTECH or RGN qualification.

Alpies Rangers with experience as play scheme leaders, children's sports coaches or trained teachers required to run adventure actvity clubs. Minimum age 18. Should have a mature, fun loving personality.

All staff must be British passport holders available from mid-June to mid-September. Ideal for anyone who has an interest in alpine activities, i.e. mountain walking and biking, white water rafting etc.

All staff assist with chalet cleaning, babysitting and hosting guests. British passport holders essential. Weekly wage, with food and accommodation, uniform, swimming pool pass and transport provided.

Applications to the above address.

SUSI MADRON'S CYCLING FOR SOFTIES: 2-4 Birch Polygon, Rusholme, Manchester M14 5HX (tel 0161-248 8282).

Company Assistants to work for a company offering cycling holidays in France. Fixed wage plus bonus. Minimum period of work 2 months between May and September. Full training in bicycle maintenance is given. Must be a keen cyclist, non-smoker, aged over 20 and speak French. Application forms can be obtained by telephoning the above number.

VENDEE LOISIRS VACANCES: 30 Parc des Demoiselles F-85160 St Jean de Monts, France (tel 0033 251-58-04-02). Linda and Mark run a small friendly business offering mobile home holidays on a campsite, with direct access to the beach in St Jean de Monts. They live locally and are on hand for help and advice.

Representative/Children's Entertainment (2) The job of the rep is to welcome, check out, and provide information for the client and to clean the mobiles. The children's entertainer runs a Children's club and shares other duties. Both organise activities like boules, quizzes, canoeing etc.

Period of work mid May to beginning of September. Wages £100 a week plus free accommodation in caravan (with TV) on site, day off, with use of company van and most afternoons free. Must be French speaker/experienced with children and enjoy meeting people. Ideal for 2 friends, or a couple.

Write to Linda Aplin at the above address enclosing a cv and photo.

VFB HOLIDAYS LIMITED: Normandy House, High Street, Cheltenham GL50 3FB (tel 01242-240355; fax 01242-570340; e-mail personnel@vfbholidays .co.uk) Est 1970. Member of AITO. Holiday operator in France and Corsica.

Resort Representatives required for season in Corsica from May to October. Applications are processed from December to April, training session to end-April.

Qualifications needed: fluent French essential. Knowledge of Corsica and lifestyle important. Age 21-35. British or French nationals. Must have confident and enthusiastic personality. Monthly wage: £550-650 depending upon age and experience, plus accommodation.

Applications should be sent to the above address.

Teaching and Language Schools

MRS JULIE LEGREE: Syndicat Mixte Montaigu-Rocheserviere, 35 avenue Villebois Mareuil, F-85607 Montaigu cedex, France (tel 02-51 46 45 45; fax 02-51 46 45 40; e-mail julie – legree@yahoo.co.uk; www.explomr.com/english).

TEFL Teacers (4) to teach English to 9-11 year old pupils in 36 different primary schools in the Vendée. Applicants should be outgoing, independent, organised and mature enough to act on their own initiative, as well as having a love of France and children.

TEFL Teacher to teach 14-21 year olds in a college and lycée as an *assitante*. Candidates will need the maturity and self-confidence to deal with teenagers, and be able to relate to a large teaching staff.

All posts require 20 hours a week teaching, per 4 day week, with no work on Wednesdays, weekends or school holidays. Full training is given and contracts run from October until May. Included in the remuneration package is free board and lodging with local families and an allowance of approx. £180 per month.

Applications by post to Mrs Julie Legree at the above address.

Voluntary Work and Archaeology

LES AMIS DE CHEVREAUX – CHATEL: Mairie de Chevreaux, F-39190 Chevreaux, France (tel/fax +33-3-84-85-95-77; e-mail accjura@aol.com; http://members.aol.com/accjura). The chateau of Cheveraux is situated in a hilltop village above the Bresse Plains.

Les Amis de Chevreaux is a place where young people of different nationalities can meet and spend time together. The work site in the Jura requires willing volunteers to help with the restoration of the 13th century castle of Chevreaux, which is also on the site of a Roman fort. Volunteers are needed for the last three weeks in July and the first three weeks in August and will be lodged on site (at the castle) in tents with a campbed; all sanitary and kitchen facilities are provided. Duties involve cleaning, reconstruction of the ruins, stone working, carpentry, archaeology and topography.

The work lasts 6 hours per day, 5 days a week. After work activities include swimming, horse riding and volleyball. At the weekends there is the opportunity to discover the rich patrimony and landscapes of the Jura. Age limits: 18-25. No special qualifications needed apart from good motivation.

Applications to Genest Jacques, President of the Association, at the above address.

 ASSOCIATION CHANTIERS HISTOIRE & ARCHITECTURE MÉDIÉVALES: 5 et 7 rue Guilleminot, 75014 Paris, France (tel 0033-1 43 35 15 51; fax 0033-1 43 20 46 82).

Volunteers required for conservation workcamps at various locations in France. The work includes restoration and repair of historic monuments, chateaux and churches. Volunteers must be at least 16 years old and in good health. Tent accommodation and cooking facilities are provided, but volunteers need to bring their own bedding and work clothes. Placements are available from April to the end of August with some camps active at other times of the year, with a minimum stay of ten days recomended. Volunteers receive on the job training under qualified supervisors and work about 6 hours per day.

For full details of the workcamps *write* to C.H.A.M. at the above address.

ASSOCIATIONS DES PARALYSES DE FRANCE: 17 Boulevard Auguste-Blanqui, F-75013 Paris, France.

Assistants required to work in holiday centres for physically handicapped adults. Pocket money given. Board and accommodation and expenses provided. Minimum age 18 years. Period of work 15-21 days during the summer vacation.

Applicants should be able to speak a little French. *Applications* to APF Evasion at the above address.

BARDOU: Klaus & Jeane Erhardt, Mons La Trivalle, F-34390 Olargues, France (tel +33-4-67-97-72-43). The hamlet of Bardou is situated at the heart of a Natural Regional Park in southern France. It attracts artists, classical musicians and nature lovers, with accommodation for volunteers and paying guests.

Volunteers to help restore and maintain 16th century stone houses and to assist with a flock of pedigree sheep in a remote mountain hamlet. Free lodging is provided in a self-catering house in exchange for 20 hours of help per week. Minimum stay 1 month between 1st March and 1st July and 1st September and 1st December. Please send a c.v. and an International Reply Coupon for details to Klaus and Jean Erhardt at the above address.

CHANTIERS D'ETUDES MEDIEVALES: 4, rue du Tonnelet Rouge, F-67000 Strasbourg, France (tel/fax 388-37-17-20).
Volunteers to work on the restoration of medieval monuments: each scheme normally involves an international team of 20-30 people. 6 hours work per day, 6 days per week. The schemes last for 15 days each and take place from the beginning of July to the end of August. Board and basic accommodation are available at a cost of around £65 for 16-18 year olds, and £55 for 18 years old upwards, for 15 days. No particular skills or experience are required of volunteers, but they should speak English or French. For details of the summer programme *contact* the above address between the beginning of February and the end of June.

CHANTIERS DE JEUNES PROVENCE COTE D'AZUR: 7 Avenue Pierre de Coubertin F-06150 Cannes, La Bocca, France (tel 0493-47-89-69; fax 0493-48-12-01; e-mail cjpca@club.internet.fr; www.club.internet.fr/perso/cjpca/).
Volunteers aged 14-17 to take part in the restoration of historic monuments and in environmental protection projects: projects consist of 5 hours work in the morning and organised activities such as sailing, climbing and diving in the afternoons/evenings. Camps take place in the country near Cannes or the island of Sainte Marguerite, and run for one or two weeks during the summer, Christmas or Easter holidays. Applicants must be sociable and speak French. For further details send two international reply coupons to the above address with a letter written in French.

CHATEAU DE SAINT-AUGUSTIN: Chateau sur Allier, F-03320 Lurcy-Levis, France (tel 470-66-43-42; fax 470-66-41-34; e-mail malaure@wanadoo.fr). An 18th century chateau and safari park, offering work for young animal lovers. 9km from the nearest town.
Voluntary Assistants (1 or 2) to offer general help in a 35 hectare safari park around an 18th century chateau. No wages are paid, but board and lodging is provided. Period of work (minimum 2 months due to the size of the house and the surrounding woodland) by arrangement with work availble *all year*. Applicants must love animals and nature and preferably hold international driving licences: the positions would be ideal for those who wish to perfect their French. A housekeeper is also required, and those staff working over the winter will be lodged in Mme de Montesquieu's part of the castle.
For more details *contact* Mme de Montesquieu at the above address.

CLUB DU VIEUX MANOIR: Abbaye du Moncel à Pontpoint, F-60700 Pont Ste Maxence, France. Founded in 1953, this is a volunteer association for young people who wish to spend some of their spare time doing rescue and restoration work on historic monuments and ancient sites. The volunteers share in the day to day organisation of the camp and site. The centres are at the Chateau Fort de Guise (Aisne), the Abbey Royale du Moncel á Pontpoint (Oise) and the Chateau d'Argy (Indre).
Volunteers required to work on the restoration of ancient monuments and similar tasks. Minimum age for volunteers is 15 years. There are no set hours to work but everyone is expected to lend a hand when the group decides to work on a project. Work is, of course, unpaid and volunteers are expected to contribute around £8 per day towards the cost of their keep. Accommodation is usually in tents. Training organised for participants of 16 years and over.
    Long-term stays are a possibility for volunteers at the Chateau Fort de Guise. After a trial period of 15 days board and lodging will be offered by the

association, minimum stay two months.
Applications to the address shown above.

CONCORDIA: Heversham House, 20-22 Boundary Road, Hove, East Sussex BN3 4ET (tel 01273-422218; fax 01273 421182; e-mail info@concordia-iye.org.uk; www.concordia-iye.org.uk).
Concordia offers young people aged 16-30 the opportunity to take part in international volunteer projects lasting 2-3 weeks, from June to September. The work is community based and ranges from nature conservation, renovation, construction and social work including children's playschemes and teaching. Volunteers pay a registration fee of approx. £85 and fund their own travel. Board and accommodation are free of charge. For further information *write* enclosing an sae to the International Volunteer Co-ordinator at the above address.

CONSERVATEUR DU PATRIMOINE: 3 rue Gregoire de Tours, F-63000 Clermont-Ferrand, France (tel 473-91-61-97/473-41-27-23; fax 473-41-27-69).
Volunteers (5) for archaeological field work in the volcanic Cantal Massif, France. To assist a dig of a mesolithic hunters settlement dated 10,000 years BC. To work 7 hours a day, 5 days a week. Volunteers required from July to August; minimum period of work 2 weeks. Accommodation provided at a cost of £120. Experience not essential but would be an advantage. Knowledge of French not necessary but useful.
Applications from March to Frédéric Surmely at the above address.

LES DEUX MOULINS: Gontard, Dauphin, F-04300 Forcalquier, France.
Volunteers to construct new buildings and improve existing amenities at this holiday centre built by and for young people of all nationalities. Minimum age of entry is 18 years and the centre is open throughout the summer. Volunteers pay part of the cost of board and accommodation. The organisation would like to stress that volunteers are unpaid but the work is by no means rigid or exacting. Further details from the address above.

ETUDES ET CHANTIERS (UNAREC): Délégation Internationale, 3 rue des Petits-Gras, F-63000 Clermont-Ferrand, France (tel 473-31-98-04; fax 473-36-98-09).
Organise voluntary work camps for the upkeep, development and preservation of the environment. Work camps lasting for two or three weeks are held over the summer. Tasks vary and include such activities as river cleaning, the preservation of old buildings and districts in small towns, organising local cultural festivals, etc. Minimum age 18 years; camps are also held for younger teenagers aged 14-17. Application fees approx. £65 (including membership and insurance).
An annual programme is produced in March. For further details *contact* the above address.

INSTITUT D'HISTOIRE: Universite du Mans, Avenue O. Messiaen, Le Mans, F-72017 France (tel 243-83-31-64; fax 243-83-31-44).
Volunteers (20) to assist on archaeological digs. 8 hour day, 5$^{1}/_{2}$ day week. Board and lodging provided free. Applicants should be in good health and enjoy working as a team. Knowledge of French or English required. Minimum period of work 3 weeks in July. *Applications* from April to Annie Renoux at the above address.

JEUNESSE ET RECONSTRUCTION: 10 rue de Trevise, Paris 9, France. **Volunteers** required to work in camps throughout France. Type of work varies from camp to camp, ranging from the construction of community centres to digging drains in wet areas. Work is unpaid, but free board and accommodation provided. About 7 hours work per day, 5 days per week. Volunteers are likely to come from all over the world. Applicants should normally be at least 18 years old, though there are some vacancies for 17 year olds. Most camps last for 3 weeks. There are also possibilities for voluntary work lasting for three months, which provides pocket money. *Applications* to the above address.

LE LOUBATAS: Centre Permanent d'Initiation a la Foret Provencale, 18 Chemin Neuf, F-13860 Peyrolles-en-Provence, France (tel 0033-4-42-67-06-70; fax 0033-4-42-57-71-25). **Volunteers** to join a workcamp from August 1-21 building a tree observatory in Provence. Mornings are spent on the project while afternoons are devoted to activities such as mountain biking, swimming, kayaking etc.. Applicants must be aged 18-25, able to get by in a camp whose main language is French, and be happy, open and interested in the project. *Applications* to Yann Abonneau, Workcamp Director at the above address.

PROFESSOR HENRY DE LUMLEY: Lab. de Préhistoire, IPH, 1 rue René Panhard, F-75013 Paris, France. **Volunteers** to take part in archaeological digs in France. To work $8^1/2$ hours per day, 6 days per week. Minimum period of work 15 days between April and June or 30 days between July and August. Minimum age 16. Applicants should be students or researchers in prehistory, archaeology or the natural sciences. *Applications* to Professor de Lumley at the above address.

NEIGE ET MERVEILLES: F-06430 St. Dalmas de Tende, France (tel 493-04-62-40; fax 493-04-88-58; e-mail Neige.merveilles@wanadoo.fr; www. neige&merveilles.com). **Volunteers** (4) to take part in international workcamps which take place between April and October. Food and accommodation provided. To work 6 hours per day, 5 days per week. Volunteers must pay their own insurance costs of approximately £50. Minimum age 18. This organisation also organises international workcamps for young people aged 15-17. For further details *contact* the Recruitment Department at the above address.

PAX CHRISTI: 58 avenue de Breteuil, F-75007 Paris, France (tel 44-49-05-30). **Volunteers** to run a temporary youth hostel operated over the summer by Pax Christi, the International Catholic Movement for Peace. During the summer months of each year it organises a centre at Lourdes for international encounters. This meeting place, offering bed and breakfast at modest prices, tries to encourage dialogue between different nations, races and religions.

The centre is run by teams of young volunteers who take care of the practical running of the house. In addition to this, however they invite visitors to join them in reflection, dialogue and prayer and in exploring Lourdes. The purpose of the centre is to give a living witness that peace is possible. Volunteers are usually between 18-30 years old and must speak French fluently. Each team runs the centre for 15 days. Their work demonstrates a very real commitment to peace.

REMPART: 1 rue des Guillemites, F-75004 Paris, France (tel 1-42-71-96-55; fax 1-42-71-73-00).
Volunteers to help restore and preserve various castles, fortresses, churches, chapels, abbeys, monasteries, farms, ancient villages, Gallo-Roman ampitheatres and underground passages on the 140 sites organised by REMPART every year, during holidays. Board and accommodation are normally provided at a cost of £4-£5 per day. Work includes masonry, woodwork, carpentry, interior decorating, restoration and clearance work. Opportunities for swimming, tennis, riding, watersports, cycling, climbing, rambling, exploring the region, crafts, music, cinema and taking part in local festivities.

Minimum age 16 or 18, with no upper age limit: anyone feeling young is welcome and some camps can accept groups. Some knowledge of French is needed. Previous experience is not necessary. *Contact* the above address for this year's programme.

LOUIS ROUSSEL: 52 rue des Forges, F-21000 Dijon, France (e-mail louisroussel@hotmail.com).
Volunteers (20) to work on an archaeological dig involving the restoration of a medieval chateau and a Gallo-Roman site near Dijon in July: in addition to digging, the jobs to be done include reassembling and drawing the finds. Accommodation is provided in exchange for around 8 hours work per day, 5 days per week and a weekly contribution of around £10. Applicants must be at least 18 years old: experience in any of the above fields would be an advantage. *Applications* to M Roussel at the above address.

LA SABRANENQUE: Centre International, rue de la Tour de L'Oume, F-30290 Saint Victor la Coste, France (tel 466-50-05-05; e-mail info@sabranenque.com). La Sabranenque is a non-profit organisation that has been working for 30 years for the preservation of rural habitat and traditional architecture.
Volunteers (10 per session) to help with the restoration of villages, sites and simple monuments in France, using traditional building methods. Work includes restoration of roofs, terraces, walls, paths or the reconstruction of small houses. Minimum period of work 2 weeks between 1st June and 30th August; at least one day each 2 week period is spent visiting the region. Board and accommodation are provided at a cost of £160 approx. per 2-week period. Applicants must be at least 18 years old and in good health. *Applications* to the above address at any time.

SERVICE ARCHEOLOGIQUE DE DOUAI: 191 rue St. Albin, F-59500 Douai, France. This is a local association for archaeology and the preservation of local cultural heritage.
Supervisors (2) to manage part of an archaeological excavation. 7 hour day, 5 day week. £500 per month. Board and lodging provided free. Period of work 2 months from July 9 to beginning of September. Applicants should have experience in field archaeology and, if possible, a knowledge of French. *Applications* to P. Demolon at the above address from April.

SERVICE REGIONAL DE L'ARCHEOLOGIE: 6, rue de la Manufacture, F-45000 Orleans, France (tel: 238-78-85-41).
Diggers and Draughtsmen (50). To work on an archaeological dig in Orleans or in one of the other digs in Central France. Should have relevant experience: some knowledge of French is desirable. 8 hour day, 5 day week. No salary, but board and lodging are provided free. Minimum period of work 2 weeks between June

and September.
Applications in April to the above address.

SERVICE REGIONAL DE L'ARCHEOLOGIE DE BRETAGNE: Hotel de
Blossac, 6 rue du Chapitre, F-35044 Rennes Cedex, France (tel 299-84-59-00; fax
02-99-84-59-19).
Volunteers (10-30 per site) to take part in various archaeological digs in Brittany
between April and September. To work 7 hours per day, 5-5¹/2 days per week.
Board and accommodation, usually on a campsite, is in most cases provided free
of charge, but on some sites there is a charge of £5 to cover insurance etc.
Minimum period of work 2 weeks. No previous experience is necessary, but a
basic knowledge of French is required. Applicants must be at least 18 years old.
The new programme will be available in April; *applications* should be sent to the
above address from March.

SOURIRE ET NATURE: chez André Risetti, rue de la Fontaine St. Marc, F-
21140 Montigny sur Armançon, France (tel 03-80-97-32-46).
Volunteers required for the renovation of a hostel 70 kms west of Dijon,
including construction of stone walls, painting, gardening, and domestic work.
Instruction offered in methods and use of tools. Work can be tailored to
applicants' particular skills. Work is available for volunteers aged 21-40 during
July and August and for volunteers aged 19-40 for the rest of the year, to work
5¹/2 days per week, minimum period of work two weeks. Board and lodging are
included. Knowledge of French (preferably), or English required.
Option 1: 33 hours work per week with approx. £10 pocket money provided.
Option 2: 15 hours work per week, with the applicant paying approx. £21 per
week towards project costs.
Applications, in writing, all year round to the above address enclosing a c.v.
and references.

UMR 6566 DU CNRS: Universités de Rennes 1, Laboratoire D'Anthropologie
CS 74205, F-35042 Rennes Cédex, France (www.sar.univ-rennes1.fr/equipes –
recherche/344.html and http://palissy.humana.univ-nantes.fr/LABOS/UMR/
index.html).
Volunteers to take part in archaeological digs in western France in the summer:
middle of August to end of September. To work from 9am-noon and 2-6pm, 5¹/2
days per week. Board provided: participants will need their own camping
equipment. Applicants must be genuinely interested in prehistoric archaeology:
knowledge of French or English is necessary. *Applications* should be sent to the
above address enclosing an International Reply Coupon.

Winter Jobs

**HARRI'S BAR: Evolution 2, Hotel Le Lavachet, F-73320 Tignes, France (tel
+33-4-79 06 48 11; fax +33-4-79 06 57 13; e-mail
evolution2hotel@wanadoo.fr). Evolution 2 is a French company based in the
ski resort of Tignes, running Harri's Bar, one of the biggest and liveliest bars
in the resort, with a mainly English speaking clientele.
Bar Staff enthusiastic, presentable, outgoing and fun-loving personalities.
Although previous bar experience is not necessary, applicants must be hard
working and able to fit into a team quickly.
Chef should have experience of ordering for and setting up three course**

menus for up to 100 hotel guests for the pre-season period. During the main season the chef will run a pub-food menu, prepare local speciality meals for up to 100 people several times a week and provide staff meals each evening. Kitchen Hands for cleaning and wash-up duties, also to fill in for chef with the pub-food menu on days off.

Staff should be willing to work as a team and infuse the bar with a positive and enthusiastic spirit. Main season (December-April) hours of work are 3.30pm-1.30am with a meal break, and there are two full days off per week. Wages start at £300 net per month not including tips and there is a discretionary end of season bonus. Good quality shared accommodation is provided as well as a daily evening meal, ski pass and ski hire. There is also the chance to take part in ski lessons and generally to ski every day.

Positions are open to male and female candidates and start around the 7th of October. *Application* forms can be obtained from the above address.

Other Employment Abroad

CENTRE D'INFORMATION ET DE DOCUMENTATION JEUNESSE: 101 quai Branly, F-75740 Paris Cedex 15, France (tel 01-44 49 12 00; e-mail cidj@cidj.asso.fr; www.cidj.asso.fr).
Advertises temporary jobs on a daily basis, mainly in Paris and the surrounding area, available to young people. It also gives information on cheap places to stay, on French university courses for foreigners and practical advice on the regulations as part of its general information serviced for young people. CIDJ also publishes booklets on a range of subjects for young people.

Please note: to get details of the jobs you must visit the centre personally; the CIDJ does not not send out information on this subject. Opening hours: 9.30 am-6pm, Monday to Friday; Saturday: 9.30am to 1pm. Nearest metro: Bir-Hakeim.

CENTRE INTERNATIONAL D'ANTIBES/INSTITUT PREVERT: 38 Bd d'Aguillon 06600 Antibes (tel 4-92 90 71 70/92 90 71 71). The Centre is situated on the French Riviera, and teaches French to more than 3000 foreign students a year.
Assistants for numerous work exchange places available including help with administration, helping in kitchens, chambermaid duties or general maintenance duties in a French language school for foreigners. No wages are paid but French courses and/or accommodation are provided. Places are available all year round for varying periods of one to six months. For more information on their various work exchange programmes, or *to apply*, contact 'Work Exchange' at the above address, or e-mail karine@cia-france.com.

MEINRAD BETSCHART: Rue du Presbytére, F-21140 Montigny sur Armançon, France (tel 0033-(0)3-80-97-18-85).
Helpers (4) to assist with the renovation of an old house belonging to a sculptor and his German speaking family. Work includes tasks from wall-building to laying carpets, and working in the garden and in the kitchen. To work 6 hours a day, 6 days a week. Wages £82 per month plus board and accommodation. Minimum period of work 2 weeks. Applicants must be willing to perform practical work and have an interest in art.

Applications to the above address one month before date on which you wish to start work.

Au Pairs, Nannies, Family Helps and Exchanges

L'ACCUEIL FAMILIAL DES JEUNES ETRANGERS: 23 rue du Cherche-Midi, F-75006 Paris, France (tel 1-42-22-50-34; fax 1-45-44-60-48; e-mail afjeparis@aol.com).
Au Pairs: (boys and girls) to assist families with housework and look after children for about 30 hours a week. Summer placements from 4 to 12 weeks possible all over France; applications for these must be received by 15 May. Also placements for the school year, preferably from the beginning of September or January to the end of June.
Paying Guest: stays for a usual minimum of 2 weeks in Paris and the suburbs (but in the provinces only during the holidays) also arranged for boys or girls aged over 18.
For further details *contact* the above address.

AQUITANE SERVICE LINGUISTIQUE: 199 Avenue Louis Barthou, 33200 Bordeaux, France, (tel 05-56 08 33 23; fax 05-56 08 32 74; e-mail aslbx@aol.com)
Au Pairs required for summer (July to September), 6 month and 12 month long positions in France, to be in charge of taking care of the children, doing housework and babysitting. Applicants should speak some French, be between 18 and 30 years old and be able to provide two letters of reference. Experience with children is needed for anyone who will be babysitting.
To work 30 hours a week (possibly more in the summer), with one full day off each week. Full board and accommodation with the family will be provided, along with about £160 pocket money per month. *Applications* to the above address.

'BUTTERFLY ET PAPILLON' SCHOOL OF INTERNATIONAL LANGUAGES & AU PAIR AGENCY: 5, Av. de Geneve, F-74000 Annecy, France (tel +3 450-67-01-33; fax +33 450-67-03-51; e-mail aupair.france@wanadoo.fr).
Au Pair: Butterfly et Papillon welcome foreign 18-26 year old students for summer and year long au-pair placements and French courses in the French Alps (Annecy is close to the Swiss border and Geneva). Pocket money at least £170 per month. Board and French lessons available. 30 hours a week plus two evenings babysitting. Age limits: 18-25. Basic French required. Driving licence and experience with children preferred.
Butterfly et Papillon will start a work exchange programme in September 2001. Under the auspices of the EU's Leonardo scheme, this programme offers foreign students the unique opportunity to live and work in France for up to 13 weeks.
Applications to Verónica Sánchez, Au Pair Placement Officer, at the above address.

CENTRE DE VACANCES D'AULON: F-65440 Guchen, France.
Assistant Group Leaders to work with children 6-12 years and 13-17 years. Approximately £105 to £115 per month according to ability. Free board and lodging. Minimum age 19 years.

INTERNATIONAL CATHOLIC SOCIETY FOR GIRLS (ACISJF) ADVISORY SERVICE: 55 Nightingale Road, Rickmansworth, Herts, WD3 2BU (tel 01923-778449 Office Hours Mon-Fri 10.30am-4pm).

Advice on au pair placements abroad, mainly in France, for English applicants. Minimum age 18 years: minimum stay 3 months approx. Any *enquiries* should be made enclosing a stamped addressed envelope, to the above address.

INSTITUT EURO PROVENCE: 69 rue de Rome, F-13001 Marseille, France (tel +33-4-91 33 90 60; fax 4-91 33 77 36; e-mail euro.provence@wanadoo.fr; http://perso.wanadoo.fr/euro.provence).
Au Pairs to look after children and carry out light housework required to work 30 hours per week plus two evenings baby-sitting. Au Pairs are required all year round, with the minimum period of work being two months in the summer and six months the rest of the year. Board and lodging are provided free.
   Applicants will need basic French, but the institute provides low cost French classes. For more details *contact* Mrs Patricia Guedj-Gandolfo.

THE NORFOLK CARE SEARCH AGENCY: 19 London Road, Downham Market, Norfolk PE3 9BJ (tel 01366-384448; fax 01366-385226; e-mail vivienneparker@hotmail.com).
Au Pair positions arranged in the South of France. All year-round for stays of three months to one year. Summer placements for 6-12 weeks in the Nice/Corsica area. Especially suitable for University students wishing to practice the French language during the summer holidays; ideal GAP year placements. Pocket money of £200 per month, plus board and accommodation. Applicants should be aged between 18 and 27 and have EU citizenship.
   For application forms phone, e-mail or write to the agency at the above address.

SEJOURS INTERNATIONAUX LINGUISTIQUES ET CULTURELS: 32 Rempart de l'Est, F-16022 Angoulême Cedex, France (tel +33-5-45 97 41 45; fax 5-45 94 20 63; e-mail contact@silc.fr; www.silc.fr).
Work Experience and **Au Pair Placements** throughout France, as well as a variety of language study courses, international summer centres, individual homestays and private tuition. For details *contact* the above address.

SOAMES INTERNATIONAL SERVICES/PARIS NANNIES: 6 Route de Marlotte, F-77690 Montieny s/Loing, France (tel 01-64 78 37 98; fax 01-64 45 91 75; e-mail soames.parisnannies@wanadoo.fr).
Au Pairs: wage approximately £45 per week.
Nannies: wage min. £160 per week.
Mothers' Helps: wage around £120 per week.
   Minimum period of work 2 months; minimum age 18. Previous childcare experience desirable. For further details *contact* the above address.

Germany

Germany is a very good prospect for seasonal work, most opportunities being in the western and southern regions. The benefits of membership of the European Union are that British and Irish jobseekers and those of the other EU states must be given the same treatment as a German when applying for a job.
   Many of the seasonal jobs available are in hotels, especially in tourist areas such as the Bavarian Alps, the Black Forest and resorts on the North Sea Coast. People going to work in a German hotel should note that managers may demand

extra hours of work from their employees, and some will not always give extra time off or pay overtime as compensation. They may also ask workers to do jobs that are not specified in their contract by asking them to fill in for other members of staff. Anyone who feels that their contract is being breached and who cannot come to any agreement with their employer should appeal to the local *Arbeitsamt* (see below) for arbitration. Jobs in other sectors in the tourist industry can be found in this chapter and in the *Worldwide* chapter at the beginning of this book.

There are also fruit-picking jobs available, although not nearly as many as in France. During the summer the best region to try is the *Altes Land* which stretches between Stade and Hamburg in north Germany and includes the towns of Steinkirchen, Jork and Horneburg. The work there consists of picking cherries in July and August, and apples in September. Try also the Bergstrasse south of Frankfurt where apples and many other fruits are grown. Germany's vineyards also provide a source of work, particularly because in recent years, German winemakers have found it increasingly difficult to find workers to help with the grape harvest. The harvest begins in October and continues into November: the vineyards are concentrated in the south west of the country, especially along the valleys of the Rhine to the south of Bonn and Moselle.

The Happy Hands programme (www.workingholidays.de) arranges working holidays on farms or in family-run hotels for British and European students who know some German. Participants are given monthly pocket money of approx. £100 and full board and lodging with families on farms or in country hotels. In return they look after children and/or horses, farm animals for 3-6 months though a six-week commitment is also allowed. There is a registration fee of approx. £100.

It may also be possible to arrange voluntary work on an organic farm: see the entry on WWOOF in the *Worldwide* chapter for details. Volunteers would receive free board, lodging and training in return for their work. For more details contact WWOOF-Deutschland, Postfach 210259, 01263 Dresden, Germany (e-mail info@wwoof.de; www.wwoof.de). Membership of the German branch of WWOOF costs about £10, and gives access to about 160 farm addresses.

On arrival in Germany, EU nationals may go the *Arbeitsamt* (employment office) in the area in which they wish to work and obtain information on job opportunities: its address will be in the local telephone directory. It is, however, simpler to arrange a job in advance through the EURES contact in your local employment office or through the Zentralstelle fur Arbeitsvermittlung (ZAV, Villemombler Str. 76, 53123 Bonn; 0228-713-0; fax 0228-713 1111; www.arbeitsamt.de) which is the official government office dealing with job applications from abroad: see their entry below. The Zentralstelle may be able to help find work in hotels, on farms, or in factories: it has a special department to help students find summer jobs, applications for which must be received before the end of February. For further information about the official German employment service and other aspects of work there consult the free booklet *Working in Germany* published by the UK Employment Service and is available from the Overseas Placing Unit (OPU), Employment Service, Level 1, Rockingham House, 123 West Street, Sheffield S1 4ER; tel 0114-259 6000 and Jobcentres throughout the UK.

Council Exchanges in New York administers a *Work in Germany Programme* for American citizens, see the Council entry on p.54 for details.

In addition to those listed in this chapter there are opportunities for voluntary work in Germany; British applicants can apply through International Voluntary Service, UNA Exchange, Youth Action for Peace and Concordia; Council: International Volunteer Projects and Service Civil International (see the IVS entry) can help US residents; their entries can be found in the *Worldwide* chapter. An advertisement in a German newspaper may bring an offer of a job; *Rheinische Post* is published at Zulpicher Strasse 10, D-40196 Dusseldorf, Germany (tel +49-211-505 2410). The following daily newspapers might also be of interest: The *Bayernkurier* Nymphenburger Str. 64, D-80005 München, Germany (tel 089-120040; fax 089-1293050; e-mail bayernkurier@t-online.de), *Die Welt* at Axel-Springer-Platz 1, GKP 20350, Brieffach 2510 (tel 040-34700; fax 040-2516071), or the *Frankfurter Allgemeine Zeitung*, which can be found at Hellerhofstr. 2 GKP 60267 (tel 069-75910; fax 069-591 1743), can also sell you an advertisement promoting your availability to work.

RED TAPE

Visa Requirements: a visa is not required by citizens of EU/EEA nations nor or Australia, New Zealand, USA and Canada for a visit for personal, tourist or business reasons to the Federal Republic of Germany of up to three months.

Residence Permits: this permit is required for any visit of more than three months or where employment is intended. Applications should be made to the Visa Section of the nearest Embassy or Consulate General of the Federal Republic of Germany. Or in the case of EU Nationals already in Germany, to the German Aliens Authority *(Auslanderbehorde)* in the town or district *(Kreis)* of intended residence.

Work Permits: for nationals of a non-EEA country, a visa and a permit are required if employment is intended in Germany. A residence/labour permit can be issued by the Embassy on written confirmation of the prospective employer and approval from whichever aliens authority is nearest the intended place of employment; this procedure is likely to take about six weeks. Swiss and US citizens benefit from being able to apply for these documents after arriving in Germany, although if they wish to start work on arrival they should apply before travelling.

EEA Nationals intending to look for work for more than 3 months might have to show the local authority that they are self-supporting while conducting a job hunt.

Au Pair: Au pairs must be aged 17-24, have a basic knowledge of German, experience of childcare and at least one host family parent should have German as their mother tongue. Authorised agencies in Germany include IN VIA Germany (Ludwigstr. 36, Postfach 420, 79004 Freiburg; 0761-200208; invia@caritas.de) with 43 branches, and Verein für Internationale Jugendarbeit, Goetheallee 10, 53225 Bonn (0228-698952/fax 0228-694166; au-pair.vij@netcologne.de/ www.vij-Deutschland.de). The German YWCA (VIJ) has more than 20 offices in Germany and places both male and female au pairs for a preferred minimum stay of one year. Another possibility is Au Pair in Deutschland (Baunscheidtstr. 11, 53113 Bonn; 0228-957300; www.gijk.de) which is part of GIJK, a cultural exchange organisation, which is also involved in holiday job and internship placements for German young people.

Voluntary Work: there are no restrictions on work of this nature.

Hotel Work and Catering

ALPOTELS (EMPLOYMENT AGENCY): 17 High Street, Gretton, Northants NN17 3DE (e-mail alan@jobs-in-the-alps.com; www.jobs-in-the-alps.com). For those who seek seasonal work in Germany, Alpotels enjoys a good reputation

with employers, employees and is acknowledged by most universities.
Buffet Girls Chambermaids, Kitchen Staff (50), for German hotels and restaurants at lake and mountain resorts. Wages £400 net per month. To work 8 hours per day, 5 days per week. Free board and accommodation. Knowledge of German desirable. Applicants should be alert, hardworking, responsible and pleasant. Hotel experience valuable, but not essential. *Applications, from British and EU citizens only*, to the above address enclosing a s.a.e. by 15 April for the summer and 30 September for the winter.

HOTEL ALTE THORSCHENKE: Brückenstrasse 3, D-56812 Cochem/Mosel, Germany (tel 02671-7059/fax 02671-4202).
Chambermaid, Buffet Assistant, Kitchen Assistant, Wage approximately £200 per month plus free board and lodging. To work 8 hours per day, 5¹/₂ days per week. Knowledge of English and German are advantages but not essential. Applicants should be enthusiastic and experienced workers and have a friendly manner. Special clothing is necessary. Minimum period of work 4 months between May 1st and November 1st. Applications should be sent to Herr and Frau Kretz at the above address. *Applications from British and EU citizens only*.

HOTEL BAYERISCHER HOF/HOTEL REUTEMANN/HOTEL SEEGARTEN: Seepromenade, D-88131 Lindau, Germany (tel 08382-9150; fax 08382-91 55 91).
Waiting Staff (9). Must speak reasonable German.
Kitchen Assistants (8). Knowledge of German not essential.
Chambermaids (8). Knowledge of German not essential
   Wage approx. £510 (Euros 820) net per month for 8 hours work per day, 5 days per week. Board and accommodation available at a small charge. Minimum period of work 3 months. Applicants must be students. *Applications* to the above address.

BERGHOTEL JOHANNESHOHE: Wallhausenstr. 1, D-57072 Siegen 1, Germany.
Buffet Assistants (2). Wage approximately £460 per month plus free board and lodging. To work a 40 hour week. To work for at least 12 weeks; period of work by arrangement. Applicants must speak German. *Applications* should be sent to the above address from April 6th.

HOTEL BRUDERMUHLE BAMBERG: Schranne 1, D-96049 Bamberg, Germany (tel 09-51 955 220; fax 09-51 955 2255; e-mail info@brudermuehle.de; www.brudermuehle.de).
Hotel Managers, Waitresses (2) with knowledge of German and relevant professional training to work 5 days a week, 8-10 hours a day at varying times during the day. Those working in the restaurant will serve food, drinks and wine. Applicants should be prepared to work for a minimum of 3 months. Wage of about £775 per month provided.
Cook (1) with cooking qualifications and knowledge of German is required to help prepare food with the French cook. Wage of about £840 a month provided.
   Subsidised board and accommodation is available at around £100 per month. *Applications* are invited at any time to the above address.

BLOOMSBURY BUREAU: P.O. Box 12749, 37 Store Street, London WC1E 7BH (tel 020-7-813 4061; fax 020-7-813 4038; e-mail bloomsburo@aol.com).

Specialists in au pair and hotel/catering placements for thirty years the Bureau promises an individual service and personal commitment, efficient introductions and a caring, responsible attitute towards applicants. They hold a licence from the German Department of Employment.

Hotel Staff (30-40) to work as general assistants, mixed duties of chamber staff, kitchen help, general cleaning or waitressing. Also a few posts for male helpers washing up and kitchen duties. Work available in family owned hotels in Bavaria from beginning of May to mid/end October. Accommodation and free board and net wages of approx. £400 per month, for up to 45 hours work per week. Applicants should preferably be students or school leavers, over 18 and speak some German. *Only EU nationals can be considered for work in Germany.*

Applications to Marianne Dix, Principal, at the above address.

HOTEL BOLD, RINGHOTEL OBERAMMERGAU: Konig-Ludwig Strasse 10, D-82487 Oberammergau, Germany.
Commis de Rang (1/2). £350 per month. Must be experienced.
Chambermaid (1/2). Salary as above. Must be neat and clean.
Dishwasher (1/2). As above.

To work 8-9 hours per day, 5 days per week. Board and accommodation provided free. Minimum period of work from 30 May to 30 September. *Applications* before May to the above address.

HOTEL-RESTAURANT BURGFRIEDEN: J. M. Muhlental 62, D-56814 Beilstein/Mosel, Germany.
Restaurant Staff to work in a buffet, serving food and drink and cleaning. Approx. £320 per month. To work a 48 hour week from 8am-6pm or 2-9pm. Free board and lodging provided. Minimum period of work 2 months. Knowledge of German necessary.

Applications to Frau Sprenger-Herzer at the above address before the end of April.

BURGHOTEL AUF SCHONBURG: D-55430 Oberwesel/Rhein, Germany (tel +49-6744 93930; fax 06744-1613; e-mail huettl@hotel-schoenburg.com; www.hotel-schoenburg.com). Schönburg Castle is a beautiful medieval castle in the romantic Rhine Valley with a superior hotel-restaurant and interntational guests. This is a small and friendly hotel with a young and enthusiastic staff.
Chambermaid (1) to work part time in the morning, or full time from 8am-4.30pm. Duties include cleaning rooms.
Waitress to work full time, or part time in combination with position as part-time chambermaid.

Salary for each position is approx. £270 per month; both positions combined is approx. £400 per month. To work 5 days per week: full time staff work 8 hours per day, and part timers work 5 hours per day. Board and accommodation provided. Minimum period of work two months. Applicants should speak good German. *Applications* should be sent to the Familie Hüttl at the above address in March.

CITYHOTEL-METROPOL: D-56068 Koblenz am Rhein, Germany (tel 0261-350-69).
Musicians (1-3) to perform folk and popular music for evening entertainment: must already have a wide repertoire of songs. Wages by arrangement. To work around 8 hours per day, 5 or 6 days per week. Board and accommodation

available. Period of work by arrangement. *Applications* to the above address at any time.

HOTEL DEUTSCHES HAUS: D-91550 Dinkelsbuhl, Weinmarket 3, Germany. **Kitchen Assistants** (2). Pay negotiable. Hours: 09.00-14.00, 18.00-21.00, 6 days per week. Free board and accommodation. Minimum period of work 2 months. *Applications* until April to the address above.

EUROTOQUES: c/o Schassbergers Kur-und Sporthotel, D-73667 Ebnisee/Schwäbischer Wald, Germany (tel +49-7184-292102; fax 07184-91053; e-mail office@eurotoques.de; www.Eurotoques.de).
Kitchen Assistants, Waiting Staff for placements in the restaurants of some of Germany's top cooks all over Germany. No wage, but free board and lodging is provided. To work 9 hours per day, 5 days per week. Minimum period of work three months at any time of year. Applicants should speak German. *Applications* to the above address.

FAMILIEN UND SPORTHOTEL ALLGAEUER BERGHOF: D-87544 Blaichach, Southern Bavaria, Germany (tel 08321-8060; fax 08321-806219; e-mail m.neusch@allgaeuer-berghof.de; www.allgaeuer.berghof.de). A 180 bed hotel with 50 staff situated in a hill-top ski resort, with access to world-cup races, hiking, tennis and mountain biking.
Chambermaids: knowledge of German not necessary.
Buffet, Kitchen Assistants and **Restaurant Assistants:** knowledge of German required.
Wages (Euros 613) £380 approx. net per month by arrangement for 40 hours work per week. Free board and lodging. No previous hotel experience required. Minimum age 18. *Enquiries* to Mrs Neusch at the above address.

FERIENHAUS MITTENWALD: Weidenweg 1-3, D-82481 Mittenwald, Germany (tel 08823-4477; fax 08823-4478; e-mail gehring@mittenwald.de; www.gehring-tourismus.de).
Chambermaid/Housekeeper/Childminder to help the first chambermaid, look after two boys and to help their mother with the household. Wages by arrangement. Accommodation provided in double room with own tv. Minimum period of work 6 months. Applicants should be aged 20-28, non-smokers, in good health and friendly to children. *Applications* to the Fam. M. Gehring at the above address.

REST. FRIEDRICHSHOF: D-76596 Forbach/Murgtal, Landstrasse 1, Germany.
Kitchen Assistant (female). £335 approx. per month. Hours: 9am-2pm and 6-9pm, 5¹/2 days per week. Free board and accommodation. Minimum period of work 2¹/2 months between June and the end of September. Those with allergies should note that there are cats in the hotel. *Applications* should be sent with a photo to the above address.

GASTHOF UND PENSION ADLER: Ehlenbogen 1, D-72275 Alpirsbach Schwarzwald, Kreis Freudenstadt, Germany (tel +49-7444-2215; fax 07444-4588). Family run hotel restaurant and farm in the black forest between Stuttgart and France.
Chambermaid. Around £400 per month plus board and lodging. Work includes

helping with the laundry.

Waiter/Waitress. Approximately £400 per month including tips plus board and lodging. Must have a knowledge of German and the ability to get on with people.

Kitchen Assistant to prepare vegetables and wash up (using machine). Around £400 per month plus board and lodging.

Farmhand/Groom to work around the farm and/or help with the horses. Wage c. £340 plus board and lodging.

To work eight to ten hours a day, 5¹/₂ days per week, shiftwork. Time off by arrangement. Salaries quoted are net, deductions having been made for board and accommodation. Staff should be prepared to help in other departments. Minimum period of work 2 months. *Applications* throughout the year to Georg Dietel at the above address.

HOTEL GASTSTATTE HOHN: D-65385 Rudesheim am Rhein, Postfach 1206, Germany.

Chambermaids (4). Salary by arrangement. 8 hours per day, 6 day week. Minimum age 18 years. Reasonable knowledge of German desirable. Minimum period of work 4 months July to October. *Applications* in March to the above address.

HOTEL GOGGL: H.V. Herkomer Strasse 19/20, D-86899 Landsberg-Lech, Germany (tel 08191 3240; fax 08191 324-100).

Chambermaid, Waitress, Receptionist to work five days per week, eight hours per day. Waitress to serve breakfast. Knowledge of German essential for Receptionist position.

HOTEL GROSSFELD: Schlosstrasse 4-6, D-48455 Bad Bentheim, Germany (tel: 05922-828; fax 05922-4349). A 120 bed hotel with spa, sauna, Turkish bath and restaurant/café.

General Assistants (4) to work in a hotel and cafe. Wage approximately £115 per month net with free board and lodging. To work 8 hours per day, 5 days per week between 9am and 5pm. Minimum period of work 2 months. Some knowledge of the Dutch language would be an advantage.

Applications with a passport photo should be sent to Herr Johannes Grossfeld from the beginning of the year until 1 April.

HOTEL HAMM: D-56068 Koblenz, St. Josef Strasse 32-34, Germany (tel 0261-34546; fax 0261-160972).

Chambermaids (2). 5 day week, 5 hours per day.

Waitress to serve breakfast and dinner and do some reception work. 5 day week, 8 hours per day.

Night Porter to man the reception desk between 7.30pm and 3am, 6 nights a week. Knowledge of German essential.

Wages on application. Free board and accommodation provided. Applicants must be available for at least 3 months (5 or more preferred) between May and September. *Applications* to the above address.

INTERNATIONALES HAUS, SONNENBERG: Clausthalerstr. 11, D-37444 St Andreasberg, Germany (tel +49-05882-944118; fax +49-05582-944100; e-mail sonnenberg@tu-clausthal.de).

Domestic Assistants (6) needed from 1st August for at least 3 months. The work is in the Housekeeping department and involves working in the dining hall, washing up, and cleaning in the kitchens, accommodation and conference rooms. The hours of work are 7.30am-1.45pm and 4.45-7.30pm, up to a total of 38½ hours per week. Within each four-week period there are eight days off which will not necessarily fall on weekends. Overtime is available and can be accumulated and taken as time off. Wages are £465 approx. per month and accommodation is provided at a cost of around £90 per month.

Applicants should be over 18, no previous experience is necessary but a basic knowledge of German and any requisite work permits are required. Staff may also take part in a conference towards the end of their stay.

For further details contact Joanne Evans at the centre.

HOTEL JAKOB: Schwarzeweg 6, D-87629 Fussen-Bad Faulenbach, Germany (fax 08362-913270)
General Assistants: around £300 per month, hours by arrangement. Free board and lodging provided. Period of work from mid May to mid October. A basic knowledge of German is necessary. *Applications* to Frau G. Jakob at the above address.

KEMPINSKI HOTEL VIER JAHRESZEITEN MÜNCHEN: Maximilianstrasse 17, D-80539 München, Germany (tel +49-89-2125 2500; fax +49-89-2125 2555; www.kempinski-vierjahreszeiten.de). A 5-star hotel located on one of the most elegant boulevards in the world. The 316 rooms and luxurious suites are all different, but united by the hotel's renowned service.
Waiting Service Staff (2) to serve food and beverages in one of the following areas: room service, banqueting, or the bistro restaurant. Staff should be fluent in German, with good English and have experience of fine dining service. Wages approx. £880 gross per month.
Housekeepers (1-2) to prepare guest rooms for the night and clean rooms daily. Applicants should have a good grasp of German and be well groomed. Wages approx. £705 gross per month.
Mini-bar Man to control and replenish the stocks in guest room mini-bars. Wages approx. £880 gross per month.
All posts are available from June to September. Staff work 7-8 hours per day in a 5 day week, with dates of work being set out in a schedule. Board and lodging is available for £90/£150 (twin/single room) per month.
Applications accepted from January.

KLOSTER HORNBACH: Loesch GmbH Im Klosterbezirk, D-66500 Hornbach, Germany (tel 0049-6338 91010-0; fax 0049-6338 91010-99). Kloster Hornbach used to be a monastery founded in 742, and was rebuilt over the last 5 years into a 4-star hotel with 34 rooms, 2 restaurants, a large garden restaurant and several banqueting rooms.
Hotel and Restaurant Staff required. *Applications* to Christiane und Edelbert Loesch at the above address.

HOTEL KONIGSSEE-BETRIEBE: Seestrasse 29, D-83471 Konigssee-Berchtesgaden, Upper Bavaria, Germany.
Ice-Cream Sellers (3). £285 per month net. Moderate knowledge of German required.
Chambermaids (3-4) to clean rooms and make beds. £285 per month net. Moderate knowledge of German required.
Assistant Waiters/Waitresses (2) to serve meals. £285 per month net. Moderate

knowledge of German required.
Kitchen Assistant to wash vegetables, prepare food and assist cooks. £285 per month net. Moderate knowledge of German required.

To work 8¹/₂ hours per day, 5 days per week. Minimum period of work 2¹/₂ months. Free board and lodging provided. *Applications* to the above address at any time.

ROMANTIK PARKHOTEL WEHRLE: Henningsen KG, Gartenstrasse 24, D-78098 Triberg/Black Forest, Germany (tel 07722-86020; fax 07722-860290; e-mail Parkhotel.Wehrle@t-online.de; www.parkhotel-wehrle.de). Romantic Black Forest hotel with 100 guest rooms and a 140 seat restaurant.

Chambermaids to clean rooms, foyer area, restaurant and toilets. Language skills and a hospitable nature required as the job involves some contact with guests.

Kitchen Assistants to clean plates and dishes, and help prepare vegetables and salads. Previous experience and a German kitchen hygiene certificate required.

Porters to help arriving and departing guest with their luggage, driving for transport and transfers, and moving furniture within the hotel. Should have a hospitable friendly outlook for dealing with guests, and a full driving licence.

Waitresses to serve breakfasts, lunch, dinner in the restaurant and in afternoons at the outdoor cafe. Previous experience required, and knowledge of languages preferred.

All staff work 8 hours per day over a 5 day week, for £370 approx. (Euros 600) per month. Board and accommodation are provided at a cost of £46 approx. (Euros 75) per month. Minimum period of work is 3 months and candidates should speak German and English.

Applications accepted from December to Gerald Henningsen at the above address.

POSTHOTEL: Obermarkt 9, D-82481 Mittenwald/Karwendel, Germany.
Chambermaids (2) to clean guest rooms, corridors, toilets, swimming pool etc. To work from 6.30am-4pm, with one hour break.

Kitchen Assistants/Washers Up (2) to wash tableware and cooking utensils, peel potatoes, clean vegetables, etc. To work from 7am-2pm and 5.30-9pm with 1¹/₂ hour break.

£650 per month, approximately. To work 8-9 hours per day, 5 days per week. Board and lodging available for around £100 per month. Minimum period of work 2¹/₂ months between July and October and between 20 December and 31 March.

Some knowledge of German an advantage: other languages are not essential. *Applicants only accepted from students holding EU passports or those studying in Germany who have the relevant work permit from the employment office. Applications,* enclosing proof of student status from school, college or university stating that you are a full time student there (International Student Identity Cards will not suffice) to the above address.

HOTEL PRINZ-LUITPOLD-BAD: D-87541 Hindelang/Allgäuer Alpen, Germany (tel 08324-8900; fax 08324-890379; e-mail luitpoldbad@t-online.de; website www.luitpoldbad.de). A 110 bedroom spa hotel built in 1864 in a quiet mountain location with glorious views of the Allgäu in the Bavarian Alps. Features include their private mud baths and their sulfur spring, which is the highest in Germany. The hotel is 70km from Lake Constance and 45km from the

king's castle Neuschwanstein/Füssen.
General Assistants (2). Should speak fluent German.
Chambermaids (3), **Kitchen Helps** (3).
£350 net per month, approx., plus around £55 net bonus per month. To work 5 days a week. Free board and accommodation provided. Minimum period of work 3 months all year round. Raise of £30 per month from the fourth month onwards. *Applications* from *EU passport holders only* to the above address.

QUEENS HOTEL FRANKFURT: Isenburger Schneise 40, D-60528 Frankfurt, Germany (tel 069-67840; fax 069-678 4190). Set in Germany's largest stretch of urban woodland near the old city, the Queen's Hotel is one of Frankfurt's premier hotels.
Serving Staff required for the hotel's restaurant, bar and beer-garden. To work 7¹/2 hours shift work per day not including a 30 minute break, over a 5 day week. The hours worked will vary according to the shifts. Board and lodging are available at a cost of c.£28 per month for board. Wages by negotiation. Staff should speak English and German.
Applications to Frau Sonia Thierer at the above address.

RELAIS & CHATEAUX HOTEL MÖNCH'S POSTHOTEL: D-76328 Bad Herrenhalb, Nr. Baden Baden, Germany (tel 070-837440; fax 070-8374 4122).
Waiting Assistant, General Assistant. Wages approx. £300 per month. To work 9 hours per day, 5 days per week. Board and accommodation provided free. Knowledge of low German, English or French needed. *Applications* to the above address in spring.

RHEINHOTEL LORELEY: Rheinallee 12, D-53639 Königswinter 1, Germany (tel 02223-9250; fax 02223-925100)
A tourist and conference hotel open all year, set beside the Rhine.
Chambermaids (1-2) to tidy rooms and change the beds. Approx. £300 per month. Must have previous relevant experience and knowledge of German.
Waiters (1-2) to serve food. Around £300 per month. Previous experience of waiting desirable. Must have knowledge of German.
To work 9 hours per day, 5 days per week. Working days variable. Applicants must be friendly people who are willing to work for at least three months. *Applications* to Manfred Maderer at the above address between 1 March and 15 March only.

ROMANTIK HOTEL FASANERIE: Fasanerie 1, D-66482 Zweibrücken/ Rheinland-Pfalz, Germany (tel +49-6332-9730; fax 06332-973111; e-mail fasanerie.direktion@romantik.de; www.romantikhotels.com/ zweibruecken).
Two hotels in Zweibrücken require **Waiting Staff** to work in a restaurant and buffet. Wages around £246/DM800 per month, with accommodation and meals included. To work 8-10 hours per day between 6.30am and midnight, 6 days per week. Period of work by arrangement between April and October.
Applicants should speak German and be flexible and adaptable; additional knowledge of French and English would be helpful. *Applications* should be sent to Andreas Foerster at the above address 2-3 months before the desired start of work.

SCHASSBERGERS KUR-UND SPORTHOTEL: Winnenderstr. 10, D-73667 Ebnisee, Germany (tel 07184-292-0; fax 07184-292-204; e-mail schassbergers-ebnisee@t-online.de; www.schassbergers.de). The hotel is one of the most attractive resorts in Germany, in the heart of the Swabian forest northeast of Stuttgart.

Kitchen Assistants, Waiting Staff, Housekeeping Staff to work for a spa and health resort hotel situated in the Swabian forest nature park, 40 km from Stuttgart specialising in short sporting/relaxation breaks.

Ages 18-30. Knowledge of German required. Some previous experience desirable. Minimum period of work 3 months. Board and accommodation provided. Initially no salary, but wage will be paid from the 4th month depending on performance. To work 9 hours per 5 day week. On days off there are a variety of activities available to staff both in and outside the hotel, including a Finnish sauna, tennis, swimming, hiking, fishing, horse riding and continuing education classes.

Applications should be sent to Ernst-Ulrich Schassberger at the above address at any time of year.

HOTEL SCHLOSS HUGENPOET GMBTT: August-Thyssen-Strasse 51, D-45219, Essen (tel 02054-120436; fax 02054-120453; e-mail personal@hugenpoet.de; www.hugenpoet.de). The Hotel Schloss Hugenpoet is a beautiful building, not far from Düsseldorf. It belongs to the Relais and Chateaux Hotel Group.

Gardeners, General Assistants, Chambermaids, Laundery Assistants needed. Applicants should be flexible, friendly and polite, and should speak German and/or English. Wages £365 approx. gross, monthly. Staff work eight hours per day over a five day working week during the summer months. Board and accommodation is provided at £126 per month. *Applications* are invited from six months prior to starting date if possible.

HOTEL SCHLOSS PETERSHAGEN: Schlosstrasse 5-7, D-32469 Petershagen, Germany. (tel ++49-05707-9313-0; fax 05707-2372; schloss-petershagen@t-online.de; www.romantikhotels.com/petershagen).

Kitchen Assistant, Waiter/Barman, Housekeeping Assistant. To work 5 hours per day over a 5 day week. Wages £63 approx. (Euros 103) per week plus free board and lodging. Basic knowledge of spoken German required. Applications to the above address 3 months before desired period of starting work. *E-mail application* preferred.

SCHLOSSHOTEL KRONBERG: Hainstr. 25, D-61476 Kronberg 1, Taunus, Germany (tel +49-6173-70701; fax +49-6173-701267; e-mail info@schlosshotel-kronberg.de; www.schlosshotel-kronberg.de). Built by the Empress Friedrich, this glamorous country house hotel is set in beautiful parkland in the heart of Rhein-Main 20 minutes away from Frankfurt.

Waiter (2) to serve breakfast and other meals and help set up and serve banquets. Must have silver service experience, be able to work in a team and be capable of helping clients enjoy their meal while serving.

Beverage Buffet to prepare hot and cold beverages for waiting staff, and maintaining stock control, including occasional stock-taking. Must speak German.

All staff work seven and three-quarter hours per day in a five day week. Split shifts are worked, the earliest start time is 6am and the latest finish time is 3pm. All staff earn £330 per month, board and lodging is available at a cost of: lodging £93, food £51 per month.

SCHLOSSHOTEL LISL & JAGERHAUS: Neuschwansteinstr. 1-3, D-87645 Hohenschwangau, Germany (tel 08362-8870; fax 08362-81107; e-mail: info@lisl.de).

Seasonal Staff for jobs including chambermaids, dishwashers, buffet assistants, restaurant assistants and waiting staff. Minimum wage £250 per month, approximately. To work 8 hours per day, 5 days per week: no night work required. Free board and lodging provided.

Some knowledge of German required. Minimum period of work 3-4 months from April to November. *Applications* to G. Meyer, Manager, at the above address until 31 March: replies will only be sent if a job is offered.

SCHLOSS REINHARTSHAUSEN: Hauptstrasse 41, Erbach m Rheingau, D-65346 Eltville, (tel 06123-676355; fax 06123-676490; e-mail ines.larsenschmidt@reinhartshausen.com; www.schloss-hotel.de) Small, leading 5-star hotel with 54 rooms, 11 conference rooms, 3 restaurants, a beautiful terrace and a winery. Run by a young team.

Waiting Staff (3) required to prepare or serve food, clear tables, etc. To work for about 5 hours a day, 5 days a week. Salary approx £550 per month Must be open minded, guest-orientated, friendly and enjoy serving.

Banqueting Set-Ups (3) required to prepare meeting rooms, serve food etc. To work 5 days a week. Salary £460 per month approx.

Kitchen Helpers (2) required to prepare food, especially for breakfasts and buffets. Cooking ability an advantage. 5 days work a week. Salary arond £550 per month.

Working time ranges from 5-10 hours a day for banqueting set-ups and kitchen helpers. Applicants must be prepared to work for at least 3 months, and must speak German and English. Accommodation and board may be available, depending on the number of requests, for approx £150 per month.

Applications to the above address from December.

SCHWARZWALD HOTEL: Rothaustr. 7, D-79848 Bonndorf, Germany (fax 07703-442).

Chambermaid, Kitchen Assistant, Buffet Assistant. Wage £200 per month. To work 8 hours per day, 5 days per week. Board and accommodation provided free. Minimum period of work 2 months. Applicants must be able to speak German or English. *Applications* to the Family Mohringer at the above address.

HOTEL SCHWEIZ: Goethe Str. 26, D-80336 München, Germany (tel +49-89-5436 960; fax +49-89-5436 9696; e-mail info@hotel-schweiz.de; www.hotelschweiz.de).

Receptionists, Restaurant Staff (20-30) required to work in reception and to serve breakfast in a new hotel in Munich. Applicants should speak good English, be computer literate, friendly, open-minded and in good health. Minimum period of work 6 months. Wage to be confirmed. The hotel will help to find accommodation for the successful candidates.

Applications should be made to the above address.

HOTEL SIEBENGEBIRGE: D-53639 Konigswinter, Haupstrasse 342, Germany (tel 0 22 23-2-13-59; fax 0 22 23-2-18-03).

Chambermaid/Kitchen Assistant for general help in the kitchen and around hotel. £350 per month. Free board and accommodation provided. Period of work from May to October. *Applications* before end of April to Herr Theo Münchrath at the above address.

HOTEL SONNE-POST: Klosterreichenbach, Murgtalstrasse 167, D-72270 Baiersbronn 6, Germany (tel 0744-2277).
Waiter/Waitress to serve in an a la carte restaurant. Should possess a knowledge of wines, beer etc. and possess dark clothing and a white apron/jacket.
General Assistant to clean rooms and help with the washing up.
Wages are from £320-£400 per month depending on experience, with opportunities for earning overtime. 8/9 hour day, 6 day week. Free board and accommodation. Minimum period of work 3 months, at any time of the year. Some knowledge of German is necessary. *Applications* to the Manager at the above address at any time of the year.

URBASCHEK'S GASTRONOMISCHE BETRIEBE: Haupstrasse 6, 92436 Bruck, Germany (tel 0049-9434 1206; fax 0049-9434 902923).
Waitresses/Barmaids. Wages by arrangement, accommodation provided. Experience not necessary, but applicants should be young and friendly. *Applications* with photograph to the above address.

GASTHOF & HOTEL VIKTORIA: D-87561 Rubi bei Oberstdorf, Allgäu, Germany (tel 8322-977840; fax 8322-9778486).
General Assistant (female) for buffet and housework. Wage over £320 per month. Free board and accommodation. Minimum period of work 3 months between beginning of June and mid October. *Applications* not later than mid April to Frau Julia Ess.

HOTEL RESTAURANT ZUM WAGNERSTUBLE: Wilderbaderstrasse 45, D-75335 Dobel/Schwarzall, Germany.
Assistant. Wages by arrangement. To work 8-9 hours per day, 6 days per week (10am-3.30pm and 7-10.30pm). Free board and lodging, minimum period of work 2 months. For further details *contact* the Familie Kieferle at the above address.

WARNER BROS. MOVIE WORLD GmbH & Co KG: Warner Allee 1, D-46244 Bottrop-Kirchellen, Germany (tel 02045-899540; fax 02045-899505; e-mail info@freizeitsparks.de). Hollywood movie styled theme and entertainment park in the west of Germany.
Customer Service Staff (420) for food and concession stands in the theme park. Previous experience would be useful, as staff will be serving in restaurants, bakeries, and at hamburger and ice-cream stalls. To work 20-40 hours per week according to post, from around 9am to 7pm or sometimes to 9pm and later. Applicants should be able to speak Dutch, German and English. Wages are approx £4 per hour net. Accommodation is not available but a staff canteen is provided where meals cost around £2.

HOTEL-WEINHAUS-OSTER: Moselweinstrasse 61, D-56814 Ediger-Eller 2, bei Cochem/Mosel, Germany (tel 02675-232; fax 02675-1570; e-mail hoteloster@t-online.de). A family hotel facing the magnificent river Mosel, with many attractions including the local wine festivals and wine-tastings arranged by the owner's brother.
Waiting Assistant, General Assistant. Wages approximately £320 per month plus tips and free board and accommodation. To work 7 hours per day, six days per week. Minimum period of work 3 months between May and October. Applicants must speak German. *Applications* to Mrs M.L. Meyer-Schenk at the above address from January.

WALDHOTEL FORELLENHOF: D-76534 Baden-Baden, Gaisbach 91, Germany (tel 07221-974-299).
House Assistants/Chambermaids/Waitresses (2). Salary by arrangement. Hours from 6.30am-5.30pm (with 1^1/2 hours free for meals) 5 days per week. Free board and accommodation. Knowledge of German required. Minimum period of work 5 months between 1 May and 30 September. *Applications* to Georg Huber at the above address in January.

HOTEL WITTELSBACHER HOF: Prinzenstrasse 24, D-87561 Oberstdorf, Germany (tel 08322-605-0; fax 08322-605-300; e-mail info@ wittelsbacherhof.de; www.wittelsbacherhof.de)
Chambermaids, Dishwashers, Kitchen Assistants, Restaurant Assistants (males and females) to work in a 140 bed hotel. Wages £315 approx. per month plus help with travelling expenses. 8 hours per day, 5 day week. Knowledge of German preferred. Board and lodging provided free of charge. Minimum period of work 2 months from May to July, July to October or December to March. Positions also available from 20 December to 10 January, or for both the summer and winter seasons. *Applications* from *EU citizens only* to the above address enclosing a photograph, c.v. and proof of student status.

HOTEL WOLF: Dorfstr. I, D-82487 Oberammergau, Germany (tel 08822-9233-0; fax 08822-9233-33; e-mail info@hotel-wolf.de; www.hotel-wolf.de).
Waiter/Waitress/Chambermaid/Kitchen Assistant. £400 to £600 per month, 5 days per week. Free board and lodging. Period of work May-October. *Applications* to the above address before May.

ROMANTIK HOTEL ZUM STERN: Linggplatz 11, D-36251 Bad Hersfeld, Germany (tel 06621-1890; fax 06621-189260; e-mail zumstern@romantik.de). Traditional, family-owned first-class hotel in the middle of Germany, 120 km from Frankfurt/Main. In summer an open-air theatre festival takes place in the ruin of the old monastery in the neighbourhood of the hotel.
Housekeepers (4) to clean rooms and for general housekeeping work, wages £340 per month.
Bar Staff (2),**Drinks Buffet Staff** (2) to serve drinks and light refreshments. Should have some experience of service work. Wages £340 per month plus tips and free board and accommodation.
    To work 8 hours per day over a 5 day week; dates of work are flexible, but with a minimum of 3 months. Depending on the place of work some knowledge of German is required.
    Applications should be sent to the Manager at the above address.

Sports, Couriers and Camping

3D EDUCATION AND ADVENTURE LTD: Business Support, Osmington Bay, Weymouth, Dorset DT3 6EG (tel 01305-836226; fax 01305-834070; e-mail darren@3d-education.co.uk). 3D is a specialist provider of activity and educational experiences for young people. Owned by Center Parcs, 3D has been operating since 1991 and gone from strength to strength year on year.
Activity Instructors. (500) Employed and trained as either multi-activity instructor, field studies instructor, specialist watersports instructor or IT instructor, staff will work with children at specialist holiday centres across the south of England as well as across the UK and Europe with Pontins and Center Parcs.

Field studies instructors must hold or at least be gaining a relevant degree. IT instructors need to have a broad range of IT skills. Any sports coaching awards or national governing body awards are advantageous, if applying for Activity instructor and Watersports instructor postitions, although those with relevant experience will be considered. Training courses are held from late January through to July, so there is plenty of opportunity to develop your skills and qualifications.

Most important is an applicant's enthusiasm, personality and energy, coupled with a true desire to work in the outdoor leisure industry. Excellent accommodation and catering packages are offered with payment and working hours as covered by minimum wage and working time legislation. Minimum period of work 14 weeks.

Applicants should *telephone* 01305-836226 for a recruitment pack between September and June. Before employment all applicants must complete a residential training programme in the UK.

BENTS BICYCLE & WALKING TOURS: The Blue Cross, Orleton, Ludlow, Shropshire SY8 4HN (tel 01568-780800; fax 01568-780801).
Company Representatives (4-5) for a tour operator offering cycling and walking holidays in Germany and Austria. Duties to include meeting clients at the airport, maintaining bicycles, transporting luggage between hotels and generally taking care of the needs of clients. Wages of around £600 per month with board and accommodation provided. To work varied hours as needs of work dictate, but generally around 40 hours per up to 7 day week.

Minimum period of work 8 weeks between the end of May and end of September. Applicants should speak fluent German and English and possess a full clean driving licence. *Applications* should be sent, with a photograph, to Stephen Bent at the above address from January.

CANVAS HOLIDAYS: East Port House, 12 East Port, Dunfermline, Fife KY12 7JG (tel 01383-629018; fax 01383-629071; www.canvas holidayscom). Canvas Holidays are looking for enthusiastic, resourceful people who enjoy a challenge and love the outdoor life. Main positions for 2002 include:
Campsite Courier. Varied responsibilities. Involves cleaning and preparation of customer accommodation, welcoming and looking after customers during their holiday and ensuring that they have the best holiday ever. As a campsite courier you will have new challenges every day which can lead to one of the most enjoyable summers you will ever have. Variable working hours.
Children's Courier. As a Canvas Holidays Children's Courier you will have had formal experience of working with children. You will organise and carry out a six day programme which involves four hours a day of Children's Club for children between the ages of 4 and 11. You will be prepared to help out with courier duties as and when requried. For many customers, the Children's Club is one of the main parts of the holiday. You will need to have the energy of a seven year old and the imagination of an eleven year old to succeed.

Package includes tented accommodation, medical insurance, full uniform and return travel to and from a UK port of entry. Positions are available from March until October. *Applications* are invited from individuals and couples. Contact Sandy, Karen or Michele at the above contact details for an application pack.

EUROCAMP: Overseas Recruitment Department (Ref SJ/02) (tel 01606-787522). Eurocamp is a leading tour operator in quality self-drive camping and mobile home holidays in Europe. Each year the company seeks to recruit up to 1,500 enthusiastic people for the following positions:

Courier: job involves cleaning and preparing customer accommodation, providing assistance, acting as an information service and an interpreter and performing some administrative duties. Couriers need to be flexible to meet the needs of the customer to provide them with excellent service. Minimum age 18 years. Applicants should be independent with plenty of initiative and relish a challenging and rewarding position. They should also possess a friendly and helpful personality. Some working knowledge of another European language is required and previous customer service experience would be an advantage. Applicants should be available to work from April/May to September.

Children's Couriers: work involves organising a wide range of exciting activities for children aged 4-13. Applicants should possess initiative, imagination and enthusiasm along with good safety awareness. Previous childcare experience is essential. Minimum age is 18 years and applicants should be available from April/May to September. Languages are not a requirement but would be an advantage (in particular German).

Senior Couriers: required to work alongside a team of Campsite Couriers and organise their daily workload, as well as carrying out the normal day to day duties of a Campsite Courier. Applicants should have good language skills and experience of leading a team.

Site Managers: required to lead a large team of Campsite Couriers, organising their daily workloads and ensuring they provide the very best customer service. Applicants should be 21 or over, have proven managerial experience, excellent communication skills and language ability.

In all the above positions you should be be available for the full season commencing in April/May through to September. Comprehensive training is provided together with a competitive salary, insurance and return travel. Applications are accepted from September/October and *can only be accepted from UK/EU passport holders*. Interviews will be conducted in Hartford, Cheshire between October and April.

KEYCAMP HOLIDAYS: Overseas Recruitment Department, Hartford Manor, Greenbank Lane, Nothwich CW8 1H (tel 01606-787522).

Campsite Couriers: to look after British, Dutch and Scandinavian customers on campsites in Germany. Duties include welcoming customers, providing local information, organising social activities on site and ensuring that all accommodation is prepared prior to arrival.

Children's Courier: to organise and provide up to 24 hours of activities per week for children aged 4-13 years, to advertise club activities and visit families on arrival.

Senior Couriers: incorporating the role of campsite courier with the additional responsibility of organising and managing a team and ensuring the smooth running of the Keycamp on site.

Montage/Demontage: for a period of approximately 6 weeks at the beginning/end of season to erect/dismantle equipment.

Minimum age 18 years. Accommodation, uniform and training provided. A working knowledge of German would be an advantage. Period of employment between March and July-October.

Applicants should write to the Overseas Recruitment Department, Keycamp Holidays, quoting reference SJ/02.

RIECHEY FREIZEITANLAGEN GMBH: D-23769 Wulfen-Fehmarn, Germany (tel 04371-86280; fax 04371-3723).
Kitchen Helpers (2). Duties include washing dishes, salad preparation and serving food. Must speak German.
Sales Assistants (2) to unpack goods, and see to sales and bike/tv hire. Knowledge of German and competence with German currency essential.
Children's Representatives (2) to look after and entertain children, which may include drawing and arts and crafts. Must speak German and be creative.
Catering Staff (2) to order and sell fast food. Knowledge of German and competence with German currency essential.
All staff to work 8 hours per day, 5-6 days per week. Wages approximately £420 net per month plus free board and lodging or approximately £900 gross, with self-catering accommodation available at a cost of £70 per month. Minimum period of work 8 weeks. *Applications* from 15 January to the above address.

Voluntary Work and Archaeology

ARBEITSKREIS DENKMALPFLEGE e.V.: Goetheplatz 9B, D-99423 Weimar, Germany (tel +49-3643 502390; fax +49-3643 851117; e-mail info@ak-denkmalpflege.de; www.ak-denkmalpflege.de).
Building Assistants (25), Carpenters (7), Joiners (4), Bricklayers (5), Students of Architecture (6-12), Civil Engineers (3), Office Assistants (4), Unskilled Staff (25) for **Voluntary Work** with an organisation conducting restoration work on historic monuments in eastern regions of Germany. This project involves mainly young people, mainly from abroad. No payment, but accommodation is provided; for students the work may be recognised by their place of study as practical work experience. 4-8 hours of work a day will be expected for 3-6 days per week; the normal minimum period of work is one week. Most of the projects take place between May and October, but help is needed in the office around the year. A basic knowledge of German is desirable, but English, French, Russian or Czech may be acceptable.
Applications should be sent to Bert Ludwig at the above address.

CONCORDIA: 20-22 Boundary Road, Hove, East Sussex BN3 4ET (tel 01273-422218; fax 01273 421182; e-mail info@concordia-iye.org.uk; www.concordia-iye.org.uk).
Concordia offers young people aged 16-30 the opportunity to take part in international volunteer projects lasting 2-3 weeks, from June to September. The work is community based and ranges from nature conservation, renovation, construction, to social work including children's playschemes and youth work. Volunteers pay a registration fee of approx. £85 and fund their own travel. Board and accommodation are free of charge. For further information *write* enclosing an sae to the International Volunteer Co-ordinator at the above address.

HEIMSONDERSCHULE BRACHENREUTHE: D-88662 Uberlingen, Germany (tel 07551-80070; fax 07551-800750; e-mail brachenreuthe@t-online.de).
Volunteers to work as helpers in a residential community for mentally handicapped children. Pocket money of £140, approximately, per month plus board and lodging in shared room and insurance. Most vacancies exist for a period of 6 months or longer around the year; the school is closed for July and much of August. The ideal candidates for the school would work from the end of August to the end of the following July. Minimum age 19. A knowledge of

German is essential. For further details *contact* the above address.

INTERNATIONALE BEGEGNUNG IN GEMEINSCHAFTSDIENSTEN eV: Schlosserstrasse 28, D-70180 Stuttgart 1, Germany (tel 0711-6491128; fax 711-6409867).
Volunteers to attend international youth workcamps in Germany. Projects include restoring an old castle, environmental protection, children's playschemes and media projects. Each workcamp consists of a group of about 15 people aged 18-30 from all over the world living and working together for the public benefit.
There is a registration fee of approximately £55; food and accommodation are provided free on the camps. IBG's new programme is published in March.

IJGD INTERNATIONALE JUGENDGEMEINSCHAFTSDIENSTE eV; Kaiserstrasse 43, D-53113 Bonn, Germany (tel 228-2280011; fax 228-2280024).
Volunteers (300) to work on summer projects such as environmental protection, the restoration of educational centres, and to assist with city fringe recreational activities. 30 hours per week of work for periods of 3 weeks at Easter or between June and September. Free board and accommodation provided. Applicants should be aged between 16-26. Knowledge of German required on social projects.
Applications should be made to the above address as soon as possible.

NIG E.V.: Tel 0049-381 4922914; fax 0049-381 4900930; e-mail NIGeV@aol.com.
Volunteers to work for a non-profit organisation which organises 20 workcamps, for people aged 18-30, in Germany and various countries. The camps focus on environmental protection, nature conservation, archaeology and cultural projects. Some projects are aimed at conserving the remains of concentration camps and developing museum projects there to educate people about the Jewish holocaust.
Accommodation and food are provided free, but volunteers will need to pay a registration fee of approximately £60.

NOTHELFERGEMEINSCHAFT DER FREUNDE eV: Fuggerstr. 3, D-52351 Düren, Germany (tel 02421-76569; e-mail ndf-dn@t-online.de; www.nothelfer.org).
Volunteers for spring and summer work camps arranged by the organisation. The work may involve building, gardening or social work. 35 hours per week approximately. Special workcamp with German language courses normally held mid July-mid August. Work is unpaid but free board and accommodation and insurance against sickness, accident and liability are provided.
Applicants should be aged 16-26 years. Camps normally last for 1 month. Volunteers are responsible for their own travel costs. *Applications* in April or May at the latest to the above address.

PRO INTERNATIONAL: Bahnhofstrasse 26 A, D-35037 Marburg, Germany (tel 06421-65277; fax 06421-64407; e-mail: pro-international@lahn.net; www.pro-international.de).
Following the concept of 'Peace through Friendship' Pro International organises international vacation work camps during the Easter and summer vacations. On these camps, which last for up to 3 weeks, 10 to 15 people aged between 16 and 26 years old from different countries participate. The participants work about 5 hours a day on public or social projects and spend their time together. Accommodation and food supply are free; the participants pay only their tickets and approx. £40 to cover administration. *Applications* have to be sent to the above address.

Other Employment Abroad

FAMILIENWEINGUT OSTER & FRANZEN: Calmonstrasse 96, D-56814 Bremm/Mosel am Calmont, Germany (fax 02675-1626). A small family business set in the beautiful surroundings of the Mosel Valley. A wonderful opportunity to learn about wine and vine.
Two people (preferably a couple) to work in vineyards, home and cellars, 8 hours per day, 6 days per week. Minimum age normally 24, although younger but mature applicants may be considered. The ability to speak English or German is essential. A driving licence would be an advantage. Full board and lodging provided in the family home, with a family atmosphere. Periods of work: two months between May and July and September to November. For further details contact the above address enclosing an international reply coupon.
    Applications to the above address will be considered from February onwards. *EC passport holders preferred.*

WEINGUT FREIHERR VON LANDENBERG 'SCHLOSKELLEREI': Moselweinstr. 60, D-56814 Ediger-Eller (Mosel), Germany (tel 02675-277; fax 02675-207). 500 year old vineyard and cellars in the heart of the Mosel wine region. Many connoisseurs of wine, young and old, buy direct from the estate because of its quality.
Sales Woman to sell wines and gifts in this award winning vineyard and castle's shop. To work 8 hours per day over a 6 day week for approx. £270, with free board and lodging. Applicants must speak German. Dates of work are variable between May and October.
    Applications in writing to Frau H. Trimborn von Landenberg at the above address.

ZENTRALSTELLE   FUR   ARBEITSVERMITTLUNG: ZAV, Studentenvermittlung 21-22, Villemombler Strasse 76, D-53123 Bonn, Germany. This is the official government labour agency which places German-speaking students in summer jobs throughout Germany. Applicants must be at least 18 years old, have a good command of German, (how good it must be depends on the individual job) and agree to work for at least two months. Work is available in hotels and restaurants, as chambermaids or kitchen helpers, or in agriculture. Contact the ZAV at the above address for application forms and further information; there is no fee for this service. *Apply* before March.

Au Pairs, Nannies, Family Helps and Exchanges

IN VIA: Katholische Madchensozialarbeit, Deutscher Verband eV, Ludwigstr. 36, Postfach 420, D-79004 Freiburg, Germany (tel 761-200206; fax 761-200638; e-mail schmidlm@caritas.de).
Au Pair positions in Germany; with regional offices in 43 cities there IN VIA can arrange to place au pairs between 18 and 25 years with German families. Minimum length of stay 6 months, but stays of 1 year preferred. For further information please contact the above address.

VEREIN FÜR INTERNATIONALE JUGENDARBEIT: Goetheallee 10, 53225 Bonn, Germany (tel +49-228 698952; fax 0228-694166; e-mail au-pair.vij@netcologne.de; www.vij-deutschland.org; www.au-pair-vij.de).
Au Pairs: girls and boys between 18 and 24 years can be placed as au pairs with

families in Germany. Preferred length of stay is 1 year, with an absolute minimum of 6 months. Pocket money of around £130 per month; season ticket for local transport also provided. Applicants must have a reasonable command of German. Those interested should *contact* the above address.

Great Britain

There are so many opportunities for summer work in Britain in Great Britain that the opportunities are collected together in the separate title *Summer Jobs in Britain*; for details see the *Useful Publications* chapter at the end of this book. However, a number of the employers and voluntary organisations listed in the *Worldwide* chapter can place people in the UK.

US students seeking temporary work in the UK can benefit from the 'Work in Britain Program'. This allows full-time college students and recent graduates over the age of 18 to look for work in Britain, finding jobs through programme listings or through personal contacts. Jobs may be pre-arranged, though most participants wait until arrival in Britain to job hunt. They must first obtain a 'British Universities North America Club (BUNAC) Card', which is recognised by the British Home Office as a valid substitute for a work permit ; this 'BUNAC Card' must be obtained before leaving the US for Britain, as it acts as an entry document. It allows the holder to work for a maximum of six months at any time of year: extensions are never granted. For information on the BUNAC card call toll free tel 1-888-GO BUNAC.

A similar programme, called the Student Work Abroad Programme (SWAP), is organised for Canadian students, graduates and young people, with varying age restrictions applying. It is administered by the Canadian Universities Travel Service, which has over 40 offices in Canada. For details see www.swap.ca.

Greece

Every year Greece receives around ten million foreign tourists, and it is the tourist trade with employers such as those listed in this chapter that offers the best chances of finding temporary work to the foreigner. One reason for this is that in the tourist industry having a native language other than Greek is an asset rather than a liability.

Other opportunities for foreigners involve domestic work with Greek families, helping with the housework and perhaps improving the family's English. Wages in Greece are generally low, but are enough to permit an extended stay. In recent years wage levels for unskilled work have been depressed in some areas because of the large number of immigrants – legal and otherwise – from Albania and other countries in Eastern Europe who are willing to work for low rates.

British, Irish and other EU nationals are permitted to use the Greek national employment service: local branches are called offices of the *Organisimos Apasholisseos Ergatikou Dynamikou*, or OAED (the Manpower Employment Organisation: Ethnikis Antistasis 8 str., GR-16610 Ano Glyfada, Greece; tel +30-1-9989000; www.oaed.gr). For further information consult the free booklet *Working in Greece* published by the UK Employment Service. Jobs are also advertised in the local major newspapers such as *Ta Nea, Eleftheros Typos, Eleftherotypia* and *Apogevmatini*.

Although many people have succeeded in finding casual farm work, such as picking oranges and olives, it is almost impossible to arrange this from outside Greece. Oranges are picked between Christmas and March, especially south of Corinth. Grapes are grown all over the mainland and islands, and growers often need casual help during the September harvest. Those who are prepared to take a chance on finding casual work in Greece will find further information on harvests in the book *Work Your Way Around the World* (see the *Useful Publications* chapter).

There are opportunities for voluntary work in Greece arranged by International Voluntary Service, Youth Action for Peace, Concordia and UNA Exchange for British applicants and Service Civil International and Council: International Volunteer Projects for Americans: see the *Worldwide* chapter for details.

It may be possible to obtain a job by means of an advertisement in one of the English language newspapers in Athens. The *Athens News* is a daily paper whose classified department is at 3 Christou Lada str, 10237 Athens, Greece (tel 1-3333404; fax 1-3223746). The minimum charge for an advertisement is £5 for 15 words. You can check the classified advertisements in the *Athens News* on the internet on http://athensnews.dolnet.gr.

RED TAPE

Visa Requirements: citizens of the UK and most other countries in Western Europe, Australia, Canada, New Zealand and the USA do not require a visa to travel to Greece.

Residence Permits: those wishing to stay in Greece for longer than three months require permission to do so from the Aliens Department *(Grafeio Tmimatos Allodapon)* or Tourist Police in the area. You must present your passport, a letter of intent of employment and a Medical Certificate.

Work Permits: a permit must be obtained by a prospective employer on behalf of a non-EEA national prior to arrival in Greece. Failure to follow this procedure may result in refusal of entry to the country. EEA nationals do not require a work permit to work in Greece.

Au Pair: allowed; a work permit must be obtained for non-EEA citizens.

Hotel Work and Catering

HOTEL AGIOS GORDIS: Thyris Kerkyras, Corfu, Greece.
Cooks (3) to prepare food for around 400 people daily. From £400 per month. Should have previous experience of professional cooking of international specialities, with an emphasis on Italian cooking. 8 hour day, 6 day week. No accommodation provided, but rooms are available locally for around £100-£120 per month. Minimum period of work 4 months between 10 April and 1 October.
Applications to Paul Rizos, Manager, at the above address.

ARISTOTELES HOTEL: 15 Acharnon Street, GR-104 38 Athens, Greece (tel 30-1-522 8126; fax +30-1-523 1138).
Cleaners, Bar Staff, Couriers are needed for a three star hotel. Wage £250 per month (plus commission for courier) with free accommodation and breakfast provided. Most vacancies are for the Summer, but some exist all year round. Minimum age 24.
Applications to Mr Vakis Ovvadias at the above address.

HOTEL ASTIR: 16 Agiou Andrew Street, Patras, Greece. **Catering Manager** (1), **Chef Cook** (1). To work eight hours a day, six days a week. No accommodation is provided. Previous employment and knowledge of English is required. Minimum period of work eight months from 15 October to 15 June. *Applications* to the above address.

HOTEL CAPRI: 6, Psaromilingou Street, Athens, Greece (tel 01-3252091/3252085; fax 01-3252091). **Cleaners, Bar Staff, Couriers** and **Nannies** are needed for a three star hotel. Wage £250 per month (plus commission for couriers), free accommodation and breakfast. Most vacancies are for the summer but some exist around the year. Minimum age 24. *Applications* to Mr Vakis Ovvadias.

COLOSSOS BEACH HOTEL: PO Box 105, 85100 Faliraki, Rhodes, Greece (tel 0241-85502; fax 0241-85679; e-mail colossosbeach.gr). The hotel has vacancies for work and training in the kitchens, restaurants and bars. These vacancies are only open to students who can prove their student status. Period of work is May to October; staff staying the whole period will receive a refund to cover their normal fare ticket.

In return for working 8 hours a day per 6 day week, staff will receive approximately £140 a month, full board and accommodation, training and free medical/hospital insurance.

Applicants should preferably speak English and German and have previous experience or qualifications in hotel/restaurant work. *Applications* with a recent photograph to Mr D. Rozalis at the above address before the end of February.

CORINA'S PLACE-IL GIARDINO: Logaras, Paros, Greece (tel 30-284-41049; fax 30-284-41492). **Kitchen Porter** (1), **Commis Chefs** (2), **Chef de Partie** (1), **Waitresses** (2). Salary at Greek rates with eventual possibility of free accommodation. Period of work 1 April to 15 October. Split and straight shifts; 5 day week during low season, 6 day week during high season.

Applicants for kitchen work should be male, while applicants for waitressing should be female. *All applicants should be EU nationals*, hard-working, of neat appearance and have at least 2-3 years previous experience. Send curriculum vitae and references, enclosing a recent photo, to Miss Corina Harcourt at the following address between November and March: 10 rue Carnot, Versailles 78000, France; at the above address after April or telephone the above number after 9pm.

DISCO BAR STROVILLI: Kardamylla 82300, Chios, Greece (tel 30 272 22560). **Bar Staff** required for both winter and summer seasons. To work from 10pm to 3am daily; no overtime. Applicants must be aged between 18 and 25. *Applications* to Mattae Manonhs at the above address.

DORETA BEACH HOTEL: Tholos, Rhodes, Greece (tel 82540/1/2/3/4/5; fax 82446). **Barman, Barmaid, Waitresses.** Around £450 per month. Knowledge of German required. Applications to Michalis A. Yiasiranis, Manager, at the above address.

HOTEL ERI: Parikia Paros, Greece (tel winter 01-5228126; fax 01-5231138). **Bar Staff, Couriers** needed to work in this hotel in the Cyciades, on the Island of Paros. An alternative contact is through the Hotel Rivoli (see below).

RESTAURANT KAMARES: 80100 Kapsali, Kythira, Greece (tel/fax +30-736-31-064; mobile 0944-363732).
Kitchen Helps (2-4). Some knowledge of Greek would be an advantage.
Waiters/Waitresses (4). Some knowledge of Greek is essential, and applicants should have some restaurant experience.

Wages starting at £290 per month approx with food and accommodation provided; to work shifts of 9-10 hours per day. Period of work from 1 July to 15 September. *Applications* with a full length photo should be sent to Antonis Magiros at the above address.

KIVOTOS CLUB HOTEL: Ornos Bay, GR-84600 Mykonos, Greece (tel +30-289 24094, 25795/6; fax 289 22844) H/O: 10 Thetidos St., GR 11528 Athens (tel 1-7246766/7; fax 1-7249203; e-mail Kivotos – 1@hol.gr; www.agn.hol.gr/hotls/ Kivotos/ Kivotos/.htm). Kivotos Club Hoel is a member of the Small Luxury Hotels Group.
Receptionists (2). Must have a relevant qualification in the hospitality industry. Wage approx. £330-£360 per month. Will work 7 days a week either from 7am to 3pm or from 3 to 11pm.
Waiters/Waitresses (3) reqired to serve breakfast, lunch and dinner at the main restaurant or serve at the restaurant by the pool. Must have a relevant qualification in the hospitality industry. Wage approx. £330 to £360 per month in return for 9 hrs work a day, 7 days a week.
Maitre'D (1) to be responsible for running the food and beverage departments of the hotel. To work 11-12 hours a day, 7 days a week. Wage approx. £450 a month. Must have graduated with a qualification relating to the hospitality industry.

Board and accommodation is available for all positions. Applicants should be prepared to work for a minimum of 3 months (6 months for the Maitre'd). Knowledge of English, German, Italian or French is useful.

Applications are invited from November to the address given above for the head office for work in the following summer.

HOTEL PORTO LOUTRO: Loutro, Sfakia, Crete, Greece 73011 (tel 0825-91433/91444; fax 0825-91091). The hotel is in a village on the South coast of Crete with no cars or roads and is only accessible by foot or ferry.
Breakfast/Bar Staff for duties including evening bar work and serving breakfasts in a small English/Greek family beach hotel. Wage around £300 per month plus shared tips and accommodation. To work shift work 9 hours per day, i.e. 7.30am-3.30pm or 3.30pm-midnight. Staff are needed from April 1st until mid-October.

Applicants should be aged 22-30; no experience is necessary but should be enthusistic, honest, reliable and outgoing. *Applications* enclosing a photo and telephone number from November to February, the earlier the better, to Alison Androulakakis at the following address: 21 Papanastasiou, Hania 73100, Crete (tel/fax 0821-43941).
Boatcrew: hardworking capable and adaptable person required to assist with the hotel's brand new six berth cruiser. The work will involve night excursions, island hopping, dolphin spotting and organising beach barbecues. Practical experience of engines, sea-sports and a knowledge of boats in general required, in addition to being outgoing and good with people. Wages of around £400 per month with accommodation onboard. Period of work April-October.

Applications from November 2001 for 2002 season, contact Captain Stavros Androulakis, 21 Papanastasiou, Hania 73100, Crete (tel/fax 0821-43941), enclosing a photo and telephone number.

HOTEL RIVOLI: 10, Ahilléos Street, Athens, Greece (tel 01-5226831; fax 5245743).
Bar Staff, Couriers are needed for a two star hotel. Wage £250 per month (plus commission for couriers), free accommodation and breakfast provided. Most vacancies are for the summer but some exist around the year.
Applications to Mr Staumatis Ovvadias at the above address.

SANI BEACH HOLIDAY RESORT: 53-55 Plastira Str. GR 542 50 Thessaloniki, Greece (tel +30-31-312320/317733; fax 31-317881; e-mail hrdtrain@saniresort.gr; www.saniresort.gr/). This long established ecological resort, on the Haldiki peninsula, guarantees its guests' enjoyment by focusing on the training and motivation of its staff.
Training placements available for 18-20 year-old Hotel, Catering and Tourism trainees in this popular Greek resort, the training programme includes financial, social and cultural elements, so that this is as much a cultural exchange as a working environment. **Front of Office Staff** (10), **Sales and Marketing Staff** (3), **Bar Staff** (15), **Housekeepers** (15), **Guest Relations Staff** (5), **Kitchen Staff** (5), **Restaurant** (15), **Animators** (10) **Conference Staff** (15), **Maintenance** (5).
A basic training wage is paid plus full board and lodging, for a basic 8 hour day, overtime being paid extra. Staff work 5-6 days per week according to requirements.
Places are available form April to October, minimum period of work is 5 months. Applicants should speak English or German.
For more details *contact* Dimitrios E. Koupis at the above address.

VILLAGE INN: 300 Laganas St., Mouzaki, Zakynthos 29092, Greece (tel +30-695-51033; fax +30-695-52387; e-mail village@mail.otenet.gr). A medium size resort on the Greek island of Zakynthos, catering to a mostly British clientele.
Entertainers/Bar Staff (2) to plan, organise and perform entertaining events such as music quizzes, karaoke nights etc, and to work as bar staff in the resort's pool bar. Wages approx. £400 per month according to qualifications.
Mini-Market Staff (2) to work in the resort's mini-market. Wages c.£400 per month.
Staff work 8 hour days in 6 day weeks. Work is available between 1 May and 30 October. Board and lodging is available, and candidates should speak English.
Applications to the above address are invited from 15 March.

XENIA HOTEL: Mitilini, Lesbos, Greece.
Chambermaids (3). £60 per month.
Waiting Staff (3). £75 per month.
8 hours a day, 5 days per week. Board and accommodation free. Minimum period of work 2 months between 1 June and 15 September. *Applications* from 1 April to the above address.

Sports, Couriers and Camping

GOLDEN SUN HOLIDAYS: 150 Kentish Town Road, London, NW5 2AG (tel 0870-708 5444; fax 020-7419 0695; e-mail brochures@goldensun.co.uk; www.goldensun.co.uk). A rapidly expanding Cypriot owned tour operator with 25 years experience.
Overseas Representatives (150) to work in Greece or Cyprus for at least three

months between 1 April and 31 October assisting guests at a holiday resort. Applicants should be at least 21 years old and have 5 GCSE's and some customer service experience. Representatives will work 8-9 hours a day, 6 days a week in return for free accommodation and a salary of £300 a month plus commission. Applicants should be fluent English speakers.

Applications should be made to the above address. Interviews will be held from October for positions starting in April.

MARK WARNER. Telephone 0120-7761-7300 (24 hour).
Club Managers, Accountants, Receptionists, Watersports, Instructors, Tennis and Aerobics Instructors, Chefs, Bar Staff, Nannies, Handymen and Nightwatchmen are required to work in Beachclub Hotels in Greece during the summer from April to November. Wages from £50-£230 per week plus full board, medical insurance, travel expenses and free use of watersport and activity facilities. Some reserve staff also needed throughout the season. Requirements for languages, age, experience, qualifications etc. vary according to the job applied for. For further details, please call the Resorts Recruitment Department on the above number.

OLYMPIC HOLIDAYS 1 Torrington Park, Finchley, London N12 8NN (tel 0870-429 6060; fax 0870-429 6161; e-mail julian@olympic hoildays.co.uk; www.olympicholidays.co.uk). Olympic Holidays are one of the top specialist tour operators to Greece and Cyprus. They cover most resorts from young and lively to upmarket, and ethnic.
Overseas Resort Representatives: (100) to act as ambassadors of the comany, so applicants must be prepared to have a PR role. Duties involve airport transfers, hotel visits, guiding excursions, administration, health and safety checks, complaint handling, welcome meetings. Applicants should have customer service experience, and sales experience is preferable. Maturity, and calm manner and good organisation are all necessary skills. Wages begin at £365 a month, plus commission, flights, insurance and accommodation (meals not included). Representatives work six days per week with variable hours. Employees may be on call 24 hours a day, seven days a week.
Overseas Administrators: (20) For office based administration work, arranging flights and transfers, accomodation allocation and guest related reports. Applicants should be able to use Word, Excel, and possess general PC skills. Applicants should have good organistional skills. Wages are £475 per month, and flights, insurance and accommodation (but not food) are provided. Employees work six days a week, eight hours per day between 8am and 8pm. Hours are variable.

For both positions, Greek language skills are an advantage. *Applications* should be sent to Julian Pearl at the above address. Enclose a c.v. and covering letter explaining why you would be suitable for the role.

PAVILION TOURS: Lynnem House, 1 Victoria Way, Burgess Hill, West Sussex, RH15 9NF (tel 0870-241 0425/7; fax 0870-241 0426; e-mail: sales@ paviliontours.com; www.paviliontours.co.uk). An expanding, specialist activity tour operator for students, adults and families. Watersports include: windsurfing, dinghy sailing, water skiing with a base centre in the Saronic Gulf. Keen to recruit highly motivated staff.
Watersports Instructors (10) to instruct children during the day: sailing, canoeing etc., and assisting with entertainments in the evening. Hours of work variable, 7 days a week. Wages approx. £400 per month. Minimum period of work

1 week between May and August. Board and lodging provided. *Applications* from January to the above address, please include current instructor qualifications.

SKYROS: 92 Prince of Wales Road, London NW5 3NE (tel 020-7267 4424/020-7284 3065; fax 020-7284 3063; e-mail connect@skyros.com; www.skyros.com).
Work Scholars to assist in the smooth running of Atsitsa, a holistic holiday centre on Skyros island. Duties include cleaning, bar work, laundry, gardening and general maintenance. Wages of around £40 per week plus full board and accommodation. Variable working hours, but normally between 6 and 8 per day, 6 days per week.
Period of work three months; either April to July or July to October. Work scholars live as part of the community; in exchange for their hard work they may participate in the courses (such as yoga, dance and windsurfing) where their duties allow. Applicants must be aged over 21, with experience of communal living: qualified nurses, chefs and Greek speakers preferred. *Applications* should be sent to the above address between January and February.

Teaching and Language Schools

ENGLISH LANGUAGE SCHOOL: 66 Tepeleniou Street, New Liossia, 13123 Athens, Greece (tel Athens 5014000; e-mail jackyschool@ath.forthnet.gr; jackyschool.homestead.com/init.html)
English Teachers to teach English to Greek students (mainly teenagers) in a school with easy access to the city centre and beach. Wages according to qualifications, with national insurance covered and holidays paid. To work Monday-Friday; hours by arrangement. Period of work from mid September to May. Applicants should have a BA in English literature (an EFL qualification would be an advantage), be aged 22-30 and be happy, outgoing people genuinely interested in living in Greece. Full and extensive training is given to inexperienced teachers. *Applications* to to Jacky Wilson-Vamvaka at the above address.

ESAC: Cosmos Center, 125-127 L. Kifisias, 11524 Athens, Greece (tel/fax ++6995824). English courses for children and newly established courses for adults, professionals and students preparing for British universities. Other languages are taught in small groups of 2-3 students.
EFL Teachers for schools around Greece. Wages by arrangement: accommodation provided. To teach 25-30 hours per week. Period of work either from June to 30 September or from 1 September to 31 May. Minimum qualification necessary a BA in languages or related subject. For further details *contact* the above address enclosing an International Reply Coupon.

Voluntary Work and Archaeology

ARCHELON SEA TURTLE PROTECTION SOCIETY OF GREECE: Solomou 57, GR-104 32, Athens, Greece (tel/fax +30-1-5231342; e-mail stps@archelon.gr).
Archelon is a non-profitmaking NGO founded in 1983 to study and protect sea turtles and their habitats as well as raising public awareness. Each year over 300 volunteers participate in STPS projects.
Volunteers are required for summer fieldwork on the the islands of Zakynthos, Crete and Peloponnesus, where the Mediterranean's most important loggerhead nesting beaches are to be found. Volunteers will participate in all aspects of the

projects including tagging turtles and public relations, and receive on-site training. The work can involve long nights in the cold or long days in the heat, so a resilient, positive and friendly attitude is essential, especially as the Society's work requires constructive co-existence with local communities.

The projects run from mid-May to mid-October, with free accommodation provided at basic campsites. Volunteers will need to provide their own tents and sleeping bags; warm clothing will be required for night work as the temperature can get quite cold and smart clothes are needed when working in hotels and information stations. The minimum period of participation is 4 weeks, and there are greater needs for volunteers at each end of the project (May, June, September, October).

Volunteers are also required to work at the Sea Turtle Rescue Centre near Athens. This is a new centre set up on the coast 20km from Athens to help treat and rehabilitate turtles caught in fishing nets or injured by speedboats. Volunteers will help in the treatment of injured turtles, assisting the ongoing construction of the site and carry out public relations work with visitors. A basic knowledge of animal care is helpful but not esential. Free accommodation is provided in converted railway carriages.

Would-be volunteers for either project need to be over 18 and willing to work in teams with people from other nationalities and backgrounds. Volunteers will have to provide a participation fee of around £50 which goes towards supporting the project and includes a one year membership of the Archelon, including 3 issues of 'Turtle Tracks', their newsletter. Archelon cannot provide any financial assistance but estimates that volunteers will need to allow about £6 per day to cover food costs. Volunteers should be able to communicate in English and have their own health insurance. Successful applicants will be informed within one month of application.

Application forms can be obtained by contacting the above address including an International Reply Coupon.

CONSERVATION KORONI: Poste Restante, Koroni 240 04, Messinias, Greece. Unique opportunity of helping to protect the pre-historic turtles in their natural environment, in addition to experiencing the cultural and aesthetic attractions of Greece.
Conservation Volunteers needed for five phases over the summer; from 16 May to 15 June (15), 16 June to 15 July (15), 16 August to 15 September (15), and 16 September to 15 October (15); 25 volunteers are needed from 16 July to 15 August, to clean up the local beach and surrounding habitats of the loggerhead turtle near Koroni in the Peloponnese in southern Greece. Duties also include some monitoring of their behaviour, data recording and material preparation.

Volunteers pay for their own transport costs etc. and an accommodation charge of approx. £90 for the month. To work 1-3 hours per day, 5 days per week; some leisure activities organised in time off. No special qualifications are necessary; applicants under 18 must have adult supervision.

For further details *contact* Claire Johnston and Darren Dorsett at the above address until late May enclosing an International Reply Coupon.

CONSERVATION VOLUNTEERS GREECE: Omirou 15, GR-14562, Kifissia, Greece (tel +30-1-623 1120; fax +30-1-801 1489; e-mail cvgpeep@ otenet.gr; www.cvgpeep.org).
Volunteers required for projects in Greece between July and the end of August. Volunteers will be working on projects that have a strong emphasis on Greek culture and take place in remote areas of Greece. Volunteers will work a 7-8 hour day over a 6 day week, minimum period of work two weeks. CVG provides food, shared accommodation, and accident insurance.

Applications can be sent to the above address from 1 June. Prospective volunteers from the UK can also apply through UNA Exchanges and QVA (see *Worldwide* chapter).

ENTOPOS EMPIRICAL CENTRE FOR HOLISTIC LIVING & ECOLOGY: Akteo-Marmariou, GR-34013 Evia Island, Greece (e-mail helikon@hol.gr). Entopos is one of the first initiatives within the Helikon Politia Village for culture and ecology.
Vegetarian Cook, Gardener. Entopos is situated on a plateau overlooking the Aegean Sea; the life there is one of voluntary simplicity and meditation. Volunteers work about 35 hours per week.

No allowance is paid, but volunteers receive accommodation and food. Minimum period of work one month. Applicants should be aged at least 20. *Applications* in writing only to Tina Agiorgiti Director, at the above address.

GREEK DANCES 'DORA STRATOU' THEATRE: 8 Scholiou Street, GR-10558 Athens Plaka, Greece (tel 3244395; fax 3246921; e-mail grdance@hol.gr; http://users.hol.gr/grdance). The official government-sponsored organisation for Greek folk dance, music & costume. The theatre provides: daily performances, courses, workshops, field research programmes, books, CDs, CD-roms, tapes, videos costumes and more, related to Greek dance and folk culture.
Voluntary Trainee Assistants (2) to learn theatre management between May and October. No accommodation provided, but help may be given in finding it: the

cost will be around £20 per day. No previous experience is necessary. For further information contact Dr A. Raftis, President, at the above address.

SEA TURTLE PROJECT RHODES ISLAND: CHELON, Viale val Padana 134B, I-00141 Rome, Italy (tel +39-6-812 5301; e-mail chelon@tin.it). CHELON is a research group working to protect and obtain in-depth knowledge of marine turtles.

Volunteers (12) to help protect rare loggerhead turtle nest sites on Rhodes; until recently it was assumed that the beaches of southern Rhodes were no longer suitable for turtles to nest on. Volunteers take part in nest censuses, the protection and observation of nesting behaviour, as well as helping researchers tag turtles for ongoing observation studies. The work also involves beach vegetation studies and conservation awareness raising among local people and tourists. English, Italian and Greek language skills will therefore prove useful, but no previous experience or skills are required.

Volunteers provide their own tents for accommodation, as well as meeting travel and insurance costs, The registration fee of approx £380 covers the cost of meals. The project runs between June and September and the minimum stay is two weeks, but volunteers can stay longer subject to approval. CHELON also runs projects in Italy and Thailand. *Contact* CHELON at the above address for further information and an application form.

Au Pairs, Nannies, Family Helps and Exchanges

THE ATHENIAN NANNY AGENCY: PO Box 51181, Kifissia T.K. 145.10 Athens, Greece (tel/fax 301-808-1005; e-mail: mskiniti@groovy.gr or ivalaki@yahoo.com). An Au Pair Agency specialising in placements in Greece.
Au Pairs for short stays (2-3 months) or long stays of 12-18 months. Fluent English, French or German speakers required for holiday au pairs (full time). Carefully screened families. Agency offers 24 hour support, airport pick up and arrival orientation. Wages vary according to ages and number of children. Candidates must be aged at least 21 and able to swim. Send c.v., photos and 6 IRCs. Holiday season *applications* must be received by 10th June.

AU PAIR ACTIVITIES-KALLIOPY RAEKOU: P.O. Box 76080, 17110 Nea Smyrni, Athens, Greece (tel 30-1-93-26-016; fax 30-1-93-26-016; e-mail porae@iname.com).
Au Pairs/Summer Companions/Mothers' Helps/Nannies. Main periods of work June to August, July to August, May to September. Wages from £40 per week for 6-7 active hours a day, for six days a week up to £134 depending on the hours worked, duties and qualifications. Accommodation with the family room shared with the children or own room provided. Applicants must be aged between 18 and 29; should be fun-loving, active, adaptable and open to Greek culture and mentality. *Applications* to the above address.

LUCY LOCKETTS & VANESSA BANCROFT DOMESTIC AGENCY: 400 Beacon Road, Wibsey, Bradford, BD6 3DJ (tel/fax 01274-402822; e-mail lucylocketts@blueyonder.co.uk). Est. 1984.
Au Pairs, Au Pairs Plus, Nannies (20-30) from June to September. Child care and light housework. Age limits 17-28. Working hours: au pairs 30 hours, Monday to Friday, au pairs plus 40-45 hours weekly, Monday to Friday. Weekly wages £30-£35 for au pairs and £45-£50 au pairs plus. Nannies must be qualified

and have 1/2 year's experience and be aged 19-35. Wages £100 plus per week. Long hours, some evenings free and one day off per week.

WEIGAN NANNIES: One White's Row, London, E1 7NF (tel 020-7377 2620; fax 020-7377 0787; e-mail weigan@senatorgroup.co.uk).
Nannies (10) wanted from now until September/October for positions in holiday resorts in Greece and Turkey. The work involves nannying either alone with a family or with a group of families, changing on a weekly basis. Hours of work are 9am-5pm, 6 days per week. The nanny package includes £75 per week, flights and transfers, food, accommodation, a uniform and full access to watersports facilities, tennis and a fitness centre.

Nannies must have NNEB/BTEC, be over 18 and have an EU passport or work permit. To *apply* contact Paul Nugent, Director.

Ireland

Ireland's unemployment rate has declined significantly over the past year and in the summer of 2001 was down to 3.7%, with a long-term unemployment rate of just 1.2%. Ireland offers a number of opportunities for seasonal work. The greatest demand for summer staff is in the tourist industry which is concentrated around Dublin and in the West, South West and around the coast. Dublin is a boom town at present for the tourist industry.

There is a fair chance of finding paid work on farms and also scope for organising voluntary work. Two organisations can help those wishing to work voluntarily on Irish farms or who are interested in learning organic farming techniques; Willing Workers on Organic Farms and the Irish Organic Farmers and Growers Association. To obtain details of World Wide Opportunities on Organic Farms write to c/o Rose O'Brien, WWOOF, Harpoonstown, Drinagh, Co. Wexford, Ireland. For information enclose a stamped addressed envelope or an International Reply Coupon. For membership, enclose a subscription fee of Euros 13/£8/US$12. For information on the Irish Organic Farmers and Growers Association, contact them at Organic Farm Centre, Harbour Road, Kilbeggan, Co. Westmeath, Ireland (tel +353-506-32563; fax +353-506-32063; e-mail iofga@eircom.net; www.irishorganic.ie). N.B. *website under construction until 2002.*

The European Employment Services EURES and the government's training and employment service FÁS can help EU nationals to find work in Ireland by registering job seekers as available for suitable work, and advising on the latest position with regard to opportunities. The Irish arm of EURES is located in the FÁS offices at 27-33 Upper Baggot Street, Dublin 4 (tel +353-1-6070500; www.fasjobs-ireland.com): and FÁS has offices in most towns that may be able to help people who visit them in person. For further information consult the free booklets *Returning to Ireland* published by the Department of Social, Community and Family Affairs or *Working in Ireland* published by the UK Employment Service.

Those seeking temporary work in Ireland's hospitality and leisure industry can leave their details with www.irishjobsearch.com. Potential employers can then access the website's database and contact you to invite you to apply for jobs they are offering. Those using the service must be available to work in any job offered for a minimum of 2 months. Registering for this service is free, but jobseekers must e-mail the website each month to confirm they are still seeking employment.

Foreign students are under certain employment restrictions in Ireland with the exception of students from the USA, Canada, Australia and New Zealand, which have reciprocal agreements with Ireland. Recent changes mean that students from other nations studying in Ireland may work up to 20 hours per week in term and full-time in vacations until their permission to stay expires. As their primary cause for being in Ireland is study, work permits are not required but working beyond the above limits will be construed as a breach of the students' study visa. This change in the availability of casual work for students does not remove the financial support requirements for student visas.

In addition to the opportunities listed in this chapter voluntary work can be arranged by International Voluntary Service for British applicants and Service Civil International for Americans: see the *Worldwide* chapter for details.

Placing an advertisement in an Irish newspaper may lead to a job. The *Irish Times* can be contacted at 10-16 D'Olier Street, Dublin 2 (tel +353-1-679-2022); the *Irish Independent* and *Evening Herald* (tel 1-705-5333) are based at 90 Middle Abbey Street, Dublin.

Several newspaper websites carry information on job vacancies. You might try the websites for the *Irish Examiner* (www.examiner.ie), the *Irish Independent* (www.loadza.com), the *Irish Times* (www.ireland.com), the *Sunday Business Post* (www.sbpost.ie) or the *Sunday Tribune* (www.tribune.ie).

RED TAPE

Visa Requirements: a visa is not required by citizens of most non-Balkan European countries, Australia, Canada, New Zealand, the United States and most other countries in the Americas or the South Pacific if they are entering Ireland for a visit as tourists.

Residence Permits: those planning a stay of over three months must register with the police or the Department of Justice, Equality and Law Reform and be able to provide evidence of how they are supporting themselves.

Work Permits: are not needed by nationals of the United Kingdom or any other EEA country. Non-EEA nationals taking up paid employment in Ireland must have a valid work permit before they enter the country. This must be obtained by the prospective employer from the Department of Enterprise, Trade and Employment, Davitt House, Adelaide Road, Dublin 8. (tel +353 1 6312121). Since mid-2000, new arrangements are in place for professionals in the IT, construction and nursing sectors.

Work Visas/Authorisations: The Irish Government introduced a new visa system in 2000 for certain categories of employees from non-EEA countries, mainly in IT, construction and in the nursing profession. The new system replaces the Work Permit system for professional employees in the designated categories. Further information is available from the Department of Foreign Affairs, 80 St. Stephen's Green, Dublin 2 (tel +353-1-4780822) or from the Visa Office in the Embassy of Ireland, 106 Brompton Road, London SW 1JJ (tel 020-7235 7700 between 2:30pm and 4:30pm).

Au Pair: only nationals of EEA countries, Iceland and Switzerland can be accepted as au pairs in Ireland.

Voluntary Work: a foreigner does not need a work permit in order to take part in an organised voluntary work project in Ireland providing (a) the scheme lasts for less than three months and (b) the work is unpaid.

Hotel Work and Catering

ARDAGH HOTEL: Clifden, Co. Galway, Ireland (tel 095-21384; fax 21314; e-mail: ardaghhotel@eircom.net).

Chambermaids, Waiting/Bar Staff, Chefs, Kitchen Porters, Reception/Bar Staff. Wages according to experience: accommodation provided. Period of work from April to October. Applicants must speak English, have experience in the hotel trade and be flexible and have an interest in catering. *Applications* to Mr and Mrs Bauvet at the above address.

ATLANTIC BAR: The Square, Kenmare, Co. Kerry, Ireland (064-41094).
Bar/Catering Staff to work in a busy pub for the summer season May-September. Work includes bar service and general duties. Outgoing personality and willingness to learn essential. Accommodation provided. *Applications* should be sent in writing to the above address.

CARAGH LODGE: Caragh Lake, Co. Kerry, Ireland (tel +353-66-976 9115; fax +353-66-976 9316; e-mail caraghl@iol.ie). An award winning small country house hotel with 15 bedrooms and a 40 seat restaurant.
Waitresses for morning and evening shifts 8am-1pm and 7pm-11pm, and to help with room cleaning.
Kitchen Staff for evening shifts only 7pm-11pm.
Housekeeping Staff for morning and evening shifts as above.
Staff are required from April to October and work a maximum of 45 hours per week over a 5-6 day week: the minimum period of work is 5 months. Wages are by negotiation based on previous hotel experience. Free accommodation is provided for suitable employees in a staff cottage, situated 1.5 km from the premises.
Applications are accepted from November onwards.

CASTLE LESLIE: Glaslough, Co Monaghan, Ireland (tel +353-47-88109; fax +353-47-88256; e-mail ultan@castle-leslie.ie; www.castleleslie.com). Irish country castle with specialist accommodation catering to local and international clientele.
Commis Chef to work in the restaurant kitchens under the supervision of a senior chef, preparing meals for guests. Wages £150 per week.
Restaurant Staff (3) to wait on tables under the supervision of the restaurant manager. Previous experience required but further training will be given. Wages £120-£160 per week, depending on experience.
Front of House Staff to process check-in and check-out of guests and generally look after guests' needs. Should be computer literate, with some telephone skills, further training provided. Wages £160 per week.
Restaurant and front of house staff should be fluent English speakers. Staff work a 40 hour, 5 day week, and work is available any time of year. The minimum period of work varies according to position, between 3 months (kitchen) and 6 months (restaurant/front of house). Board and lodging is available.
Applications are invited at any time to Samantha Leslie at the above address.

DELPHI LODGE: Leenane, Co. Galway, Ireland (tel +353-954 2222; fax +353-954 2296; e-mail delfish@iol.ie; www.delphilodge.com). A country hotel and fishing lodge in a stunning but remote valley in Connemara, on the west coast of Ireland.
Housekeeper (4), Waitress (4), Kitchen Help (2), Chef/Cook required to work as part of a team running this remote fishing lodge/country house hotel. Wages £150 per week. Board and lodging is included.
Staff work 8 hours per day, five days per week. Work is available from February to October, and the minimum period of work is two months. Applicants should have a good grasp of English.
Applications for these posts will be accepted from February.

EVISTON HOUSE HOTEL: Killarney, Co. Kerry, Ireland. The Eviston House is a family run hotel in the centre of beautiful Killarney. It comprises 75 rooms, the 'Colleen Bawn' restaurant, the famous 'Danny Mann' Pub and 'Scoundrels' nightclub. Staff are admitted free to pub and nightclub when off duty.
Bar Staff. Minimum age 18 years. Wages on application.
Chefs all grades of chef required.
Receptionists experience preferred.
Waiter/Waitress. Wages on application. Preferably with experience. Minimum age 18 years.
Minimum period of work 4 months between May and September. *Applications* during March/April to the above address.

GOLF LINKS HOTEL: Glengariff, Co. Cork, Ireland.
Waitresses (3). Wages on application. Average 55 hours per week. Minimum age 17 years.
Barmaid. Wages and hours as above. Minimum age 19 years.
Hall Porter. Wages and hours as above. Minimum age 18 years.
Laundry Maid. Wages as above. Average 40 hours per week. Minimum age 18 years.
Housemaids (2). Wages and hours as above. Minimum age 17 years.
Chef/Cook. Wages and hours as above. Must have some experience of commercial catering. Free board and accommodation. Minimum period of work 5 weeks between mid-May and September. *Applications* from April to the above address.

THE OLDE RAILWAY HOTEL: The Mall, Westport, County Mayo, Ireland (tel +353-98-25166; fax 353-98-25090; e-mail railway@anu.ie; www.anu.ie/ railwayhotel). Charming 18th Century coaching inn, situated alongside the Carrowbeg river in the centre of the pretty town of Westport. Plenty to do in time off; new town leisure centre, beaches, walks, fishing etc.
Cooks, Chefs and **Waiting Staff** (4) to work 40 hours per five-day week. Pay from £700 per month plus free board and lodging. Must have relevant experience/qualifications. Minimum period of work 2 months; staff required all year round. Knowledge of English essential. *Applications* to Karl Rosenkranz at the above address.

PARK LODGE HOTEL: Park, Spiddal, County Galway, Ireland (tel 091-553159; fax 091-553494).
Chef to cook 30-40 mainly *table d'hote* dinners per day. Duties to include planning and providing full meals of starters, soups, main courses and desserts in straightforward Irish/English cuisine. Wage of approx. £700 per month. Normal working hours from 1-9pm, 5 days per week. Board and accommodation provided free of charge in basic/spartan accommodation shared with other staff; meals on a 'help yourself' basis. Minimum period of work by arrangement between early June and late September. *Applications* to Geraldine Foyle at the above address as soon as possible.

SINNOTT HOTELS: Furbo, Co. Galway, Ireland 9 (tel 091-592108). This quality employer hotel is a leading four star property in the west of Ireland, and is part of a progressive group. There is a strong emphasis on professional customer service.
Chefs/Commis Waiting Staff, House Assistants, Bar Staff, Porters. Wages by arrangement, depending on experience. For shift work, five days per week. Minimum period of work three months between April and October. Applicants

should be able to speak English; previous experience is desirable but not essential. *Applications* to the above address from January.

ZETLAND COUNTRY HOUSE HOTEL: Cashel Bay, Connemara, Co Galway, Ireland (tel 095-31111; fax 095-31117; e-mail zetland@iol.ie; www.connemara.net/zetland/). A 4-star country house hotel on Ireland's west coast.

Receptionist for reception desk work, welcoming guests etc.
Commis Chef (2) for breakfast and dinner catering.
Waiter/Waitress (4) to serve guests at breakfast and dinner.
Housekeeper to oversee upkeep of house and guest rooms.
Chambermaid (4) to clean and tidy guest rooms.
Kitchen Porter (2) for general kitchen duties.

Apart from the kitchen porter and chambermaid positions some previous hotel/catering experience is necessary. Staff wages are £480 (except for Housekeeper £600) per month live in. Hours of work are 8-10 per day within a 5¹/2 day week. Period of work 1 April-31 October, with a minimum period of work of one month. All staff should speak English.

Applications from 1st March to the above address.

Sports, Couriers and Camping

ERRISLANNAN MANOR: Clifden, West Galway, Ireland (tel 353-95-21134). The manor is situated on Ireland's western seaboard, where the Gulf Stream allows palm trees and fuschias to grow. The local habitat of sandy beaches and rockpools is home to wonderful seabirds, sea shells and wildflowers.

Au Pair, Receptionist and Coffee Shop Assistant. £50 per week. To work between June and August, also to help in the stables.
Junior Trek Leader. £50 per week. Flat provided. Knowledge of languages essential.
Senior Trek Leader and Instructor £100 plus per week (negotiable). Should have BHSAI or ICES qualifications. Flat provided.

To work with 30 Connemara ponies on a trekking and riding centre mainly for children, the manor also breeds and schools ponies. Hours from 8.30am-5.30pm daily. Minimum period of work 3 months between early April and the end of September. Knowledge of French or German an advantage. *Applications* to Mrs S. Brooks at the above address during January and February.

Voluntary Work and Archaeology

THE BARRETSTOWN GANG CAMP FUND: Barretstown Castle, Ballymore Eustace, County Kildare, Ireland. (Tel: + 353 45 864115; fax + 353 45 864711; email anne-marie.browne@barretstowngc.ie; www.barretstowngc.ie)
The camp provides a powerful activity-based, therapeutic recreation programme for seriously ill children aged from seven to sixteen years, and their families, from twenty countries throughout Europe.
Volunteers are a vital part of the camp's programme and generously donate their time over a weekend during spring or autumn, or ten days during one of our summer sessions. Meals and accommodation are provided.
Paid Staff (Caras and Activity Leaders) required for the summer programme, period of work available June until mid-September 2002. These places are residential positions, meals and accommodation are provided. Candidates must

be available for the full summer period.

Cara – responsible for attending to the daytime and night-time needs and providing emotional support for the children in their care. They encourage the children to participate fully in all aspects of camp and gain maximum benefit from their experience.

Activity Leader – Responsible for the designing, planning, and leading groups of children in one or more of the following activities: Arts & Crafts, Archery, Camping, Canoeing, Drama, Film, High Ropes, Low Ropes, Creative Writing, Equestrian, Fishing, Music, Nature, Photography, Pottery, Woodwork.

All staff must be a minimum of 19 years old, before April 2001 *and fluent in English*. Application packs, forms and further information can be obtained through the website or by post from Anne-Marie Browne, European Staff Recruitment Co-ordinator at the above address. Closing date for the receipt of applications is Monday 15 February 2002.

PILGRIM ADVENTURE: 120 Bromley Heath Road, Downend, Bristol BS16 6JJ (tel 0117-957 3997). Pilgrim Adventure groups travel light, sharing fellowship and food while exploring Ireland and also the remoter Celtic parts of Great Britain. Pilgrim Adventure is an ecumenical Christian organisation founded in 1987.

Volunteers (4) to help lead groups of all ages 10-25 people and assist with worship and general chores in Ireland and Great Britain. Volunteers receive full board accommodation and travel. To work on average 35 hours a week. Minimum period of work 6 weeks between May and October. Help occasionally required at other times, including opportunities to join a year-round team of volunteers who plan and reconnoitre Pilgrim journeys. Must have experience and an interest in outdoor activities, especially hill walking.

Applications from January to David Gleed, Chair, at the above address.

CONSERVATION VOLUNTEERS IRELAND: The Green, Griffith College, South Circular Road, Dublin 8, Ireland (tel/fax 01-454 7185; fax 01-454 6935). Conservation Volunteers Ireland is an agency that co-ordinates, organises and promotes environmental working holidays. Volunteers are required to work on the conservation of Ireland's natural and cultural heritage: no previous experience is required as full training is provided on site, but a knowledge of English is essential. Volunteers work 8 hours per day. Please note that this work is unpaid; board and lodging are provided at a reasonable cost. Work ranges from 3 days to 2 weeks all year round. *Applications* to the above address for further information and a booking form.

SIMON COMMUNITY OF IRELAND: St Andrews House, 28-30 Exchequer Street, Dublin 2, Ireland (tel +353-1 671 1606; fax +353-1 671 1098; e-mail catri.okane@iol.ie; www.simoncommunity.com). The Simon Community of Ireland has Communities in Cork, Dundalk Dublin and Galway. They aim to provide accommodation and services for the homeless and long term to eliminate homelessness.

Volunteers required to work alongside homeless men and women in Ireland. The main duties of the volunteer include befriending residents and general housekeeping. Volunteers work shifts and receive full board and lodging. In addition they receive £50 per week allowance and regular holidays. A minimum commitment of 6 months is required. Applicants must be 18 years of age. For more information contact Catri O'Kane at the above address.

VOLUNTARY SERVICE INTERNATIONAL: 30 Mountjoy Square, Dublin 1, Ireland (tel 855-1011; fax 855-1012; e-mail vsi@iol.ie; http://homepages. iol.ie/vsi). **Volunteers** to work with VSI (the Irish branch of Service Civil International). The aim of the organisation is to promote peace and understanding through voluntary service in Ireland and throughout the world. VSI organise 30 short term voluntary workcamps in Ireland each summer and we welcome the participation of volunteers from other countries. Enquiries must go through your local SCI Branch or workcamp organisation.

Other Employment Abroad

AILLWEE CAVE CO. LTD.: Ballyvaughan, Co. Clare, via Galway, Ireland (tel +353-65-7077036; fax 065-7077107; e-mail aillwee@eircom.net; www.aillweecave.ie). Ireland's premier show cave, Aillwee Cave is situated in a remote rural area of the famous region the 'Burren'. It is a place of wonder, beauty and discovery. From the terrace there are breathtaking views of Galway Bay and the Connemara Mountains.

Cave Tour Guides (5) to lead a maximum of 35 persons on a 45 minute tour through the caves. Wages are (Euros 810) £500 approx. per month gross, plus tips. Training will be given. Knowledge of geology a help but not essential.

Catering Staff (6) to work as counter hands for the salad bar, fast food outlet and potato bar. From (Euros 889) £550 gross per month. Experience necessary.

Sales Staff (4) to work in the gift shop. From £550 per month. Previous experience an advantage.

Sales Staff (2) to work in a farm shop in which cheese is made daily on the premises. Wage as above.

For all positions, hours of work are 40 hours over 5 days a week. Minimum period of work 2 months; work commences March, majority of staff needed by the end of April. Board and shared accommodation are available at the staff hostel at a cost to be arranged. Proficiency in English essential and a genuine wish to work in tourism. *Applicants from outside the EU must be in possession of a current work permit and health insurance.*

Applications from December to Susan Johnson, Director, at the above address.

Au Pairs, Nannies, Family Helps and Exchanges

DUBLIN SCHOOL OF ENGLISH: 10-12 Westmoreland Street, Dublin 2, Ireland (tel 01-677 3322; fax 01-671 8451/679 5454; e-mail: Admin@dse.ie; www.dse.ie/dse).

Au Pairs placed with Irish families for periods of from 3 to 12 months. 30-35 hours per week. Pocket money allowance of around £140 per month, plus free board and accommodation. Minimum age 18, maximum age 24. Basic knowledge of English required: suited to students of limited means who wish to improve their English. Attendance of English classes is compulsory.

Italy

The rate of unemployment in Italy stands at approximately 12%. The best chances of obtaining paid employment in Italy are probably with the tour operators in this and the *Worldwide* chapter at the beginning of the book. Other possibilities involve teaching English as a foreign language, though most who get jobs have a TEFL qualification and are prepared to stay longer than a few months of the summer. If you want to try and find this sort of job once you are in Italy look up *Scuole di Lingua* in the *Yellow Pages*. Those with special skills are most likely to find work: for example an experienced secretary with a good knowledge of English, Italian and German would be useful in a hotel catering for large numbers of German, British and American tourists. Otherwise it is surprisingly difficult to find work in hotels and catering. People looking for hotel work while in Italy should do best if they try small hotels first: some large hotel chains in northern resorts take on staff from southern Italy, where unemployment is especially high, for the summer season and then move them on to their mountain ski resorts for the winter season.

Although Italy is the world's largest producer of wine, a similar problem exists with the grape harvest (*vendemmia*): vineyard owners traditionally employ migrant workers from North Africa and other Arab countries to help the local work force. Opportunities are best in the north west of the country, for example in the vineyards lying south east of Turin in Piemonte, and in the north east in Alto Adige and to the east and west of Verona. The harvest generally takes place from September to October. For details of the locations of vineyards consult the *World Atlas of Wine* by Hugh Johnson (Mitchell Beazley, £30) in a public library; the same publishers also produce the useful *Touring in Wine Country: Tuscany* (£12.99).

There are other possibilities for fruit picking earlier in the year, but again there will be competition for work. Strawberries are picked in the region of Emilia Romagna in June, and apples are picked from late August in the region of Alto Adige and in the Valtellina, which lies between the north of Lake Como and Tirano. More information about finding casual farm work is given in *Work Your Way Around the World* (see the *Useful Publications* chapter). When in Italy you should be able to get information on local harvest work from *Centri Informazione Giovani* (Youth Information Offices) which exist throughout the country for the benefit of local young people: consult telephone directories for their addresses.

EU nationals are allowed to use the Italian state employment service when looking for a job in Italy; its head office is the *Ministero del Lavoro* at Via Flavia 6 in Rome. To find the addresses of local employment offices in Italy either write to the above Italian address or look for the *Ufficio del Lavoro* in the telephone directory of the area where you are staying. Note that these offices will only deal with personal callers. For further information consult the free booklet *Working in Italy* published by the UK Employment Service.

International Voluntary Service (IVS), Youth Action for Peace, UNA Exchange and Concordia can assist British applicants to find voluntary work in Italy, and Service Civil International and Council: International Volunteer Projects can aid Americans; see the *Worldwide* chapter for details.

An advertisement in an Italian newspaper may produce an offer of employment. Smyth International, 1 Torrington Park, London N12 9GG deal with *La Stampa* (Turin daily), and other provincial papers. The Milan paper *Il Giornale* is published at Via Gaetano Negri 4, I-20123 Milan.

RED TAPE

Visa Requirements: full citizens of the United Kingdom, of the United States, Australia, New Zealand and most western European countries do not require a visa for visits of up to 3 months.

Residence Permits: visitors staying in a hotel will be registered with the police automatically. Those intending to stay for more than 3 months should apply to the local police at the *Questura* (local police headquarters) for a *permesso di soggiorno* which is valid for 90 days. If you arrive with the intention of working, EEA nationals must first apply to the police *(questura)* for a *Ricevuta di Segnalazione di Soggiorno* which allows them to stay for up to three months looking for work. Upon production of this document and a letter from an employer, you must go back to the police to obtain a residence permit – *Permesso di Soggiorno*. Then in some cases you will be asked to apply for a *Libretto di Lavoro* (work registration card) from the town hall or *Municipio* (although, in theory, this should not be necessary for EU nationals).

Work Permits: a work permit is issued by the local authorities to the prospective employer, who will then forward it to the worker concerned. Non-EU citizens must obtained the permit before entering Italy.

Au Pair: work permits are normally required except for EU/EEA nationals and those of countries holding agreements with Italy such as New Zealand.

Domestic Work

A.R.C.E.: Attività Relazioni Culturali con l'Estero, Via XX Settembre, 20/124, 16121 Genova, Italy (tel 010-583020; fax 010-583092; e-mail arceita@tin.it; http://space.tin.it/associazioni/chiorl). Their Italian families are well selected and applicants can choose placements between large and small towns, as well as being able to rely on A.R.C.E. for support.

Au Pairs (100)/Mothers' Helps (50) for placements in Italy; to babysit and perform a little light housework. Au pairs work 6 hours a day, mothers' helps work 8 hours a day, 6 days a week. Wages approx. £150-£240 per month. Board and accommodation provided. Applicants should be aged between 18 and 30. Minimum period of work 1 month from June/July to end of August/September. Childcare experience essential. Knowledge of English and possibly Italian required.

Applications (male or female) from April to the above address.

Hotel Work and Catering

THREE HOTELS ON ITALY'S LAGO D'ORTA: Hotel L'Approdo, Villa Crespi, Hotel Giardinetto: for address see below. The Lake D'Orta is a popular tourist destinatin, full of marvellous gardens and green meadows in a Mediterranean haven. Attracions on offer include watersports, horse-riding, golf and tennis.

Assistant Receptionists (2-3) required for reception tasks, language skills helpful.
Chambermaids (2-3) to clean hotel rooms.
Waiting Staff (2-3) to serve meals and beverages.
Kitchen Staff (2-3) to help prepare food for meals and desserts.

Staff required for all posts from May until September, minimum period of work 3 months. Staff work 8-9 hours per day over a $5^1/2$ day week. All posts come with board and accommodation in addition to wages varying between £130-£190 approx. according to position. Applicants should speak at least English and Italian.

To apply contact Caterina Primatesta at the Hotel Giardinetto, Via Provinciale 1, Pettenasco, ITALY (tel +39-323-89118; fax +39-323-89219; e-mail hotelgiardinetto@tin.it; www.lagodortahotels.com).

ALBERGO RISTORANTE COLIBRI: Via Cristoforo Colombo 57, I-17024 Finale Ligure (Savona), Italy.
Commis Waiters to set and clear tables and clean dining room. Some hotel experience an advantage.

Chambermaids for general cleaning duties and room service. Experience and some knowledge of languages an advantage.
Dishwashers to operate dish washing machine, assist cooks and clean the kitchens.
Salaries for all positions approximately £530 per month. To work 9 hours per day, 6 days per week. Free board and accommodation provided. Applicants must be available for at least 4 months between March and October and be at least 18 years of age. *Applications* as soon as possible to the above address.

HOTEL CANNERO: I-28821 Cannero Riviera, Lake Maggiore, Italy (tel +39-323-788046; fax +39-323-788048; e-mail info@hotelcannero.com).
Receptionist. To work 10 hours per day, 6 days per week. Free board and accommodation. Knowledge of English, basic German and Italian required. Period of work 5 months between April and September.
Chambermaid. To help in the bar and the garden. Working hours and period of work approximately as for receptionist
Applications at the above address.

HOTEL CAPO SUD: I-57037 Lacona, Isola d'Elba, Italy.
Waiter. Knowledge of Italian and German required.
Receptionist. Knowledge of Italian and German required. Applicants must be of good appearance.
Night Porter. With cleaning duties
Applications from January to the above address.

HOTEL CAVALLINO D'ORO: I-39040 Castelrotto (BZ), Sudtirol, Dolomites, Italy (tel 0-471-706337; fax 0-471-707172; e-mail cavallino@cavallino.it; www.cavallino.it). This carefully renovated hotel in the old village square of Kastelruth, dates from 1393, thus it has a history of hospitality spanning 600 years.
Assistant Manager (1), **Waiters**(2), **Kitchen Helps**(2), **Dish Washers** (2), **Chambermaids** (2). Wage depends upon experience and qualifications. To work 8 hours per day, 6 days per week. Minimum period of work 10 weeks. Free board and lodging provided. Knowledge of German and/or Italian would be an advantage, and is essential for the managerial position. *Applications* to the above address from January.

HOTEL CONTINENTAL: I-44024 Lido di Spina/FE, Italy.
Kitchen Staff (2 females). £200-£220 per month. To do general kitchen work.
Waitresses (5). Salary as above.
Room Maids (5). Salary as above. To clear rooms.
Staff work an average of 8 hours per day, 6 days a week. Board and accommodation free. Minimum period of work 4 months between May and October. *Applications* for both to Ennio E. Casacci at the Hotel Continental.

HOTEL EDEN GIGLI: Viale Morelli 11, I-60026 Numana (AN), Riviera del Conero, Italy (tel 071-9330652; fax 071-9330930). This 35 bed, family-run hotel is situated by a sheer drop overlooking the sea, near Mount Conero. The hotel places emphasis on peace and restfulness, and the owners aim to meet the needs of their employees as well as their customers.
Waiters (2-3) Must have a good knowledge of Italian and at least two years' experience. To work 8 hours per day, split shifts. Wages £575-735 depending on experience.

Bar Staff: male or female applicants must have a good knowledge of Italian and experience in mixing cocktails (at least four years). To work 5:30pm to 1:30 am. Wages £735-895 depending on experience.
Receptionist Applicant must have a good knowledge of Italian/German, and a thorough knowledge of computers. To work seven hours a day, split shifts. Wages £510-640 depending on experience.
Employees for all positions will work eight to nine hours per day, seven days a week. Minimum period of work is three months between 10th June and 10th September. Board and accommodation is provided free of charge. *Applications* accepted from March 2002 onwards.

COUNTRY HOTEL FATTORIA DI VIBIO: Doglio, I-06057 Montecastelo di Vibio (PG), Italy (tel 075-8749607; fax 075-8780014; e-mail info@ fattoriadivibio.com; www.fattoriadivibio.com). A family-run country house.
Barman/Waiter required to serve at tables in the restaurant/bar.
Chambermaid required to clean rooms and carry out other general cleaning jobs.
    Salary approximately £265 per month, board and accommodation provided.
Applicants should have relevant experience, be 20 to 35 years of age and have a basic knowledge of spoken Italian and English. Minimum 2 month stay required between 15 June and 15 September, working 8 hours a day, 6 days a week.
    Applications are invited to the above address from February 2002.

HOTEL DES GENEYS SPLENDID: Bardonecchia, Italy (fax +39-122-999295; e-mail geneys@libero.it). A hotel with a youthful and family atmosphere. An ideal place to learn Italian, to study and to rest in a beauty spot.
Chambermaids (2) for general duties. Wages by arrangement. 6 day week of 48 hours. Free board and accommodation. Knowledge of French required. Minimum period of work July and August. *Applications* from May to the above address.

GRAND HOTEL CESENATICO: Forli, Italy.
Secretary. Duties include bookkeeping and reception work. Knowledge of several languages required.
Waiters: duties by arrangement.
    8 hours per day. Wages by arrangement, with free board and accommodation provided. Must have knowledge of French and German. Minimum period of work 3 months between 1st June and 20th September. *Applications* in February to the address above.

HOTEL PENSIONE LA LANTERNA: Via Osteria, I-53030 Livigno (50) Italy.
Kitchen Staff: (2 females). £160-£180 per month to do general kitchen work.
Waitresses (5). Salary as above.
Room Maids (2). Salary as above. To clear rooms.
    Staff work an average of 9 hours per day, 6 days a week. Free board and accommodation. Minimum period of work 2 months between May and October. *Applications* to Ennio E. Casacci at the above address.

POSTA HOTEL POST: I-39043 Chiusa-Klausen, Sudtirol, Italy (tel 0472-847514; fax 0472-846210).
Chambermaid. Wage approximately £500 per month. To work 6 days per week. A knowledge of German and Italian would be an advantage, but is not essential. *Applications* to Johannes Reiserer at the above address.

RELAI CA' MASIERI: I-36070 Trissino, Italy (tel 445-490122; fax 445-490455). **Waiters/Waitresses, Kitchen Staff.** Wages around £80 per week. To work 8-12 hours a day, 5-6 days a week. Free board and accommodation provided. Period of work 3-6 months between end of March and end of October. Knowledge of German, Italian or French required. *Applications* as soon as possible to Mr Vassena Angelo.

PARKHOTEL VILLA GRAZIOLI: Via Umberto Pavoni 19, I-0046 Grottaferrata, Rome (tel 0039-06-9454001; fax 0039-06-9413506; e-mail info@villagrazioli.com; www.villagrazioli.com). This historic sixteenth century hotel, sited 20km from Rome, belongs to the international association, 'Relais and Chateaux'.
Waitresses (2). To work in restaurant and bar. Some English and French required. Wages c.£310 (Euros 500) per month.
Reception Clerk Must speak English and French. Wages c.£310 (Euros 500) per month.
Chambermaid. Wages c.£245 (Euros 400) per month.
All employees to work eight hours per day, five days a week between mid July and the end of August. Board and accommodation is provided. *Applications* should be sent to the above address from March.

HOTEL VILLA S.MICHELS: via Della Chiesa 462, Masa Pisana, 55050 Lucca, Italy (tel 0039.0583.370276; fax 0583.370277; e-mail tlvillasmichele@ tin.it; www.hotelsivllasanmichele.it). This hotel is featured in all major hotel guides.
Receptionists (2) to carry out standard receptionist duties, and also help with secretarial and hostessing work. Fluency in English is important, and a knowledge and willingness to learn French or Italian would also be useful. Knowledge of eastern European languages advantageous. The successful applicants will work 7 hours a day, 6 days a week, for at least a week between 1 March and 30 November. Minimum age 20. Board and accommodation are provided with a salary of £600 per month.
Applications are invited as soon as possible to the above address. Please enclose c.v. and photo.

Industrial, Sales and Office Work

WELCOME HOTELS & RESORTS: Via Bologna 1043, I-44100, Ferrara, Italy (tel 0039-532-713604; fax 0039-532-713609; e-mail welcotel@tin.it).
Translator and Computer Application Person and **Telephone Marketing Person** (1) to translate text from Italian to English and put text on computer for a readership of tourists, writing English messages and news for an English newspaper. Bed and breakfast accommodation provided plus £25 weekly. To work 4 hours, 5 days a week. Minimum period of work 2 weeks between June and 10 August. Applicants must be Italian and English speaking, and provide a reference and personal assurance. This position is not centrally located and requires people who like to live a simple life. *Applications* from 1 May at the above address; e-mail communication will be preferred.

Sports, Couriers and Camping

CANVAS HOLIDAYS: East Port House, 12 East Port, Dunfermline, Fife KY12 7JG (tel 01383-629018; fax 01383-629071; www.canvas holidayscom). Canvas

Holidays are looking for enthusiastic, resourceful people who enjoy a challenge and love the outdoor life. Main positions for 2002 include:

Campsite Courier. Varied responsibilities. Involves cleaning and preparation of customer accommodation, welcoming and looking after customers during their holiday and ensuring that they have the best holiday ever. As a campsite courier you will have new challenges every day which can lead to one of the most enjoyable summers you will ever have. Variable working hours.

Children's Courier. As a Canvas Holidays Children's Courier you will have had formal experience of working with children. You will organise and carry out a six day programme which involves four hours a day of Children's Club for children between the ages of 4 and 11. You will be prepared to help out with courier duties as and when requried. For many customers, the Children's Club is one of the main parts of the holiday. You will need to have the energy of a seven year old and the imagination of an eleven year old to succeed!

Package includes tented accommodation, medical insurance, full uniform and return travel to and from a UK port of entry. Positions are available from March until October. *Applications* are invited from individuals and couples. Contact Sandy, Karen or Michele at the above contact details for an application pack.

EUROCAMP: Overseas Recruitment Department (Ref SJ/02) (tel 01606-787522). Eurocamp is a leading tour operator in quality self-drive camping and mobile home holidays in Europe. Each year the company seeks to recruit up to 1,500 enthusiastic people for the following positions:

Courier: job involves cleaning and preparing customer accommodation, providing assistance, acting as an information service and an interpreter and performing some administrative duties. Couriers need to be flexible to meet the needs of the customer to provide them with excellent service. Minimum age 18 years. Applicants should be independent with plenty of initiative and relish a challenging and rewarding position. They should also possess a friendly and helpful personality. Some working knowledge of another European language is required and previous customer service experience would be an advantage. Applicants should be available to work from April/May to September.

Children's Couriers: work involves organising a wide range of exciting activities for children aged 4-13. Applicants should possess initiative, imagination and enthusiasm along with good safety awareness. Previous childcare experience is essential. Minimum age is 18 years and applicants should be available from April/May to September. Languages are not a requirement but would be an advantage.

Senior Couriers: required to work alongside a team of Campsite Couriers and organise their daily workload, as well as carrying out the normal day to day duties of a Campsite Courier. Applicants should have good language skills and experience of leading a team.

Site Managers: required to lead a large team of Campsite Couriers, organising their daily workloads and ensuring they provide the very best customer service. Applicants should be 21 or over, have proven managerial experience, excellent communication skills and language ability.

In all the above positions you should be be available for the full season commencing in April/May through to September. Comprehensive training is provided together with a competitive salary, insurance and return travel. Applications are accepted from September/October and *can only be accepted from UK/EU passport holders.* Interviews will be conducted in Hartford, Cheshire between October and April.

HAVEN EUROPE: 1 Park Lane, Hemel Hempstead HP2 4YL. Haven Europe Ltd have provided self-drive family camping holidays for over 20 years. They are part of the Bourne Leisure Group, who are the largest, privately owned leisure company in the UK.

Courier Staff to work on campsites in Italy. Staff receive free accommodation, a competitive salary, uniform and insurance. Duties include preparation of guest accommodation, reception and problem solving. Working hours are long and variable. Applicants should be available from March to the end of September. Previous experience would be an advantage. Mature couples are invited to apply.

Children's Courier Staff to work on the same parks; duties include organisation and implementation of an activity programme for children. Staff receive free accommodation, uniform and a competitive salary. Experience with children an advantage and a genuine liking of working with children is essential. Applicants should be available from March/May to early September, be at least 19 years of age. Italian an advantage but not essential.

Please write to the above address requesting an application form.

HEADWATER HOLIDAYS: 146 London Road, Northwich, Cheshire CW9 5HH (tel 01606-813333; fax 01606-813334; e-mail info@headwater.com; www.headwater-holidays.co.uk). Holidays travelling at the customers pace, on foot by bike or in a canoe through beautiful unspoilt regions.

Overseas Representatives to work for an activity holiday company in Italy. Duties include meeting clients at airports and stations, supervising local transportation for them and their luggage, hotel and client liaison, bike maintenance and on the spot problem solving. Good working Italian, and full clean driving licence required. Organisational skills, resourcefulness and cheerfulness essential. Minimum age 21 years.

Wages from £100-£150 per week; accommodation provided. To work hours as required. Staff required full season from April to October. Further information and on-line applications to be found on their website, or an applicaton form can be requested from the above address.

KEYCAMP HOLIDAYS: Overseas Recruitment Department, Hartford Manor, Greenbank Lane, Nothwich CW8 1H (tel 01606-787522).

Campsite Couriers: to look after British, Dutch and Scandinavian customers on campsites in Italy. Duties include welcoming customers, providing local information, organising social activities on site and ensuring that all accommodation is prepared prior to arrival.

Children's Courier: to organise and provide up to 24 hours of activities per week for children aged 4-13 years, to advertise the club activities and visit families on arrival.

Senior Couriers: incorporating the role of campsite courier with the additional responsibility of organising and managing the team and ensuring the smooth running of the Keycamp operation on site.

Montage/Demontage: for a period of approximately 6 weeks at the beginning/end of season to erect/dismantle equipment.

Minimum age 18 years. Accommodation, uniform and training provided. A working knowledge of Italian would be an advantage. Period of employment between March and July-October.

Applicants should write to the Overseas Recruitment Department, Keycamp Holidays, quoting reference SJ/02.

MARK WARNER: Telephone 020-7761-7300 (24 hour).
Club Managers, Accountants, Receptionists, Watersports Instructors, Tennis and Aerobics Instructors, Chefs, Waiting and Bar Staff, Nannies, Handymen and Nightwatchmen are required to work in Beachclub Hotels in Italy and Sardinia during the summer from April to November. Wages from £50-£230 per week plus full board, medical insurance, travel expenses and free use of watersport and activity facilities. Some reserve staff also needed throughout the season. Requirements for languages, age, experience, qualifications etc. vary according to the job applied for. For further details, please call the Resorts Recruitment Department on the above number.

Work With Children

SMILE: v.Vignolese 454, I-41100 Modena, Italy (tel +39-059-363868; fax 059-363868).
Tutors (8-10) required to take classes in English and supervise games and sporting activities involving groups of 10-12 children. Applicants should be between 20 and 25 years old, well-behaved and cheery with an interest in culture, be keen and able sportsmen and should play a musical instrument. Experience of working with children and any relevant special abilities would be an advantage. Applicants will work from 9am to 5pm from Monday to Friday and for two hours on Saturday morning. There will be a day of training in Modena before the placement begins.
    Applicants should be prepared to work between either 12 June and 15 July or 28 Aug and 16 Sept. Free accommodation and food will be provided, as will a wage of between £100 and £120 per week. There will also be the opportunity to travel in Italy; SMILE may be able to pay for a part of the cost of a flight to Italy.
    Applications to the above address.

SUMMER CAMPS: Via Roma 54, 18038 San Remo, Italy (tel/fax +39-0184-506070; e-mail: info@acle.org; www.acle.org). Summer Camps is a non-profit association which was the first in Italy to teach English through Theatre in Education and organise drama courses recognised by the Italian Ministry of Education.
Summer Camp Counsellors/Tutors required in camps throughout Italy. Working in association with the Italian Ministry for Education, ACLE provides full immersion English camps for Italian children. Staff would be expected to work eight to ten hours a day, at residential and non-residential camps, providing fun and exciting programmes in English for children between 5 and 16. Applicants must be over 18, native Englsih speakers and have the ability to create English lessons involving songs, games, sport, art and drama. Successful applicants will be invited to San Remo for full training and introductory TEFL course prior to working between 2 and 10 weeks. Applicants must love working with children and have energy and enthusiasm. *Application forms* and details on the web site. Applications accepted between January and April.

THEATRINO: Via Roma 54, I-18038 San Remo, Italy (tel/fax +39-0184-506070; e-mail info@acle.org; www.acle.org). Theatrino is part of ACLE, a non-profit organisation, which was the first to teach English to children and teenagers through Theatre in Education (TIE), and to organise drama courses recognised by the Italian Ministry of Education for Teachers. This small touring English language theatre company and the small routing French language theatre company both recruit from January to April, April to June and September to December (auditions one month prior to tour start).

English Speaking TIE Actors and **French Speaking TIE Actors** To work in teams of three (two female, one male) travelling around Italy providing interactive graded language shows to Italian children between 5 and 19. Scripts range from basic nursery rhymes to Shakespeare, with a wide range of acting talents requrd. Actors would work a minimum of four hours a day with a combination of shows and worksops. Each team must drive on average 100km per day and be responsible for shows, workshops, props, finances and daily reports. ACLE provide flights, training, accommodation (on bed and breakfast basis), travel while working, insurance (does not cover personal items) and approx. £100 per week with a bonus system at the end of a successful tour. *Applicants* should send CV and photo to San Remo office or look in *The Stage* for audition advertisements.

Voluntary Work

ABRUZZO NATIONAL PARK: Viale Tito Livio 12, 00136 Rome - Italy (tel 06-35403331; fax 06-35403253; e-mail post@pna.it).

Volunteers to spend 15 days working with other young people who are interested in protecting flora and fauna in an outpost of the Abruzzo National Park. Participants collaborate with the operators, researchers, technicians and guards of the Park in activities such as assisting and educating visitors, maintenance and research. Volunteers should have experience in the field of nature and be able to spend time in the mountains even in tough living conditions. Minimum age 18. Accommodation and a contribution towards food expenses are provided.

For more information contact the above address, or better still, both their International Centre in Villetta Barrea (tel ++39-086489102; fax ++39-086489132; e-mail pna.international:flashnet.it) and the International Parks Centre in Rome (above).

AGAPE: Centro Ecumenico, I-10060 Prali (Torino), Italy (tel +39-0121-807514; fax +39-0121-807690; e-mail campolavoro@agapecentroecumenico.org). AGAPE is situated in the village of Prali in the Germanasca valleys, about eighty miles from Turin. The centre organises national and international meetings during the holiday period. Its isolated position provides the oportunity to experience life away from modern stresses, although this means that the volunteers should be good at entertaining themselves.

AGAPE is an 'ecumenical centre', where believers of different faiths and denominational backgrounds can meet with non-believers in an open and relaxed atmosphere.

Volunteers for manual work alongside the permanent staff. Job includes helping with cooking, cleaning, laundering etc. Board and lodging provided. To work for from 20 days to five weeks between the middle of June and September. Shorter workcamps are also held at Christmas and Easter. Applicants must be aged at least 18; knowledge of Italian an advantage. *Applications* should be sent to the above address.

ASSOCIAZONE CULTURALE LINGUISTICA EDUCATIONAL (ACLE): Via Roma 54, San Remo, Italy (tel/fax +39-0184-506070; e-mail info@acle.org; website www.acle.org). ACLE is a non-profit organisation which was the first in

Italy to teach English through Theatre in Education and organise drama courses recognised by the Italian Ministry of Education for Teachers.

Restoration Volunteers required to help in the restoration of medieval houses. The houses will form part of an artist community and retreat hosting workshops and courses. The houses are situated in the village of Bajard, 900m above sea level. On a clear day it is possible to see the snow capped French Alps and the sea in the bay of San Remo. Vounteers are given the opportunity to relax in this idyllic setting in exchange for five hours work per day. The work involves a fair amount of physical labour, and an idea of basic restoration tasks is desirable. We will provide gloves, dust masks, goggles and tools. Volunteers must provide their own working clothes and sleeping bags. Due to the nature of the project, positions are available working alone or with a group from April to October. *To apply*, complete an on-line application form and forward with the dates you wish to be considered for to info@acle.org.

Office Volunteer: required in the head office in San Remo. In return for a small flat and pocket money, you would be working as part of a small team recruiting Counsellors for the Summer Camps positions. You must be computer literate, a native English speaker and experienced in an office environment. The position is abaibable from October to September and applicants must be available for the full contract. Knowledge of Italian language and culture an advantage. Call to discuss availability.

Web Site Designer required for the head office in San Remo. In return for accommodation and pocket money succesful applicants would work on a recruitment website for ACLE. Knowledge of Italian language and culture an advantage. Call to discuss availability.

CHELON MARINE TURTLE CONSERVATION & RESEARCH PROGRAMME: Viale val Padana 134B, I-00141 Rome, Italy (tel +39-06-8125301; e-mail chelon@tin.it). Founded in 1992 CHELON is a research group within the Tethys Institute; its researchers work to obtain in-depth knowledge of the biology of marine turtles and aid their conservation.

Volunteers to help researchers studying loggerhead turtles in the Mediterranean (Greece, Italy) between June and September. Volunteers will assist in gathering data on nesting behaviour, tagging turtles for observation and taking part in conservation awareness raising among local people and tourists. English and Italian language skills in particular will prove useful.

Volunteers contibute about £380 per two weeks, this covers food and accommodation. Travel and insurance costs are not included. The minimum stay is two weeks, but volunteers can stay longer subject to approval. CHELON also runs projects in Thailand. *Contact* CHELON at the above address for further information and an application form.

LA SABRANENQUE: Centre International, rue de la Tour de l'Oume, F-30290 Saint Victor la Coste, France (tel 466-50-05-05; e-mail info@sabranenque.com). La Sabranenque is a non-profit organisation working with volunteers toward the preservation of traditional Mediterranean architecture. Participants learn skills, share experiences within a diverse group and live in these beautiful villages.

Volunteers (10 per season) to help with the restoration of villages, sites and simple monuments, using traditional building methods, in Altamura, Southern Italy and the hamlet of Gnallo, Northern Italy. Work includes restoration of walls, paths or the reconstruction of small houses. Period of work 2-3 weeks between early July and August.

Board and accommodation is included in the project cost, which is equivalent to £180 per 3 week project. At least one day during each 2-3 week session is spent visiting the region. Applicants must be at least 18 years old and in good health. *Applications* to the above address at any time.

Au Pairs, Nannies, Family Helps and Exchanges

AU PAIR INTERNATIONAL: Via S Stefano 32, 40125 Bologna, Italy (tel +39-051-267575/238320; fax 051-236594; e-mail info@au-pair-international.com; www.au-pair-international.com).
Au Pairs (150) for either summer (June-September) or longer term (6, 9 or 12 months) placements in Italy. The work is mostly childminding, with some light housework. Pocket money of approx. £40 per week plus full board and lodging. Around 6 working hours per day, with 1 complete day and 2/3 evenings free per week. Applicants should be aged 18-30; experience of babysitting an advantage. *Applications* to Au Pair International at the above address, there is no fee to be placed in Italy.

Luxembourg

The official language in Luxembourg is Luxembourgish but German and French are spoken and understood by almost everyone, and casual workers will normally need a reasonable knowledge of at least one of these. EU citizens can use the State Employment Service when they are looking for work. Its headquarters can also give general information on the current work situation: write to the *Administration de l'Emploi*, 10 rue Bender, L-1229 Luxembourg (tel +352-478 5300; www.etat.lu/ADEM/adem.htm). There is also useful information in the free booklet *Working in Luxembourg* published by the Employment Service (see the *Useful Publications* chapter towards the end of this book).

In recent years Luxembourg has consistently had one of the lowest unemployment rates in the EU and currently has the lowest level of all at less than 3% and so prospects of finding temporary work there are good. Employment agencies specialising in temporary work include *Manpower-Aide Temporaire*, 42 rue Glesener, L-1630 Luxembourg (tel +352-48 23 23; fax +352-40 35 52; e-mail cmathenot@manpower.lu). Employment agencies are listed in the yellow pages under *Agences de Travail*.

For information about holiday jobs, students are advised to contact the *Administration de l'Emploi* at the above address where a special service run by EURES counsellors – the *Service Vacances* – exists: this must be visited in person by those interested. In April of each year, a special forum for summer jobs is organised by the Youth Information Centre in Luxembourg City, where students can meet employees and firms offering summer jobs and be informed about their rights. The centre also runs a special service for summer jobs from April to August. The Youth Information Centre can be found at *Centre Information Jeunes*, 26 place de la Gare, L-1616 Luxembourg (tel +352-26 29 32 00; fax +352-26 29 32 03; e-mail CIJ@info.jeunes.lu; website www.cij.lu).

The Luxembourg Embassy in London can also be of use by supplying a list of the main British firms based there, and another of hotels, some of which may be willing to take on temporary workers (please send a sae or IRC when asking for these lists).

People are sometimes needed to help with the grape harvest, which normally begins around the 20th September and continues for four or five weeks. To advertise in newspapers contact *Tageblatt* at 44 rue du Canal, L-4050 Esch-Alzette (tel +352-54 71 31; fax +352-54 71 30; www.tageblatt.lu) who also publish a French weekly called *Le Jeudi* aimed at foreigners living in Luxembourg. There is a weekly English language newspaper, the *Luxembourg News* at 25 Rue Philippe II, L-2340 Luxembourg (tel +352-46 11 221; fax +352-47 00 56); the same publisher also produces *Luxembourg Business*, a monthly business magazine.

RED TAPE

Visa Requirements: no visa is necessary for entry into Luxembourg by members of an EEA country or citizens of the USA, Canada, Australia or New Zealand.
Residence Permits: if you wish to stay in Luxembourg for longer than three months, you must obtain permission in advance from the Administration Communale of the Municipality of Residence unless you are an EU national. Non-EU nationals must produce a medical certificate and radiographic certificate issued by a doctor established in Luxembourg as well as the other documents required by all applicants: proof of identity and proof of sufficient means of support or a *Déclaration Patronale*.
Work Permits: are necessary for any non-EEA national wanting to work in Luxembourg. Permits are issued by the *Administration de l'Emploi* to the prospective employer. Non-EEA nationals must obtain a job and a work permit before entering Luxembourg.
Au Pair: permitted in Luxembourg. However the prospective employer must obtain an *Accord Placement Au Pair*. This agreement describes in detail the conditions governing the au pair's stay, as well as her and her employer's obligations. The host family is responsible for filling in this agreement and forwarding it to the au pair for signature. The agreement is then submitted for approval to the *Administration de l'Emploi*. This contract must be concluded before the au pair leaves her country of residence.
Voluntary Work: foreigners are free to carry out voluntary work for recognised international bodies.

Hotel Work and Catering

HOTEL DE L'ABBAYE: 80 Grand'rue, L-9711 Clervaux, Luxembourg.
Waitresses (1/2). £440-£550 per month, plus tips and share of service charge. A little cleaning work. Knowledge of French or German required. Minimum period of work 3 months under contract.
General Assistants (1/2 girls). £470-£530 per month plus tips. To help in the kitchen and with cleaning.
8-12 hours per day, 6/7 days per week. Free board and accommodation. The order of the house must be accepted by those wishing to live in. A married couple would be acceptable. Minimum period of work 3 months between 15 March and 15 October. Training may be given. *Applications to* Mr Paul Wagner, Director.

HOTEL LE ROYAL: 12 Boulevard Le Royal, L-2449 Luxembourg, Luxembourg (tel +352-241 6161; fax +352-225948; e-mail humanresources@ hotelroyal.lu; www.hotelroyal.lu). Located in the heart of Luxembourg City, this 5 star hotel has 210 rooms and suites, and prides itself on the attentive but discreet service of its staff.

Stagiares (2) required to take up six month placements in this leading hotel. Successful candidates may be employed as restaurant and banquet waiting staff or assistant receipt controllers and auditors. Staff will earn around £170 per month for working 40 hour weeks, with board and lodging available. Applicants should ideally speak English and French or German. The minimum period of work is six months and these periods run from 1 January to 30 June and 1 July to 31 December, so applications are invited immediately.

Applications should be sent to Albanse Millot-Royer, Human Resources Manager at the above address.

SHERATON AEROGOLF HOTEL LUXEMBOURG: Executive Hotels Sarl, BP 1973, L-1019 Luxembourg.

Driver/Bellboy to operate a bus shuttle, take care of the luggage of clients, welcome clients and perform other tasks in the hotel. Wage approximately £500 per month net. To work 8 hours per day, 5 days per week. Free accommodation provided in a staff house. Period of work from 1 August to 30 September. Applicants must hold a driving licence and speak English, French and basic German. *Applications* should be sent to Beatrice Bockholtz, Personnel Manager, at the above address.

Sports, Couriers and Camping

CANVAS HOLIDAYS: East Port House, 12 East Port, Dunfermline, Fife KY12 7JG (tel 01383-629018; fax 01383-629071; www.canvas holidayscom). Canvas Holidays are looking for enthusiastic, resourceful people who enjoy a challenge and love the outdoor life. Main positions for 2002 include:

Campsite Courier. Varied responsibilities. Involves cleaning and preparation of customer accommodation, welcoming and looking after customers during their holiday and ensuring that they have the best holiday ever. As a campsite courier you will have new challenges every day which can lead to one of the most enjoyable summers you will ever have. Variable working hours.

Children's Courier. As a Canvas Holidays Children's Courier you will have had formal experience of working with children. You will organise and carry out a six day programme which involves four hours a day of Children's Club for children between the ages of 4 and 11. You will be prepared to help out with courier duties as and when requried. For many customers, the Children's Club is one of the main parts of the holiday. You will need to have the energy of a seven year old and the imagination of an eleven year old to succeed!

Package includes tented accommodation, medical insurance, full uniform and return travel to and from a UK port of entry. Positions are available from March until October. *Applications* are invited from individuals and couples. Contact Sandy, Karen or Michele at the above contact details for an application pack.

EUROCAMP: Overseas Recruitment Department (Ref SJ/02) (tel 01606-787522). Eurocamp is a leading tour operator in quality self-drive camping and mobile home holidays in Europe. Each year the company seeks to recruit up to 1,500 enthusiastic people for the following positions:

Site Managers: required to lead a large team of Campsite Couriers, organising their daily workloads and ensuring they provide the very best customer service. Applicants should be 21 or over, have proven managerial experience, excellent communication skills and language ability.

Campsite Courier: job involves cleaning and preparing customer accommodation, providing assistance, acting as an information service and an interpreter and performing some administrative duties. Couriers need to be flexible to meet the needs of the customer to provide them with excellent service. Minimum age 18 years. Applicants should be independent with plenty of initiative and relish a challenging and rewarding position. They should also possess a friendly and helpful personality. Some working knowledge of another European language is required and previous customer service experience would be an advantage. Applicants should be available to work from April/May to September.

Children's Couriers: work involves organising a wide range of exciting activities for children aged 4-13. Applicants should possess initiative, imagination and enthusiasm along with good safety awareness. Previous childcare experience is essential. Minimum age is 18 years and applicants should be available from April/May to September. Languages are not a requirement but would be an advantage.

Senior Couriers: required to work alongside a team of Campsite Couriers and organise their daily workload, as well as carrying out the normal day to day duties of a Campsite Courier. Applicants should have good language skills and experience of leading a team.

In all the above positions you should be be available for the full season commencing in April/May through to September. Comprehensive training is provided together with a competitive salary, insurance and return travel. *Applications* are accepted from September/October and *can only be accepted from UK/EU passport holders.* Interviews will be conducted in Hartford, Cheshire between October and April.

The Netherlands

The Netherlands has one of the lowest unemployment rates in the EU, dropping to 2.5% in 2001. Most Dutch people speak excellent English, and so a knowledge of Dutch is not essential for those looking for unskilled seasonal jobs. The tourist industry employs large numbers of extra workers over the summer: it is worth noting that the bulb fields attract tourists from spring onwards, and so the tourist season begins comparatively early for Europe. Early application is therefore important.

Although this chapter lists only details of paid employment in the Netherlands, there are in fact a number of opportunities for voluntary work. International Voluntary Service, Youth Action for Peace, Concordia and UNA Exchange recruit Britons and Council: International Volunteer Projects and Service Civil International (see the IVS entry) in the USA recruits Americans for camps there; see the *Worldwide* chapter for details.

Holland has many private employment agencies (*uitzendbureaus*) which are accustomed to finding short term jobs for British and Irish workers. These jobs normally involve unskilled manual work, such as stocking shelves in supermarkets, working on factory production lines, or washing up in canteens. Most of the agencies will only help people who visit them in person. To discover nearby addresses look up *uitzendbureaus* in the *Gouden Gids* (Yellow Pages); Randstad, ASB, Unique and Manpower are among the best known names.

Some agencies handle vacancies for work in flower bulb factories, which need large numbers of casual workers from mid-April to October to pick asparagus, strawberries, gherkins, apples and pears: the peak period is between the middle of June and the beginning of August. At the same time of year there are jobs in greenhouses and holiday parks. These jobs are popular with locals and usually can be filled with local jobseekers. From the end of September/beginning of October until January of the following year, jobs might be available in the bulb industry (bulb picking and in factories) and sauerkraut. Although bulbs are grown elsewhere in Holland, the industry is concentrated in the area between Haarlem and Lisse, especially around the town of Hillegom. There are also a limited number of jobs every year in the fruit and vegetable producing greenhouses of the 'Westland' in the province of Zuid-Holland.

EU (EEA) nationals can make use of the service of the European Employment Services (EURES) represented in their own Public Employment Service and in the Netherlands. EURES provides jobseekers with information and advice about living and working in another country of the EEA. The Euroadvisers also have an overview of temporary and permanent vacancies available in the Netherlands. Contact the nearby local employment office for more information. In the Netherlands addresses of local Dutch Euroadvisers can be obtained through the *Landelijk Bureau Arbeidsvoorziening*; look up *Arbeidsbureau* in a telephone directory. For further information consult the free booklet *Working in The Netherlands* published by the UK Employment Service.

Those wishing to place advertisements in Dutch newspapers may contact *De Telegraaf*, a major Dutch newspaper, at Basisweg 30, 1043 AP Amsterdam, The Netherlands (tel 010-20-5852208; e-mail com.bin@telegraaf.nl).

RED TAPE

Visa Requirements: citizens of the United Kingdom, United States, EEA countries, Canada, Australia, New Zealand and Japan plus many other countries do not need a visa.

Residence Permits: EEA nationals who intend to stay for more than three months must acquire a sticker in their passport from the local aliens police (*Vreemdelingenpolitie*) or Town Hall, normally over-the-counter, within 8 days of arrival. Evidence of means of support and suitable local accommodation – hostel addresses will normally suffice – must be shown. The passport should then be taken to the local tax office to apply for a *sofinummer* or '*sofi*' (social/fiscal number). Normally you will have to complete both these steps before being allowed to register with employment bureaux or take up a job, though in some cases the *sofi* will suffice. To turn the initial sticker into a residence permit *(Verblijfsvergunning* or *verblijfskaart)* after three months, you will have to show a genuine work contract or letter of employment from an employer (not an agency) and pay a fee. The contract will have to show that the legal minimum wage and holiday pay are being paid and the proper tax and deductions are being made.

Work Permits: North Americans, Antipodeans and others who require no visa to travel to the Netherlands are allowed to work for less than three months, provided they report to the Aliens Police within three days of arrival and their employer has obtained a *tewerkstellingsvergunning* (employment permit) for them. In practice, the *tewerkstellingsvergunning* is unlikely to be issued for casual work. Non-EU nationals wishing to work for longer than three months must obtain a work permit before arrival in the Netherlands. In the first instance an authorisation for temporary stay or *machtiging tot voorlopig verblijf* (MVV) must be granted before the employer can apply for an employment permit from the CBA (Centraal Bestuur Arbeidsvoorziening). The MVV can be applied for through the Dutch Embassy in your country.

Entry may be refused to all travellers who are unable to show that they have the means to support themselves whilst in the Netherlands and to buy a return onward ticket.

Au Pair: such arrangements are allowed, subject to the conditions outlined above.
Voluntary Work: permission to take work of this type may be obtained on your behalf by the sponsoring agency in the Netherlands.

Agricultural Work

VAN WAVEREN B.V.: Pastoorslaan 30, P.O. Box 10, N-2180 AA Hillegom, Netherlands (tel 31-(0)252-516141; fax 31-(0)-252-523112).
Flower Bulb Packers to work 7.30am-5/6pm. £615-£730 per month as per collective labour agreement. Minimum period of work 6 weeks from about 15 July to 30 September. Accommodation available on campsite nearby. Knowledge of English essential. *Applications* from April to the above address.

Hotel Work and Catering

HOTEL MALIE: Malienstraat 2, N-3581 SL Utrecht, The Netherlands (tel +31-30-2316424; fax 030-2340661; e-mail info@maliehotel.nl)
Chambermaids wanted for June, July, August to work 8 hours per day per 5 day week. Wages by arrangement, with board and lodging available according to space. Staff should speak a foreign language: English, French, German, Italian or Spanish and if possible Dutch. The minimum period of work is three months and *applications* are invited from January marked for the attention of Mr E.R. van Driel at the above address.

GRAND HOTEL & RESTAURANT OPDUIN-TEXEL: Ruyslaan 22, 1796 AD De Koog, Texel, The Netherlands (tel 0031-222-317445; fax 0031-222-317777; e-mail info@opduin.nl; www.opduin.nl). A luxurious 4 star hotel with 100 rooms, 50 employees, gourmet restaurant, and swimming pool. It is just 200 metres from the beach on a beautiful island in 'the top of Holland'
Kitchen Porters (2) for general kitchen work including dishwashing and cleaning. No previous experience necessary.
Assistant Waiters (2) for general work in their service department during breakfast, lunch and dinner. Previous experience is recommended but not necessary. Good appearance essential.
Chambermaids (2) for general cleaning work in the hotel. Good health essential.
  Applicants for these positions must be available for at least 3-4 months during the period March to November. *Applications* with photograph from January to Mr C den Ouden Esq. at the above address .

HOTEL WILHEMINA/HOTEL KING: Koninginne Weg 167-169, NL-1075 CN Amsterdam, The Netherlands.
Receptionists (2), Chambermaids (3). Approximately £700 gross per month. To work 4-8 hours per day, 5 days per week. No accommodation available. Applicants must speak English. *Applications,* enclosing a processing fee of £10, to the above address as soon as possible.

Sports, Couriers and Camping

3D EDUCATION AND ADVENTURE LTD: Business Support, Osmington Bay, Weymouth, Dorset DT3 6EG (tel 01305-836226; fax 01305-834070; e-mail darren@3d-education.co.uk). 3D is a specialist provider of activity and educational experiences for young people. Owned by Center Parcs, 3D has been operating since 1991 and gone from strength to strength year on year.

Activity Intsructors (500) Employed and trained as either multi-activity instructor, field studies instructor, specialist watersports instructor or IT instructor, staff will work with children at specialist holiday centres across the south of England as well as across the UK and Europe with Pontins and Center Parcs.

Field studies instructors must hold or at least be gaining a relevant degree. IT instructors need to have a broad range of IT skills. Any sports coaching awards or national governing body awards are advantageous, if applying for Activity instructor and Watersports instructor postitions, although those with relevant experience will be considered. Training courses are held from late January through to July, so there is plenty of opportunity to develop your skills and qualifications.

Most important is an applicant's enthusiasm, personality and energy, coupled with a true desire to work in the outdoor leisure industry. Excellent accommodation and catering packages are offered with payment and working hours as covered by minimum wage and working time legislation. Minimum period of work 14 weeks.

Applicants should telephone 01305-836226 for a recruitment pack between September and June. Before employment all applicants must complete a residential training programme in the UK.

EUROCAMP: Overseas Recruitment Department (Ref SJ/02) (tel 01606-787522). Eurocamp is a leading tour operator in quality self-drive camping and mobile home holidays in Europe. Each year the company seeks to recruit up to 1,500 enthusiastic people for the following positions:

Campsite Courier: job involves cleaning and preparing customer accommodation, providing assistance, acting as an information service and an interpreter and performing some administrative duties. Couriers need to be flexible to meet the needs of the customer to provide them with excellent service. Minimum age 18 years. Applicants should be independent with plenty of initiative and relish a challenging and rewarding position. They should also possess a friendly and helpful personality. Some working knowledge of another European language is required and previous customer service experience would be an advantage. Applicants should be available to work from April/May to September.

Children's Couriers: work involves organising a wide range of exciting activities for children aged 4-13. Applicants should possess initiative, imagination and enthusiasm along with good safety awareness. Previous childcare experience is essential. Minimum age is 18 years and applicants should be available from April/May to September. Languages are not a requirement but would be an advantage .

Senior Couriers: required to work alongside a team of Campsite Couriers and organise their daily workload, as well as carrying out the normal day to day duties of a Campsite Courier. Applicants should have good language skills and experience of leading a team.

Site Managers: required to lead a large team of Campsite Couriers, organising their daily workloads and ensuring they provide the very best customer service. Applicants should be 21 or over, have proven managerial experience, excellent communication skills and language ability.

In all the above positions you should be be available for the full season commencing in April/May through to September. Comprehensive training is provided together with a competitive salary, insurance and return travel.

Applications are accepted from September/October and *can only be accepted from UK/EU passport holders.* Interviews will be conducted in Hartford, Cheshire between October and April.

Work with Children

ACTIVITY INTERNATIONAL: PO Box 7097, NL-9701 JB Groningen, the Netherlands (tel 050-3-130-666; fax 050-3-131-633; e-mail info@ activity.aupair.nl;/www.activity.aupair.nl).
Au Pairs (500) for placements in the Netherlands. Pocket money of approx. £175 per month in exchange for around 30 hours childcare and light household duties per week, with extra money paid for babysitting and medical insurance covered, travel to and from the Netherlands is also paid for by the host family. Placements are for between 6 and 12 months. Applicants should have an interest in Dutch culture and learning the Dutch language. Once in the Netherlands au pairs can join the agency's *Go Dutch* club and join activities such as city tours and weekend trips. *Applicants should be from EEA countries*, speak English, be aged 18-25, have experience of childcare and be able to provide references. Activity International work with a number of partner agencies throughout Europe, applicants should therefore contact the above address for details of the nearest agency to them.

Norway

Even though Norway voted not to join the European Union a few years ago, it is a member of the European Economic Area (EEA) which means that EU nationals can enter and look for work for up to 6 months. They can seek work through local offices of the Norwegian employment service and work without needing work permits.

The EURES department of the *Arbeidsmarkedsetaten* (Employment Service) assists job-seekers in person; contact the Euroadviser, Øvre Slottsgate 11, Postboks 420 Sentrum, 0103 Oslo; 22 42 41 41/fax 22 42 44 38). A temporary work unit *(Vikartjenesten)* operates from the same address (22 42 60 00/fax 22 42 10 08) and the ordinary job centre is nearby at Akersgate 1-5. The main employment service website www.aetat.no is only in Norwegian. Try also a telephone job line *Grønn Linje* 8000-33166, which provides information on vacancies registered with the Employment Service and is free within Norway.

The rate of unemployment in Norway is currently less than half the EU average which makes the country a good prospect for the job-hunter. There are a number of well-paid jobs available in Norwegian hotels over the summer. English is widely spoken and so a knowledge of Norwegian is not essential: but, as elsewhere in Europe, the tourist industry appreciates people who can speak more than one language. People who are in Norway may also be able to find unpleasant but lucrative work in fish processing factories in such towns as Trondheim, Bergen or Vardo, but over-fishing has reduced the possibilities of finding such work. When looking for work it is worth bearing in mind that Norwegian students are on vacation between 15 June and 15 August (approximately), and so there will be more opportunities before and after these dates.

However those aged 18-30 can take advantage of a 'Working Guest' programme whereby visitors can stay with a Norwegian family in a working environment such as a farm or in tourism; details of the farm work can be found under the entry for Atlantis Youth Exchange and application forms can be obtained from Concordia in the UK or Interexchange in the US.

The Norwegian employment service (*Arbeidsdirektoratet*) is unable to help people looking for summer jobs. British citizens may be able to find voluntary work in Norway through Concordia or International Voluntary Service and Americans through Service Civil International (see the *Worldwide* chapter for details).

Oslo has a Use It office (Ungdomsinformasjonen), one of whose aims is to find work and accommodation for young visitors while offering a range of services, as in Copenhagen. Use It is located at Møllergata 3, 0179 Oslo (22 41 51 32/fax 22 42 63 71; e-mail Post@unginfo.oslo.no) and is open year round from 11am to 5pm with longer opening hours during the summer. Their website www. unginfo.oslo.no/streetwise in English carries tips for living and working in Oslo.

Those wishing to advertise in Norwegian newspapers may contact Crane Media Partners Ltd, 20-28 Dalling Road, Hammersmith, London W6 OJB (020-8237 8601; fax 020-8735 9941), who handle the national daily *Dagbladet*. *Aftenposten* is published at Akergt. 51, POB 1178-Sentrum, N-0107 Oslo.

RED TAPE

Visa Requirements: a visa is not normally required by people of most western countries for a visit of less than three months, provided that employment is not intended.

Residence Permits: this permit must be obtained before entering Norway for any stay of more than three months by non-EEA nationals unless a work permit has already been obtained. This should be applied for at least 3 months before you intend to travel to Norway. EEA nationals, with the firm intention of taking up employment, may enter and stay in Norway so long as they can prove that they have sufficient funds to finance their stay for up to 6 months while seeking work, but after 3 months they too must obtain a residence permit. Although this does not apply to cross-border workers who return home once a week. An application has to be submitted to the local police with proof of employment within the time frame given above.

Work Permits: British, Irish and nationals of other EU/EEA/EFTA countries do not need work permits in Norway, but if the intention is to work and stay for more than three months a residence permit must be applied for. Non-EEA citizens must obtain a work and residence permit before entering Norway. Permits should be applied for at least 3 months before you intend to arrive in Norway. Having been offered a job and a place to live, you should obtain application forms for a work permit from the nearest Norwegian Embassy or Consulate General, which will send the completed applications to the Directorate of Immigration in Oslo for processing.

Working Holiday Visas. A working holiday visa scheme has been in place between Norway and Australia since August 2001. Applicants must be Australian nationals, intend primarily to holiday in Norway for up to a year, be aged between 18 and 30 years at time of application, possess reasonable funds and travel insurance, be travelling without dependent children, not have a criminal record and not have held a working holiday visa previously. To apply travellers should complete the application forms in duplicate and supply 2 recent passport-style photos, a valid passport, a return ticket or proof of funds to buy one, proof of financial means and travel insurance documents. Applications can be made through the consular offices of the Royal Norwegian Embassies in Australia or London.

Au Pair. Atlantis runs a programme for 100-150 incoming au pairs who must be aged 18-30, able to speak English and willing to stay at least six months but preferably 8-12 months. Details are available on their website www.atlantis-u.no. Atlantis charges a registration fee of kr1,000, a quarter of which is non-refundable if the placement doesn't go ahead. Au pairs from an EEA country can

obtain the residence permit after arrival whereas citizens of non-EU countries must arrange the paperwork before arrival.
Voluntary Work: this is permitted, but is subject to the regulations outlined above.

Agricultural Work

ATLANTIS YOUTH EXCHANGE: Kirkegata 32, 0153 Oslo, Norway (tel +47-22 47 71 70; fax 47-22 47 71 79; e-mail post@atlantis-u.no; www.atlantis-u.no).
Atlantis, the Norwegian Foundation for Youth Exchange, arranges stays on Norwegian farms for people of any nationality who are aged 18-30 and speak English. Participants share every aspect of a farmer's family life, both the work and the leisure; free board and lodging are provided. The work may include haymaking, weeding, milking, picking berries, fruit and vegetables, caring for animals etc.: pocket money of approx. £56 per week is paid for a maximum of 35 hours work a week.

Stays are for between eight and twelve weeks all round the year. EU applicants can apply for up to twenty-four weks though. *Applications* must be received 3-4 months before desired date of starting work for non-EFTA/EU applicants: EU/EFTA applicants may be accepted closer to the arrival date. For further details and an application form contact the above address. British applicants can apply through Concordia. The registration fee is approx. £100 (£200 for a placement of 12-24 weeks); if not placed all but approximately £20 is returned.

Hotel Work and Catering

HOVRINGEN HOGFJELLSHOTEL: N-2679 Hovringen, Norway.
Waitresses (2). Wages according to experience.
Chambermaids (2). Wages as above.
Pantry Maids (2). Wages as above.
Kitchen Assistants (2). Wages as above.
A 7^{1}/$_{2}$ hour day, 6 day week is worked. Board and accommodation provided at 40p per day. Minimum period of work 6 weeks between 1 June and 30 September. This is a small family hotel in the mountains. *Applications* from mid-April to the above address.

LINDSTROM HOTEL: N-5890 Lardal, Norway. Tel 056-66202.
Hotel Staff (20) to work in the kitchen, dining room and cafeteria and to clean rooms. Payment on an hourly basis at £5 per hour. Board and lodging available at a charge. To work 8 hours per day, 5 days per week. Minimum period of work 6 weeks between 1 May and 30 September. Applicants should be aged at least 18, speak English and to work in the kitchen will need some experience of cooking.
Applications to Karen Margrethe Lindstrom at the above address from January.

STALHEIM HOTEL: N-5715 Stalheim, Norway. This busy first class, family run hotel is beautifully situated in the Fjord country of western Norway, 140km from Bergen. It has an International clientele and is open from May to October.
Chefs (8). Wages approx. £1,300 per month, must be fully trained, experienced, and hold appropriate certficates.
Chambermaids (8), Waiters/Waitresses (10), Pantry Boys/Girls (8), Cooks (5). All paid approximately £1,200 per month. Previous experience a plus.
Sales Girls (5) for the gift shop. £1,200 per month. Must be sales minded.
All staff work 7^{1}/$_{2}$ hours per day, 5 days a week, occasional overtime required. Salaries taxed at approximately 25%. Board and accommodation provided at

approximately £184 per month. Uniforms available. Minimum period of work 3 months between 10 May and 25 September. *Applications* giving date of birth and details of education, experience, references and dates available and enclosing a recent photograph should be sent to Ingrid Tonneberg, Managing Director, at the above address.

HOTEL ULLENSVANG: N-5774 Lofthus, Hardanger, Norway.
Waiters, Waitresses, Chambermaids, Kitchen Assistants, Cooks. Wages by arrangement according to qualifications. 38 hours per 5 day week. Board and accommodation available at £60 per month. Period of work 1 May to 1 November. *Applications* as soon as possible to the above address.

HOTEL VORINGFOSS: N-5783 Eidfjord i Hardanger, Norway.
Waitresses and **Chambermaids.** Board and accommodation available. Experience preferred but not essential. Minimum period of work 3 months between April and October. *Applications* in March-April to the above address. Do not send International Reply Coupons: reply not guaranteed.

Portugal

Although unemployment in Portugal is currently lower than the European Union average, the best chances of finding paid employment are with tour operators (see below and the organisations in the *Worldwide* chapter), or teaching English as a foreign language, or in hotels in tourist areas such as the Costa do Sol and the Algarve. Private employment agencies such as Manpower may however be able to provide casual jobs for which a knowledge of Portuguese is necessary.

British and Irish citizens and other EU nationals are permitted to use the Portuguese national employment service: look under *Centro do Emprego* in a telephone directory. There are also a number of private employment agencies, principally in Lisbon and Oporto: for agencies specialising in temporary work look under *Pessoal Temporário* in the yellow pages (*Páginas Amarelas*). For further information consult the free booklet *Working in Portugal* published by the Employment Service.

Short-term voluntary work can be arranged for British travellers by UNA Exchange, International Voluntary Service/Service Civil International and Youth Action for Peace. Their entries in the *Worldwide* chapter give more details about their organisations.

An advertisement in the English language *Anglo Portuguese News (APN)* may lead to a job offer; its address is Apartado 113, P-2766-902 Estoril, Portugal (tel +351-21-466 1551; fax 21-466 0358; e-mail apn@mail.telepac.pt). *Expresso* is published at Rua Duque de Palmera 37-2, P-1296 Lisbon (tel 21-526141; fax 21-543858).

RED TAPE

Visa Requirements: for holiday visits of up to three months a visa is not required by full citizens of EEA countries. The maximum period is two months for US citizens. Australians will need a visa even for holiday visits.
Residence Permits: for stays longer than three months a residence permit should be obtained from the nearest immigration office (*Serviço de Estrangeiros e Fronteiras*). The address of the headquarters of the *Serviço de Estrangeiros* is Rua Conselheiro José Silvestre Ribeiro 4, 1600-007 Lisbon (tel 21-711 5000),

while the regional Lisbon office is at Avenida António Augusto Aguiar 20 (tel 21-315 9681). To obtain a residence permit, you must be able to provide a letter from your employer in Portugal confirming your employment.

Work Permits: EU/EEA nationals do not require work permits to work in Portugal, only a residence permit as above. Non-EU nationals must provide an array of documents before they can be granted a work visa, including a residence visa obtained from the Portuguese Consulate in their home country, a document showing that the Ministry of Labour *(Ministerio do Trabalho)* has approved the job and a medical certificate in Portuguese. The final stage is to take a letter of good conduct provided by the applicant's own embassy to the police for the work and residence permit.

Au Pair: permitted but not customary; a work permit is required.

Voluntary Work: there are no restrictions applied to work of this nature.

Hotel Work and Catering

HOTEL ESTALAGEM VALE DA URSA: Cernache do Bonjardim, P-6100 Serta, Portugal (tel 274-90981; fax 274-90982).

Waitresses/Restaurant Assistants (1/2), Kitchen Porters (1/2) to help in the dining room, bar and kitchen. Some experience in the catering industry would be an advantage.

Applications should be sent to the Manager at the above address in April and May.

LAWRENCES HOTEL: Rua Consiglieri, Pedroso, 38-40, Vila de Sintra,Sintra, Portugal (tel 21-910-5500; fax 21-910-5505; e-mail lawrences_hotel@ hotmail.com; www.portugalvrtual.pt/lawrences). A five star hotel and restaurant situated in the beautiful heritage town of Sintra.

Kitchen Staff (3), Restaurant Staff (3), Receptionists (3) required to work 5 days a week for a minimum of three months between 1 May and 15 October. Salary £150 per month approx. Knowledge of English is required. Some knowledge of French, Portugese or German would be advantageous.

Applications are invited from February to the above address.

MAYER APARTMENTS: Praia Da luz, 8600-157 Luz Lagos, Algarve, Portugal (tel 00351-282-789313; fax 00351-282-788809).

Bar Person. Outgoing, hardworking, independent individual to serve drinks and snacks at a busy poolside bar. Wages are £92 per month plus commission. No experience necessary as full training is given. To work 10am to 7pm from 1st May to 31st October. Board and accommodation is included. Applicants must speak English

To apply send c.v. and photo to Mr Adrian Mayer at the above address from February onwards.

QUINTA DO BARRANCO DA ESTRADA: 7665-880 Santa Clara A Velha, Portugal (tel +351 283-933065; fax +351-283-933066; e-mail paradiseinportugal@ mail.telepac.pt; www.paradise-in-portugal.com; www.birding-in-portugal.com). This small, family-run hotel is in some of the most remote and unspoilt countryside in Europe. On the shore of a vast freshwater lake, the hotel is ideal for nature lovers and those interested in watersports.

Bar Staff, Gardeners, Entertainers, Waiters/Waitresses, Cooks. All staff are required to work eight hour per day, five days per week. Minimum period of work is six months between March and October. Wages vary according to experience; board and accommodation are provided. A knowledge of Portugese, English, French and German would be useful. Driving licence, and knowledge of ornithology or nature are also useful. *Apply* in early 2002 to Frank and Lulu McClintock

Sports, Couriers and Camping

CLUB TRAVEL 2000: Jackson House, Sibson Road, Sale, Manchester M33 7RR (tel 0161-968-2000; fax 0870-241-9341; juliea@club-travel2000.co.uk; www.club-travel2000.co.uk). Club Travel 2000 is a small company which has been in business for 17 years. It has a very friendly environment and is strongly customer service focused.

Overseas Holiday Representatives (5+). Duties include airport transfers, welcome meetings, visiting guests in properties, preparing paper work, reports and guiding excursions. Wages of £450 per month, depending on experience.

Head Representatives (3+) To perform the same duties as Overseas Holiday Representatives. Wages £650 per month, depending on experience.

For both positions, applicants must be educated to GCSE level, and have achieved at least a Grade C in Maths and English. Applicants must be prepared to work long hours, have plenty of stamina and a good sense of humour. Knowledge of Spanish is preferred but not essential. Working hours are 9am to 1pm and 5pm to 8pm, six days per week. Employees must be prepared to work overtime when required. Season of employment is April to November; minimum working period of three months. Accomodation is provided. Send *applications* to Julie Allanson, Overseas Manager at the above address.

Voluntary Work and Archaeology

ATEJ/TURISMO ESTUDANTIL: Apartado 4586, P-4009 Porto Codex, Portugal. **Volunteers** to work on farms, archaeological digs, with the handicapped, etc. To work 5-8 hours per day. Free board and lodging provided. Period of work from 1 July to 30 September. Knowledge of Spanish and English or French required. *Applications*, enclosing a curriculum vitae, to the above address in April, or March at the latest.

Au Pairs can also be placed in Portugal by this organisation. For further information, write to the above address in February or March.

COMPANHEIROS CONSTRUTORES: R. Pedro Monteiro, 3-1. Coimbra, Portugal.
Volunteers for construction camps on behalf of the socially, physically and mentally underprivileged. 8 hours per day. Free board, accommodation and insurance. Cost of travel to and from camp is the responsibility of the volunteer.

2-4 week periods from June to September. An application fee of $200 is payable. Applications should be made 2 months before start of work period to the above address. There also exist vacancies for long term volunteers.

Spain

Unemployment may have dogged the Spanish economy in recent years but a recent upswing is changing things for the better, the economy has seen growth rates of 4% for 2000 and 3.1% for 2001 so far (these figures are from the Spanish Embassy, correct for July). So with unemployment dropping those looking for temporary work there will find things slightly easier than in previous years. Opportunities for foreigners are best in the tourist industry or teaching English, both areas where the knowledge of another language is an asset.

Many jobs in the tourist industry are described both in this chapter and the *Worldwide* chapter at the beginning of the book. Some of the best opportunities for work in Spain are in hotels so that applications to hotels in tourist areas could result in the offer of a job. Since many of these hotels cater for tourists from Northern Europe, a good knowledge of languages such as German, Dutch, French and English will be a great advantage to foreign workers. The website www.gapwork.com has information about working in Ibiza and provides the web addresses for clubs and other potential employers. It is estimated that about 6,000 Britons try to find work on Ibiza each year so it is important to offer a relevant skill.

It should be remembered that hotel workers in Spain work very long hours during the summer months and foreign workers will be required to do likewise. In many cases at the peak of the tourist season hotel and restaurant staff work a minimum of 10 hours per day and bar staff may work even longer hours. A 7-day week is regarded as perfectly normal during the summer. Despite these long hours, salaries are generally somewhat lower than elsewhere in Western Europe.

A knowledge of English and Spanish may help an experienced secretary to get bilingual office work with companies in large cities. There are also a number of jobs for teachers of English: the definitive guide to this type of work is *Teaching English Abroad* (see the *Useful Publications* chapter).

British and Irish citizens and other EU nationals who are in Spain and confident of their knowledge of Spanish may use the Spanish national employment service: look under *Oficina de Empleo* in a telephone directory. Private employment agencies are known as *Empresas de Trabajo Temporal:* for addresses consult the Yellow Pages (*Páginas Amarillas*). For further information consult the free booklet *Working in Spain* published by the UK Employment Service (see the *Useful Publications* chapter towards the end of this book). Alternatively you can contact your nearest embassy: the Spanish Embassy in London produces information leaflets, one of which is entitled *Working in Spain* which gives a general guide to the travelling employee. Others are aimed at students and voluntary workers.

It is always worth checking the English language press for the sits vac columns which sometimes carry adverts for cleaners, live-in babysitters, chefs, bar staff, etc. Look for *SUR in English* (www.surinenglish.com) which has a large employment section and is used by foreign and local residents throughout southern Spain. It is published free on Fridays and distributed through supermarkets, bars, travel agencies, etc. If you want to place your own ad, contact the publisher Prensa Malaguena, Avda. de Maranon 48, 29009 Malaga.

Advertisements can be placed in Spanish newspapers including *El Mundo*, a national daily, which is handled by Smyth International, 1 Torrington Park, London N12 9GG. *El Pais*, the leading national daily, is published at Prisa, Miguel Yuste 40, E-28037 Madrid.

There are also opportunities for voluntary work in Spain arranged by Concordia, UNA Exchange, Youth Action for Peace and International Voluntary Service for British citizens, and Council: International Volunteer Projects and Service Civil International for US nationals; see the *Worldwide* chapter for details.

RED TAPE

Visa Requirements: a visa is not required by citizens of the United Kingdom, United States and of EEA countries for visits to Spain, although if they obtain a job or stay for more than 90 days they will need to obtain a residence permit.

Those non-EEA nationals taking up a paid job must obtain a visa from the Spanish Consulate before travelling to Spain: this can take 3 months to process. To avoid delay, anyone requesting information or visa forms should write stating their nationality and the purpose of their intended stay, enclosing a stamped addressed envelope.

Residence Permits: those who intend to stay more than three months must apply for a residence card *(Tarjeta de Residencia)* within 30 days of arrival. Application should be made to the local police headquarters *(Comisaría de Policia)* or to a Foreigners' Registration Office *(Oficina de Extranjería)*. The documents necessary for the *residencia* are a contract of employment, three photos, a passport and (sometimes) a medical certificate. This information can be confirmed with the Labour & Social Affairs Counsellor's Office of the Spanish Embassy (20 Peel St, London W8 7PD; 020-7221 0098; spanlabo@globalnet.co.uk) and with the British Consulate-General in Spain (c/ Marqués de la Ensenada 16-2°, 28004 Madrid; 91-308 5201). Their notes *Settling in Spain* include detailed advice on sorting out red tape as well as the addresses of all 14 British Consulates in Spain.

Work Permits: are not required by EEA nationals. The immigration situation for non-EU citizens has become increasingly difficult forcing employers of non-Europeans to embark on an expensive, complex and lengthy process. Non-EU nationals must first obtain a *visado especial* from the Spanish Embassy in their country of residence after submitting a copy of their contract, medical certificate in duplicate and authenticated copies of qualifications. In some cases a further document is needed, an *antecedente penale* (certificate proving that they have no criminal record). The employer must obtain a work permit on your behalf from the Spanish Ministry of Labour through the relevant *Delegacion Provincial de Trabajo y Seguridad Social.*

Au Pair: The status of an au pair is between that of a worker and a student. If from a non-EEA country au pairs should apply for a student visa before leaving their country of residence. Once in Spain, they should report to the local police authorities and show a letter from the family and another one from the school where they are studying Spanish.

Voluntary Work: there are no restrictions applied to work of this nature.

Hotel Work and Catering

HOTEL ANCORA: Lloret de Mar, Costa Brava, Spain.
Receptionist. Wages on application. Hours approximately 9am-1pm and 4-8pm, shift work. Board and accommodation provided free of charge. Knowledge of Spanish and English essential, German useful. Must be able to work minimum of 3 months, from May to end of September. *Applications* from February to the Director.

HOTEL BONSOL: Paeso de Illetas 30, 07181 Illetas, Mallorca (tel 971-4021-11; fax 971-40-25-59; e-mail barnsol@fehm.es; www.la-chateau.com/bon-sol). This family run hotel has 92 rooms and three restaurants.
Nanny (2) to care for and entertain children. Must be kind and be able to care for babies. Wages £525 (Euros 850) per month.
Beach Boys (2) to look after the pools, beach and garden. Applicants must be qualified pool attendants, and should be friendly, professional and kind. Wages £545 (Euros 880) per month.
Waiter (2) to serve meals and drinks. Must be friendly, kind and professional. Wages £545 per month. (Euros 880).
Commis Waiter (2). To assist the waiter. Wages £525 (Euros 850) per month.

Dish washer (2) should be clean and professional. Wages £525 (Euros 850) per month.

Trained Cook: (2) To organise the working of the kitchen. Should be professional with good experience of working in a kitchen. Wages c. £930 (Euros 1,500) per month.

Buffet and Snack Kitchen Helper (2) to prepare food and assist with buffet. Should be clean, with a knowledge of cooking. Wages £545 per month.(Euros 880)

For all positons, employees will work 40 hours over a five day week. Minimum of two months work betwen June and October. Accommodation is shared and costs £220 (Euros 360) per month. For all positions except kitchen staff, a knowledge of German, English and Spanish is necessary. *Applications* from March onwards.

HOTEL BON REPOS: Calella (Barcelona), Spain.

Receptionist. Wages on application. Must be able to type. Average 10 hours work per day. Board and accommodation provided free of charge. Knowledge of Spanish and English essential, of German or French helpful. Minimum period of work 3 months between beginning of May and end of September. *Applications* from February to the above address.

HOTEL-RESTAURANT CAN BOIX DE PERAMOLA: Can Boix, S/N, E-25790, Peramola, Spain (tel +34-973 470266; fax +34-973 470281; e-mail canboixperamola@infonegocio.com; www.jpmosa.com). A small hotel situated in the low Catalan pyrenees run by the Pallarès family for many generations. Well known restaurant.

Waiter(s) (1/2) to work in the restaurant or in the bar. Wage £400 approx or above depending upon skills.

Cook (1). Wage £400 approx or above depending upon ability.

Chambermaids (1/2) required to clean and prepare the rooms, public areas and laundry service. Wage £400 or above depending upon ability.

To work for a minimum of 4 months between April and October. 5^1/2 days a week, 9 to 10 hours a day. Board and accommodtion are available free of charge. A good knowledge of both English and Spanish is required.

Applications are invited at any time to Mr. Joan Pallares at the above address.

HOTEL CAP ROIG: 17250 Playa de AroCtr, Spain (tel +34-972 652000; fax 972-650850). The hotel is situated directly over the sea. It is frequented by international clients and is open all year round.

Waitresses (2), Waiters (3), Bar Assistants, Bar and Pool Assistants (2), Chambermaids (3) with relevant experience required. Salary approx. £500 per month.

Cook (Assistant) (1) with relevant experience required. Salary approx. £575.

6-8 hours work a day, 6 days a week, either between 8am and 4pm or between 2pm and 10pm. All applicants must be prepared to work for a minimum of 6 to 8 weeks between June and September. Board and accommodation is included. Those who can speak relevant languages such as Spanish are preferred. All applicants must have a valid EU passport.

Applications are invited as early as possible to Peter Siebauer at the above address.

HOTEL CASTILLO DE MONZON S.L.: Carretera Santander, Monzon de Campos 34410, Palencia, Spain.

General Assistants (2) to work in a hotel as cleaners and waitresses. Approximately £165 per month. Board and accommodation provided. Period of work from 2 to 6 months. Applicants should have an experience of hotel work and be able to speak Spanish and French. *Applications* to Jose Diez Sedano at the above address in June.

HOTEL CUEVA DEL FRAILE: Hoz del Huecar, E-16001 Cuenca, Spain (tel 34-966-21-15-71; fax 34-966-25-60-47).
Waiters (5), Cooks (2) to work in a restaurant and at an outside barbecue. Wages depend upon qualifications, experience etc.; free board and lodging provided. To work 8 hours per day, 5-6 days per week. Minimum period of work 2 months between 1 June and the end of September.

Knowledge of Spanish, English and French would be advantageous. *Applications* should be sent to Mr Borja Garcia at the above address from March.

HOTEL DURAN RESTAURANT: Lasauca 5, E-17600 Figueres, Spain.
Waiters (2), Cook (1), to carry out usual catering duties: the cook will be expected to prepare easy meals. Approximately £380 per month. 8 hours work a day, 5¹/2 days a week. Board and accommodation are provided free of charge. Minimum period of work one month between 1st June and 30th September. Applicants must be able to speak French and English, and must be of smart appearance. *Applications* should be sent to the above address one or two months before the desired period of work.

HOTEL FESTA BRAVA: Lloret de Mar (Costa Brava), Spain.
Receptionist. Wages on application plus commission and tips. Knowledge of Spanish and English essential, German useful.
Chabmermaids. Wages as above.

Board and accommodation provided free of charge. Minimum period of work 3 months between May and end of September. *Applications* from February to Sr Angel Panes Rius, Director, at the above address.

HOTEL FLAMINGO: Lloret de Mar (Costa Brava), Spain.
Assistant Receptionist (female). Salary on application. Average 9-10 hours daily, shift work. Free board and accommodation. Knowledge of Spanish, English and German essential. Minimum period of work beginning of May to beginning of October. *Applications* from February to the above address.

LANGLEY S.L.: Edificio Xaloc, Local No. 1, San Augustin, E-07029 Ibiza, Spain (tel/fax +34-971-342815). Bar and entertainment staff required for the Ibiza scene; Langley run 6 fun pubs and one Irish Theme Bar in the resort and seek lively and committed staff.
Bar Staff, Public Relations, Party Organisers (40) to work on a rota. PR Staff greet passers-by in the street and inform them of that night's activities or themes in Langley's 6 fun pubs, the others organise themes or work behind the bar. Staff will also help decorate pubs for party nights and liaise with DJs about events, as well as serving and preparing all types of drinks and pub type food, from behind a busy bar, with some waiting on tables. Work also includes re-stocking, cleaning and organising the bar and seating areas. Applicants should be lively and able to join in the fun to create a good entertainment atmosphere. Irish staff preferred for the Irish Theme Bar. Wages approx. £320 per month.
Irish Musician/Entertainer (2) to entertain an audience of 18-30 year olds who want to party all night and have a craic in an Irish bar in Ibiza. A repertoire of

typical songs and singalongs is essential as is a good mix of music styles to suit all tastes. Applicant must have experience of microphone work and a sense of humour, as well as the ability to keep the show as lively as possible. All PA equipment provided. Wages around £600 per month.

Food Preparation Chef (7) to prepare pub-style food for a chain of 5 pubs which can easily be served by bar staff at a later time. Creativity, ingenuity and originality in terms of menu choice is essential. Wages approx. £400 per month.

DJ/Entertainer (7) to entertain an audience of 18-30 year olds who want to party all night, microphone work is essential, as is the ability to mix and play all types of music, compere theme nights, competitions and karaoke. All equipment and music provided. Wages approx. £500 per month.

Stock Control and Deliveries Personnel (2) to check deliveries to a central warehouse and daily onward delivery to outlets. Daily stock takes and reports are required and the preparation of central warehouse orders. Previous experience and a full clean driving licence required. Wages approx. £500 per month.

Free accommodation and a meal before the shift starts are provided, and staff can drink up to 6 half pints of soft drink or Spanish lager free while working, except for the stock control and deliveries personnel who are restricted to soft drinks for safety reasons. No smoking is allowed at work.

No qualifications are required but previous experience in these fields of work either in the UK or abroad, an outgoing personality, enthusiasm, dedication and the ability to work hard are necessary. Foreign language skills are not essential but are beneficial. Staff work 56 hours per week in 8 hour shifts. All wages are paid monthly in Spanish pesetas via a local bank account.

While the cost of travelling to interview is borne by the candidate, on completion of the contract Langley S.L. will refund the cost of travel to take up employment. Contracts are for 6 months although shorter periods of work are possible. *Applications* are invited from 1st December.

HOTEL LAS VEGAS: Carretera de Francia, Calella (Barcelona), Spain.
Receptionists (2). £300 per month. 8 hours per day, 6 day week. Free board and accommodation. Good knowledge of German and Spanish essential. Period of work 1 July to 30 August. *Applications* from January to the above address.

HOTEL MIREIA: Lloret de Mar (Gerona), Costa Brava, Spain.
Waiters for night club (2). Wages on application plus tips. Hours: 9pm-5am. Board and accommodation provided free of charge. Knowledge of Spanish and English essential, and German helpful. Must be able to work from beginning of May until the end of September. *Applications* from February to the above address.

HOTEL MONTE CARLO: Lloret de Mar (Costa Brava), Spain.
Waiters (2). Wages on application plus tips. Hours: 8-10am, 1-3pm and 8-10pm. Board and accommodation provided free of charge. Knowledge of Spanish and English essential. Must be able to work for a minimum of 5 months, from April to October. *Applications* from March to the address above.

HOTEL MONTEMAR: Calle Puntaires 20, Pineda de Mar (Barcelona), Spain (tel +93-767 00 02; fax +93-767 15 79).
Assistant Animateur. Must be Dutch.
Receptionist. £550 per month. Must be Dutch.
To work 7 hours per day, 6 days per week. Board and accommodation provided free of charge. The ability to speak Dutch, Spanish and German is

essential and some knowledge of French is required. Applicants must be Dutch and available for at least 4 months from May to October. *Applications* from February to the above address.

NICO-HOTEL: CN-II km 150, 42240 Medinaceli (Sozia) Spain (tel 975-326111; fax 975-326474). This hotel is in an historic village 150km from Madrid, with a high class Spanish clientele.
Kitchen Staff needed all year round. Wages on application. To work 7 hours per day, 6 days per week.
Waitresses (5). Wages on application. To work 8 hours per day, 6 days per week. Previous experience preferred. Some knowledge of Spanish required. Minimum period of work 3 months.
Chambermaids (4). Wages and conditions as above, although slightly shorter hours are worked.
Secretary. Wages on application. To work 6 hours per day, 6/7 days per week. Some knowledge of Spanish required. Minimum period of work 2 months.

Free board and accommodation provided. All applicants must be at least 18 years of age. The work period is April to October. The Manager of this hotel wishes to stress that Medinaceli is not situated on the coast. *Applications* from February to the Manager at the above address, enclosing a full-length photograph. There are also vacancies at the Hotel Duque de Medinaceli, CN-II 150, Medinaceli (Soria), Spain.

HOTEL PICASSO: Torroaella de Monteri, Girona, Spain.
Waiters. £400 per month.
Maids. £400 per month.

To work at least 5 hours per day, 7 days per week. Board and accommodation available. Minimum period of work between July and August. Experience required. *Applications* to J.M. Ferrer at the above address in spring.

HOTEL RIGAT: Playa de Fanals, Lloret de Mar, Costa Brava, Spain. (e-mail rigat@ctv.es; website www.rigat.com) A 4 star Mediterranean hotel located on the sea, close to Barcelona. Those with or without hotel work experience are welcome to apply.
Receptionist/Barmaid: must be able to type. Wages by arrangement according to job and qualifications. 8 hours per day, 6 day week. Free board and accommodation. Age 19-28. A knowledge of French and German is required. Applicants must be considerate, polite and in good health. Girls should take a blue knee-length skirt and white blouses. Minimum period of work July and August but there are vacancies from June to September. *Applications* from February to Mr Felipe Rigat, Cadena Hotelera Rigat, c/o Ave de America No.1, Lloret de Mar (17) Spain.

HOTEL RIVIERA: Malgrat de Mar (Barcelona), Spain.
Receptionists. Must be able to type. Approximately £45 per week plus tips and commissions. Average 8 hours daily shift work. Board and accommodation provided free of charge. Knowledge of English and Spanish essential. Must be able to work from beginning of May until end of September. *Applications,* with photo, from March to the address above.

RESTAURANTE ROMAN OASIS & INNER SANCTUM HOTEL: Camino Los Banos de la Medionda, Manilva 29691, Malaga Costa del Sol, Spain (tel +34-952-892380; fax 952-890192; e-mail romanoasis@europe.com; www.insanctum.

com) The Roman Oasis Restaurant is an exotic and busy countryside restaurant, (seating 120) English owned for 20 successful years, and attached to it is a small luxury hotel, The Inner Sanctum. Both businesses are open June to September.
Bar, Floor and Kitchen Staff: for the restaurant. To work 7 nights a week, late nights, as is Spanish custom. *Applicants must hold an EU passport,* enjoy meeting people from many nations, be outgoing, energetic, hard-working, punctual and take pride in their appearance. Some Spanish or other languages necessary. Non-smokers given preference. Evening meal provided.
Hotel Staff. Two responsible live-in staff, who do not necessarily have to have experience. Two people, either a couple, or two men/two women because the accommodation is shared.

The hotel and restaurant are located between Marbella and Gibraltar, 3km from the beach and the nearest town Manliva (2km). Positions are available for the full season (hotel only) but some are available for mid-June to end of August. Accommodation is available. Wages depending on the shift. For a rough guide, longest shift is 4:30 p.m. to closure; wages after tax and cost of accommodation deduction, approx. £300 per month plus about £75 in tips. Please *apply to* Mr P Hickling at the special e-mail address insanctum@hotmail.com with full cv and photo before March 15th.

SALATS INVERSIONS S.A.: C/Deveses 23-25, l'Estartit, E-17258 Girona, Costa Brava, Spain (tel 972-75 15 77 17; fax 972-75 10 59).
Kitchen Staff (2) to cook basic pub food either alone or with an assistant. To work 10 hours per day, 6 days per week. Applicants should be aged over 21 and fast, competent workers with basic experience of food/cooking; training will be given.
Bar/Entertainment Staff (7) to work for a very busy theatre theme bar; duties to include serving drinks and food, stock control plus involvement in amateur shows. Applicants must be aged at least 21 with experience of bar work, hardworking and honest, with bubbly personalities; training will be given. The ability to sing or dance would be advantageous.

Wages of around £120 per week plus tips. Accommodation provided in a shared house with food and drink (but not water and electricity) and medical cover included. Contracts will be issued. Period of work April-October. The bar is looking for staff who are good all-rounders and who work well as part of a team.

Applications to Kate Gray, Personnel Manager, at the above address.

Sports, Couriers and Camping

ACORN ADVENTURE: 22 Worcester Street, Stourbridge DY8 1AN (tel 01384-446057; fax 01384-378866; e-mail topstaff@acornadventures.co.uk). An adventure activity holiday company offering groups multi-activity camping holidays in North Wales, the Lake District, France, Spain and Italy.
Seasonal Staff (300); instructors, maintenance staff, administrators, catering staff and nurses needed mid-April to September (some shorter contracts). Activities include sailing, canoeing, kayaking, climbing, abseiling and caving. Living allowance of approximately £50 plus supplement/bonus subject to centre and location. Please send an application letter for the attention of Recruitment to recieve a full information pack.

CAMPING GIOBO ROJO: Barangé-Brun C.B., Carretera Nacional II, km 660'9 08360 Canet de Mar (Barcelona), Spain (tel/fax 93-794 1143; e-mail cgrojo@teleline.es; www.globo-rojo.com).

Receptionist, Waiter/Waitress, Qualified Swimming Pool Guard required for this campsite near Barcelona (40km). All staff should be polite, with relevant experience. The wages are c. £375 per month for 8-9 hour days over a 7 day week, with free board and lodging. Ideally applicants should speak English, German, and some Spanish, while the job provides an excellent chance to improve Spanish.

The work is available between 1 July and 30 August, and *applications* are invited from April onwards.

CANVAS HOLIDAYS: East Port House, 12 East Port, Dunfermline, Fife KY12 7JG (tel 01383-629018; fax 01383-629071; www.canvas holidayscom). Canvas Holidays are looking for enthusiastic, resourceful people who enjoy a challenge and love the outdoor life. Main positions for 2002 include:
Campsite Courier. Varied responsibilities. Involves cleaning and preparation of customer accommodation, welcoming and looking after customers during their holiday and ensuring that they have the best holiday ever. As a campsite courier you will have new challenges every day which can lead to one of the most enjoyable summers you will ever have. Variable working hours.
Children's Courier. As a Canvas Holidays Children's Courier you will have had formal experience of working with children. You will organise and carry out a six day programme which involves four hours a day of Children's Club for children between the ages of 4 and 11. You will be prepared to help out with courier duties as and when requried. For many customers, the Children's Club is one of the main parts of the holiday. You will need to have the energy of a seven year old and the imagination of an eleven year old to succeed!

Package includes tented accommodation, medical insurance, full uniform and return travel to and from a UK port of entry. Positions are available from March until October. *Applications* are invited from individuals and couples. Contact Sandy, Karen or Michele at the above contact details for an application pack.

CLUB PUNTA ARABI: Apartado Correos 73, Es Cana/Santa Eulalia del Rio, Ibiza, Balearic Islands, Spain (tel 971-33 06 50/51).
Staff for a wide range of jobs in one of 2 holiday centres in Ibiza. Work includes sports instruction, including sailing, windsurfing and tennis, disc jockeys, theatre work where experience in make up, costumes and lighting is needed, etc. German essential and Spanish useful.
Amateur Entertainers for club shows-sketches, mime etc.
Guitarist/Folk Singer/Busker for parties, excursions etc.
Managers:with experience of running bars, restaurants etc.

Wages by arrangement. Applicants should have a reasonable knowledge of German: Spanish also useful. Period of work 1 May to 15 October. *Application forms* available from Miss Sarah Steiner, Director, Club Punta Arabi.

EUROCAMP: Overseas Recruitment Department (Ref SJ/02) (tel 01606-787522). Eurocamp is a leading tour operator in quality self-drive camping and mobile home holidays in Europe. Each year the company seeks to recruit up to 1,500 enthusiastic people for the following positions:
Campsite Courier: job involves cleaning and preparing customer accommodation, providing assistance, acting as an information service and an interpreter and performing some administrative duties. Couriers need to be flexible to meet the needs of the customer to provide them with excellent service. Minimum age 18 years. Applicants should be independent with plenty of initiative and relish a challenging and rewarding position. They should also possess a

friendly and helpful personality. Some working knowledge of another European language is required and previous customer service experience would be an advantage. Applicants should be available to work from April/May to September.
Children's Couriers: work involves organising a wide range of exciting activities for children aged 4-13. Applicants should possess initiative, imagination and enthusiasm along with good safety awareness. Previous childcare experience is essential. Minimum age is 18 years and applicants should be available from April/May to September. Languages are not a requirement but would be an advantage.
Senior Couriers: required to work alongside a team of Campsite Couriers and organise their daily workload, as well as carrying out the normal day to day duties of a Campsite Courier. Applicants should have good language skills and experience of leading a team.
Site Managers required to lead a large team of Campsite Couriers, organising their daily workloads and ensuring they provide the very best customer service. Applicants should be 21 or over, have proven managerial experience, excellent communication skills and language ability.
In all the above positions you should be be available for the full season commencing in April/May through to September. Comprehensive training is provided together with a competitive salary, insurance and return travel. Applications are accepted from September/October and *can only be accepted from UK/EU passport holders*. Interviews will be conducted in Hartford, Cheshire between October and April.

HAVEN EUROPE: 1 Park Lane, Hemel Hempstead HP2 4YL (tel 01442-203287; fax 01442-241473; www.haveneurope.com). Haven Europe Ltd, a leading self-drive, mobile home and camping company, provide seasonal job opportunities in France, Spain and Italy. Haven Europe Ltd. offers a competitive salary, accommodation on park, free uniform, travel to and from place of work, training, and medical insurance.
Courier Staff to work on campsites in Spain. Staff receive free accommodation, a competitive salary, uniform and insurance. Duties include preparation of guest accommodation, reception and problem solving. The hours are long and variable. Applicants should be available from March to end of September. Previous experience an advantage. Mature and sensible couples are invited to reply.
Children's Courier Staff to work on the same parks, organising and implementing children's activity programmes. Free accommodation, uniform and competitive salary. Experience with children is an advantage, and a genuine liking of working with children is essential. Applicants should be available from the April to early September and be at least 19 years of age. Spanish an advantage but not essential.
Please write to the above address for an application form.

KEYCAMP HOLIDAYS: Overseas Recruitment Department, Hartford Manor, Greenbank Lane, Nothwich CW8 1H (tel 01606-787522).
Campsite Couriers: to look after British, Dutch and Scandinavian customers on campsites in Spain. Duties include welcoming customers, providing local information, organising social activities on site and ensuring that all accommodation is prepared prior to arrival.
Children's Courier: to organise and provide up to 24 hours of activities a week for children aged 4-13 years, to advertise Le Club activities and visit families on arrival.

Senior Couriers: incorporating the role of campsite courier with the additional responsibility of organising and managing the team and ensuring the smooth running of the Keycamp operation on site.

Montage/Demontage: for a period of approximately 6 weeks at the beginning/end of season to erect/dismantle equipment.

Minimum age 18 years. Accommodation, uniform and training provided. A working knowledge of Spanish would be an advantage. Period of employment between March and July-October.

Applicants should write to the Overseas Recruitment Department, Keycamp Holidays, quoting reference SJ/02.

OPEN HOLIDAYS: 29 Guildbourne Centre, Worthing, West Sussex BN11 1LZ (tel 01903-201864; fax 01903-201225; e-mail: donna.elias@ openholidays. co.uk). Upmarket tailor-made villa, apartment and hotel holidays, specialising currently in Pollensa and Cala D'Or in Majorca and various resorts in Menorca and the Algarve.

Resort Representatives to assist clients and operate tours in Majorca and Menorca. To work 8 hours per day, 6 days per week. Salary £500-£700 per month. Board and accommodation negotiable. Minimum period of work 6 months from April to October. Minimum age 21. Knowledge of Spanish preferred. Must hold a full UK driving licence.

Applications from September-December to the General Manager at the above address. Successful applicants attend a training course in the UK during February.

PAVILION TOURS: Lynnem House, 1 Victoria Way, Burgess Hill, West Sussex RH15 9NF (tel 0870-241-0425; fax 0870-241-0426; e-mail sales@paviliontours. com; www.paviliontours.co.uk). Specialist activity tour operator for students, adults and families. Watersports, golf, tennis and team sports organised mainly on the Costa Brava.

Watersports Instructors (10) to work on the Costa Brava to instruct children during the day in sailing, canoeing etc., and to assist with entertainments in the evening. Hours of work variable, seven days a week. Wages approx. £400 per month. Minimum period of work is one week between May and August. Board and lodging provided. Applications from January to the above address. Please include current Instructor qualifications.

SOLAIRE HOLIDAYS: 1158 Stratford Road, Hall Green, Birmingham, B28 8AF (tel 0121-778-5061; fax 0121-778-5065; e-mail jobs@solaire.co.uk; www.solaire.co.uk). Solaire Holidays provides self-drive, self-catering holidays to Spain and France.

Site Couriers (20) to look after clients and prepare accommodation. Knowledge of Spanish desirable. Wage £280-£400 per month.

Children's Couriers (4) to run a children's club. Previous experience of working with children is required. Wage £280-£400 per month.

Cleaners (4) to clean site facilities. No experience or qualifications required. Wage £280-£340 per month.

Bar Staff (2) to work in site bar. Previous bar work experience required. Wage £280-£340 per month.

General Site Managers (4) required to keep site and facilities tidy. Wage £280-£340.

Maintenance Staff (2) required to carry out on-going site and accommodation maintenance. Previous experience in maintenance work required. Wage £400-£600 per month.

Applicants can apply for work between April and October, May and September or July and August. Hours of work vary according to demand, but applicants can expect to work for six days a week, on a rota system. Accommodation is provided as part of contract. Food is not provided. Applications are invited from October onwards to the above address.

Teaching and Language Schools

ABC ENGLISH: Calle Sol de Abajo 3, Antoñana, E-01128 Alava, Spain. ABC English organise summer language camps in the Basque country. They are not a language academy.

English Teachers (6) required in July to teach English and organise activites for children aged between 8-14. Applicants must be at least 18 years old, and while a teaching certificate is not necesary for all positions, applicants should have outdoor skills and a creative nature.

Applications, from *EU citizens* only, should be sent to Tulio Browning at the above address.

ENGLISH EDUCATIONAL SERVICES: C/ ALCALA 20-29, 28084 Madrid (tel 34-91-531-4783; fax 34-91-531-5298; e-mail movingparts@excite.com).

English Teachers (80-110) with recognised EFL qualfication such as CELTA or TESOL Trinity College required by recruitment specialists for EFL in Spain. Positions available in various parts of the country including Madrid. Standard length of contact is 9 months; teaching mainly in the evenings from 5pm onwards. Salary depends on the client school the teacher is employed by, as does provision for accommodation. Most client schools will help their teachers find a place to live.

EU Citizens are preferred. Interviews may be carried out in the UK and Ireland at peak times. *Applications* should be made to the above address.

ITC INTERNATIONAL TEFL CERTIFICATE, BARCELONA: Rocafort, 104, 08015 Barcelona, Spain (US Voice mail 1-800-915-5540; US Fax (815) 550-0086; tel (Barcelona) (34) 93 423 9482; e-mail info@itc-training.com; www.itc-training.com).

ITC International TEFL Certificate 110 hour intensive training courses in Prague or Barcelona give you practical experience living, working, and interacting abroad before you even begin teaching. Caring support staff, lifetime job assistance worldwide. ITC offers in Spain the internationally recognised 4-week TEFL Certificate Course that qualifies graduates to teach English worldwide. Sessions are held year-round and on a monthly basis. Upon completion of the course ITC can guarantee a job in Eastern Europe, provides lifetime job guidance worldwide and has employment contacts throughout the globe. Over 1,500 teachers have graduated from ITC and are now working throughout the globe.

Trainees receive extensive supervised teaching practice with foreign students during the course and housing is available during the course. ITC is registered by the Ministry of Education in Spain. ITC also maintains a list of summer teaching opportunities in Spain and nearby countries. See the *Czech Republic* chapter for information on ITC's Prague programme.

THE MANGOLD INSTITUTE: Marques de Sotelo 5, Pasaje Rex, Valencia E-46002, Spain (tel 96-352-77-14 or 351-45-56; fax 96-351-45-56; e-mail: mangold@mangold-valencia.com; www.mangold-valencia.com).

Teachers. To teach general English including the technical aspects of the language. 30-34 hours work per week for wages of £550-£750 per month. No accommodation available. Applicants must be university graduates and hold an E.F.L. certificate or similar. They should be dynamic and outgoing. Minimum period of work 9 months, October to June. *Applications* in May to the above address or come in person.

RELACIONES CULTURALES INTERNACIONALES: Callez Ferraz no. 82, Madrid E-28008, Spain (tel 91-541-71 03; fax 91-559-11-81).
Supervisors, Language Assistants. Approx. £100 per month. 5-8 hour day. 5 to 6 days per wk. Should like children and have studied at higher education establishment. Teaching and/or sport orientated applicants preferred. Minimum period of work 1 to 2 months around the year.
English Language Teachers for private Spanish colleges and kindergartens. Wages from £130 per month. To teach English and look after children aged from 4 years onwards. Should be qualified teachers, preferably with EFL experience. Minimum period 1 month all year round.
Au Pairs to live and help with light household chores in a Spanish family, or take care of children and help teach English. Ages 18-28 years. Placements all over Spain and over the whole year. Full social assistance during the stay is provided by RCI. Summer stays from one to three months, or around the year for 6 to 12 months. No special requirements are necessary. Paying stays are also arranged.
Counsellors (80) to supervise and teach English sports on 3 summer camps.
   Applications to the above address as soon as possible.

Work with Children

C.P.N. AZTERLARIAK: Apartado número 3191, 01002 Vitoria-Gasteiz, Spain (tel 945-281794; e-mail azterlaria@euskalnet.net). C.P.N. Azterlariak, run nature camps in sessions of two weeks during the summer to provide a balanced programme of leisure activities for children and teenagers aged 8-18. The camps take place near Urbion's beautiful mountains.
Volunteers are required to work for two weeks 15th-30th July.
Monitors (2) to be responsible for the children 24 hours a day; overseeing activities, looking after their personal belongings, planning their outdoor activities. monitors should be energetic, imaginative patient and sensitive. Being an extrovert is not necessary. Monitors will also be involved in general cleaning/camp maintenance duties. Some knowledge of Spanish is essential and Monitors are required to attend a short training course preceding the camp.
Cooks (1-2) Experience of cooking for large numbers is useful, and applicants will preferably hold a relevant qualification. Cooks must be prepared for outdoor cooking.
   For all positions, employees receive full board, accommodation in tents and liability insurance. Monitors are unpaid volunteers: Cooks receive £130-£185 depending on numbers attending.
   Apply by e-mail, or to the address above.

KURSOLAN: c/Sandalo, 5, E-28042 Madrid, Spain (tel 91-320 7500; fax 91-320 7753).
Monitors (40) to take care of, and teach English and sports to, Spanish children. Wages by arrangement; free board and lodging provided. To work at least 9^1/2 hours per day, 7 days per week with two 24 hour periods free per week. Period of

work from the middle of June to September. Applicants should have experience of teaching and sports. *Applications* to the Camp Director at the above address.

VIGVATTEN NATUR KLUB: Apartado 3253, E-01002 Vitoria-Gasteiz, Spain (tel 945-28-17-94; fax 945-28-17-94). Staff needed to live and work with children in the outdoors in the most beautiful places in Spain; the Klub offers a unique and unforgettable international experience.

Monitors (15) to be responsible for children 24 hours a day, with duties including planning, organising and directing outdoor activities. Wage of approx. £290 per month. Previous experience of working with children is essential,

Support Staff (12) to see to the maintenance and cleaning of the camps and food preparation, serving and clearing away after meals. Wage of approx. £290 per month. Possession of a certificate of competence in food hygiene would be helpful.

Cooks (3) to be responsible for the daily cooking. Wage of approximately £290 per month. Must have experience of cooking for large numbers of people and should preferably hold a relevant qualification.

Camp Nurses (3) to be responsible for the health and welfare of the children and staff. Wage of approx. £290 per month; must hold nursing qualifications.

Full board and accommodation provided. Minimum period of work two weeks over the summer. Applicants should speak English; knowledge of Spanish is also desirable. Applicants are required to make and pay for their own travel arrangements. *Applications* to Laureano Varela, Director, at the above address in February or March.

Voluntary Work and Archaeology

CANARY NATURE: Atlantic Whale Foundation, St Martins House, 59 St Martins Lane, Covent Garden, London WC5H (e-mail edb@huron.ac.uk; www.whalefoundation.f2s.com).

Aimed at more mature **volunteers** than those who sign up with Proyecto Ambiental (see below), this project carries out more intimate research with pilot whales and bottlenose dolphins, on a dedicated researcg boat, with volunteers assisting the researcher more directly. Accommodation is provided in tourist quality rural housing. This volunteer opportunity is entirely research orientated, with specialist talks on cetacean issues.

PROYECTO AMBIENTAL TENERIFE: c/o 59 St Martins Lane, Covent Garden, London, WC2N (e-mail edb@huron.ac.uk; www.whalefoundation.f2s.com).

Volunteers to help on popular whale and dolphin conservation and research projects in the Canaries, in multinational groups of 30-40 volunteers at a time, between June and October. Work involves working with the whale-watching industry on research on the impact of boats, photo-identification of pilot whale and bottlenose dolphin communities, pollution studies, educational workshops and public art programmes and helping prepare workshops and educational materials. The projects also involve work with the local communities. The participation cost of £95 per week includes half board accommodation, all training and funds the projects.

A positive attitude is most essential although knowledge of European languages is particularly useful. Projects are based in Tenerife. For qualified divers, there is also a sublittoral marine habitat survey in Tenerife for which, again, there will be a surcharge payable.

Contact the above address for an information pack enclosing a 31p s.a.e. or two international reply coupons.

THE SUNSEED TRUST: Apdo. 9, E-04270 Sorbas, Almeria, Spain (tel +34-950 552 770 10am-Midday; e-mail sunseedspain@arrakis.es). The Sunseed Trust is a British registered charity looking for ways to contain or reclaim deserts.
Volunteers and longer term plaement volunteers are sought to participate in the work of their centre in Southern Spain. Typical projcts may involve germination trials, erosion control techniques, solar oven development, pasteurisation processes, hydroponic growing etc. There is also a need for an input into community tasks such as gardening, building and catering.

Applicants must pay for their own travel to the centre and make a weekly contribution of £45+ towards expenses (depending on the season and type of stay). For further details please send three International Reply Coupons to Sunseed, PO Box 2000, Cambridge, CB4 3UJ England, or contact the Spanish centre directly.

Au Pairs, Nannies, Family Helps and Exchanges

ABB AU-PAIR FAMILY SERVICE: Via Alemania 2, 5ºA, E-07003 Palma de Mallorca Spain (tel +34-971-752027; fax +34-971-298001). Friendly au pair agency with high quality services and carefully chosen host families.
Au Pairs required to help families look after children and carry out general housekeeping work. Applicants should have a mature outlook, be responsible and have a love of children. Au-pairs normally work 25-30 hours over a 5-6 day week. Placements are available all year, with a minimum stay of 3 months in the summer.

Applicants should speak either English and Spanish, English and French or English and German. *Applications* accepted all year, and should be sent to Clara Managin at the above address.

CENTROS EUROPEOS PRINCIPE, S.L.: C/Principe 12, 6A-28012 Madrid, Spain (tel +34-91 532 72 30; fax +34-91 521 60 76; e-mail ccprincipe@inicia.es).
Au Pairs to work 30-35 hours per week; pocket money of around £32 to £45 per week. Placements of 2/3 months are possible over the summer, but it is easier to arrange placements of 9/10 months for the whole school year, or for 6 months from January or April.
Paying Guests for stays in Madrid, Alicante, Segovia, Salamanca, Valencia, Toledo, Barcelona, Cordoba, Granada, Seville or Santander.
Exchanges also arranged between Spanish and British students aged 12-25 for 2-4 weeks.
Applications to the above address.

Sweden

As Sweden is a member of the European Union, nationals of EU and EEA countries are free to enter to look for and take up work. Although the rate of unemployment is considerably lower than it has been (4.3% in August 2001), there are strict limits on the number of foreigners allowed to work in Sweden.

The Swedish labour service cannot help jobseekers from non-EEA countries to find work in Sweden. General information and addresses of local employment offices may be obtained from *Arbetsmarknadsstyrelsen* at Kungstensgatan 45, S-113

99 Stockholm, Sweden (tel +46-8-5860 6000; e-mail arbetsmarknadsstyrelsen@ ams.amv.se; www.ams.se which is in English). It is up to the individual to get in touch with employers. Long-term vacancies and summer jobs can now be sought by those with a knowledge of the Swedish language on the internet: http://jobb.amv.se.

There are also opportunities for voluntary work in Sweden arranged by International Voluntary Service for British people and Service Civil International for Americans: see the *Worldwide* chapter for details.

Advertisements in Swedish newspapers may be placed through Crane Media Partners Ltd, 20-28 Dalling Road, Hammersmith, London W6 OJB (tel 020-8237 8601; fax 020-8735 9941), who handle *Dagens Nyheter, Goteborgs Posten* and *Sydsvenska Dagbladet.*

RED TAPE

Visa Requirements: EU citizens excepted, a visa is required by many nationalities for a tourist visit to Sweden.

Residence Permits: EU citizens can apply for residence permits from within Sweden by contacting the Immigration Board Office (Statens Invandrarverk, Box 6113, S-600 06 Norrköping; tel 011-156000; e-mail invandrarverket@siv.se) and completing the application forms. Applicants should note that the procedure of obtaining a Residence Permit can take between 2 and 5 months.

Non-Europeans must submit to their local Swedish Embassy a written offer of work on form AMS PF 101704, at least two months before their proposed arrival. The procedure involves an interview at the Embassy. Immigration queries should be addressed to Migrationsverket, the Swedish Migration Board (601 70 Norrköping; 11-15 60 00; www.migrationsverket.se). Full details are posted in English on their web pages or you can request printed leaflets.

Work Permits: Citizens of EU countries do not need work permits in order to work in Sweden. For others a work permit requires an offer of employment to have been obtained, application forms for the necessary permit should then be obtained from your nearest Swedish Embassy. The application will be processed by the Swedish Immigration Service and the procedure can take 1-3 months. Applications for work permits are not accepted from foreign visitors who are already in Sweden.

Au Pairs: Au pairs are subject to the same regulations as all other foreign employees so non-EU nationals must obtain a work permit before leaving their home country. The Scandinavian Institute in Malmö (Box 3085; 040-93 94 40/fax 040-93 93 07; info@scandinavianinst.com) makes au pair placements in Swedish families and throughout Scandinavia.

Agricultural Work

CARL-HENRIK NIBBING: Skillinggrand, 9, S-11120 Stockholm, Sweden.
Farm Assistant. Wages by arrangement: free travel. Board and lodging provided; helper lives as member of the family. General duties around summer residence/farm in southern Sweden. Age 14-19 years. Applicants should be competent and good natured. Period of work June to August. *Applications* to C.H. Nibbing.

Hotel Work and Catering

PENSIONAT HOLMHALLAR: S-62010 Burgsvik, Sweden (tel 0498-4980-30; fax 0498-498056).

Hotel Workers (2) to clean rooms and work in the kitchen and restaurant. £860 approx. per month. To work 40 hours per week of hotel work. *Applications to Carl Hansen at the above address in February/March.*

Switzerland

Switzerland has managed to keep one of the lowest unemployment rates in the world, and to preserve that state it imposes strict work permit requirements on all foreigners who want to work there. It is significant that unlike most of the other non-EU members of Western Europe, Switzerland did not join the EEA a few years ago, although there are long-term plans for it to do so. However, a bilateral treaty on free movement of persons has been concluded with the EU. This agreement is new for 2002, and the main obstacles to free movement will be abolished in 2004. Information on this can be found on-line at www.europa.admin.ch.

Switzerland has always needed extra seasonal workers at certain times of the year, and traditionally issues a quota of short-term work permits. The tourist industry in particular needs staff for both the summer and winter seasons (July to September and December to April).

Jobs in the tourist industry are described both in this chapter and the *Worldwide* chapter at the beginning of the book (for example see the entry for Village Camps). Students looking for hotel work should note the entry below for the *Schweizer Hotelier Verein* (Swiss Hotels' Association). Hotel work can be hard: in the past some workers have found they have been expected to work longer hours than originally promised without any compensation in the form of overtime payments or extra time off, or be asked to do jobs other than those specified in their contracts. In return, however, wages should be higher than average for hotel work in Europe.

Farmers also need extra help at certain times of the year: see the entry below for the Landdienst-Zentralstelle, which can arrange working stays on Swiss farms. Opportunities in the short but lucrative grape harvest in October (particularly in the Lausanne area) would be greater were it not for the difficulty of getting work permits. Some knowledge of German or French is normally needed, even for grape-picking. Italian is also spoken, particularly in the canton of Ticino.

Placing an advertisement in a Swiss paper may lead to the offer of a job. *Tribune de Geneve* is published at 11 rue des Rois, CH-1211 Geneva (www.edicom.ch/tdg).

There are opportunities for voluntary work in Switzerland with the organisations named at the end of this chapter and British applicants can also apply through Concordia and International Voluntary Service, and Americans through Service Civil International; see the *Worldwide* chapter for details.

RED TAPE

Visa Requirements: citizens of the United Kingdom, the United States, Canada, Australia, New Zealand and most other European countries do not normally require visas for tourism. Nationals of most other countries need a visa.

Residence/Work Permits: the Swiss Residence Permit (*Aufenthaltsbewilligung* or *autorisation de séjour*) covers both the right of abode and employment. These are required for all persons entering to take up employment and entitle the holder to live in a specific canton and work for a specified employer. They can only be applied for from outside Switzerland and processing of the application takes 6-8 weeks. Hence if you wish to work in Switzerland, you must secure a job before entering the country.

The permits come in several types; for anyone looking for temporary work, the relevant ones are: *A Permits* for seasonal employment up to a maximum of 9 months for jobs in the tourist and building industry. *B Permits* are valid for one year for one specific job. Once you have obtained a job your prospective employer must obtain a work and residence permit on your behalf. When the permit has been granted you can contact the embassy and pick up your visa. After arrival you should register with the Aliens Police within 8 days and before starting work.

Au Pairs also require a work permit as above.

Voluntary Work: a work permit is required as above.

Agricultural Work

LANDDIENST-ZENTRALSTELLE: Postfach 728, CH-8025 Zurich, Switzerland (tel 1-261-44-88; fax 1-261-44-32; e-mail admin@landdienst.ch; www.landdienst.ch). Landdienst is a non-profit making, publicly subsidised organisation which each year places around 3,000 Swiss and 500 foreign farmers assistants.

Farmers' Assistants to work on family farms. Wages £190 per month plus free board and lodging. To work 8 hours per day, 6 days per week. Minimum period of work 3 weeks between the spring and autumn. Knowledge of German and/or French essential. *Applications* are invited at least 4 weeks prior to desired starting date. Individual applicants must be nationals of a country in western Europe and pay a registration fee.

British applicants can obtain more information by sending a sae to Concordia, Heversham House, 20/22 Boundary Road, Hove, East Sussex BN3 4ET; Danish applicants should contact EXIS, Postboks 291, DK-6400 Sonderborg; Dutch applicants through Travel Active Programmes, Postbus 107, NL-5800 AC Venray; Portuguese applicants through International Friendship League, R. Ruy de Sausa Vinagre 2, P-2890 Alcochete. A six-week group stay for applicants from Eastern Europe will also be arranged from mid-August to late September: contact the above address for contact addresses in Poland, the Czech Republic, Slovakia and the Baltic States.

Hotel Work and Catering

CHALET-HOTEL ADLER: Fam.A & E Fetzer, CH-3718 Kandersteg, Switzerland (tel 033-675 8010; fax 033-675 8011; www.chalethotel.ch). This hotel is set in the mountains of Switzerland, with rail access allowing excursions across the country.

Barmaids, Chambermaids. Waitresses to work from 8^1/2hours, 5 days a week. Salary approx. £690 per month. Minimum period of work 2^1/2 months from May/June to September/October. Accommodation provided. Knowledge of German required.

Applications, with a photo, from April to the above address.

HOTEL ALPENBLICK: Oberdorf, CH-3812 Wilderswil, Switzerland (tel +33-828 3550; fax +33-828 3551). The hotel is situated in the Ferienort Wilderswil near the Jungfrau. It has an excellent reputation for the high standard of its cooking, and a friendly, co-operative and cosy atmosphere.

Cook to prepare meals for the à la Carte restaurant and also prepare the menu and meals for half-board hotel guests. Good cooking abilities, and the ability to cope with the stresses of a busy restaurant are prerequisites.

Waiting Staff to serve breakfast, evening meals and light afternoon snacks. Applicants should have a sound knowledge of German, experience of waiting on tables and a well groomed appearance.

Housekeeper to clean the hotel and restaurant and to look after children; the applicant should have a love of order and a way with children.

All posts pay £940 gross per month, for 45-48 hours per week; board costs c.£190 and lodging c.£90 per month. Period of work is from early June to mid September, with the minimum period of work being 2-3 months. All staff should speak German. *Applications* are accepted from October onwards, addressed to Richard Stöckli at the above address.

HOTEL BAHNHOF: CH-8201 Schaffhausen, Switzerland (tel 52-624 19 24; fax 52-624 74 79).

Hotel Staff (2) for housekeeping and work in the dining room. Wages up to £1,300 per month. 8 hours per day, 5 days per week. Knowledge of German required. Minimum period of work 4 months between 1 June and 30 September. *Applications* from the spring to Arnold W. Graf at the above address.

HOTEL BELLEVUE: CH-3901 Simplon-Pass, Switzerland (tel 027-979 1331; fax 027-979 1239).

Secretary to work on reception desk and take care of all correspondence. Knowledge of German, French and Italian essential. Good secretarial and hotel experience required.

Chambermaid. Knowledge of German, French and Italian an advantage.

Waiters/Waitresses (4). Must have experience in similar work. Knowledge of some German, French and Italian required. Suit trainee wishing to widen experience.

Wages on application. Free board and accommodation provided. Minimum age 18 years. Minimum period of work 2 months during the summer season. *Applications* from January to the above address.

HOTEL BERNINA SAMEDAN: CH-7503 Samedan, Switzerland (tel 081-852 12 12; fax 081-852 36 06; e-mail hotel-bernina@bluewin.ch; website www.hotel-bernina.ch). The Hotel Bernina is a traditional hotel for holiday-makers (in summer: hiking, biking and mountain climbing) with 100 beds, an à-la-carte Italian restaurant, bar, park, tennis courts and sun-terrace.

Porters, Waiters/Waitresses (3) with experience in hotel/restaurant work. Wages about £1,200 per month. To work 8¹/2 hours per day, 5 days per week. Minimum period of work is three months between June and October. Board and accommodation is available at a cost of £250 per month. Must have previous experience and knowledge of German. *Applications* to Th. Bonjour, Director at the above address until May at the latest.

BURGENSTOCK HOTELS & RESORT: CH-6363 Bürgenstock, Switzerland (tel +41-41-612 9910; fax +41-41-612 9901; e-mail human.resources@ buergenstock-hotels.ch). Luxury standard 5-star hotels 20km from Lucerne, open from April to October.

Chef de Rang (15), Commis de Rang (10), Kitchen Staff (15) for a la carte and banquet catering and service, all applicants should have high standards, previous experience and speak German. Wages from £980 per month according to experience.

Bar Staff (3) should have previous experience of bar work, wages by negotiation according to experience.

Chambermaids (10) wages from £960 per month.

Staff work a 45 hour week, with the period of work running from April to October, with dates of work varying according to position. Board and lodging is available at a cost of c.£160 and £77-£155 respectively. Staff should speak German, English or French.

Applications are invited from November onwards to Frau Regine Bartsch, Human Resources Manager at the above address.

HOTEL CASA BERNO: CH-6612, Ascona, Switzerland (tel 091-791-3232; hotel@casaberno.ch; www.casaberno.ch). This four star hotel is situated above Ascona, with magnificent panoramic views.

Kitchen/Office Staff. (2) No special qualifications nor languages necessary.

Laundry Staff: for light work/ironing. No special qualificatons necessary, nor languages.

For both positions, the minimum period of work is 2 months between 15th March and 31st October 2002. Board and accommodation available for approx. £310 per month. Wages are approx. £1,100 per month. *Apply* to Pierre Goetschi, the Director, at the above address.

HOTEL CLUB: 71 rue du Parc, CH-2300 la Chaux-de-Fonds, Switzerland (tel 041-32 914 15 16; fax 041-32 914 15 17).

Bar Assistant to serve drinks and attend to customers; training will be given.

Trainee Receptionist to welcome clients, take reservations, operate the telephone switchboard and computer, run the front office, and help serve breakfasts when things are quiet.

Breakfast Assistant to prepare a buffet breakfast, serve tea and coffee and generally clean up.

Chambermaids for general cleaning duties in all parts of the hotel, work in the laundry and to perform general errands.

Wages approx. £920 per month. To work a 42 hour, 5 day week; working hours will vary according to need. Board and lodging available for around £100 per month. Period of work by arrangement between July and August and December and January. Applicants who can speak French are preferred; knowledge of Swiss-German, German, French, English and/or Italian would be advantages. The hotels' clients tend to be businessmen so efficiency of service is of importance. *Applications* to Madame J. Koegler, Director, at the above address at any time. Due to large number of applications only candidates who might be hired will receive replies.

CONTINENTAL PARKHOTEL: CH-6900 Lugano, Switzerland (tel 91-966-11-12; fax 91-966-12-13). This holiday hotel set in a sub-tropical park, overlooks Lake Lugano and the mountains.

Waitress £700 net or more, depending on previous experience, per month. 45 hour, 5 day week. Free board and accommodation provided. Season from 1 April to 30 October. Knowledge of German or experience of hotel work necessary to see to get a working permit (citizens of EU only). *Applications* to E. Fassbind at the above address.

HOTEL CRISTALLO: Poststrasse, CH-7050 Arosa, Switzerland (tel 081-377 2261; fax 081-377 4140).
Waiter/Waitress (1-2). £1,500 per month. Must have previous experience. Staff work about 9 hours per day, 5 days per week. Board and accommodation provided at £300 per month, deducted from gross salary. Knowledge of German essential. Minimum period of work 12 weeks between the middle of June and the end of September. *Applications* to the above address in March and April.

HOTEL FORNI: Marzio Forni, CH-6780 Airolo, Switzerland (tel 91-869 12 70; fax 91-869 15 23; e-mail: INFO@forni.ch).
Kitchen Staff and Waitress to serve in the bar and restaurant. Must be presentable. Approximately £1,000 per month. To work 9 hours per day, 5 days per week. Board and accommodation available for £340 per month. *Applications* to the above address.

BERGHAUS GFELALP: CH-3718 Kandersteg, Switzerland (tel +41-33-6751161). This hotel is situated in Kandersteg, an area of outstanding beauty, and renowned for its hiking possibilities.
Waiting and Chamber Staff: required between 15th July and 15th September, to work 45 hours per week over 5-6 days. The posts are available as either 2 female or 2 male jobsharers, or one male/female working full time. Job sharing would mean both employees working at weekends with one free during the week to travel or go sightseeing. Wages are 1,000 SFr (£405 approx.) per month and free accommodation is provided. Employees must be able to speak German.
To *apply* write to Fam. Schärer at the above address.

GRAND HOTEL BELLEVUE: CH-3789 Gstaad, Switzerland (tel 033-748 31 71; fax 033-724 21 36).
Waiting Assistants (2). Wage approx. £900 per month. To work 42 hours per week, with board and lodging available for around £285 per month. Period of work by arrangement between Christmas/New Year and July/August. Applicants should speak German, English and French. *Applications* to Mr Ferdinand D. Salverda, General Manager, at the above address.

THE HIKING SHEEP GUEST HOUSE: Villa La Joux, CH-1854 Leysin, Switzerland (tel/fax +41(0)24-494 3535; e-mail hikingsheep@leysin.net; www.leysin.net/hikingsheep). A guesthouse in the Swiss French Alps nestled beside forest and snow-capped mountains, looking towards the Trient Glacier and the Mont Blanc massif.
General Staff required to assist in the running of the guest house. Should speak basic French and English; speaking German would be an asset. Applicants must be outgoing, friendly, flexible and trustworthy. To work 4-5 hours a day 7 days per week, all year round; minimum period of work 1 month. Board and lodging are provided. *Applications* may be made at any time of year to Gérard at the above address.

HOTEL HIRSCHEN: Passhöhe, CH-9658 Wildhaus, Switzerland.
Counter Assistants/Waiting Staff (1/2) to serve hotel guests at mealtimes, present buffets, wash glasses, prepare coffee, breakfast etc. Wages approx. £1,100 per month. 9-9½ hours work per day, 5 days per week. Board and lodging provided. Minimum period of work 3 months between June and October. Knowledge of German and previous experience of hotel work essential. *Applications* to S. Walt at the above address from February.

JOBS IN THE ALPS (EMPLOYMENT AGENCY): 17 High Street, Gretton, Northants NN17 3DE (e-mail alan@jobs-in-the-alps.com; www.jobs-in-the-alps.com).

Waiters, Waitresses, Chambermaids, Kitchen Helps, Hall and Night Porters (200 in the winter, 150 in summer) for good Swiss hotels, cafes and restaurants at mountain resorts. Wages of £500 per month for 8¹/₂ hours work per day, 5 days per week. Free board and accommodation. Knowledge of French and/or German required for most positions. Applicants should be alert, intelligent, hardworking, responsible and pleasant. Hotel experience preferable but not essential. Periods of work: June to September (minimum period three months including July and August), or December to April (whole season only). *Applications, from British and EU citizens only*, enclosing a s.a.e. by 30 April (summer season) or 30 September (winter season).

HOTEL JUNGFRAUBLICK UND BEAUREGARD: Haupstrasse, CH-3803 Beatenberg, Switzerland (tel 41-33 841 15 81; fax 41-33 841 20 03).

Waiting Staff. Wages £825 per month, approximately. To work 8¹/₂ hours per day, 5 days per week. Board and lodging available for £270 per month. Period of work at least 4 months from June to October or November. Knowledge of German required. Applicants should be reliable workers who can take pleasure in their work. *Applications* to Herr Heinrich at the above address.

HOTEL LANDHAUS: CH-7299 Davos Laret, Switzerland.

Waitress for general dining room duties. £500-£600 per month. Preferably with previous experience and some knowledge of French and German.

Stillroom Maid for general and buffet duties. £150-£180 per month. Some knowledge of French and/or German an advantage.

8¹/₂ hours per day, at least 5 days per week. At the height of the season a 7 day week may be worked. Free board and accommodation. All applicants must be available for the whole of the period 1 July to mid September and be over 18 years old. *Applications* with recent photograph and international reply coupon from April to the above address.

HOTEL MEIERHOF: CH-7260 Davos-Dorf, Switzerland (tel 41-81 416 82 85; fax 41-81 416 39 82; e-mail: meierhof@email.ch). Traditional and charming mountain resort-hotel with 80 rooms, set in the heart of the village next to all the attractive sport and leisure facilities of Davos.

Waiter/Waitress £900 per month, for a 44 hour week, 9 hours per day. Board and accommodation provided. Knowledge of German essential. Must be able to start work on the 15 June. *Applications* in March and April to R. Frey, the Manager, at the above address.

HOTEL MEISSER: CH-7545 Guarda, Switzerland (tel 81-862-21-52; fax 81-862-24-80). A medium-sized hotel, 2¹/₂ hours from Zurich, led by a young dynamic team.

Service Workers (1-2) Wage about £775 per month. Should have relevant experience.

General Workers (1-2) Wage around £775 per month.

Both positions involve 8-9 hours work a day, 5 days per week. To work from 15 June to 31 August or as contracted. Board and accommodation are available, the cost to be deducted from wages. Ability to speak English is important; knowledge of German, French or Italian would also be useful.

Applications are invited to Benno Meisser at the above address from January onwards.

HOTEL MOND: Dorfstrasse 1, CH-6375 Beckenried, Switzerland (tel +41-620 1204; fax +41-620 4618; e-mail info@hotel-mond.ch; www.hotel-mond.ch). The 'Mond' hotel was built in 1870. Since then it has been owned and run by the same family. The hotel has 60 beds, 2 restaurants and a bar and is located at Beckenreid, on the edge of Lake Lucerne.

Buffet Assistants to serve drinks.

Waiting Staff to serve in a la carte restaurant.

Wages approximately £1,250 per month gross. To work 8-9 hours per day, 5 days per week. Period of work from the beginning of June to the end of September: minimum period of work 2 months. Applicants must speak German. *Applications* to Monica Egli-Amstad at the above address before the end of January.

HOTEL MOTEL KRONE: CH-3074 Berne-Muri, Switzerland.

Assistant Waiter. Some waiting experience and a little German essential.

Buffet Assistant (male). To prepare snacks and drinks. Some knowledge of German essential.

Dishwasher (1), Kitchen Porter (1). No previous experience required but a little German is required.

All staff work 9 hours per day, 5 days per week, probably on split shifts. Board and accommodation is provided free of charge. All applicants should be available for at least 2¹/₂ months, between 18-25 years of age and EU members. *Applications* as soon as possible to Herrn Bachler at the address above.

MOTEL-RESTAURANT MON ABRI: 3658 Merligen, Switzerland (tel 033-511380; fax 033-513671).

Temporary Waiting Assistant to work in a good standard *a la carte* restaurant. Wage according to turnover, with a minimum of £950 per month. To work 8 hours per day, 5 days per week. To work shifts either from 7am-3.30pm or from 3.30pm-midnight, each with a 30 minute meal break. Accommodation available for approx. £130 per month. Minimum period of work three months. Applicants should be friendly and speak English and German; knowledge of French would be an advantage. *Applications* to Fam. C. Rijke-Wyler at the above address in April and May.

MOTOTEL POSTILLON: CH-6374 Buochs, Switzerland.

Waiting Staff to work in a busy restaurant on a motorway. Approximately £940 per month. To work 8¹/₂-10¹/₂ hours per day, 5 days per week. Board and accommodation available for £95-£115 per month approx. Knowledge of German and English is necessary. *Applications* to Rene Ulrich, Director, at the above address.

PARKHOTEL BAD RAGAZ: CH-7310 Bad Ragaz, Switzerland.

Waiting Staff (2), General Assistants (2). Wages by arrangement. 42 hours per 5 day week. Minimum period of work 5 months between April and October. Board and accommodation available for around £200 per month. Applicants should speak German and have some previous experience. *Applications* to the Manager at the above address as soon as possible.

PARK HOTELS WALDHAUS: CH-7018 Flims-Waldhaus, Switzerland (tel +41-81-928 4848; fax 81-928 4858; e-mail info@park-hotels-waldhaus.ch; www.park-hotels-waldhaus.ch).
Assistant Waiters/Waitresses: must have previous experience of serving and speak German and French or Italian.
Swimming Pool Attendant to care for the pool, pool bar and information kiosk as well as to do cleaning work. Must speak German and either French or Italian.
    Net wages approximately £900 per month, with board and lodging provided for approx. £300 per month.applications, with a photograph, should be sent to the above address from February; *only applicants from EEA countries will get work permits for Switzerland.*

RESIDENCE AND BERNERHOF HOTELS: CH-3823 Wengen, Switzerland.
Waiters/Waitresses, Buffet Assistants, Laundry Maids, General Assistants. Wages on application. Staff work 9 hours per day, 5 days per week. Accommodation (30) days. Meals: lunch/dinner (no breakfast) for 22 days. 2 hotel restaurants; à-la-carte, and pizzeria. Guests almost always English, German, US, and Swiss. In the centre of Wengen. Period of work from December to April, and June to October. Knowledge of German required; knowledge of French an advantage. *Applications* to Rudolph Schweizer at the above address.

RESTAURANT BLAUES ROSSLI: CH-3668 Utzigen, Switzerland.
General Assistants (2, preferably girls) to help clean rooms, serve in the restaurant and help at the counter coffee bar, wash dishes, help with the laundry. To work 5 days per week. Salary approximately £400, net, per month. Board and accommodation provided free of charge. Minimum period of work 8 weeks, although preference will be given to those who can work for the whole season, April to October. Knowledge of German preferable. *Applications* to Mrs Kilchör at the above address at any time.

HOTEL RIGIBLICK AM SEE: Seeplatz 3, CH-6374 Buochs, Switzerland (tel 41-41-624 4850; fax 41-41-620 6874; e-mail hotelrigiblick@freesurf.ch; www.a-o.ch/6374-rigiblick_am_see). A 4-star hotel and restaurant on the lakeside.
Trainee Assistant (Waiter/Waitress), Trainee Chef to work 44 hours, 5 days a week. Wages approx. £1050 per month. Period of work May/June-August/September. Board and accommodation provided for £260 per month. *Applicants must hold an EU passport* and have a very good knowledge of German.
    Applications as soon as possible to the above address.

ROMANTIK HOTEL SANTIS: CH-9050 Appenzell, Switzerland (tel +41-71-788 1111; fax +41-71-788 1110; e-mail romantikhotelsaentis@bluewin.ch; www.romantikhotels.com/Appenzell). A traditional family-run 4-star hotel in one of the most beautiful areas of Switzerland, Appenzell is in the German-speaking region. The staff are mostly young people from around the world.
Waiter/Waitress; wage approx. £1,025 per month. To work 9 hours per day, 5 days per week. Board and accommodation available for approx. £221 per month. Minimum period of work 4 months between June and September. Applicants must have experience and speak German. Work permits are only available for EU/EFTA nationals. *Applications* to Stefan A. Heeb at the above address.

ROMANTIK HOTEL SCHWEIZERHOF: CH-3818 Grindelwald, Switzerland (tel 033-853-22-02; fax 033-853-20-04; e-mail schweizerhof@grindelwald.ch).

The Schweizerhof, a truly traditional hotel in Grindelwald, world famous holiday and winter sports centre at the foot of the Eiger in the Bernese Oberland.
Chambermaids (4-5) to clean rooms and do laundry.
Maintenance Assistants (3) to carry out general maintenance tasks on house and in garden.
Assistant Cooks (2) to assist in the kitchen with preparation and washing-up.
Laundry Assistants (2)
     Wages about £960 per month. To work a 42-hour 5-day week. Period of work is from 1 June to 15 October. Board and accommodation is available at a cost to be arranged. Knowledge of German is required. *Applications* to the above address between January and March at the latest.

SCHWEIZER HOTELIER-VEREIN: Monbijoustrasse 130, Postfach, CH-3001 Bern, Switzerland (tel 41-31-370-43-33; e-mail hoteljob.be@swisshotels.ch; www.hoteljob.ch). The 'Swiss Hotel Association' has around 2500 hotels and restaurants as members.
General Assistants from EU and EFTA countries to work in hotels in German-speaking Switzerland. Wages approximately £1,100 per month. Duties include helping with cooking, service and cleaning. Wages by arrangement. To work 8 hours and 25 minutes per day, 5 days per week. Period of work 3-4 months between June and September.
     Board and accommodation available at a cost of approximately £325 per month. Good knowledge of German essential. Please note that jobs in the French and Italian speaking parts of Switzerland can not be arranged. Applicants must possess valid passports etc. A registration fee of approximately £30 is payable. *Applications* accepted all year round.

SEEHOTEL WILBERBAD: CH-6062 Wilen am Sarnersee, Switzerland (tel 041-662 70 70; fax 041-662 70 80).
Waiter/Waitress (1-2) for lido and terrace restaurant. Must speak fluent German. Wages of around £610 per month. All staff to work 8¹/2 hours per day, 5 days a week. Board available at approx. £110 per month; accommodation in a double room costs approx. £58 per month. Minimum period of work 4 months. *Applications* in the autumn to Herr Bruno Odermatt, Director, at the above address.

HOTEL SONNE: CH-9658 Wildhaus, Switzerland (e-mail beutler-hotels@bluewin.ch; www.beutler.hotels.ch).
Waiters/Waitresses (3). £700, net, per month. Good knowledge of German required.
Buffet Staff (2). £600, net, per month. Good knowledge of German required.
     Staff work 81/2 hours per day, 5 days a week. Board and accommodation available at £216 per month. Minimum period of work 10 weeks. Winter season December to March and Summer season July to October. *Applications* as soon as possible to the proprietor, Paul Beutler, at the above address.

TRUMMELBACH FALLS: Gletscherwasser-Fälle, CH-3822, Lauterbrunnen, Switzerland.
Restaurant Assistant to work in the self-service restaurant at the entrance to the falls. The position calls for an all-rounder as duties include assisting behind the

counter, operating the cash register, clearing tables and cleaning.
Elevator Operator/Restaurant Assistant to operate a funicular lift inside a mountain, taking people to see the waterfalls. Time to be divided between operating the lift 2-3 days per week and working in the restaurant.

Wages £800-£900 per month for working a 5 day week. To work approximately 8-10 hours a day with a half hour lunch break. Applicants must speak fluent English and some basic German; knowledge of French would be an advantage. Must hold an EU passport and be aged at least 22. Applicants should send a full c.v. and a passport photo to Herr Urs von Almen at the above address by January.

HOTEL WALDHAUS: CH-7514 Sils-Maria, Engadin, Switzerland (tel 081-838 5100; fax 081-838 5198; e-mail staff@waldhaus-sils.ch; www.waldhaus-sils.ch). A five-star family hotel with up to 70% regular guests from all over the world.
General Assistants (2) to play an extensive role in service for the guest-rooms, lounge and terraces, and to see to the welfare of 220 guests as well as taking responsibility for their meals, under the direction of a superior. Wages £715-£858 per month. Must have knowledge of German, and the ability to take pleasure in working for guests.

To work 8-9 hours per day, 5 days per week. Minimum period of work is 3-4 months in the summer or winter seasons. Food and accommodation are available at the following prices; a double-room costs about £70 per person per month. *Applications* are invited up until mid-March for the summer season, or mid-August for the winter, and should be sent to Irene Ryser, Personnel Manager, at the above address.

HOTEL ZUM WEISSEN ROSSLI: CH-6487 Goschenen, Switzerland (tel +41-886 80 10; fax 886 80 30).
Waiting Assistants, Buffet Assistants, Chambermaids. Wages and hours of work by arrangement. Board and lodging provided. Period of work by arrangement, minimum contract of 6 months. Good knowledge of German required. *Work permits cannot be obtained for applicants from eastern Europe. Applications* to the above address 8 weeks before the desired beginning of work.

Sports, Couriers and Camping

CANVAS HOLIDAYS LIMITED: 12 Abbey Park Place, Dunfermline, Fife KY12 7PD (tel 01383-644018; fax 01383 620481; www.canvas.com). Canvas Holidays are looking for enthusiastic individuals who enjoy camping and a real challenge. Main positions available for 2001 include:
Campsite Couriers. Varied responsibilities, but largely responsible for the cleaning and preparation of customer accommodation, welcoming and looking after customers on-site, helping with any problems that might arise and organising activities for children and adults. Variable working hours.

Package includes tented accommodation, medical insurance, full uniform and travel expenses to and from UK port of entry. Period of work from end March to mid-October. Good working knowledge of German essential. *Applications* are invited from Septmber to Michèle, Karen or Sandy to the above address. No upper age limit!

EUROCAMP: Overseas Recruitment Department (Ref SJ/02) (tel 01606-787522). Eurocamp is a leading tour operator in quality self-drive camping and mobile home holidays in Europe. Each year the company seeks to recruit up to

1,500 enthusiastic people for the following positions:

Campsite Courier: job involves cleaning and preparing customer accommodation, providing assistance, acting as an information service and an interpreter and performing some administrative duties. Couriers need to be flexible to meet the needs of the customer to provide them with excellent service. Minimum age 18 years. Applicants should be independent with plenty of initiative and relish a challenging and rewarding position. They should also possess a friendly and helpful personality. Some working knowledge of another European language is required and previous customer service experience would be an advantage. Applicants should be available to work from April/May to September.

Children's Couriers: work involves organising a wide range of exciting activities for children aged 4-13. Applicants should possess initiative, imagination and enthusiasm along with good safety awareness. Previous childcare experience is essential. Minimum age is 18 years and applicants should be available from April/May to September. Languages are not a requirement but would be an advantage (in particular German).

Senior Couriers: required to work alongside a team of Campsite Couriers and organise their daily workload, as well as carrying out the normal day to day duties of a Campsite Courier. Applicants should have good language skills and experience of leading a team.

Site Managers: required to lead a large team of Campsite Couriers, organising their daily workloads and ensuring they provide the very best customer service. Applicants should be 21 or over, have proven managerial experience, excellent communication skills and language ability.

In all the above positions you should be be available for the full season commencing in April/May through to September. Comprehensive training is provided together with a competitive salary, insurance and return travel. *Applications* are accepted from September/October and *can only be accepted from UK/EU passport holders*. Interviews will be conducted in Hartford, Cheshire between October and April.

SWISS TRAVEL SERVICE: 55-59 High Road, Broxbourne, Herts, EN10 7DT (tel 01992-456236; fax 01992-448855; e-mail swiss@bridge-travel.co.uk; www.swisstravel.co.uk). Swiss Travel Services is a UK market leader for holidays to Switzerland with over 50 years experience. Posts are available both in summer and in winter.

Resort Reps (20) required to meet and greet clients, liaise with suppliers and sell tickets for excursions. Ability to speak German, Italian or French would be advantageous.

Driver (1) needed to transport clients from the station to the hotel, to carry baggage and to perform some rep duties. Applicants must have a full clean driving licence.

During the summer season the minimum period of work is 3 months between 1 April and 1 October; generally working from 8:30am to 7:30pm 6 or 7 days a week. Board, accommodation and a wage of around £400 per month are provided.

Applicants should be at least 21 years old, have good client handling skills and experience of dealing with older people. *Applications* can be made through the above website and are invited from EU and EFTA nationals or those who have obtained permission to work in Switzerland.

Work with Children

THE HAUT LAC INTERNATIONAL CENTRE: CH-1669 Les Sciernes, Switzerland (tel +41-26-928 4200; fax +41-26-928 4201; e-mail admin@haut-lac.ch; www.haut-lac.ch). The Haut Lac Centre is a family run business organising language and activity courses for an international clientele. A high client return rate is due to the Centre's work and play philosophy.

Language Teachers; French (6), English (3), German (2) to take four 40 minute classes (Monday, Tuesday, Thursday, Friday) and one 40 min. study per day, supervise one test per week and have two days off per week. Candidates should have a degree and a TEFL qualification or equivalent, or be studying for a Language or Teaching degree.

Sports Activity Monitors (6) to organise and run a wide variety of sports and excursions. One day off per week.

Maintenance Person to carry out garden upkeep, decorating tasks and repair work, should have previous experience.

Wages for all positions are from £100 per week according to qualifications and experience. Board and accommodation are included as is laundry. Staff work 45-54 hours per 5-6 day week. Period of work mid-June until mid-August, with a minimum requirement of 4 weeks work. Applicants should speak English, French or German, and *applications* are invited at any time to the above address.

Voluntary Work and Archaeology

GRUPPO VOLUNTARI DALLA SVIZZERA ITALIANA: CP 12, CH-6517 Arbedo, Switzerland (tel 079-3540161 (NATEL) 091-8574520 (office); fax 071-6829272; e-mail Fmari@vtx.ch).

Volunteers (15 per camp) to take part in work camps in Maggia, Fusio and Borgogne helping mountain communities, clearing woods etc. 4 hours work per day. Board and accommodation available for £2.50 approx per day: in special circumstances they may be provided free. Minimum period of work one month between June and September.

Applicants should speak Italian, German or French. *Applications* to the above address. Volunteers must be able to present valid documents and a residence permit.

INTERNATIONALE BEGEGNUNG IN GEMEINSCHAFTSDIENSTEN eV: Schlosserstrasse 28, D-70180 Stuttgart 1, Germany (tel 0711-6491128; fax 711-6409867).

Volunteers to attend international youth workcamps in Switzerland. Typical projects might include restoring an old castle, environmental protection, children's playschemes and media projects. Each workcamp consists of a group of about 15 people aged 18-30 from all over the world living and working together for the public benefit.

There is a registration fee of approximately £55; food and accommodation are provided free on the camps. The programme for 2002 is published in March.

INTERNATIONALE UMWELTSCHUTZ STUDENTEN: IUS-AWSR, Postfach 1, CH-9101 Herisau, Switzerland (tel/fax 071-351 5103).

International Student Exchange Placements for voluntary work during the summer.

Volunteers aged between 18 and 28 to help on mountain clearing and conservation projects. The projects last 10-20 days in the Alps around Davos, Zermatt and Engelberg. The work invoves clearing rubbish from ski slopes and footpath networks and repairing footpaths. Volunteers receive pocket money of £2 per day and accommodation is offered in tourist camps offering traditional Swiss food.

Volunteers must meet their own travel costs, and obtain health, accident and third-party insurance before arriving. A registration fee is also required and details of that are in the application form. In addition to being in good physical condition applicants should be surefooted with some mountain experience.

The nature of the work is such that applicants must be German speakers, willing to participate in camp life and over 18. Further details and an application form are available from IUS at the above address.

MOUNTAIN FOREST PROJECT: STIFTUNG BERGWALDPROJEKT: Hauptstrasse 24, CH-7014 Trin, Switzerland (+41 81-630-4145; fax +41-81-630-4147; e-mail info@bergwaldprojekt.ch).; www.bergwaldprojekt.ch). An organisation of workcamps for volunteers from 18 to 80, working in the mountain forests of Switzerland, Austria and Germany.
Volunteers; 10-15 places per week available in 50 camps per year. Work involves reforestation and forest maintenance, building footpaths for access and fences. No experience is necessary. Camps run from April to October. Volunteers may stay for one week per year. Free board and lodging is provided.

Programme details for 2002 will be available from January and *applications* will be accepted from then onwards.

Au Pairs, Nannies, Family Helps and Exchanges

PRO FILIA: 51, rue de Carouge, 1205 Geneva, Switzerland (tel/fax 022-329 84 62). **Au Pairs** can be placed with families in the regions of Switzerland and Geneva for stays of a minimum of 12 months. The office is manned from 8.30am-11am Monday-Friday and from 2.30-5pm on Wednesday. For further details contact the above address.

ROMANTIK HOTEL SÄNTIS: CH-9050 Appenzell, Switzerland (tel 0041-71 788 11 11; fax 0041-71 788 11 10; e-mail: romantikhotelsantis@bluewin.ch; www.romantikhotels.com/Appenzell). A traditional family-run 4-star hotel in one of the most beautiful areas of Switzerland; Appenzell is in the German-speaking region. The staff are mostly young people of various nationalities.
Au Pair/Nannny required to look after 3 small children, and carry out light household duties, must speak English with the children (they are bilingual). To work 9 hours per day, 5 days a week, wages negotiable. Accommodation in nearby staff houses offering the chance to meet many young people from different nationalities working at the hotel. Work permits are only available for EU/EFTA nationals.
Applications to Stefan A. Heeb at the above address.

Eastern Europe

Belarus

Short-term voluntary work in Belarus can be obtained for UK nationals through the International Voluntary Service, UNA Exchange, Youth Action For Peace and Concordia; US nationals need to contact Service Civil International or Council: International Volunteer Projects; see their entries in the *Worldwide* chapter for details. The following organisation can also act as an advisory service for those interested in finding voluntary work in Belarus.

ATM BELORUSSIAN ASSOCIATION OF INTERNATIONAL YOUTH WORK: P.O. Box 64, 220119 Minsk, Belarus (tel 0172-278183; fax/tel 0172-222714).
Volunteers (150) for workcamps in Belarus in different fields including ecology and various social issues. Volunteers from abroad come to the Belorussian workcamps every year to take part in activities and study programmes, or to help with office work, or to lead the camps and help with the co-ordination of the summer exchange. Applicants of any nationality are welcome and will be assisted with visas, etc.

No special skills are needed, apart from Russian language skills for some of the programmes. German and English are the other camp languages. The minimum age limit is 18 years and there is no upper limit. Disabled applicants welcome, but they must contact the organisation prior to application. The usual length of placement is three or four weeks between June and September, although some volunteers can be placed for two to four months. Volunteers must pay an application fee, but during the workcamp they are provided with free food, accommodation and health insurance. Accommodation is provided in student hostels.

For further information contact the above address.

The Czech Republic

The chances of finding paid summer work in the Czech Republic and Slovakia are low, but voluntary work can be arranged for British people by International Voluntary Service, UNA Exchange, Youth Action For Peace and Concordia; Council: International Volunteer Projects in New York helps to place Americans as does Service Civil International (see the International Voluntary Service entry). Details of the above organisations can be found in the *Worldwide* chapter.

RED TAPE

Visa Requirements: A visa is required by British nationals and citizens of many other countries when travelling to the Czech Republic for non-tourist purposes.

Those unsure about whether they require a visa should check with their nearest Czech consulate. When applying for a visa, applicants must be able to present a passport valid for at least 15 months (or 9 months for a short term traveller) from the date of issue of the visa, two passport-sized photographs, a document proving the purpose of the stay (e.g. a work permit or a Long Term Residence visa) confirmation of available accommodation, proof of health insurance and proof that they have sufficient funds to cover their living expenses in the country.

Residence Permits: A new Residency Law came into force in 2000 making it necessary to apply for a long-stay Czech visa before arrival in the country. Full details are available from the Czech Embassy in your country (in Britain phone 020-7243 1115; fax 020-7243 7988 or in the USA www.czech.cz/washington). Anyone who intends to work or for any other reason stay in the Czech Republic for longer than 90 days must obtain the visa in advance. Necessary documents include a work permit issued by the employer, proof of accommodation, etc. all presented in the original or a notarised copy.

Work Permits: Must be obtained by your future employer from the local employment office *(Urad práce)*. They will need a signed form from you plus a photocopy of your passport and the originals or notarised copies of your education certificates. Work Permits will only be granted where the employer can prove that they cannot find a suitable Czech candidates to carry out the job. All of this takes at least three months.

Teaching and Language Schools

ITC – INTERNATIONAL TEFL CERTIFICATE, PRAGUE: Main Office, Kaprova 14, 110 00 Praha 1, Czech Republic (tel/fax (420 2) 2481-7530/4791; US voice-mail tel 800-915-5540; US fax (815) 550-0086 e-mail info@itc-training.com; www.itc-training.com)

ITC International TEFL Certificate 110 hour intensive training courses in Prague or Barcelona give you practical experience living, working, and interacting abroad before you even begin teaching. Caring support staff lifetime job assistance worldwide. ITC offers the internationally recognised 4 week TEFL Certificate Course that qualifies graduates to teach English worldwide. Sessions are held year-round on a monthly basis. Upon completion of the course ITC can guarantee a job in Eastern Europe, provide lifetime job assistance worldwide and put you in touch with employment contacts around the world. For each session ITC organises a job workshop and provides career counselling during and after the course. ITC has graduated over 1500 teachers who are now working throughout the globe. There is an on-site EFL school with employment opportunities for ITC graduates. Trainees receive extensive supervised teaching practice with foreign students during the course. Housing and work Visa advice available. ITC is a member of the American Chamber of Commerce in Prague. See the *Spain* chapter for information on their Barcelona program.

Voluntary Work

BRONTOSAURUS MOVEMENT: Brontosaurus Council CR, Bubenska 6, Praha 7, Czech Republic 170 00 (tel 42-2 667 102 45).

Volunteers (2,000 per year) to take part in environmental summer workcamps around the Czech Republic. The Movement is an independent body co-ordinating the efforts of local groups which must be applied to directly: *contact* Jan Dusik, International Co-ordinator, enclosing an International Reply Coupon for a copy of the list of summer camps open to foreigners.

CONCORDIA: Heversham House, 20-22 Boundary Road, Hove, East Sussex BN3 4ET (tel 01273-422218; fax 01273 421182; e-mail info@concordia-iye.org.uk; www.concordia-iye.org.uk).
Concordia offers young people aged 16-30 the opportunity to take part in international volunteer projects, lasting 2-3 weks, from June to September. The work is community based and ranges from nature conservation, renovation, construction and social work including childrens' playschemes and youth work. Volunteers pay a registration fee of £85 and fund their own travel. Board and accommodation are free of charge. For further information *write* enclosing an sae to the International Volunteer Co-ordinator at the above address.

Hungary

In addition to the opportunities listed below there are also opportunities for voluntary work arranged by Youth Action for Peace, International Voluntary Service and UNA Exchange for UK nationals, and for US nationals through Service Civil International: see the *Worldwide* chapter for details.

AVALON '92 AGENCY: Budapest 1075, Karoly Krt. 21, Hungary (tel 36-13513010; tel/fax 36-13426355).
English Teachers (up to 10). Hours depending on schedule. A BA is the minimum qualification acceptable.
Secretarial Positions. Hours and pay negotiable. Must have language and word-processing skills and be creative.
Nannies (up to 30) to work in Hungary. Mostly live-in. Part/full time, live-out also available. Wages £100-£130 per month. Duties include housekeeping. 6-8 hour day; 5 day week. Preferably aged 21-30 with childcare experience.
Au pair positions all over Europe also arranged. *Applications* must be sent 60 days before entry into Hungary. Contact the above address.

Voluntary Work

BIOKULTURA/WWOOF: Hungarian Association of Organic Growers, Mr Zsolt Meszaros, Biokultura Egyesulet, 1023 Budapest, Toruk u. 7 em 1, Hungary.
Volunteer Farm Workers: placements on organic farms and gardens in Hungary can be arranged by the Biokultura Association, the Hungarian Association of Organic Growers, in co-operation with WWOOF. Work can include weeding, animal husbandry and helping with the harvest. Applicants must speak German or English or French; knowledge of Russian might be useful. It is recommended that applicants arrange insurance for themselves and have an anti-tetanus injection. Those interested should contact the address above.

Latvia

The following organisation can help people to find employment in Latvia. In addition UK nationals can arrange voluntary work there through International

Voluntary Service, Youth Action for Peace or UNA Exchange and US nationals through Service Civil International (see the *Worldwide* chapter for details).

RED TAPE

Visa Requirements: EU and US citizens do not require a visa to enter Latvia. Applicants from some countries (not Australia, New Zealand and Canada) will require an invitation which must be signed and stamped by the Department of Citizenship and Immigration in Riga.

Residence Permits: In order to obtain a residence permit for Latvia an applicant must submit an application form, a photocopy of a valid travel document and an invitation certified by the Department of Migration and Citizenship Affairs. If an applicant intends to work in Latvia, an invitation approved by the State Labour Department must be obtained.

INTERNATIONAL EXCHANGE CENTRE: 35 Ivor Place, London NW1 6EA (tel 020-7724 4493; fax 020-7724-0849; e-mail outbounder@btconnect.com; www.isecworld.co.uk).

The International Exchange Center works to promote positive, enjoyable cultural exchanges. Overseas work is offered in various countries for various types of work. See website for details. Non-students welcome. No language requirement.

Camp Counsellors Programme: Camp Leaders/Activity Instructors/Language Teachers needed to work in cildren's summer camps in Russia and Ukraine, looking after children aged 8-15 years old. Energetic and friendly personality and a genuine desire to work with kids is essential; specialists in sports, music etc. are epecially welcome. Free board and accommodation. Pocket money is low by western standards but is equivalent to the basic wage of local camp staff. Placement fee of £100.

English Teachers to work on EFL teaching programme. English teachers are placed at language schools, summer language centres in Latvia, Russia and Ukraine. Some teaching experience/qualifications desirable. Placement fee of £100.

Work and Study Experience Russia. This programme allows foreign participants to get involved in Russian daily life and culture. Participants are enrolled into 4 week language courses (10 hours per week) based at universities in Moscow, followed by work experience in a company in Moscow and other cities in Russia for a period of 2-4 months. Whenever possible. The programme cost of £240 (US$350) includes the cost of 4 weeks of study and accommodation in a University dormitory room, pick up on arrival to Moscow and a work placement. Salary may be low by Western standards – £34-£138 (US$50-200) per month. Participants can extend their study period while they are in Russia by paying directly to the University £82 (US$120 for 4 weeks of study). Jobs are at entry level positions mainly in hospitality but may be in other areas.

Participants can also choose to find a job themselves while studying at language courses: however they need to be aware that unemployment rate is Russia is high. IEC will provide informational support but will not find an actual job for such participants. (If finding own job, the programme costs $330).

Applications must be submitted at least 3 months before the earliest program start date for those wishing to be placed through IEC and 1¹/2 months for those wishing to find their own job. Students must arrange their own medical insurance and visas must notify IEC of their arrival dates at least one week before arrival.

Malta

It may be possible to arrange a holiday job in Malta with the following organisation:

MALTA YOUTH HOSTELS ASSOCIATION (MYHA): 17 Triq Tal-Borg, Pawla PLA O6, Malta (tel +356-693957; e-mail myha@keyworld.net). The MYHA offers temporary, free accommodation to persons needing social assistance. It also receives young travellers and workcamp volunteers to assist in the achievement of this aim. The MYHA operates workcamps all round the year, whereby volunteers are accommodated in return for a minimum of 3 hours per day of unpaid work as directed by the MYHA.

Volunteers to work on a Short-term Workcamp. Volunteers, (aged 16-30) from all countries may stay for between two weeks and three months. Accomodation is in the youth hostels.

Volunteers to work on Long-term Workcamps. Volunteers may stay six, nine or twelve months. *EU applications only.* Volunteers should be aged 18-25.

For both positions *apply* sending three International Reply Coupons. Where IRCs are unavailable, two US dollars will suffice. Application forms should be received six months before the camp is due to start.

Poland

Teaching work in Poland can be found with the organisations listed below. In addition, voluntary work in Poland can by arranged through Youth Action for Peace, UNA Exchange and International Voluntary Service for British people, and Council: International Volunteer Projects and Service Civil International for Americans: see the *Worldwide* chapter for details.

RED TAPE

Visa Requirements: EEA nationals and those from the USA do not require visas to enter Poland but their stay is limited to anything from 14 to 90 days depending on country of origin, and 180 days for British citizens. Note: there are several types of visa obtainable such as visitors, transit and business; for more details contact your nearest Embassy or Consulate of the Republic of Poland.

Work Permits: A work visa (Visa 06) must be applied for in your country of origin. Original or notarised copies of your degree diploma and TEFL Certificate (if applicable) must be presented along with a promisory work permit from your future employer to the Polish Consulate in your country of residence. The Consulate then issues a residence visa. After arrival the residence visa and interim work permit are taken to the regional employment office *(Wojewódzki Urzad Pracy)* to obtain a proper work permit. The handout from the Polish Consulate entitled 'Visas for Teachers' sets out the procedures and states that the current cost of the multi-entry residence visa is £104. Ring the Polish Embassy for details (020-7580 0475; www.polishworld.com/polemb).

Language Schools

ANGLO-POLISH UNIVERSITIES ASSOCIATION (APASS): 93 Victoria Road, Leeds LS6 1DR (tel (emergency only) 0113 2758121, 8-10am/4-6pm). The Spirit of Adventure Teaching Holiday is a joint project between APASS and the Polish Ministry of Education. It offers a 3-4 week free holiday in one of most interesting Central European countries.

Native English Speakers (British educated) required for 'teaching holidays' in Poland (mainly conversation with groups of 8-10 Polish grammar school teenagers). Teaching experience welcomed, but not essential. Applicants should be young people, but older persons interested in education are welcomed, as are parents with teenage children. Succesful applicants will work 15 hours per week, for 3 weeks in July/August, The 3 weeks of teaching will be followed by a week touring Poland. Visiting Warsaw, Krakow, Auschwitz, Tatra Mountains etc. All expenses paid by the Polish host. Successful candidates *from the EU* will have visa and work permit fees waived. Assisted travel available and full hospitality including recreational activities will be provided in Poland.

Applications from March onward. Send a £3 cheque (payable to APASS) and a 9 by 6 inch self-stamped (£0.41) addressed envelope for the comprehensive information pack.

THE ENGLISH SCHOOL OF COMMUNICATION SKILLS (ESCS): Attn. Personnel Department, ul. Sw. Agnieszki 2/Ip, 31-068 Kraków, Poland (tel/fax 0048 12 422 85 83; e-mail personnel@escs.pl).

Teachers of English (60) wanted for full-time positions at ESCS schools in: Kraków, the cultural heart of Poland; Tarnów, where the locals are reputedly the friendliest people in Poland; Nowy Targ, where they take their skiing seriously; Myslenice, the best of both worlds, close to the big city and in the beautiful countryside; and Katowice, the rock 'n' roll capital of Poland.

Period of work from October to June. Job involves teaching English to Polish students of all ages. Salary according to experience and qualifications. Applicants must hold an EFL methodology certificate and have a degree level education. ESCS holds EFL training courses in September.

Summer School: (15) same as above for July and August.

Summer Camp: (6) TEFL teachers wanted. Job involves teaching English for 4-8 hours per day to Polish students of all ages in an informal atmosphere at the beautiful Polish seaside. Duties include participating in sports events (baseball) and other activities. Accommodation, food and travel to and from Krakow provided. Minimum age 21. Applicants should be educated to degree level, with bright, confident personalities and be enthusiastic about sport.

PROGRAM BELL: 61-701 Poznan, ul Fredry 7, pok.22-26 Poland (tel 061-85-36 972; fax 061-85-30-612). Part of the renowned international network of Bell schools. Situated in central Poznan, a historic city of 6 million inhabitants. The school welcomes teachers to camps in an attractive area of Poland. The Poznan location is excellent for travelling, with Berlin 3 hours westward and Warsaw to the east.

English Teachers to teach groups of 10-12 children and teenagers for three or four hours per day, and later to organise activities and look after children at language camps; duties include being responsible for the children 24 hours a day.

10-12 staff needed in all. Wages by arrangement plus full board and lodging. The camps each last 2 weeks and take place in July and August. Applicants should be aged between 22 and 30 and preferably have TEFL qualifications and experience of working with children. There is also the possibility of one-year contracts.

Russia

While there are occasional opportunities for finding paid temporary work in Russia it is still easier to find voluntary than paid work there. In addition to the opportunities listed below British people should contact Youth Action for Peace, International Voluntary Service, UNA Exchange and Concordia while Americans should contact Council: International Volunteer Projects and Service Civil International; for details see the *Worldwide* chapter. The Russian state body 'Goskomtrud' is responsible for the hiring of manpower from abroad. The address of the Department is: The Goskomtrud of Russia, 1 Square Kuibysheva, 103706, Moscow, Russia.

INSTITUTE OF ARCHAEOLOGY OF ALMATY: International Scientific Projects, Tole Bi 21, Room 22, 480100 Almaty, Kazakhstan (tel +7-3272 917338; fax +7-3272 916111; e-mail ispkz@nursat.kz).
Volunteers for archaeological fieldwork, to take part in three programmes of summer fieldwork. Under instruction from specialists from the institute volunteers will receive training in steppe archaeology, paleoecology, methodology, aerial surveying and documentation.
Programme costs are between US$250-300 (£175-£210 approx.) per week, in return volunteers will be provided with food and accommodation.
For more details contact Renato Sala or Jean-Marc Deom at the Institute.

INTERNATIONAL EXCHANGE CENTER: 35 Ivor Place, London NW1 6EA (tel 020-7724-4493; e-mail; outbounder@btconnect.com; www.isecworld.co.uk). International Exchange Center works to promote positive, enjoyable cultural exchanges. Overseas work is offered in various countries for various types of work. See website for details. Non-students welcome. No language requirement.
Camp Counsellors Programme: Camp Leaders/Activity Instructors/Language Teachers needed to work in cildren's summer camps in Russia and Ukraine, looking after children aged 8-15 years old. Energetic and friendly personality and a genuine desire to work with kids is essential; specialists in sports, music etc. are epecially welcome. Free board and accommodation. Pocket money is low by western standards but is equivalent to the basic wage of local camp staff. Placement fee of £100.
English Teachers to work on EFL teaching programme. English teachers are placed at language schools, summer language centres in Latvia, Russia and Ukraine. Some teaching experience/qualifications desirable. Placement fee of £100.
Work and Study Experience Russia. This programme allows foreign participants to get involved in Russian daily life and culture. Participants are enrolled into 4 week language courses (10 hours per week) based at universities in Moscow, followed by work experience in a company in Moscow and other cities in Russia for a period of 2-4 months. Whenever possible. The programme cost of £240 (US$350) includes the cost of 4 weeks of study and accommodation in a University dormitory room, pick up on arrival to Moscow and a work placement. Salary may be low by Western standards – £34-£138 (US$50-200) per month. Participants can extend their study period while they are in Russia by paying directly to the University £82 (US$120 for 4 weeks of study). Jobs are at entry level positions mainly in hospitality but may be in other areas.

Participants can also choose to find a job themselves while studying at language courses: however they need to be aware that unemployment rate is Russia is high. IEC will provide informational support but will not find an actual job for such participants. (If finding own job, the programme costs $330).

Applications must be submitted at least 3 months before the earliest program start date for those wishing to be placed through IEC and 1½ months for those wishing to find their own job. Students must arrange their own medical insurance and visas must notify IEC of their arrival dates at least one week before arrival.

Slovenia

The following organisation organises voluntary work in Slovenia. British people can also find this type of work there through International Voluntary Service or UNA Exchange, while US citizens can apply to Service Civil International; see the *Worldwide* chapter for details.

ZAVOD VOLUNTARIAT: Service Civil International Slovenia, Breg 12 Sl-1000 Ljubljana, Slovenia (tel +386-1-4258067; fax +386-1-2517208; e-mail placement@zavod-voluntariat.sl; www.zavod-voluntariat.sl). Voluntariat is a non-profit and non-governmental organisation which co-ordinates voluntary work and international work camps in Slovenia. Voluntariat aims to promote social justice, sustainable development and solidarity through voluntary service. **International Work Camp Volunteers.** Voluntariat organises between 15 and 20 work camps in Slovenia every year. Most work camps are held from June to September and last two or three weeks. The main topics of the work camps are: ecology, Bosnian refugees, children and handicapped people. Most work camps do not require any special skills. Accommodation and food is provided. *Applications* should be made through the applicant's nation branch of SCI. **Long and medium-term voluntary work:** projects of LTV and MTV are based mostly in Ljubljana and they include: refugee projects, projects for youngsters from undepriviledged backgrounds and projects for elderly people. Voluntariat also offers long and medium-term voluntary work abroad.

Turkey

Opportunities for paid work in Turkey normally involve either teaching English or working for a tour operator. There are opportunities for volunteer work with the organisations listed below or through UNA Exchange, Youth Action for Peace, International Voluntary Service and Concordia for British citizens, or Council: International Volunteer Projects and Service Civil International for Americans; see the *Worldwide* chapter for details.

Please note that those who enter Turkey as tourists with or without a tourist visa are not permitted to take up employment in the country.

RED TAPE

Visa Requirements: All British and Irish nationals can obtain a 3 months/multiple-entry visa at their point of entry to Turkey. American nationals also now need visas; they can obtain these either in advance or on arrival. Australian, Canadian, New Zealand citizens do not need visas for stays of up to

3 months as tourists. Citizens of some countries requiring visas can obtain them while entering Turkey: contact a Turkish Embassy or a Consulate General for details. Any UK national entering Turkey is advised to have a minimum of 6 months validity on their passports from the date of their entry into Turkey. In the UK up to date details of visa and permit requirements can be obtained by telephoning 09068-347348 (calls cost 60p per minute).

After obtaining a work/resident visa you must register with the local police headquarters within a month following your arrival in Turkey and obtain a residence permit.

Residence Permits: are required by those who are staying in Turkey for reasons other than tourism.

Work Permits: a contract of employment by the private sector is required before application to the Turkish Consulate General is made. A letter of approval from the Undersecretariat for the Treasury is also required from those who will be employed as technical staff in the private sector. Prospective English teachers must have a degree and TEFL certificate. Should the employer be related to the tourism business, a letter of approval should be obtained from the Turkish Ministry of Tourism before visa application. Permits must be applied for and obtained before departure for Turkey. Applicants should allow at least 8 weeks for their permit application to be processed. Employment is only likely to be offered to those with special qualifications. Visa fees range from £38 to £60. If a work visa is granted the holder is required to register with the local police within a month of their arrival and obtain a residence permit.

Au Pair: work permits are required.

Voluntary Work: work permits are required.

Sports, Couriers and Camping

MARK WARNER. Telephone 020-7761 7300 (24 hour).
Club Managers, Accountants, Receptionists, Watersports Instructors, Tennis and Aerobics Instructors, Chefs, Bar Staff, Nannies, Handymen and Nightwatchmen are required to work in Beachclub Hotels in Turkey during the summer from May to October. Wages from £50-£230 per week plus full board, medical insurance, travel expenses and free use of watersport and activity facilities. Some reserve staff also needed throughout the season. Requirements for languages, age, experience, qualifications etc. vary according to the job applied for. For further details, please call the Resorts Recruitment Department on the above number.

Voluntary Work and Archaeology

CONCORDIA: 20-22 Boundary Road, Hove, East Sussex BN3 4ET (tel 01273-422218; fax 01273 421182; e-mail info@concordia-iye.org.uk; www.concordia-iye.org.uk).
Volunteers aged 16-30 are needed for international volunteer projects lasting 2 weeks from July to September. Work is mainly on construction and manual projects in villages. Basic food and accommodation are provided. Volunteers pay a registration fee of £85 and organise their own travel and insurance. Send a stamped addressed envelope to the above address for further information.

GSM YOUTH SERVICES CENTRE: Bayindir Sokak, No.45/9 Kizilay, 06450 Kizilay-Ankara, Turkey (tel +90-312-417-11 24/417-29-91; fax +90-312-425-81-

92; e-mail gsmser@superonline.com).
GSM organises around 20 workcamps throughout Turkey in co-operation with the local municipalities and universities. The projects, usually taking place in towns or on campus sites, can involve environmental protection, restoration and/or festival organisation.

The age limits are: 18-28 in all of the projects. The projects last for 2 weeks from July until the end of September. Volunteers work 5 hours a day, weekends are free with organised excursions available. Board and lodging are provided in dormitories, small hotels/pensions, camp houses or with families. Volunteers pay their own travel costs and pay a contribution fee of approx. £45.

Applications through partner organisations including Concordia, Quaker International Social Projects and the United Nations Association (Wales): see the *Worldwide* chapter for details.

Au Pairs, Nannies, Family Helps and Exchanges

ANGLO PAIR AGENCY: 40 Wavertree Road, Streatham Hill, London SW2 3SP (tel 0208-674 3605; fax 0208-674 1264; e-mail anglo.pair@btinternet.com).
Nannies (50 or more) to work 40-45 hours per week with babies and young children in Turkey. Weekends normally off. Wages £150-£250 per week if qualified or £100 or more per week if unqualified, with accommodation provided and other living expenses covered. Placements are either for the summer (May-October) or at any time of year. Applicants must be native English speakers and normally aged 20-35. Unqualified nannies must have experience in child care.
Au Pairs (50 or more) for summer and year round placements in Turkey; applicants from overseas also placed in the UK. Pocket money of £45-£65 per week plus living expenses and accommodation. Duties include childcare and light housework 25-35 hours per week. Applicants should be aged 19-27 and should have some childcare experience.

The agency has its own office in Istanbul to offer support to those placed in Turkey. *Applications* to Mrs Kim Kirtley at the above address.

GENCTUR TRAVEL EDUCATION AGENCY LIMITED): Prof. F. K. Gökay Cad. 21, Denizli Ap. Kat. 1, Hasanpasa, Istanbul, Turkey (tel 90-216-347 8484; fax 90-216-336 6878; e-mail: edu@genctur.com.tr).
Counsellors needed for summer children's/teenagers' camp, with experience and/or interest in working with children/teenagers. Abilities in sports, arts, music, drama or handicrafts is a must. Native speakers of English, German and French preferred. Camps last for 2 weeks and it is possible to work in more than one camp.

This is voluntary work, but return transport, full board and accommodation and pocket money are provided.

WEIGAN NANNIES: One White's Row, London, E1 7NF (tel 020-7377 2620; fax 020-7377 0787; e-mail weigan@senatorgroup.co.uk).
Nannies (10) wanted from now until September/October for positions in holiday resorts in Greece and Turkey. The work involves nannying either alone with a family or with a group of families, changing on a weekly basis. Hours of work are 9am-5pm, 6 days per week. The nanny package includes £75 per week, flights and transfers, food, accommodation, a uniform and full access to watersports facilities, tennis and a fitness centre.

Nannies must have NNEB/BTEC, be over 18 and have an EU passport or work permit. To *apply* contact Paul Nugent, Director.

Ukraine

Apart from the voluntary work available in the Ukraine through the Latvian-based International Exchange Centre (see chapter on Latvia), short-term voluntary work can be arranged for UK nationals through Concordia, International Voluntary Service and UNA Exchange. US citizens can arrange placements through Council: International Volunteer Projects and Service Civil International. Voluntary work can also be obtained through the organisation listed below.

UNION FORUM: Lychakivskastr. PO 5327; Lviv-10, Ukraine, 79010. (tel +380322 726934; fax +38 0322 759488; e-mail ukrforum@ipm.lviv.ua).
Short-term Volunteers (40) between 18 and 35 years of age required to carry out reconstruction and environmental work during July and August 2001. No special qualifications are required. Board and accommodation are provided free of charge.
Applications should be made to Arkadiy Sharkov at the above address.

YOUTH VOLUNTARY SERVICE: 11/60 Lystopadna, LVIV, 290034, Ukraine (tel/fax 00-380-322 423658).
Volunteers (15) required to take part in short term social projects (2-3 weeks) from late June until the end of August. To work 5 hours a day, Monday-Friday. Board and accommodation provided.
Applications through national organisations or directly to the above address.

Yugoslavia

Short-term volunteer projects in Yugoslavia can be arranged for British citizens by Youth Action for Peace and in Serbia by UNA Exchange. See their entries in the *Worldwide* chapter for more details. The following organisation offers opportunities to work in Yugoslavia.

GALINDO SKOLA STRANIH JEZIKA (SAVA CENTAR & VOZDOVAC): Milentija Popovica 9, 11070 Novi Beograd, Yugoslavia (tel 11-311 4568; fax 11-455785; e-mail galindo@net.yu). The first private language school in the country, located in Novi Beograd's congress and shopping centre. Excellent working atmosphere, with students from pre-school to executives.
English Teachers (3) to work with Yugoslavian children, adolescents and adults. Minimum wage approximately £280 per month, working 6 or 7 hours per day, 5 days per week.
Applicants should be enthusiastic and responsible, and have a BA in English and TEFL, TESL or TESOL qualifications. Knowledge of some Serbo-Croatian would be an advantage. *Applications* should be sent to Nada Gadjanski at the above address.

Africa and the Middle East

Egypt

Chances of finding a paid summer job in Egypt are slight but there may be possibilities in the tourist industry for example in the diving resort of Dahab. Otherwise opportunities for temporary work are normally restricted to voluntary work.

Hotel Work and Catering

ZAMALEK HOTELS & TOURISM: c/o Welcome Hotels & Resorts, Via Bologna 498, I-44100 Ferrara, Italy (tel 0039-532-977105; fax 0039-532-970238; e-mail: welcotel@tin.it).

Trainee Chef for El Cairo and Red Sea Hotels. Work involves cooking Italian cuisine. Salary £182 per month plus full board and accommodation. Applicants must be interested in joining this international organisation as a chef or maitre; minimum period of work is 6 months training after which half of the applicant's air fare will be reimbursed. Knowledge of English and Italian required.

Applications should be sent with references from September 1 to the above address; e-mail communication preferred.

Sports, Couriers and Camping

EMPEROR DIVERS: 22 High Street, Sutton, Ely, Cambridgeshire CB6 2RB (tel 01353-778096; fax 01353-777897).

Diving Instructors to provide diving instruction to holidaymakers in the Red Sea, Egypt. Wage £364 per month plus 20% commission on each course. To work 5-8 hours per day, 6 days per week. Accommodation available. Minimum period of work one year.

Applicants must hold at least PADI OWI qualifications, plus BSAC AI if possible. The ability to speak German, French, Italian and/or Spanish would be an advantage. *Applications* should be sent to the Administration Department at the above address as soon as possible.

Teaching and Language Schools

INTERNATIONAL HOUSE: International Language Institute Heliopolis, 2 Mohamed Bayoumi Street, Off Merghany Street, Heliopolis, Cairo, Egypt (tel 202-291295/418 9212; fax 202-415 1082; e-mail ili@idsc.net.eg;

www.ihworld.com).

Teachers of English (6) required to teach intensive English courses to adults and young learners aged 5-15. Applicants should be Cambridge/RSA or CELTA qualified and preferably have experience of working with young learners. 20-25 hours of work per week between June and September, minimum period of work 6 weeks. Wages c.£600 per month with free accommodation. Depending on the length of contract worked there is a bonus of a percentage paid towards the cost of the flight to Egypt, e.g. 50% for 12 weeks worked, up to a limit of £380.

Applications to the above address from February.

Voluntary Work and Archaeology

WIND SAND & STARS: 2, Arkwright Road, Hampstead, London NW3 6AD (tel 020-7433 3684; e-mail office@windsandstars.co.uk; www.windsandstars. co.uk). Wind Sand & Stars is a small specialist company that organises a wide range of journeys and projects within the desert and mountain areas of South Sinai.

Participants for work on an annual environmental, scientific, historical expedition operated during August in the desert and mountains of Sinai. There is a fee attached for travel to the area. All applicants must be over 16 years of age. *Applicants* should contact the above address any time.

Ghana

Voluntary work for Britons in Ghana can be organised by UNA Exchange and Youth Action for Peace. A summary of their work is listed along with their addresses in the *Worldwide* chapter. The organisations below also offer opportunities to work in Ghana.

BUNAC: 16 Bowling Green Lane, London EC1R 0QH (tel 020-7251 3472; fax 020-7251 0215; e-mail africa@bunac.org.uk).

BUNAC runs a *Work Ghana* programme which enables recent graduates (2000 and 2001 for the 2002 programme) to spend a minimum of three months working and travelling in West Africa. Work opportunities range from teaching positions to development projects to administrative roles. Departures are in January and July.

BUNAC also runs a *Teach in Ghana* programme which arranges teacher placements in secondary schools in Ghana between September and July. Applicants should have some teaching experience and preferably a teaching qualification (for example, PGCE, QTS or BEd). There is one departure at the end of August.

Participants of either programme will receive local rates of pay which will sufficiently cover living costs; the schemes, however, should not be viewed as 'money-making' opportunities.

For further details about these programmes contact BUNAC at the above address or visit www.bunac.org.

Voluntary Work and Archaeology

FIOH/WWOOF GHANA: P.O. Box 154, Trade Fair Site, La-Accra, Ghana (tel/fax 23321-766825). WWOOF is concerned with organic farming and FIOH runs tree planting and environmental projects. Both organisations require a large number of participants for their annual WORKCAMPS. Their schools help train children from poor families, participants get to experience traditional and proverbial Ghanaian hospitality.

Voluntary Farm Workers to work on both organic and traditional farms in Ghana. Work includes weeding with a hoe or cutlass and harvesting of food and cash crops including maize, cassava, oranges, cocoa etc. Volunteers with experience of organic farming especially welcome.

Volunteers to work in a bicycle repair workshop currently being set up; no wage paid at present but there is the possibility of pocket money in the future. Two volunteers needed every six months. No particular qualifications are necessary, but applicants should be have experience of repairing bicycles.

Other schemes are also operated such as: summer workcamps on which volunteers work on construction conservation projects and tree planting activities in rural areas; placement schemes for qualified teachers are also organised. Practical lessons in traditional African drumming and dancing are available too. For further information send two international reply coupons to Mr Ebenezer Nortey-Mensah, Co-ordinator, at the above address.

SAVE THE EARTH NETWORK: Save the Earth Network, PO Box CT 3635, Cantonments-Accra, Ghana, West Africa (tel 233-21-236362; fax 233-21-231485; e-mail sten@gppo.africaonline.com.gh or eben_sten@hotmail.com). Save the Earth Network is an organisation dedicated to promoting sustainable development, agroforestry, environmental conservation and cultural exchange through voluntary work in Ghana.

Volunteer Teachers required to teach English language and mathematics in primary and junior secondary schools in Accra and surrounding villages at any time between mid-September to mid-December, mid January to mid-March or mid-April to early September. Other projects available (during the same periods) are assisting in giving free basic education to street and financially disadvantaged children at Save the Earth Network Centres and assisting in educating the youth in communities, schools and STEN centres about drug abuse, teenage pregnancy and HIV/AIDS.

Conservation Volunteers to assist in the conservaton of the tropical rainforest through tree nursing and planting. Volunteers could participate at anytime of the year, though mainly between April and October.

Volunteers to assist in nursing and planting fruit trees at agroforestry farms or harvesting the fruits. The purpose is to promote agroforestry and also protect the watershed. Volunteers could participate at anytime of the year. Please note that the fee for participation in the agroforestry program is negotiable; the standard fee may be reduced by between 10 and 35 per cent.

Volunteers can participate in a program from a period of 1 week to 1 year. The fee for participating is approximately £115 a month for participation with food included, or around £50 a month for participation without food provision. Payment should be made in cash on arrival in Ghana (in local currency equivalent). Volunteers will work 5 days a week for 4 hours a day, and are provided with accommodation with a host family or in a STEN hostel, with water, electricity and a bed. Travel is not included. Volunteers must be aged 18 or above.

For more information or to *apply,* write to the above address.

VOLUNTARY WORKCAMPS ASSOCIATION OF GHANA (VOLU): PO Box 1540, Accra, Ghana (tel 233-21-663486; fax 233-21-665960).

VOLU organises workcamps in the rural areas of Ghana for international volunteers. Tasks involve mainly manual work; construction projects, working on farm and agro-forestry projects, tree planting, harvesting cocoa and foodstuffs, working with mentally retarded people, teaching, etc. Around 1,500 volunteers are needed for workcamps at Easter, Christmas and from June to October. Volunteers can stay throughout each period.

No special skills or experience are required but volunteers should be over 16 years old and fit to undertake manual labour. Volunteers pay their own travelling costs and an inscription fee of approximately £120 but accommodation and food are provided at the camps. VOLU supplies offical invitations to enable volunteers to acquire visas before leaving for Ghana.

Israel

A foreigner wishing to take up paid work in Israel must find a job and hold a work permit (obtained by his or her employer) before entering the country. A special visa exists for volunteers, and fortunately for those who wish to find a place on a kibbutz or moshav once they are in the country it can in some circumstances be obtained after arrival; see below for details. However it is usually preferable to arrange a kibbutz place before leaving for Israel.

There are some opportunities for paid employment in the tourist industry, especially around the resort of Eilat on the Red Sea and the Old City in Jerusalem. However, most people who wish to work in Israel for a few months choose to work on kibbutzim or moshavim. These are almost wholly self sufficient settlements which take on volunteers for a normal minimum of eight weeks. The main difference between the two is that the property is shared on a kibbutz, while most houses and farms are privately owned on a moshav. So on one volunteers work and share the farm tasks with permanent staff, while on the latter they are paid and there is less communal spirit. However, the whole kibbutz system is set to undergo some potentially dramatic changes as plans are in hand to transfer kibbutzim from state to private ownership. It is very possible that the kibbutz system will eventually disappear, or become more like the moshavim movement in which private ownership of land is the norm.

On a kibbutz the work may consist of picking olives, grapes or cotton in the fields, domestic duties, or factory work; on a moshav the work is agricultural. In return for a six day week volunteers receive free accommodation, meals, laundry and cigarettes. Volunteers are normally given pocket money on kibbutzim, while on a moshav a small wage is paid but the working hours are liable to be longer. Other programmes available on kibbutzim include Kibbutz Ulpan (which is intensive Hebrew study) and Project Oren Kibbutz Programmes (which is intensive Hebrew study, as well as travel and study of Israel).

The addresses in the *Kibbutz* section below who help people who want to arrange work on a kibbutz are based in London. Americans can contact Kibbutz Program Center at 21st Floor, 633 Third Ave., New York, NY 10017 (tel 1-800247 7852 or 212-318-6130; fax 212-318-6134; e-mail kibbutzdsk@aol.com, ulpankad@aol.com or projoren@aol.com); volunteers need to bear in mind that with this organisation they must be prepared to make a commitment of at least two months. There are many other placement offices around the world: Israel's diplomatic missions should be able to advise on the nearest one to you.

The following organisation may be able to place people who are actually in Israel. In recent years the authorities have been discouraging volunteers from travelling to Israel on one way tickets without having a written assurance of a place on a kibbutz, and with insufficient money for their fare home: the official line is that volunteers must have a return ticket and a reasonable sum of money (around £150/$225) in their possession when they enter the country. Contact the Kibbutz Program Centre: Volunteers Department; 18 Frishman Street, 3rd Floor, Cr. Ben Yehuda Tel Aviv 61030 (tel 03-524-6156 or 03-524-8874; fax 03-523-9966; e-mail kpcvol@inter.net.il; www.kibbutz.org.il); it is open 9am-2pm, Sunday-Thursday. The centre advises people who do not pre-arrange a place before entering Israel that there might be a wait of days or even weeks before one is found, especially in the summer. However in the current political circumstances, there is a general shortage of foreign volunteers. All volunteers must be available for a minimum of 2 months, be between the ages of 18 and 35, speak a reasonable level of English and be in good mental and physical health.

The other major form of voluntary work in Israel consists of helping with archaeological excavations, often of Old Testament sites. The minimum stay for volunteers is normally two weeks. In the majority of cases volunteers must pay at least £15/US$25 a day for their expenses on a dig. British citizens wishing to find voluntary work in Israel can obtain placements through Concordia.

Those wanting to know more about not only work on kibbutzim and moshavim, but also all other forms of short-term work in Israel should consult the book *Kibbutz Volunteer* (see the *Useful Publications* chapter).

Placing an advertisement in the English language paper *The Jerusalem Post* may also lead to an offer of a job. They can be contacted at the *Jerusalem Post* Building, P.O. Box 81, Romena, Jerusalem 91000 (fax 2-377646).

RED TAPE

Visa Requirements: for a tourist visit to Israel a visa is not normally required prior to arrival by citizens of the UK, USA and some Western European countries. However, a visa is necessary before entering the country if work is intended.

Residence Permits: on entering the country, a visitor is likely to be given permission to stay for up to three months. Permission for a longer stay should then be obtained from the Ministry of the Interior, Hakirya Ruppin Road, no.2, Jerusalem.

Work Permits: your prospective employer should obtain the necessary permit from the Ministry of the Interior in Israel. You should have the permit with you when you enter the country.

Voluntary Work: a B4 Volunteer Visa is required of participants doing voluntary work (which includes kibbutzim and moshavim). The fee is NIS675 ($20) which covers 3 months. If you have pre-arranged your stay before arrival and have a letter of invitation you can obtain the B4 at the point of entry: otherwise, you can obtain it within 15 days of beginning voluntary work, provided you obtained the position through official channels. The B4 can be renewed only once.

Kibbutzim and Moshavim

KIBBUTZ PROGRAMME CENTER: P.O. Box 3167, 18 Frishman St. (corner of Ben Yehuda St.), Tel Aviv 61030, Israel (tel 03-527 8874/03-524 6156; fax 03-523 9966; e-mail kpcvol@inter.net.il; www.kibbutz.org.il). The Kibbutz Programme Center is the only office officially representing all the 250 kibbutzim. The center is responsible for their volunteers and provides for them from arrival until they leave the kibbutz.

Kibbutz Volunteers required all year round, to work 7-8 hours per day over a 6 day week. Period of work 2 months (minimum) to 6 months. Volunteers receive full board and accommodation, free laundry and £50 pocket money per month.

Volunteers need to pay a registration fee of £32, and be able to converse in English. To apply contact the centre with details of your name and date of birth, date of arrival, passport number and a covering letter describing yourself. *Applications* are accepted all year round, but at least one week in advance of your arrival in Israel.

KIBBUTZ REPRESENTATIVES: 1A Accommodation Road, Golders Green, London NW11 8ED (tel 020-8458 9235; 020-8455 7930; e-mail: enquiries@kibbutz.org.il). Has sent volunteers to Kibbutzim for over thirty years; offer full orientation, flexible of group or individual placement, and post departure care.

Working Visitors to learn the way of kibbutz life and its various aspects. Minimum stay 8 weeks; maximum stay 6 months. Accommodation, food, entertainment and occasional short trips arranged free in return for working 8 hours a day, 6 days a week, with a 3-day break in addition each month. Age 18-32 years. Medical certificate and two character references required. Informal interview and full orientation given, plus choice of group or individual travel.

Working Hebrew Scheme: as above but with chance to learn some Hebrew, with a 36 hour working week and 12 hours per week of Hebrew lessons; the course lasts for 3 months. Places are limited. Cost £175 plus approx. £10 for books.

Send s.a.e to above address for application forms and further information.

PROJECT 67 LTD: 10 Hatton Garden, London EC1N 8AH (tel 020-7831 7626; e-mail project67@aol.com). The longest-established office in Britain dealing with Kibbutzim and Moshavim, Project deals with most of the Kibbutzim and Moshavim in Israel.

Project 67 arranges working holidays for young people between the ages of 18 and 35. Volunteers can choose to work either on a Kibbutz where they work an 8 hour day, 6 day week in exchange for free meals, accommodation, laundry, recreational facilities and occasional excursions and monthly pocket money. Or on a Moshav where they work for an Israeli farmer in exchange for accommodation and from £200 a month.

Departures for either a Kibbutz or a Moshav are all year round and the minimum stay is 8 weeks. For a free brochure telephone or send a stamped addressed envelope to the above address or if in London call into the office to see the video and have a chat with one of the staff. Open 9am-5.30pm.

Voluntary Work and Archaeology

DEPARTMENT OF CLASSICAL STUDIES: Tel Aviv University, Ramat Aviv, Tel Aviv, Israel (fax 3-6406243; e-mail: fischer@post.tau.ac.il; www.tau.ac.il/~yavneyam). Since 1992 five seasons of archaeological excavations have been carried out at the ancient port site of Yavneh Yam, with the help of hundreds of volunteers from about ten countries, offering them an unique possibility of both reconstructing the past and encountering the complexity of modern Israeli society. The partcipation fee of £470 for two weeks includes a full board accommodation at the modern Youth Village 'Ayanoth', a lecture series on archaeology, geography and history of the Holy Land, field trips, a wonderful swimming pool, the blue Mediterranean...

Volunteers (up to 40) needed to take part in archaeological excavations. Volunteers are recruited for two week periods in July and August; it is possible to stay for more than one period. Volunteers must pay for their own food and accommodation (cost around £470 per two week period). Applicants should speak English, French or German: previous archaeological experience is an advantage but not essential. For further details *contact* Prof. Moshe Fischer at the above address.

ELI SHENHAV: JNF: 11 Zvi Shapira Street, Tel Aviv, Israel.
Volunteers (17) to work on an excavation of a Roman theatre three miles from Caesarea, a Roman Theatre in Shuni. Working hours are from 5.30am-noon, 5 days per week. Minimum period of work 1 week in July and August. Board and accommodation provided for around £10 per day. For further details *contact* Eli Shenhav at the above address.

FRIENDS OF ISRAEL EDUCATIONAL TRUST 'BRIDGE PROGRAMME': P.O.Box 7545, London NW2 2QZ (fax 020-7794 0291; e-mail foiasg@foiasg.free-online.co.uk). A British foundation established to promote an understanding of the geographies, histories, cultures and peoples of Israel, and to forge working links between the UK and Israel.
Scholarships are offered to 12 British applicants per year to enable them to take part in kibbutz work and community action and do some teaching in a developing town. The scholarships cover travel, insurance, board and lodging: there is no pay. 5-6 hours per day, 6 days per week between February and August.
   Applicants should be resident in the UK, prepared to work hard and to show initiative. *applications*, enclosing a stamped addressed envelope or an International Reply Coupon, must be made to the above address by 1 July for the following year.

ISRAEL YOUTH HOSTEL ASSOCIATION: c/o Youth Travel Bureau, 1 Shezer Street, P.O. Box 6001, Jerusalem 91060, Israel (tel 972-2-655 84 00: fax 972-2-655 84 32; e-mail: iyha@netvision.net.il; http://youth-hostels.org.il).
Volunteers interested in working in a youth hostel in Israel should write to the hostels directly. A list of youth hostels is available from the association at the above address.

Unipal: BCM Unipal, London WC1N 3XX (tel/fax 01227-272590). Written enquiries preferred. Unipal (Universities' Trust for Educational Exchange with Palestinians) runs a summer programme of teaching in the West Bank, Gaza and Lebanon.
Volunteers to teach children, aged 12-15 from mid-July to mid-August. Volunteers must be native English speakers, based in the UK and at least 20 years old. Cost approx. £380. Closing date for *applications* is the end of February.

WEIZMANN INSTITUTE OF SCIENCE: P.O.Box 26, Rehovot 76100, Israel (fax 972-8-9344492; e-mail greta1.rosenberg@weizmann.ac.il; www.weizmann. ac.il/acadsec/students.html).
Undergraduate Research Students to join a research project involving the Life Sciences, Chemistry, Physics and Mathematics and Computer Science. A small stipend is provided. Projects last for between 10 weeks and 4 months in the summer. Applicants must have finished at least 1 year at university and have some research experience.

Application forms are available on the Internet at the Weizmann Institute homepage (www.weizmann.ac.il/acadsec/students.html) and should be sent to the Academic Secretariat, the Summer Program for undergraduate students, at the above address; they must arrive by 31 December, of each year.

YOUTH TRAVEL BUREAU: 1 Shazer Street, P.O. Box 6001, Jerusalem 91060, Israel (tel 972-2-655 84 00: fax 972-2-655 84 32; e-mail: iyha@netvision.net.il; http://youth-hostels.org.il). Can help groups of Youth Hostel Association members to participate either in archaeological excavations for a minimum period of 2 weeks, or help individuals volunteer in the hostels (for room and board and pocket money) for a minimum of 2 months.
    Apply to the above address for details.

Au Pairs, Nannies, Family Helps and Exchanges

AU PAIR INTERNATIONAL: 2 Desler Street, 51507 Bnei Brak, Israel (tel 03-619 0423; fax 03-5785463; e-mail shulmitg@zahave.net.il; website www.aupair-international.co.il).
Nannies, Mothers' Helps, Housekeepers (age 22+) to work in Israel. Wages of £440 or more per month, plus accommodation with families. To work 9 hours per day, plus baby-sitting. Placements all year-round. One year stays preferred but short stays can also be arranged. *Applications* to Veronica Grosbard, Manager, at the above address.

PROJECT 67 LTD: 10 Hatton Garden, London, EC1N 8AH (tel 020-7831 7626; e-mail project67@aol.com).
Au Pairs and **Mothers' Helps** for placements in Israel, all year round for stays of a minimum 6 months. 30-45 working hours a week and au-pairs are expected to assist with general housework, children and light cooking. Pocket money from £450 a month depending on working hours. Age limit 20-45. English speaking families and other languages also available.

Kenya

Chances of finding a paid summer job in Kenya are minimal, but there are opportunities to participate in voluntary work with the following organisations. In addition, UNA Exchange can place British, and Service Civil International, American nationals in voluntary work in Kenya: see the *Worldwide* chapter for details.

KENYA VOLUNTARY DEVELOPMENT ASSOCIATION: PO Box 48902, GPO Nairobi, Kenya (tel/fax 254-02-225379, or 254-02-247393; e-mail kvdakenya@yahoo.com).
Volunteers to work on projects in remote villages aimed at improving amenities in Kenya's rural and needy areas, working alongside members of the local community. The work may involve digging foundations, building, making building blocks, roofing, awareness campaigns etc. Short term camps take place in January, April, June, July, August, November and December, and there are normally 20-25 volunteers per camp with six hours of work per day, six days per week. The long term programmes take place all year round, entailing placements of three or more months, in Kenyan communities on a professional basis as social

workers, agriculturalists etc.

Accommodation is normally provided in school classrooms or similar buildings; foreign participants are expected to adapt to local types of foods, etc. The camps normally last for 2 or 3 weeks. Minimum age 18. There is a registration fee to be paid on arrival, of approximately £130/£220 for July and August). For further details send three International Reply Coupons to the Director at the above address.

TAITA DISCOVERY CENTRE: The Tsavo Kasiagu Wildlife Corridor, PO Box 48019, Nairobi, Kenya, (tel 254-2-331191 or 254-2-222075; fax 254-2-330698 or 254-2-216528; e-mail tdc@wananchi.com; www.Taita Discovery.com). Surrounding the unique Mount Kasigau are a number of relatively small and isolated rural communities. With the assistance of The African Wildlife Foundation's programme, these communities have committed themselves to participating in a conservation project to retain the unparalleled biodiversity of the region and preserve its currently untouched landscape.
Volunteers (max 20 at any time) live in basic conditions in the village, and are left to complete their chosen projects independently, although support is available 'on request' and in an emergency.
Community Service Projects Teachers needed for art, music, sport and drama.
Community Based Micro Enterprises Projects to develop the use of edible and useful plants of the bush, develop herbal rememdies, develop a Bonsai tree enterprise. There are also projects in elephant dung paper and products, and aquaculture, sericulture and apiculture enterprise.
Conservation Data Collection Volunteers to take part in data collection, inventories of invertebrates, birds, plants, etc. Volunteers also needed for ecological plot sampling and behavioural studies of birds.
Other Projects include putting oral accounts of the Taita people onto paper, rural health programmes, primary school infrastructure development, economic studies and the development of alternative fuels.

Project costs start at US$30 per banda per night (a banda sleeps 4 volunteers) and the minimum stay is one month. To *apply* contact the projects at the above address.

Morocco

Work permits are necessary for employment in Morocco: they are generally only given to people who speak French and/or Arabic, and have some particular skill or qualification that is in demand (e.g. teaching or IT).

There are, however, possibilities of seasonal work in the expanding tourist industry, especially around the resorts of Agadir, Marrakesh and Tangier. Several European holiday companies operate in Morocco and employ summer staff. A knowledge of French will normally be expected: this is also the language most likely to be used in voluntary workcamps, although English should be understood.

In addition to the voluntary opportunities listed below, International Voluntary Service, Youth Action for Peace and UNA Exchange can help UK nationals, and Council: International Volunteer Projects and Service Civil International Americans, find voluntary work in Morocco: see the *Worldwide* chapter for details. Students can arrange places in work camps listed.

RED TAPE

Visa Requirements: a visa is not required by citizens of most Western European countries, Australia, Canada, New Zealand and the United States if they are entering Morocco as tourists.

Residence Permits: those planning a stay of over three months must register with the police and be able to provide evidence of how they are supporting themselves.

Work Permit: any foreigner taking up paid employment in Morocco must have a valid work permit: this will be obtained by the prospective employer from the Ministry of Labour. Work permits can be obtained while in Morocco if a job is found.

Au Pair: not customary.

Voluntary Work: a foreigner does not need a work permit or special visa in order to take part in an organised voluntary work project in Morocco providing (a) the scheme lasts for less than three months and (b) the work is unpaid.

Sports, Couriers and Camping

MOUNTAIN TREKS & TRAINING LTD: 17 Lilley Lane, West Heath, Birmingham B31 4JY (tel/fax 0121-680 3507).

Expedition Leaders (10), **Expedition Organisers** (10) to lead 6-week expeditions for young people in Morocco between 3 June and 3 September. Also some possibilities for work in Zimbabwe and Namibia later in the year. Wages from £50 per week. Applicants need a Mountain Leader's certificate and an NVQ level 3 in Outdoor Education.

Applications to Jeff South, Director, at the above address.

Voluntary Work

LES AMIS DES CHANTIERS INTERNATIONAUX DE MEKNES: PO Box 8, 50001 Meknes, Morocco (fax +212-5-517772; e-mail acim_b@hotmail.com). International non-profit making organisation.

Volunteers and professionals are needed to take part in work camps throughout Morocco from July-August. Minimum period of work 3 weeks. The aim of A.C.I.M is heightening awareness of conservation projects through workshops, guided tours, lectures, courses and architectural and archaeological workcamps. Activities are aimed at 17-35 year olds. Volunteers are insured by the organisation when they are in the camp. *Applications to* Zouhir Ouzzine, General Secretary, at the above address.

CHANTIERS SOCIAUX MAROCAINS: BP 456, Rabat, Morocco (tel 07-79 13 70).

CSM organises workcamps in Morocco which concentrate on projects intended to benefit the local community. About

300 Volunteers a year are involved, spending two or three weeks of the summer on the sites with fellow workers from many European and African countries.

Applicants should be between 18 and 30 years old, and in good health. Food and accommodation are provided, but the volunteer is responsible for all his or her personal expenses.

Those interested can either *apply through* their national branch of the CCIVS (which is International Voluntary Service in Britain), or directly to the President at the above address.

MOUVEMENT TWIZA: A.M.T, 23, Rue Echiguer Hammandi, Hay Salam B.P. 77, 15000 Khemisset, Morocco.

Mouvement Twiza organises weekend and summer work camps for volunteers in Morocco. It recruits about 500 volunteers per year to participate in a range of socio-cultural activities including work in the slums and in schools and construction work.

Applicants of any nationality are accepted, but volunteers must speak French and English, and preferably be outgoing and sociable. The minimum age limit is 18 years of age, and applicants must be healthy, willing and able. Volunteers are required in the summer for a maximum of three weeks. Accommodation is provided but pocket money is not.

Those interested should write to the above address.

Nigeria

Opportunities for paid temporary work in Nigeria are rare. The following organisation can arrange voluntary placements there.

VOLUNTARY WORKCAMPS ASSOCIATION OF NIGERIA:, G.P.O. Box 2189, Lagos, Nigeria (tel 01-821568).

VWAN organises workcamps centred around community projects for youths of different cultural backgrounds and nationalities throughout Nigeria. Between 120 and 150 volunteers per year participate in the workcamps; the work is mainly unskilled manual labour. This includes bricklaying, carpentry, sport, games, excursions, debates and discussions. VWAN also undertakes short and medium term programmes in the year.

Applicants of any nationality are welcome, but a knowledge of English is required. Volunteers must also be physically fit. The usual length of placement is between one and two months (i.e. July to September). Volunteers must pay a registration fee of approx £130 while feeding, board and lodging are provided for selected volunteers throughout the duration of the camps.

There is a charge of $20 for an application form, brochure and placement for the camps. Only applications received with the prescribed fee before the month of May will be treated each year. *Applications* to the Secretary General at the above address.

South Africa

The government is (understandably) not keen to hand out work permits to Europeans and other nationalities when so many of their own nationals are unemployed. Work permits are granted only in instances where South African citizens or permanent residents are not available for appointment or cannot be trained for the position.

Most people who do casual work have only a three-month tourist visa, which must be renewed before it expires. A 90-day extension can be obtained from the Department of Home Affairs in Johannesburg or Cape Town for a fee. After you have done this a few times, the authorities will become suspicious.

One solution to the problem is to consider BUNAC's work and travel programme in South Africa. Full-time students and recent graduates under the age of 27 may be eligible for a 12-month working holiday permit (see entry).

Voluntary work is organised for British citizens in South Africa by UNA Exchange and Youth Action for Peace. See their entries in the *Worldwide* chapter for details. Work can be found in South Africa through the organisations below.

FOREIGN PLACEMENTS CC: P.O. Box 912, Somerset West 7129, South Africa (tel 04457-7677; fax 04455-32680).
The agency Foreign Placements can arrange short-term casual work in South Africa as well as contracts for medical staff and skilled workers. For details contact the above address.

WORK SOUTH AFRICA: BUNAC, 16, Bowling Green Lane, London EC1R OQH (tel 020-7251 3472; fax 020-7251 0215; e-mail africa@bunac.org.uk; www.bunac.org).
BUNAC administer a new scheme that enables students who graduated last year or who are to graduate this year and who are aged under 27 to take up legally any job anywhere in South Africa: BUNAC can provide help in arranging work on arrival. Many participants work in hotels and restaurants or in jobs within the tourist industry. Many also take up shop-based or office work or community developmental work. The work visa is valid for up to 12 months and departures from the UK are in July, October and January. BUNAC arranges flights, visas, insurance and the first three night's accommodation.
For further details contact BUNAC at the above address or visit their website www.bunac.org.

SANCCOB – THE SOUTH AFRICAN NATIONAL FOUNDATION FOR THE CONSERVATION OF COASTAL BIRDS: P.O. Box 11116, Bloubergrant 7443, Cape Town, South Africa (tel +27-21-557 6155; fax 21-557 8804; e-mail sanccob@netactive.co.za; www.sanccob.co.za).
Volunteers required to help with the cleaning and rehabilitation of oil-soaked coastal birds. The main tasks involve keeping the hospital clean (scrubbing pools and pens), feeding the birds and checking that the centre is prepared for a major oil spill. The coastal waters of South Africa are a major shipping route and oil pollution is a recurrent problem, the main bird types dealt with are African penguins, gulls, gannets, tern and cormorants.
Volunteers must be willing to work in hard conditions with wild and difficult birds. Help is given with finding Bed & Breakfast accommodation and volunteers must meet their own living costs (approx. US$30-40/£ per day). The period May-October is the busiest but spills can happen at any time, the minimum stay is two weeks and applicants must be at least 16 years old.
To apply contact SANCCOB at the above address.

Tanzania

In addition to the following entry, UNA Exchange can offer short-term volunteer projects to Britons wishing to work in Tanzania for a few months: while Americans may be able to apply through Service Civil International; their entries in the *Worldwide* chapter give more details.

VolunteerAfrica: PO Box 24 Bakewell Derbyshire DE45 1TA (www.volunteerafrica.org). Providing support to a community based organisation working in the Singida and Tabora Regions of Tanzania, VolunteerAfrica is run entirely by volunteers to keep down running costs.

Volunteers to spend three months living and working alongside villagers on locally initiated projects such as the building of new schools or village health centres.

The cost of participating during 2002 is approximately £2,500 which consists of £650 for training, food, accommodation and travel costs in Tanzania, £1,000 towards the cost of the projects, a maximum of £250 towards UK administration costs and approximately £600 for flights and insurance.

Applicants must be aged 18 or over when they are due to travel overseas and applications can only be made through the organisation's website.

Togo

Apart from obtaining a voluntary work place through UNA Exchange (see *Worldwide* chapter for details), the following organisations can provide voluntary work opportunities in Togo.

JEUNESSE EN ACTION: S/C WWOOF-TOGO, B.P. 25 Agou Nyogbo, Togo (tel +228-471030; fax +228-471012; e-mail wwooftogo@hotmail.com). Jeunesse en Action is a non-profit making organisation, aiming to bring young people together while carrying out reforestation and conservation work.

Volunteers required for workcamps in Togo, between July-August and August-September. Camps cost approx. £60 which covers board and lodging. Volunteers must speak French.

Applications are invited all year, although for the summer camps the deadline for applications is 30 June. To obtain further information send two International Reply Coupons to S. Y. Agbeko at the above address. Information on these camps can also be obtained from MOACTIMO, Annie Jossaume le Bessin, F-50510 Cerences, France (fax +33-2-33 51 94 30).

WWOOF-TOGO: B.P. 25 Agou Nyogbo, Togo (tel +228-471030; fax +228-471012; e-mail wwooftogo@hotmail.com). Part of the worldwide organisation of organic farms WWOOF-TOGO can provide information on organic farms in Togo and west Africa, in return for two International Reply Coupons.

The Americas

Brazil

US nationals may be able to obtain voluntary work in Brazil through Council: International Volunteer Projects, allowing for yearly changes in their project planning.

ASSOCIAÇÃO BRASILIA DE INTERCAMBIO CUTURAL-INTERNATIONAL CHRISTIAN YOUTH EXCHANGE (ABIC-ICYE BRAZIL): Rua Espirito Santo, 362 cep 90.010-370 Porto Alegre/RS, Brazil (tel/fax 55-51-221-9075; e-mail abic@cpovo.net). ABIC is part of International Christian Youth Exchanges, a non-profit non-governmental organisation which aims to promote friendship between youth and adults worldwide through its youth exchange programmes.
Volunteers aged 18-25 required to take part in exchanges, living with local families and taking part in local projects. The Brazilian projects involve working with Amnesty International and other projects.

Canada

The employment of foreigners in either short or long term work in Canada is strictly regulated. Even with Canada's booming economy it is illegal to work in Canada without an employment authorisation; with some exceptions, a job must be obtained from outside the country, and even then the employer will face difficulty in obtaining permission to employ you unless they can show that they are not depriving a Canadian citizen or permanent resident of the job.

Anyone seeking employment in Canada should write directly to Canadian employers before arrival to enquire about employment prospects. Information on jobs in Canada can also be obtained by reviewing Canadian newspapers or trade journals which are available at larger new agencies. Addresses of potential employers can also be found in the *Canadian Trade Index* or the *Canadian Almanac and Directory*, both of which can be found at large libraries.

Teachers from British Commonwealth nations may be able to arrange exchange placements by contacting *The League for the Exchange of Commonwealth Teachers*, Commonwealth House, 7 Lion Yard, Tremadoc Road, London SW4 7NQ (tel 020-7498 1101; fax 020-7720 5403).

To work legally in Canada, you must obtain an Employment Authorization from a Canadian High Commission or Embassy before you leave your home country. The Canadian government offers in the neighbourhood of 17,000 temporary authorisations each year to full-time students to work temporarily in Canada. Participants in the official work exchange must be aged 18-30 years and must have proof that they will be returning to a tertiary level course of study on their return to the UK.

Interested students should check the website www.canada.org.uk/visa-info or obtain the general leaflet 'Student Temporary Employment in Canada' by sending a large s.a.e. with a £1 stamp and marked 'SGWHP' in the top right-hand corner to the Canadian High Commission (Immigration Visa Information, 38 Grosvenor St, London W1K 4AA; 09068-616644 60p a minute). Students who already have a job offer from a Canadian employer may be eligible for 'Programme A'. They can apply directly to the High Commission in London for an Employment Authorization (reference 1102) which will be valid for a maximum of 12 months and is not transferable to any other job.

The other and more flexible possibility is to obtain an unspecified Employment Authorization from BUNAC (see Worldwide). BUNAC's Work Canada programme offers about 1,300 students (including gap year students with a university place and finalists with proof that they will return to the UK) the chance to go to Canada for up to a year and take whatever jobs they can find. Students on this programme can depart at any time between February and December. The great majority of participants go to Canada without a pre-arranged job and spend their first week or two job-hunting.

In Ireland enquiries should be directed to Programmes Department, usit NOW, 19-21 Aston Quay, O'Connell Bridge, Dublin 2 (tel +353-1-602 1667; e-mail programmes@usitworld.com).

UNA Exchange can organise voluntary work in French-speaking Quebec; the Council International Volunteer Projects can arrange voluntary work in Canada for Americans: for details see the *Worldwide* chapter.

RED TAPE

Visa Requirements: Citizens of the United Kingdom and most other countries in western Europe, of UK dependent territories, Australia, New Zealand, most other Pacific islands, the United States, Mexico and most Caribbean islands do not normally require a visa for a visit to Canada. Citizens of other countries may need to obtain one. No matter what the length or purpose of the proposed stay, permission to enter and remain in Canada must be obtained from the Immigration Officer at the port of entry. If the purpose is any other than purely for a tourist visit to Canada, you should consult the Canadian High Commission abroad before departure.

The length of stay in Canada is decided at the port of entry. Normally entry is granted for six months.

Employment and Student Authorization: Authorises an individual to work 'at a specific job for a specific period of time for a specific employer'. It must be applied for before arrival. Some details of the Work Authorizations available through BUNAC (16 Bowling Green Lane, London EC1R 0QH; tel 020-7251 3472; www.bunac.org.uk) are given above.

Voluntary Work: A special category of work permit covers voluntary work which takes about a month to process if you have found a placement through a recognised charitable or religious organisation.

Agricultural Work

WILLING WORKERS ON ORGANIC FARMS (CANADA): RR2 Carlson Road, S.18, C.9, Nelson, British Columbia, Canada VIL 5P5 (tel/fax 250-354 4417; e-mail www.wwoof.ca). Hundreds of young people, from 30 different countries, every year go 'wwoofing' in Canada. Hosts available from the east to the west coast of Canada.

Volunteers to work on 400 organic farms in Canada ranging from small homesteads to large farms. Duties include general farm work and may include going to market, working with horses, garden work, milking goats, etc. No pocket money but board and lodging provided free of charge. Opportunites may be available all year round. Minimum age 16.

Only EEA nationals with valid tourist visas need apply. *Applications*, enclosing three International Reply Coupons and C$30 (cash) for a farm list and description booklet, should be sent to the above address.

Voluntary Work and Archaeology

FRONTIERS FOUNDATION/OPERATION BEAVER: 2615 Danforth Avenue, Suite 203, Toronto, Ontario, Canada M4C 1L6 (tel 416-690-3930; fax 416-690-3534; e-mail frontiersfoundation@on.aibn.com; www.frontiersfoundation. org). Frontiers Foundation is a non-profit voluntary service organisation supporting the advancement of economically and socially disadvantaged communitites in Canada and overseas.

Volunteers are recruited from across the world to serve in native and non-native communities across Canada for a variety of community construction and recreation projects. The organisation works in partnership with requesting communities in low-income rural areas. Projects help to provide and improve housing, to provide training and economic incentives and to offer recreational/educational activities in developing regions.

Volunteers must be 18 or older and available for a minimum period of 12 weeks. Skills in carpentry, electrical work and plumbing are preferred for construction projects; previous social service and experience with children are sought for recreational/educational projects. The greatest need for volunteers is in June, July and August. Group size is usually between 2 and 8.

All accommodation, food and travel, within Canada is provided. Travel to and from Canada is the responsibility of the volunteer. Accommodation is normally provided by the community; volunteers must be prepared to live without electricity, running water or roads in some communities. Long term placements of up to 18 months are possible provided that the volunteer's work is deemed satisfactory after the initial 12 week period.

Application kits and information are available from the above address; please provide 3 International Reply Coupons. Once an applicant has sent in application forms there can be a delay of 3-12 weeks as references come in and possible placements are considered. Acceptance cannot be guaranteed.

Other Employment Abroad

INTERNSHIP CANADA PROGRAMME: Council on International Educational Exchange (Council Exchanges), 52 Poland Street, London W1F 7AB (tel: 020-7478 2020; fax 020-7734 7322; e-mail infouk@councilexchanges.uk). Assisting 1500 students undertake practical training in North America each year, Council Exchanges is a worldwide organisation helping people develop skills and acquire knowledge for working in a multicultural, interdependent world.

The programme enables students who hold *British or Irish passports* to complete a period of work experience of up to one year in Canada. Minimum age 18. Applicants must be enrolled in full-time further or higher education (HND level or above) or a recent graduate within 12 months of finishing, or a gap year student with an unconditional offer of a university place. Before applying applicants must have secured a full-time work placement in Canada directly related to their studies.

Programme costs start at £270 for a two month stay and particpants must have Council's insurance cover for the length of their stay. Official documentation and assistance with visa application are provided, as are orientation materials covering taxes, housing, Canadian culture and transportation; plus 24-hour emergency assistance with any problems whilst in Canada.

Applications can be made at any time of year, but should be made at least two months before the desired date of departure.

WORK CANADA: BUNAC, 16 Bowling Green Lane, London EC1R 0QH (tel 020-7251 3472; e-mail canada@bunac.org.uk).
There are approximately 1,500 places on the Work Canada programme for full-time students (degree, HND, NVQ 4/5 or those in a gap year with a confirmed place for the following Autumn). The Work Authorisation is valid for one year and enables participants to work and travel anywhere in Canada. You can apply either with (1) a definite job offer plus $600 support funds, (2) a letter of sponsorship from a Canadian citizen plus support funds of $600, or (3) $1,000 support funds only.

Approximately 90% of participants go to Canada without a pre-arranged job and take an average of six days to find one. BUNAC also offers advice on job-hunting, various travel deals and on-going support services whilst in Canada. For further details contact the above address or visit the website www.bunac.org.

Colombia

The following organisation has vacancies for suitably qualified employees in Colombia.

CENTRO COLOMBO AMERICANO: Cra. 45 No. 53-24, Medellìn, Colombia (tel 574-513-4444; fax 574-513-2666; e-mail lshem@colomboworld.com; www.colomboworld.com).
TEFL Teachers required, preference of nationality: U.S., Canadian or British. Other countries also welcome, conditions may vary. Applicants must have BA or MA (Education, Language teaching, TESOL). Teachers are employed on one-year contract (renewable), 6 contact hours per day. English for children and adults. Salary: 1,500,000 1,800,000 pesos (£445-£535 approx.) per month, plus round trip ticket and all visa expenses paid. Assistance in finding housing. Pre-service and in-
service training provided. Medical benefits and Spanish lessons provided.

Candidates should apply directly to the school, selection is made through references and phone interview. Send CV and three letters of recommendation to Lai Yin Shem, Academic Director or Steve Ingham, Academic Coordinator.

Costa Rica

Under Costa Rican law it is illegal for foreigners to be offered paid work, but the organisations listed in this chapter offer voluntary work. US nationals may be able to obtain voluntary work through Council: International Volunteer Projects, allowing for yearly changes in their project planning. Britons may find opportunities arranged by UNA Exchange.

AGROPECURIA BALVE S.A.: Am hohlen Stein 54, D-58802 Balve, Germany (tel/fax +49-2375 21 70).
or Finca Bella Vista, Raizal Colorado de Abangares, Guanacaste, Costa Rica (tel +506-6780464; fax +506-6780467; e-mail: balvesa@racsa.co.cr; www.homepages. compuserve.de/RicaUrlaub).
Volunteers are needed to help run and work on a tropical ecological farm in Costa Rica. Typical work duties include small scale agriculture, gardening , construction, carpentry, fishing and maintenance work. Relevant skills and experience are useful, but not essential, though it is recommended that volunteers have some basic knowledge of Spanish. An interest in ecology and biological farming is a plus. Applicants over 16 years are accepted. The minimum stay is one month, and there is no upper limit. Volunteers are expected to pay $100 a week to cover food and lodging in rooms usually rented to tourists. Wages cannot be paid, but volunteers can enjoy a lot of privileges like use of the swimming pool, horse or cycle riding, excursions, and working and living with Costarricans to learn Spanish rapidly. Those wishing to learn Spanish whilst they are there are encouraged to apply. Those interested should contact Rudolf Micknass, President, at the above address, preferably by e-mail. Alternatively, contact Am Hohlen Stein 54, D-58802 Balve, Germany (tel/fax 0049 2375-2170). Please note only Spanish speakers should telephone the Costa Rica number.

ARBOREA PROJECT FOUNDATION: Boca Taboga, Sierpe de Osa, Costa Rica, Ap.do Postal 65-8150 Palmar Norte (tel 506-786 65 65; fax 506-786 63 58; e-mail mapache@greenarrow.com; www.greenarrow.com/travel/mapache.htm).
The Arborea Project, established in Costa Rica, is a non-profit Foundation whose goal is to protect and defend nature. Work includes the purchase of virgin lands to protect them from becoming pastures or being cultivated intensively, and the reforestation of lands that have been affected by human activity.
    Volunteers are required between November and April to help either on land owned by Arborea or to work with Rangers in the National Parks of Corcovado and Cano Island. Work on Arborea land may consist of animal and plant surveys, forest wardening, working in tree nurseries or general wardening: in the Parks it may consist of improving the walks or putting up notices around the paths, camping areas and archaeological sites.
    No special qualifications are needed. Volunteers will stay either in one of the lodges surrounding Arborea or at Rangers' stations. Contributions of approx. £18 a day towards expenses plus around £30 for 2 weeks towards transport etc. are expected.
    For more information about the Foundation and its aims contact the Arborea Project at the above address.

IYOK AMI: P.O. Box 335-2100, Guadalupe, San José, Costa Rica, Central America. (tel +506-387-2238 (Spanish is preferred); fax 506-771-200 or 506-223-1609; e-mail iyokbosque@yahoo.es).
Volunteers to work at Iyok Ami, an extensive private reserve that includes both tropical cloud and tropical rain forests, and an Indian reserve. These wild areas have been set aside to protect flora, fauna and water resources, and also to serve

as areas of scientific and research study.

Volunteers' help is needed to build and maintain trails and for reforestation, help with labelling and transplantation of flowering plants around the trails, making topographical and pictorial maps of the area, constructing signposts, teaching English in schools, protecting and stimulating the Quetzal bird reproduction. Volunteers also help with the classification of plants, birds and fungi, and other work depending on the volunteer's interest and specialist knowlege.

Volunteers will receive a free daily hour of basic Spanish teaching. Anyone is welcome to apply. Iyok Ami is a private organisation that receives no funding and so volunteers pay $600 per month, to cover board, laundry and accommodation (overlooking the forest, the Irazu, and Turrialba volcanoes). Volunteers are expected to work five hours per day, Monday to Friday. Weekends are free for visiting other places (the beach etc.).

RAINFOREST CONCERN: 27 Lansdowne Crescent, London, W11 2NS (tel 020-7-229 2093; fax 020-7-221 4094; e-mail info@rainforestconcern.org; www.rainforest.org). Rainforest Concern is a non-political charity dedicated to the conservation of vulnerable rainforest. They invite support for the sponsorship of acres of tropical rainforest and encourage volunteers to help out with research and reserve maintenance.

Turtle Monitors (20) The chief purpose of the programme is to protect the leatherback turtle. The work includes protecting the beach from egg-collecting poachers, monitoring and tagging turtles and cleaning trails. Hours of work are 8pm-4am, on a variable number of days per week, between mid-March and the end of August. Minimum period of work is 1 week. Board and lodging is provided at a cost of $100/£62 per week. No special skills are required, although Spanish would be helpful, but applicants must have a sincere interest in conservation, be over 18 and generally fit.

Applications can be sent to the above address at any time of year.

Cuba

The following organisation recruits people for a working holiday scheme in Cuba.

THE CUBA SOLIDARITY CAMPAIGN: c/o Red Rose Club, 129 Seven Sisters Road, London N7 7QG (tel 020-7-263 6452; fax 020-7-561 0191; e-mail office@cuba-solidarity.org.uk; www.cuba-solidarity.org.uk, www.cubaconnect. co.uk). CSC's aim is to promote friendship and solidarity between Cuba and the UK. People are encouraged to join CSC and take part in a wide range of activities.

Volunteers to take part in a scheme in Cuba involving 3 week's work on a self-contained camp near Havana. The work involves building and agricultural work. 4¹/₂ day working week, with transport to Havana provided during time off and excursions arranged on Sundays. There are many opportunities to meet Cubans, and a number of optional educational visits and lectures. Two work brigades are organised each year, one in the summer and one in the winter.

Some knowledge of Spanish would be useful. Participants must cover their own travel costs and make a contribution for accommodation, food and travel (approximate cost £770). The Campaign organises the necessary visa. Contact the above address for further information. Contact CSC for application deadlines and further information.

Ecuador

UNA Exchange and Youth Action for Peace offer short-term International Volunteer Projects to Britons in Ecuador, while Council: International Volunteer Projects can do the same for US citizens. See their entries in the *Worldwide* chapter for more details.

BENEDICT SCHOOLS OF LANGUAGES: PO Box 09-01-8916, Guayaquil, Ecuador (tel 4-444418; fax 4-441642; e-mail benecent@telconet.net).
TEFL Teachers: (15) required for several schools in Guayaquil (Urdesa, Centro, Garzota, Centenario, Entrerios). Applicants should ideally be British, American, Canadian or Irish, hold a teaching certificate or college degree and be proficient in English.

Minimum period of work 4 months (two courses), although the school prefers it if teachers can stay at least 10 months. Help is given with finding accommodation and the salary is US$2-3 per hour. Applications accepted and work available all year round, to *apply* contact Mercedes de Elizalde, General Director at the above address.

FUNDACIÓN GOLONDRINAS/ THE CERRO GOLONDRINAS CLOUDFOREST CONSERVATION GROUP: c/o Calle Isabe La Católica 1559, Quito, Ecuador (tel 593-2-226602; e-mail manteca@uio.satnet.net (subject: volunteer); www.ecuadorexplorer.com/golondrinas).
Volunteers required to help conserve 25,000 hectares of highland cloudforest on the western slopes of the Andes. The project's work involves the introduction of sustainable agroforestry techniques, soil conservation, research and the reintroduction of tree species. Volunteers will be involved in these activities in two field sites; some general labouring also required.

Minimum stay 1 month. Some experience of horticulture/permaculture, and advanced Spanish are prerequisites, and a contribution to costs of c. £148/$240 per month. Special financial arrangements will be made by the group for those with advanced skills in gardening, agroforestry, permaculture and those who wish to stay more than 3 months.

Volunteers accepted all year round, but contact Fundacion at least 3 months in advance of desired dates of placement. Volunteers must arrange their own travel, visas and field kit. Details of work and kit requirements can be obtained from the above address.

RAINFOREST CONCERN: 27 Lansdowne Crescent, London, W11 2NS (tel 020-7229 2093; fax 020-7221 4094; e-mail info@rainforestconcern.org; www.rainforest.org). Rainforest Concern is a non-political charity dedicated to the conservation of vulnerable rainforest. They invite support for their sponsorship of acres of forest and encourage volunteers to help out with research and reserve maintenance.
Research Assistant/Rainforest Maintenance Volunteers (18) required at any time. The work involves an element of research or physical labour, such as reforestation or compiling species lists, depending on the projects being undertaken at the time.

Hours of work are flexible, and places are available all year-round. Minimum period of work is 3 days. Board and lodging is provided at a cost of $20/£12 per day. No special skills are required, although Spanish would be helpful, but applicants must have a sincere interest in conservation, be over 18 and generally fit.

Applications can be sent to the above address at any time of year.

Mexico

Paid employment is difficult to find in Mexico and must be approved by the immigration authorities in Mexico City before a visa will be issued to enter Mexico. Visitors entering Mexico as tourists are not permitted to engage in any paid activities under any circumstances.

There are a growing number of opportunities for voluntary work in Mexico. British applicants can find voluntary work in Mexico through UNA Exchange or Youth Action for Peace, US nationals through Council: International Volunteer Projects; see the *Worldwide* chapter for details.

AMERICAN FRIENDS SERVICE COMMITTEE: 1501 Cherry Street, Philadelphia, Pennsylvania 19102, USA.
Volunteers to work in remote rural villages in Mexico improving and constructing schools or other community facilities and to help with agricultural projects. Work generally lasts for 7 weeks from early July to late August. Applicants should be 18-26 years old and speak Spanish. Limited scholarships available some years. Participants are responsible for their own travel costs and must make a contribution of around $400 to cover orientation, food and accommodation and health and accident insurance

For details American applicants should write to the above address enclosing an international reply coupon before 1st March; European applicants should apply directly to SEDEPAC, Apartado Postal 27-054, 06760 Mexico DF, Mexico (fax 52-5-584 3895; e-mail sedepac@laneta.apc.org)

Please note that no paid jobs are available in Mexico or US through the AFSC or SEDEPAC.

BUSCA (BRIGADA UNIVERSITARIA DE SERVICIOS COMUNITARIOS PARA LA AUTOGESTION): Casa de la Cultura Raul Anguiano, Parque Ecologico Huayamilpas, Yaqui esq. Nezahualcoyotl s/n, Colonia Ajusco Huayamilpas, Mexico, D.F. 04390 Mexico (tel/fax 525-6 66 47 71; e-mail busca@laneta.apc.org.).
Volunteers to work with young local people in indigenous communities in Mexico on development projects concerned with areas such as health, education, human rights, the environment, community work etc. Volunteers live and work in teams of five or six people. No pocket money is paid, and participants must pay a fee of approx. £310 towards costs of food, accommodation and transport inside Mexico. Minimum period of work 7 weeks between 25 June and 15 August. Volunteers should be aged 18-26, must have a good knowledge of Spanish and be willing to share and exchange experiences.
Volunteers are also required to join 20 Mexicans in a 2,000 km bicycle journey across Mexico which has the objects of promoting the bicycle as a form of transport and raising funds for community development projects. Volunteers must raise sponsorship of $0.50 per km and need at least a basic knowledge of Spanish.

Should be aged 17-27.
     Participants must pay for their own travel to and from Mexico. *Applications should be sent to the above address between January and May 1st.*

Peru

The following organisation has vacancies for suitably qualified employees in Peru.

TAMBOPATA JUNGLE LODGE: P.O. Box 454, Cusco, Peru (tel/fax +51-84-245695; e-mail tplcus@terra.com.pe; www.tambopatalodge).
Nature Guides to lead nature walks for tourists and accompany them during their stay at a jungle lodge in the rainforest of Southern Peru within the Tambopata National Reserve. Working hours required may be any time between 4am and 8pm, as the tour programme dictates. Those taken on will be qualified students and scientists. The exchange programmes are: people who participate in 20 days per month of guiding will receive in exchange return air travel between Lima or Cusco and Puerto Maldonado per 90 days and £100 per month, or guide 10 days per month and receive in exchange a return air ticket for each 90 days worked and the remainder of the month free for research, etc. Applicants can also combine these two programmes.
     The minimum stay is 180 days at any time of year. Applicants will ideally stay for six months, have a background in nature studies, speak English and Spanish; knowledge of French and German would be an advantage. Those interested should contact the above address including a curriculum vitae.

USA

The American economy is currently in the position that with 4% unemployment employers are having trouble finding staff to fill temporary and summer vacancies. Walt Disney World, for example, found themselves so short of workers for summer 2000 that they put on a lavish recruitment party at one of their parks to try and attract new workers. Opportunities for summer work in the United States are so numerous that apart from those listed below, there are thousands covered in detail by a separate publication *Summer Jobs USA 2002* which lists thousands of vacancies in resorts, theatres, hotels, ranches, business, national parks, etc. throughout the USA; it also gives details on the different work visas necessary for any non-American citizen wishing to work in the USA. This book is published in the USA at $18.95 under the name *Summer Jobs for Students* by Peterson's Guides (PO Box 67005, Lawrenceville, NJ 08648-4764) and is available in Britain in good bookshops for £12.95 or (plus £1.50 postage) direct from its European distributors, Vacation Work, 9 Park End Street, Oxford OX1 1HJ. Vacation Work also distribute for the same publishers the book *Internships* (US price $26.95), a guide to career-related summer jobs for students in the USA. The UK price is £18.95 plus £3 postage. Both can be obtained with a discount on the cover price through Vacation Work's website www.vacationwork.co.uk.
     Placing an advertisement in an American paper may lead to the offer of a job. *The New York Times* is published by A.O. Sulzberger, of 229 West 43rd Street, New York, NY10036. It has a UK office at 66 Buckingham Gate, London, SW1 6AU (tel 020-7799 2981)

The au pair placement programme allows thousands of young Europeans with childcare experience to work for American families for exactly one year on a J-1 visa. They apply through a small number of sponsoring organisations which must follow the guidelines which govern the programme, so there is not much difference between them. The arrangement differs from au pairing in Europe since the hours are much longer and, if the au pair comes from the UK, there is no language to learn. The basic requirements are that you be between 18 and 26, speak English, show at least 200 hours of recent childcare experience and provide a criminal record check.

Voluntary work can be found in the USA through the Winant-Clayton Volunteer Association (entry below), Youth Action for Peace, UNA Exchange, Concordia, International Voluntary Service, Council: International Volunteer Projects, and Service Civil International. See the *Worldwide* chapter for details.

RED TAPE

Visa Requirements: since the introduction of the Visa Waiver Program, the tourist visa requirement is waived in the case of 29 nationalities, including British and Australian citizen passport holders. Nationals of the 29 VWP countries may enter the U.S. for up to 90 days for tourism or business, provided they meet all of the regulations for visa free travel. Note: Certain travellers are not eligible to travel visa free, for instance those who have been arrested and/or convicted of an offence. The Rehabilitation of Offenders Act does not apply to U.S. visa law. For a full list of the 29 visa free countries, including the criteria which must be met to travel visa free, and further information on those not eligible to travel under the VWP, contact your nearest Embassy or Consulate, or visit the Department of State's website at http://travel.state.gov.

Anyone entering the United States to work requires the appropriate work visa. Under no circumstances can a person who has entered the U.S. as a take up any form of employment paid or unpaid.

Residence Permits: Anyone seeking to take up permanent residence in the U.S. requires the appropriate immigrant visa. In general immigration is family or employment based. For further information, contact your nearest Embassy or Consulate, or visit the Department of State's website as above.

Work Permits: Anyone taking up temporary employment, whether paid or unpaid, requires the appropriate work visa. There are a number of possible visas for temporary workers, au pairs, exchange visitors and cultural exchange visitors. Most of the opportunities listed in this chapter are covered by the J-1 Exchange Visitor visa, which is arranged by the organisations with entries. Employment-based H-2B visas are available through major employers of seasonal workers (as in ski resorts) only after the employer receives Labor certification from the Department of Labor (which takes 3-6 months).

Au Pair: J-1 visa available through officially approved exchange visitor programmes overseen by the Public Affairs Division of the Department of State.

Voluntary Work: Individuals participating in a voluntary service program benefitting U.S. local communities, who establish that they are members of and have a commitment to a particular recognised religious or non-profit charitable organisation may, in certain cases, enter the United States with business (B-1) visas, or visa free, if eligible, provided that the work performed is traditionally done by volunteer charity workers, no salary or remuneration will be paid from a U.S. source other than an allowance or other reimbursement for expenses incidental to the stay in the United States, and they will not engage in the selling of articles and/or solicitation and acceptance of donations. Volunteers should carry with them a letter from their U.S. sponsor which contains their name and date and place of birth, their foreign permanent residence address, the name and address of their initial destination in the U.S., and the anticipated duration of the voluntary assignment.

Summer Camps

www.campamerica.co.uk

for the summer of a lifetime...

- free return flights
- free meals and accommodation
- great choices of work
- pocket money
- 10 weeks to travel the USA

CAMP AMERICA   Camp America 37a Queen's Gate London SW7 5HR
                      020 7581 7333
                      email brochure@campamerica.co.uk

CAMP AMERICA: Dept. SJA, 37A Queen's Gate, London SW7 5HR.
Camp America is looking to recruit Youth Leaders/Specialist Counsellors to work on American summer camps for 9 weeks from June. The work could include childcare and teaching of specialist activities such as sports, music, arts and drama.

Applicants are offered free London-New York return flight, board and lodging at camp, J1 Cultural Exchange Visa, pocket money and up to 2 months' independent travel. Anyone who applies must be 18+ and free from June to September.

CAMP COUNSELORS USA: UK Offices: Green Dragon House, 64-70 High Street, Croydon CR0 9XN (tel 020-8688 9051; e-mail Inquiry@ccusaweusa.co.uk; www.ccusa.com) and 27 Woodside Gardens, Musselburgh, nr. Edinburgh EH21 7LJ (tel 0131-665 5843; e-mail 101355.257@compuserve.com; www.ccusa.com). US Office: 2330 Marinship Way, Suite 250, Sausalito CA 94965, USA.

Camp Counselors USA is a high quality programme that places young people at American Summer Camps. Counselors are only placed at camps that have a good reputation with CCUSA. Each year CCUSA staff inspect the camps and interview Counsellors, so that improvements can be made if necessary. CCUSA require people with sports and/or arts and crafts qualifications or willing to assist with the physically and mentally handicapped.

In addition CCUSA require well motivated young people who are willing to be role models for the camps (to look after the children whilst they are at camp). In the coming year Camp Counselors will also be recruiting support staff, who must be full time students. All applicants must be available for interview in Europe. For further information write to the above address.

CAMPOWER: Dept. SJA, 37a Queen's Gate, London SW7 5HR.
Camp America is looking to recruit students to work on American summer camps or resorts for 9 weeks from June. The work might be in the kitchen or laundry or involve driving or general maintenance; it represents an ideal camp alternative for those not wishing to work directly with children.

Applicants are offered free London-New York return flight, board and lodging at camp, a J1 Cultural Exchange Visa, pocket money and up to 2 months' independent travel. Applicants must be students aged at least 18 and free from June to September. For details contact the above address.

KAMP: BUNAC, 16 Bowling Green Lane, London EC1R OQH (tel 020-7251 3472; fax 020-7251 0215; e-mail: camps@bunac.org.uk).
KAMP is a low cost fare-paid programme for summer camp staff who are not afraid of two months' hard fairly physical work in an ancillary capacity. Working in the kitchen and maintenance areas, staff do not look after children and have access to many of the camps' facilities during time off.

BUNAC places applicants, arranges the special work/travel visa, flight and travel to camp. In addition, participants are given free board and lodging at camp, a salary and up to six weeks of independent travel afterwards. The programme is open to those who are currently enrolled at a British university, studying full time at degree (or advanced tertiary or postgraduate) level, and gap year students with an unconditional offer of a university/college place to return to. The programme fee was £62 in 2001.

SUMMER CAMP USA: 16 Bowling Green Lane, London EC1R 0QH (tel 020-7251 3472; fax 020-7251 0215; e-mail: camps@bunac.org.uk).

A low-cost, non-profit camp counsellor programme run by BUNAC (the British Universities North America Club), placing over 5,000 people in US and Canadian summer camps. Provides job, work papers, flights, salary, board and lodging, and a flexible length of independent holiday time after the 9 week work period. Applicants must be aged 18-35, have experience of working with children *and be living in the UK at the time of making their application.* For details contact the above address or visit the website www.bunac.org. The programme fee is £62 in 2001.

Voluntary Work and Archaeology

HAWAIIAN INSTITUTE OF TROPICAL AGRICULTURE: c/o Andy's Organic, PO Box 1729, Pahoa, HI 96778, USA (tel 808 965-0069; e-mail andysorganic@hotmail.com). A certified organic farm striving to become a school for tropical agriculture, specialising in yellow ginger but also growing diverse tropical crops. The farm is located in a rural and beautiful agricultural area on Hawaii's largest island. Tide pools, hot ponds, a small lake and a healing centre where one can take yoga classes can be found nearby.

Voluntary Farm Hands with extensive experience who wish to deepen their understanding of sustainable agriculture in the tropics. Farm work includes planting, cultivating, harvesting, washing and packing as well as other tasks that may arise. Apprentices are required to work 12 hours a week in exchange for room and food from the garden, and are expected to contribute to community chores as well. Applicants should be prepared to stay for at least 4 months; a stay of 8 to 12 months is recommended.

Applications should be made to the above address at any time

INTERNATIONAL CENTER FOR GIBBON STUDIES: P.O. Box 800249, Santa Clarita, CA 91380 (tel 661-943 4915 hours of operation 10am to 7pm (Pacific Time); fax 661-296 1237; e-mail: gibboncntr@aol.com; www.gibboncenter.org).

Volunteer Primate Keepers (up to 3 at any one time) to work with gibbons at the centre. Duties include preparing food and feeding, changing water, cleaning enclosures, observing behaviour (if time permits), entering data into computer (Apple Mac), maintaining grounds etc. To work from approx. 6.30am-5pm, 7 days a week; opportunities for time off depend on the number of volunteers. Volunteers must make their own travel arrangements and buy their own food locally; accommodation is provided.

Applicants must be aged at least 20, well motivated, love animals, be capable of retaining unfamiliar information, get along with a variety of people, be in good physical condition and able to work outside in extreme weather conditions. They will need to have the following medical tests: stool cultures, ova and parasite stool test, standard blood chemistry and haematology, tuberculosis (or written proof from a doctor certifying that they have been vaccinated against tuberculosis) and Hepatitis B. Also required are vaccinations against tetanus (within the last 5 years), rubella, measles and Hepatitis B (if not already immune).

Applications to Patti Dahle, Volunteer Co-ordinator, at the above address or by e-mail.

THE INTERNATIONAL VOLUNTEER PROGRAMME: La Sociètè Française de Bienfaisance Mutuelle, 210 Post Street, Suite 502, San Francisco, CA 94108, USA (tel 415-477-3667; fax 415-477-3669; www.ivpsf.com).

Founded in 1991 this cultural and volunteer exchange programme sends applicants from the Britain or France to the USA.

Volunteer exchange staff required for six weeks in California, to work in a range of placements such as hospitals, homeless shelters, and the offices of not for profit organisations. Places of work are located throughout California. Programme fees of £900 (UK applicants)/Euro 1500 (French applicants) cover round trip flights, board and lodging and transport to and from the airports to the places of work.

Further information can be obtained by contacting Rebecca Jewell, Programme Director at the above address.

KALANI OCEANSIDE ECO-RESORT: RR 2 Box 4500, Pahoa, Beach Road, Hawaii 96778 (tel +808 965-7828 (business) +800 800-6886 (registration); fax +808 965-0527; e-mail kalani@kalani.com; www.kalani.com). Kalani Oceanside Eco-Resort is a non-profit inter-cultural conference and retreat centre located on an island twenty acres of pristine land, surrounded by tropical forest and the Pacific Ocean.

Volunteers: the retreat centre operates with the assistance of approximately 20 resident volunteers who help to provide services to the guests of the Resort. To participate in the programme volunteers must stay a minimum of three months. In exchange for thirty hours of volunteer time per week participants receive mainly vegetarian meals, shared lodging, and a week long vacation during the three month placement. Opportunities for volunteering exist in food service, grounds/maintenance, and housekeeping. The cost of the Resident Volunteer Programme is $900/£610 for the three month term. Volunteers must be at least 20 years old and in good health; experience in the area for which the applicant volunteers is preferred.

Application form and free brochure are available from the above address.

WINANT-CLAYTON VOLUNTEER ASSOCIATION (WCVA): 179 Whitechapel Road, London E1 1DU (tel 020-7-375 0547; fax 020-7-377 2437; e-mail wcva@dircon.co.uk). WCVA operates an annual exchange of volunteers between the UK and USA. It hopes to promote friendship and understanding between the two countries as well as to provide valuable life experiences.

Volunteers (20) for voluntary work including working with the homeless, the elderly and children, psychiatric rehabilitation, drug rehabilitation and helping on HIV/AIDS programmes. Placements are largely in New York and Eastern States. Pocket money, board and accommodation provided while working, but volunteers must pay for their own air fare and other travel expenses. However, some bursaries are available for volunteers from Ireland and East London. Period of work 8 weeks from the middle/end of June to the beginning of September, followed by a two/three week period for independent travel.

Applicants must be UK passport holders. No particular qualifications are essential, but previous experience of voluntary work is useful. For further details send a large s.a.e. to the above address. Applications must be received by mid-January, as interviews are held in February.

WWOOF USA AND HAWAII (Willing Workers on Organic Farms): RR2 Carlson Road, S.18, C.9, Nelson, British Columbia, Canada V1L 5P5 (tel/fax 250-354-4417; e-mail wwoof@usa.com; www.wwoofusa.com). US youths and hundreds of people from all over the world go 'wwoofing' every summer. Farm Hosts are available in most states and on all the Hawaiian islands.

Volunteer experiences range from small homesteads to large farms. Duties include general work, milking goats etc. Pocket money is not usually provided, but board and lodging are provided free of charge. Opportunities may be available all year round. Minimum age of sixteen. If not a US citizen, *only EEA nationals with valid tourist visas* need apply. *Applications* available on-line. Otherwise, send full name, mailing address and registration fee. US membership is $30 and Hawaii membership is $15 plus postage. Cash or cheques (made payable to Kate Noble) are accepted. WWOOF will then send you the booklet of host farms.

Other Employment

AU PAIR IN AMERICA: Dept. SUM, 26 Shakespeare Road, Bedford, MK40 2ED (tel 07002-287247; fax 01234-351070; e-mail elizabeth@ elizabethelder.co.uk; www.aupairamerica.co.uk).
Au Pair in America operates the largest and most experienced legal childcare programme to the United States. Au Pairs and Nannies are placed with a carefully screened family for a 12 month placement providing 45 hours childcare per week. Benefits include free return flights between major European cities and New York, free board and lodging and $139.05 (approx. £84) weekly payment, 4-day Orientation programme held near New York, legal Exchange J-1 visa, $500 tuition allowance, medical insurance, 2 weeks paid holiday, optional 13th month to travel, year-long support from US Community Counsellor and placement in an established 'cluster' group.
    Au Pair in America introduced a new programme in 1998 for qualified and experienced (2 years full-time) childcare providers - Au Pair Extraordinaire. American families value highly the training, expertise and professionalism off these applicants and in return they recieve $200 (approx. £130) per week, in addition to the benefits listed above.
    Applicants must be 18-26, have recent practical experience with children (e.g. babysitting), hold a full driving licence and be available for 12 months.
    For information on either programme and a chance to speak to a returned au pair, call 07002-287247 or contact the above address.

CHALLENGE EDUCATIONAL SERVICES LTD: 101 Lorna Road, Hove, East Sussex, BN3 3EL (tel 01273-220261; fax 01273-220376; e-mail enquiries@challengeuk.com; www.challengeuk.com). Challenge Educational Services Ltd. organise 1-4 month work placements in the USA. Individual searches are undertaken for each applicant, to find an internship which suites their individual needs.
Internships are offered in all areas of business and industry, e.g. banking, marketing, finance and journalism. All internships are offered on a voluntary basis (unpaid).
    Prices range from £1,450 for a one month internship without accommodation to £4,190 for a four month internship including accommodation. Most placements are in the San Fransisco area.

INTERNATIONAL EXCHANGE CENTER: UK Office: 35 Ivor Place, London NW1 6EA (tel 020-7724 4493; e-mail isecinfo@btconnect.com; www.isecworld.co.uk). The International Exchange Center works to promote positive, enjoyable cultural exchanges. Overseas work is offered in various countries for various types of work. See their website for full details.
Work and Travel in the USA Programme: Choice of various entry-level jobs

around the US in cities, resorts and national parks. From ride operators at amusement parks to waitresses in Cape Cod. Working hours around 40 a week, pay £ ($5.25+) per hour. Subsidised accommodation arranged. Applicants must be university students aged 18+. Enthusiasm and commitment the key to great time. The programme runs from May-July.

To *apply* contact the above address.

INTERNSHIP USA PROGRAMME: Council on International Educational Exchange (Council Exchanges), 52 Poland Street, London W1F 7AB (tel: 020-7478 2020; fax 020-7734 7322; e-mail internusa@councilexchanges.org.uk; www.councilexchanges.org.uk). Assisting over 1500 students to find work in North America each year, Council Exchanges is a worldwide organisation helping people develop skills and acquire knowledge for working in a multicultural, interdependent world.

This scheme enables students and recent graduates to complete a period of course-related work experience/training for a period of up to eighteen months in the US, with an optional travel period preceding or following placement. Minimum age 18. Applicants must be enrolled in full-time further or higher education (HND level or above) or be a recent graduate (within 12 months of finishing). Students must find their own training placements, related to their course of study, and either through payment from their employer or through other means, finance their own visit to the United States.

Participants pay an administrative fee of £270 with £30 increments for each additional month of stay. Council provides the legal sponsorship required to obtain the J-I visa, as well as orientation materials covering issues such as social security, taxes, housing, American culture and transportation; plus 24-hour emergency assistance with any problems whilst in the United States and comprehensive insurance. Council's website (www.councilexchanges.org.uk) has a searchable database of internships in the USA. *Applications* can be made at any time of year, but should be made at least six weeks before desired date of departure.

WORK AMERICA: BUNAC, 16 Bowling Green Lane, London EC1R OQH (tel 020-7251 3472; fax 020-7251 0215; e-mail: workamerica@bunac.org.uk).
Work America is a general work and travel programme open to students through BUNAC. The programme enables participants to take virtually any summer job in the US and provides the opportunity to earn back living and travelling costs. A special work and travel visa allows students to work and travel from June to the beginning of October.

BUNAC provides a Job Directory which is packed with jobs from which to choose and arrange work before going. The programme is open to those who are currently enrolled at a British University or college studying at degree (or advanced tertiary or postgraduate) level and gap year students who have an unconditional offer of a university place to return to at the end of summer. The programme fee was £89 in 2000. Early application is strongly advised. Visit www.bunac.org for more details and a list of local treks.

WORK & TRAVEL USA: Council on International Educational Exchange (Council), 52 Poland Street, London W1F 7AB (tel 020-7478 2020; freephone 0800 731 9076; fax 020-7734 7322; e-mail: watusa@councilexchanges.org.uk). Council is a worldwide organisation placing people in casual work, internships and teaching positions across the world.

This scheme enables full-time students to work and travel anywhere in the USA from early June to mid October. It is not necessary to pre-arrange jobs, but Council's website (www.councilexchanges.org.uk) has a searchable database of over 18,000 jobs in the USA. Assistance with finding jobs, and job lists are provided at the comprehensive arrival orientation. Students choose their flight dates and can fly into New York, Chicago or San Francisco.

Minimum age 18. Applicants must be enrolled in full-time higher education, be a recent graduate or on a gap year. The programme includes flights, insurance, job listings, travel information, pre-departure orientation materials, first night's accommodation and practical orientation on arrival, visa service, and 24 hour emergency assistance with any problems while in the United States.

Apply from January to June.

WORK EXPERIENCE USA: c/o Camp Counsellors, UK Offices: Green Dragon House, 64-70 High Street, Croydon CR0 9XN (tel 020-8688 9051; e-mail Inquiry@ccusaweusa.co.uk; www.ccusa.com) and 27 Woodside Gardens, Musselburgh, nr. Edinburgh EH21 7LJ (tel 0131-665 5843; e-mail 101355.257@compuserve.com; ccusa.com). US Office: 2330 Marinship Way, Suite 250, Sausalito CA 94965, USA.

Camp Counsellors' Work Experience USA work and travel programme is a US government authorised programme which runs between June and September. Applicants for this programme must be full time students between the ages of 20 and 28.

The only work limitations are that you cannot work as a domestic help or as a nanny; other than that the sky's the limit and the job is arranged before you leave the U.K. Wages will generally be at entry level and equivalent to those of Americans doing the same work.

For further information contact the above address.

WORLDNETUK: Southern Office, Avondale House, Sydney Road, Haywards Heath, West Sussex; Central Office, Emberton House, 26 Shakespeare Road, Bedford MK40 2ED (tel 01234-352688; fax 01234-351070; e-mail info@worldnetuk.com; www.worldnetuk.com). Leading work and travel specialists offering the following programmes: Camp USA; Nanny/Childcare Programmes to USA;

Ski/Summer Resort Nannies; Work and Travel USA; Study Programmes USA – Educare and Academic Year Abroad. Destinations include 180 clusters throughout the USA, France, Corsica, Spain, Belearics, Turkey, Italy, Sardinia, Greece, Austria and Switzerland..

Nanny/Childcare Programme USA for 18-26 year olds with childcare training, NNEB, Btec National Diploma in Nursery Nursing or NVQ level III. Full clean driving licence required. Departures every month. Opportunity to travel at end of year.

Au Pair Programme USA: for 18-26year olds with 200 hours childcare/babysitting. Full clean driving licence. Departures every month. Opportunity to travel at end of year.

Camp USA: 19-28 year olds needed to take up posts as Counsellors or Support Staff for min 8-10 weeks during summer months. All departures in June. Opportunity to travel at end of stay.

Ski/Summer Resort Nannies for work with all major travel companies; applicants must be qualified /experienced in childcare to work either in activity clubs, creche or with individual families and available for either the full summer or ski season. No age limit. Applicants must be available for either the full summer or ski season (some shorter term placements sometimes available)

Work & Travel USA: exciting opportunity to work in US for between 2.5 and 4 months. Summer jobs in hotels, restaurants, theme parks, county fairs, camping centres and national parks. Winter jobs in ski and recreation areas and warm weather tourist destinations.. Summer programme begins May - August and winter programme begins in December.

Study Programmes offered by Worldnetuk include:

Educare: a chance for 18-26 year olds to study part-time at college or University whilst working with school age children and living with an American family.

Academic Year America: opportunity for 15- 8 year olds to spend either one term or a full academic year with an American family and attending a US High School. Departures August and January. Programme sponsored by the American Institute for Foreign Study

For a full brochure call 01234-352688, fax 01234 351070, email info@worldnetuk.com or visit www.worldnetuk.com.

Au Pairs, Nannies, Family Helps and Exchanges

CHILDCARE AMERICA: Childcare International Ltd., Trafalgar House, Grenville Place, London NW7 3SA (tel 020-8906 3116; fax 020-8906 3461; e-mail: office@childint.co.uk; www.childint.co.uk).

Au Pair and **Nanny** stays in the USA. Childcare America offer a visa-supported one year stay to applicants aged 18-26 with good childcare experience. Applicants must drive and be non-smokers. Families provide full round trip air fare, medical insurance and part time college course plus two weeks' paid holiday. Salary up to $165 per week for qualified nannies and a minimum of $139.05 per week for au pairs. Choose from a wide range of approved families from across the USA. Full local counsellor support is provided to introduce friends and give guidance with every aspect of the stay. *Applications* to the above address.

EDUCARE IN AMERICA: c/o WorldNetUK (Work and Travel Specialists), Emberton House, 26 Shakespeare Road, Bedford MK40 2ED (tel 01234-352688.).

A great new opportunity for international young people to spend a year in the USA, studying part-time at college or university whilst working and living with an American family. Study courses offered to enhance future careers at US colleges include business administration, marketing, psychology and media studies. In exchange for full accommodation and full board applicants will become a companion to school age children for a max time of 30 hours per week. Also gives the opportunity to travel. For full brochure *contact* the above address.

Asia

China

British nationals can find voluntary work in China through the UNA Exchange see the *Worldwide* chapter for details. The following organisation offers the opportunity to work in China.

TEACH IN CHINA: Council Exchanges, 52 Poland Street, London W1F 7AB (tel 020-7478 2020; fax 020-7734 7322; e-mail: tic@councilexchanges.org.uk). Sending more graduates to China than any other organisation, Council Exchanges is a worldwide organisation helping people develop skills and acquire knowledge for working in a multicultural, interdependent world.

Teach in China offers an opportunity for graduates to spend 5 or 10 months teaching English in a university, college or school in China. There is no age limit, and teaching/TEFL qualifications are not required in order to apply. Successful applicants attend a one week training course on arrival in Beijing focusing on learning Chinese, understanding Chinese culture and giving an insight to TEFL. Host institutions in China provide private accommodation (usually a teacher's apartment on or near the campus), and a monthly salary which is generous by Chinese standards. Participants are responsible for paying their outward air fare and training fee, as well as a programme fee to Council Exchanges to cover the costs of arranging the placement, processing all paperwork required for visas and work permits, visa fees, the training centre and 24 hour emergency support while in China. Return fare is paid by the host institution on completion of a 10 month contract.

Council Exchanges sends participants on this programme in late August and early February in accordance with the Chinese semester system, and *applicants* are encouraged to return forms and application materials at least 3 months beforehand in order to ensure that a suitable placement is found. US applicants should apply to Council Exchanges' New York Office: 633 Third Avenue, 20th Floor, New York, 10017-6706.

India

Despite its vast size India offers few opportunities for paid temporary work, particularly for those without any particular skill or trade to offer an employer: there are untold thousands of Indians who would be delighted to do any unskilled job available for a wage that would seem a pittance to a westerner. Anyone determined to find paid employment there should explore the possibility of working for tour operators who specialise in organising holidays to India, and they would normally only consider applicants who are familiar with the country.

There are, however, a number of opportunities for taking part in short-term voluntary schemes in India. One of the most famous is Mother Teresa's Missionaries of Charity in Calcutta which takes on part-time volunteers to care for and feed orphaned children, the sick and dying, mentally or physically disabled adults and children or the elderly at its children's home in Calcutta (Shishu Bhavan, 78 A.J.C. Bose Road), in the Home for Dying Destitutes at Kalighat and other houses run by the Missionaries of Charity in Calcutta and other Indian cities, but no accommodation can be offered. To register, visit the Mother House at 54A A.J.C. Bose Road, Calcutta 700 016. Further information is also available from their London office at 177 Bravington Road, London W9 3AR (020-8960 2644).

Council: International Volunteer Projects and Service Civil International can place Americans on voluntary schemes in India, and UNA Exchange can offer similar placements for Britons: see the *Worldwide* chapter for details. Please note that as is normal with short-term voluntary opportunities, those taking part must pay for their own travel expenses, and will often be required to put something towards the cost of board and lodging.

RED TAPE

Visa Requirements: a tourist visa is required by all non-Indian nationals entering India for a visit as tourists.

Residence Permits: those planning a stay of over 3 months must register with the Foreigners Regional Registration Office within 14 days of arrival and be able to provide evidence of how they are supporting themselves. It is not possible to change a tourist visa to a long stay visa within India.

Employment Visas: any foreigner taking up paid employment in India must have a valid work permit before they enter the country: they should apply to the nearest Indian consulate, enclosing a copy of their contract.

Au Pair: not customary.

Voluntary Work: details of the voluntary work to be undertaken should be sent to the Indian consulate when applying for a visa at least 2 months in advance as they have to be forwarded to India. If you do want to attach yourself to a voluntary organisation for more than three months, you should aim to enter India on a student or employment visa (see Indian Embassy website www.hcilondon.org).

BHARAT SEVAK SAMAJ (BSS): Nehru Seva Kendra, Gugoan Bye Pass Road, Mehrauli, New Delhi 30, India (tel 657609).

The Samaj was founded by Shri Jawaharlal Nehru, the first Prime Minister of India, as a non-political national platform for mobilising people's spare time, energy and resources for national reconstruction as a part of the first Five Year Plan. It has a network of branches all over the country, with a membership of over 750,000, 10,000 members working on projects, and about 50 foreign volunteers helping each year.

Any person who offers his services for a minimum of two hours a week can become a member of the Samaj. Its normal programme includes the organisation of urban community centres in slum areas, night shelters, child welfare centres, nursery schools, training camps for national reconstruction work, family planning camps and clinics, and publicity centres for the Plans. The work also encompasses relief and reconstruction work after natural calamities, such as famine, drought, cyclones and earthquakes as well as the construction of houses for the Schedule Caste (lowest caste) and tribes and low cost latrines in villages.

Both skilled and unskilled workers are welcomed. Foreign volunteers, who can serve for between 15 days and three months, should be prepared to live in simple accommodation and respect local customs and traditions. They must finance their own stay, and it is preferred that they speak English.

Applicants should contact the General Secretary at the above address for further details enclosing International Reply Coupons.

DAKSHINAYAN: c/o Siddarth Sanyal, A-5/108 Clifton Apartments, Charmwood Village, Eros Gardens, Surajkind Road, Faridabad 121009 (tel 0129-525 3114 or 525 3165, cellphone 9811192133; e-mail dakshinayan@vsnl.com).
Volunteers to work with a registered trust engaged in providing education and medical assistance to tribes in the Rajamhal Hills and the surrounding plains. The project requires two volunteer health workers, who should be qualified/trainee doctors or nurses, to provide first aid, dispense medicines and train village women in health work. Any number of unskilled volunteers aged at least 18 are also needed to help on other development projects. Volunteers normally work 4-6 hours a day, 6 days a week for between 4 weeks and 6 months. Help is needed throughout the year. No expenses are paid and individuals are expected to contribute approx. £3 per day for food and a one-time fee of approx. £30 for processing applications and other administrative charges.

All applicants must be at least 18 years old, socially sensitive and willing to work in remote locations. Living conditions on most rural development projects are very basic. Knowledge of Hindi an advantage.

Applications, at least 30 days in advance of desired departure date, to Siddharth Sanyal, Executive Trustee, at the above address. Participants must arrive in Delhi in the first week of the month for orientation and placement. Please enclose and international postal coupon.

JAFFE INTERNATIONAL EDUCATION SERVICE: Kunnuparambil Buildings, Kurichy, Kottayam 686549, India (fax 91-481-430470).
Voluntary Teachers to teach in summer schools all over India. Subject areas include: Beauty Therapy, Creative Writing, Cooking, English, French, Gardening, Journalism, Music, Painting, Photography, Travel and Tourism. Due to foreign currency restrictions, no salary is paid but free board and lodging is provided. Hours of work are flexible; minimum 3 hours a day, Monday to Friday. Volunteers required from 1 April to 31 May; minimum period of work 4 weeks. Applicants must have at least an undergraduate degree in the subject of specialisation and proficiency in the English language. *Applications* from 1 January to the address above.

JOINT ASSISTANCE CENTRE: G-17/3, DLF City, Phase 1, Gurgaon, Haryana-122002, India (tel +91-124-6352141 or 6353833; fax 0091-124-6351308; e-mail: jacindia@mantraonline.com). JAC offers a unique opportunity of an exciting and challenging nature carrying out humanitarian works in close unison with local agencies as well as the UN and other international groups.
Volunteers can join 'learn while you travel' scheme and perform various jobs for a voluntary action group (registered as a charity) concerned with furthering disaster preparedness through training programmes, exhibitions and seminars. It also has cultural schemes, fund raising, camps, digs, workcamps and related publications. Tasks include helping with office work, editing, writing, teaching, social work, joining youth workcamps, helping run seminars and giving demonstrations and lectures, etc. on first aid, camping, trekking, rock climbing

etc. There are opportunities for learning natural cures (chromopathy), yoga, meditation, Indian language and about Indian life philosophy through cheap travel and visits to several other projects through the JAC travel scheme.

Any number of volunteers are accepted, but for specific projects, to suit personal applicant profile, volunteers must be able to work for a minimum of three months. Working hours are 8 hours a day and 5 days per week with free days or weeks by mutual arrangement. Simple but safe and secure accommodation is provided in a rural camp style in huts or tents, in the slum or rural areas. Longer term placements in other projects according to skills/interests are also arranged. Three day long orientation programmes about India, its history, culture and thought, are organised every month. Students wanting to do internships or study and research in any field can also be accepted.

No special qualifications required but some experience of first aid, typing or scouting would be helpful. Minimum age 18 years. Help is needed from volunteers for periods of from 4-26 weeks, around the year. Participants are required to send a processing fee of £30 with their application. They must then contribute a further £100 for the first month to cover food, accommodation, administration, and airport pickup).

Contact Narendra Kumar Jain, Convener, at the above address for application forms, enclosing 3 International Reply Coupons for reply by Air Mail.

RURAL ORGANISATION FOR SOCIAL ELEVATION: Social Awareness Centre, Kanda Bageshwar 263631, Uttarancahal,, India. R.O.S.E. is a small charity, based in a beautiful location at the foot of the Himalayas. It provides volunteers with the opportunity of experiencing true rural Indian life while providing education and improving local sanitation and health care facilities.
Volunteers (1-10) to carry out voluntary work in rural areas including teaching English to children, construction, poultry farming, environmental protection, agricultural work, recycling paper to make hand-made greetings cards, office work, compiling project proposals, reports and health care. Groups of volunteers can be organised into work camps lasting 10 to 30 days, but individuals are also welcome to apply. Volunteers work 5 hours a day, five days a week. Accommodation in a family house provided in addition to three delicious meals a day. Volunteers must pay their own travel costs and about £4 a day towards board and lodging, costs, administration and R.O.S.E's school expenses.
Applications should be addressed to Mr Jeevan Lal Verma at the above address. Please enclose 3 international reply coupons and a large envelope.

Japan

The range of short term casual jobs open to Westerners in Japan is extremely limited, particularly so at a time when unemployment in Japan is reaching record high levels. However, longer term opportunities do exist, particularly in the area of teaching English: it has been estimated that 11% of all Japanese people attend English 'conversation classes'. A native English speaker therefore possesses a marketable skill if he or she has a degree; experience or qualifications in teaching English as a foreign language are added advantages.

For further information on teaching work in Japan see *Teaching English Abroad*. Anyone who is serious about wanting to spend some time in Japan should read *Live and Work in Japan*, a thorough guide for anyone hoping to live and work there. See the *Useful Publications* chapter for details of these books.

Council: International Volunteer Projects and Service Civil International can help US residents, as can Concordia, Youth Action for Peace, UNA Exchange and International Voluntary Service UK residents, to find short term voluntary work in Japan; see their entries in the *Worldwide* chapter for details.

RED TAPE

Visa Requirements: nationals of the UK, USA, Ireland, Germany, Switzerland and Austria can visit Japan as tourists without a visa for up to 3 months and extend this to 6 months. Most other nationalities can visit for up to 3 months, as long as they have a return or onward ticket and sufficient funds.

Work Permits: A position must be secured and working visa obtained before you enter the country. Applicants for working visas must submit their application to the Consulate in person. If the person obtains a certificate of eligibility from Japan a visa can be issued in three days.

Working Holiday Visas. Holders of British, Australian, Canadian and New Zealand passports can apply for working holiday visas: these must be applied for at the Japanese Embassy of their home country. The rules are generally the same, but full details can be obtained from the nearest Japanese Embassy or consulate.

For British readers, working holiday visas may be granted provided they are:
(a) British citizens resident in the United Kingdom;
(b) intend primarily to holiday in Japan for a period of up to one year from date of entry;
(c) aged between 18 and 25 years inclusive at time of application, except where the competent authorities of the Government of Japan agree to extend the limitation upwards to 30 years;
(d) unaccompanied by children or spouses, except where the spouse also possesses a working holiday visa;
(e) in possession of a valid passport, return travel ticket or sufficient funds to purchase such reasonable funds for normal maintenance purposes during the initial part of the proposed stay in Japan;
(f) in good health;
(g) willing to leave Japan at the end of their stay;
(h) able to confirm that they have not previously been issued with such a visa.

There is a non-refundable processing fee for a working holiday visa (£7 in the UK).

400 Working Holiday Visas are available to British citizens between April and the following March, applications are accepted from the 17th of April. To apply one each of the following must be supplied to the Japanese Embassy or Consulate-General in addition to a valid British passport: visa application form, a 35mm x 45mm photograph, a typed CV or personal history, a proposed itinerary for the first six months in Japan to include details of any prearranged employment, a typed reason for applying, evidence of travel tickets/reservations and evidence of funds (for ticket holders this is £1,500, confirmed reservation holders £2,500). Application forms and explanatory material can be obtained from the Japanese Consulate-General in London or Edinburgh.

There is a support organisation the *Japanese Association for Working-Holiday Makers* with offices in Tokyo, Osaka and Kyushu (Tokyo office: Sun Plaza 7th Floor, 4-1-1 Nakano, Nakano-ku, Tokyo 164-8512, Japan; tel 03-3389-0181) which can be found on-line: www.jawhm.or.jp.

Japanese Working Holiday visas are single entry, so if you have to leave Japan for any reason you must obtain a re-entry permit from the competent immigration authorities before leaving. On arrival in Japan travellers should register with their embassy or consulate, and inform them of changes in address. For clarification of these points and news of any changes in the regulations please contact the nearest Japanese Embassy or consular mission.

Au Pair: not possible.

Voluntary Work: not customary, but a visa would be required.

Teaching and Office Work

THE JAPAN EXCHANGE AND TEACHING (JET) PROGRAMME: Council on International Educational Exchange, 52 Poland Street, London W1F 7AB (tel 020-7478 2010; fax 020-7434 7322; e-mail: JETinfo@ councilexchanges.org.uk). Working with many governments across the globe, Council is a worldwide organisation helping people develop skills and acquire knowledge for working in a multicultural, interdependent world.

The JET programme is a Japanese governmental scheme. Graduates from thirty-nine countries are recruited annually to assist Japanese English teachers in secondary schools or to work in local government offices for a period of one year. In 2001, 736 UK graduates joined over 6,000 graduates worldwide and took up positions on this programme. By 2002, the JET Programme hopes to be placing 10,000 graduates in high schools throughout Japan.

Participants receive remuneration of 3,600,000 yen (equivalent to £23,000) per year and a return air ticket to Japan, orientation programmes are provided both pre-departure and post-arrival, as well as assistance with finding accommodation. *Application forms* are available from early October each year and UK applicants must return them to the JET Programme Desk at the above address by the 7th December deadline. Successful applicants will depart for Japan in late July 2001

JET applicants in the USA should contact the Embassy of Japan at 2520 Massachusetts Avenue NW, Washington DC 20008 (tel 202-939-6772). Graduates from Australia, Brazil, Canada, China, France, Germany, Ireland, Israel, Italy, New Zealand, Mexico, Peru, Portugal, the Republic of Korea, the Russian Federation and Spain should contact the Japanese Embassy in their country of origin.

SHIN SHIZEN JUKU (NEW NATURE SCHOOL): Tsurui-Mura, Akan-Gun, Hokkaido 085-1207 Japan (tel 0154 642821).

Volunteers (up to 4) Kind, honest, responsible and enthusiastic wanted to teach English to Japanese people. Free food and accomodation are provided, in return for teaching and gardening work, minimum period of volunteering 6 weeks. Hours and programme vary from day to day but there is plenty of time for recreation. An interest in learning Japanese is encouraged. Applicants with an international driver's licence essential. *Applications* with photo to Hiroshi Mine, Manager, at the above address.

Voluntary Work

ARK ANIMAL REFUGE KANSAI: 595 Noma Ohara, Nose-Cho, Toyono-Gun, Osaka-Fu, Japan (tel 0727-37-0712; fax 0727-37-1645; e-mail arkbark@wombat.or.jp; www.wombat.or.jp/arkbark).

Volunteer Workers (2) to help at an animal sanctuary with over 200 dogs and 100 cats for 3 months over the summer. Return airfare (to a maximum of £700) with food and accommodation provided. To work 8am-5pm 6 days per week helping to walk, feed and care for the animals. Applicants should have veterinary skills or have proven experience in the animal welfare field or at least be be experienced in handling dogs and cats. *Applications to* Jeff Bryant (Volunteer Co-Ordinator) at the above address, or e-mail jeriko@portnet.ne.jp

. **Nepal**

Nepal is one of the most promising destinations for young people who want to spend a few months as a volunteer in a developing country, assuming national stability can be re-established after the tragic death of the King and his family in June 2001.

People who find voluntary openings in Nepal will be faced with a visa problem. Tourist visas (which can be purchased on arrival for $25 cash) are valid for 30 days whereupon they have to be renewed. This is straightforward for the first three months for a fee of $1 a day. A four-month visa can be applied for at the Immigration Office in Thamel, Kathmandu (tel 01-470650). Normally these will not be granted unless the request is supported by an official organisation. People who overstay their visas have in the past been fined heavily or even put in prison.

An impressive range of non-governmental organisations makes it possible for people to teach in a voluntary capacity. Although volunteers must bear the cost of travel and living expenses, the cost of living is very low by western standards.

UNA Exchange and Youth Action for Peace can arrange short-term voluntary work placements in Nepal. See their entries in the *Worldwide* chapter for more details. The following organisations are also looking for volunteers to work in Nepal.

FRIENDSHIP CLUB NEPAL (FCN): P.O. Box 11276, Maharajgunj, Kathmandu, Nepal (tel 977-1-427406; fax 977-1-429176; e-mail fcn@ccsl.com.np).
The following are voluntary positions for which the participants are expected to make a contribution of around £100 per month towards expenses. Basic accommodation is provided for all volunteers. There are vacancies all year round and written enquiries should be accompanied by 2 international reply coupons.
English Teachers (36) to teach English in school/college 3-5 hours per day, 6-day week. BA minimum qualification.
Secretaries (10) to work at main FCN office in Kathmandu or office in Chitwan. 6 hour day, 6 day week.
Project Expert (15) to visit and assess rural areas and prepare relevant project proposals. Pocket money provided.
Contact Prakash Babu Paudel, President at the above address.

GRAHUNG KALIKA: Walling Municipality, 2 Walling Bazaar, Syangja, Nepal. A non-governmental organisation set up in 1996 in a remote area of Nepal (about 260km west of Kathmandu) to improve the teaching of English to primary school children.
Volunteers required for short and long term placements (minimum stay 4 weeks) to teach English, develop western farming practices and help raise awareness of issues and practices for healthy childbirth. No teaching experience necessary; volunteers must adopt a practical and creative approach and be able to muck in with the local community.

Apart from the opportunity for first hand experience of Nepalese rural life, volunteers can enjoy mountain trekking, white-water rafting and sightseeing in the Himalayas.

Volunteers should be aged at least 17 and will need to pay a registration fee of $20 (£13 approx), their own travel and insurance costs, as well as contributing approx. £40 towards the project's costs. Board and lodging are arranged by the project at a rate of £30 per month. Applications should be made at least one month in advance of the proposed visit to Nepal, especially in June-July when the monsoon closes many project schools.

An information sheet giving further details of the project can be obtained by writing by registered post (enclosing an International Reply Coupon) to the above address. Enquiries should be to Mr Dol Raj Subedi, P.O. Box 11272, Kathmandu, Nepal (tel +977-1-532674; fax +977-1-527317; e-mail mail@multcon. wlink.com.np).

INSIGHT NEPAL: P.O. Box 489, Pokara, Nepal (tel +977-061-30266; e-mail insight@mos.com.np; www.south-asia.com/insight). Insight Nepal was established with a view to providing an opportunity to those who are interested in gaining a unique cultural experience by contributing their time and skills for the benefit of worthwhile community service groups.

Volunteer Teachers (15) to teach various subjects in primary, secondary and vocational schools in Nepal. To work 5 to 6 hours per day, 5 or 6 days per week. Insight Nepal organises homestays for the volunteers, and the host family provide accommodation and two meals per day. Period of work either from February to May or August to November.

Applicants should be aged between 18 and 60 and be educated to at least A level standard. Experience of teaching is advisable but not essential. Applicants with games, sporting and artistic skills preferred. Short-term volunteer placements also can be arranged upon request.

PEOPLE'S WELFARE COMMITTEE: G.P.O. 12137, Kathmandu, Nepal (fax 0977-1-412997; e-mail jbardewa@wlink.com.np)
Volunteer Agriculturalists (5 per month)
Volunteer Teachers (10 per month) to teach English in primary schools.

The above are needed to work for 60 hours per month. For further details send an International Reply Coupon to Mrs Srijana Bardewa at the above address.

SANGAM ENGLISH SCHOOL: PO Box 11969, Kathmandu, Nepal (fax +977-1-417590; e-mail sangam_school@hotmail.com). Established in 1987 by local educationalists, the Sangam English School is situated in Shivanagar Village in the Nawalparasi district of Nepal, some 190km south-west of Kathmandu. It is near Chitwan National Park and the Narayani river.

Volunteers are needed to teach in the school for one to six months. In return the volunteers are offered a comfortable room in a house with local village people. Volunteers will be invited to participate in cultural activities within the community and will have the opportunity to teach English, Maths, Science, the Environment etc. In addition volunteers will have the chance to pursue their own interests in activities such as trekking, sightseeing and rafting. Volunteers can also become invloved in social work or community development projects aimed at improving health, the environment, agriculture, etc., depending upon their individual interests and experience. They can also learn the local language of Nepal and about its culture if they are interested. Volunteers are free to arrange their own programmes of activities which directly help the students' education. Volunteers must be enthusiastic, creative and physically energetic. Age and qualifications are not important. However, an interest in sports or playing musical instruments would be an advantage. Volunteers are placed with a host family, who provide low cost food and accommodation. Where possible, toilet facilities, water and lighting will be provided, although this is not guaranteed. Volunteers contribute approx. £35 (US$50) to cover administration and communication expenses and an additional £35 per month approx. to the host family for food and accommodation. An application fee of approximately £15 (US$20) is payable in advance along with the application form.

For more information and an *application form* contact the above address.

VOLUNTARY WORK OPPORTUNITIES IN NEPAL (VWOP): PO Box 4263, Kathmandu, Nepal (tel +977-1-488773; fax +977-1-416144; e-mail vwop2000@hotmail.com). VWOP is a voluntary programme which coordinates between international volunteers and the schools/organisations which provide voluntary jobs and opportunities in urban and remote areas of Nepal, including teaching English in schools, being involved in environmental programmes, health programmes and research programmes. Volunteers may also arrange and implement their own ideas/prgrammes/activies, which directly help the local community. VWOP also help those who intend to invest in education, agriculture, livestock, health, environment, research etc. in rural areas of Nepal.

Qualifications and experience are not essential, but should have some knowledge of environment and health programmes. Interested volunteers are invited to have first hand experience of living and working with local village people. Volunteers are invited to participte in cultural activities and will have the opportunity to explore other parts of Nepal where thay can engage in trekking, white water rafting, and sightseeing.

Volunteers stay with a local family during placement sharing their home, food and amenities. For further information and an *application form*, contact the Chairman, VWOP, at the above address.

Thailand

In addition to the conservation project listed below UNA Exchange and Youth Action for Peace offer British volunteers the chance to work in Thailand. Council Exchanges operate a *Teach in Thailand* scheme: see their advertisement on page 9.

GIBBON REHABILITATION PROJECT: Wildlife Animal Rescue Foundation, 235 Sukhumvit Soi 31, Bangkok, 10110 Thailand (tel 266-662 0898; fax 266-261 9670; e-mail econet@asiaaccess.net; www.war-thai.org). The Gibbon Rehabiliation Project was set up in 1992 to rehabilitate captive raised White-handed Gibbons and is based in the Khao Phra Thaew National Park.

Volunteers needed to help with preparing food for and feeding gibbons, building, maintaining and cleaning cages and footpaths and lecturing and showing tourists around. Longer stay volunteers can take part in behavioural research.

Volunteers should be in good physical condition, enthusiastic, able to work unsupervised and ideally have experience in construction or working with animals. Biology anthropology or vetinary students/graduates are especially welcome.

Stays are for 3-8 weeks (3 weeks is the minimum possible) and volunteers pay US$1,169 (£790) for the first 3 weeks and US$130 for each additional week.

Volunteers arranging to stay longer than 8 weeks pay US$975 and $65 respectively. These costs do not cover flights, food, visas or insurance but accommodation is provided in Thai village bungalows.

To *apply* contact W.A.R. at the address above.

SEA TURTLE PROJECT PHRATHONG ISLAND: CHELON, Viale val Padana 134B, I-00141 Rome, Italy (tel +39-06-8125301; e-mail chelon@tin.it). CHELON an Italian based research group, works to obtain in-depth knowledge of the biology of marine turtles and aid their conservation. They work in collaboration with the Marine Biological Centre in Phuket.

Volunteers to help researchers studying Olive Ridley, Green, Leatherback and Hawksbill turtles in the south of Thailand between December and May. Volunteers will assist in gathering data on nesting behaviour, tagging turtles for observation and taking part in conservation awareness raising among tourists and local people.

The presence of volunteers helps deter poaching of turtle eggs and young as well as involving the local community in the project. The work often involves long walks patrolling the three beaches to estimate the number of nests and the species of turtle nesting there. Visits to villages are used to involve the locals and to collect information on trade in turtle eggs, and talks given in the evenings at the Golden Buddha Beach resort increase understanding of turtle conservation amongst tourists.

Volunteers are accommodated in huts at the Golden Buddha beach resort, this and meals at the resort clubhouse are covered by the registration fee of £375, per two weeks. The minimum stay is two weeks, but volunteers can stay longer subject to approval. Travel and insurance expenses are met by the volunteer.

Contact CHELON at the above address for further information and an application form.

Australasia

Australia

The short length of this chapter does not bear any relation to the vast range and number of temporary opportunities available in Australia. However, there are a few factors to bear in mind when considering Australia as a destination for a summer job. The first factor is the reversal of seasons: the Australian summer takes place in what is winter to much of the rest of the world and so jobs on their fruit harvests and at the peak of their tourist industry occur at the wrong time of year for anyone hoping to find work between July and September. There is also the financial factor: the cost of a return ticket to Australia makes going there for a paid job for just a few weeks very uneconomic – even though in real terms the cost of getting to Australia is at its cheapest ever – the cost is still such that it makes better financial sense to stay for months rather than weeks.

Luckily for the foreigner Australia has a working holiday scheme which can ease the formalities for those going there to pick up casual work. Some guidelines for those hoping to do so are given below, but working holidays in Australia are covered in greater depth in *Work Your Way Around the World* (see the *Useful Publications* chapter) and in the information available from Australian High Commissions and Embassies. A third point to consider is that Australia is one of the most popular destinations for working travellers, and the limited number of visas means that you need to begin the application process well in advance of your intended travel.

Although Australia now has a declining unemployment rate, those job-seekers must be prepared to devote time and energy to the job hunt. One tip is to look for work away from the big cities, where other new arrivals from overseas may be competing for the same jobs. A valuable source of rural jobs is Employment National (EN), the government's privatised job agency. Enquiring in one office will allow you to uncover harvest work near one of the more than 200 other offices across the country. Employment National encourage working holidaymakers to contact their specialist fruit and crop-picking department on 1300-720126 or to check their website (www.employmentnational.com.au).

The fruit harvests of Northern Victoria employ a massive 10,000-12,000 people in the Australian summer (January-March). The town of Shepparton is about two hours north of Melbourne with easy accessibility via rail or bus services. From Sydney, catch a train to Albury and from there take the bus to Shepparton. Information can be obtained from the Northern Victoria Fruitgrowers' Association Ltd, PO Box 394, Shepparton 3632 (21 Nixon St, Shepparton; 03-5821 5844; nvfa@mcmedia.com.au) and the Victorian Peach and Apricot Growers' Association, PO Box 39, Cobram 3644 (30A Bank St, Cobram; 03-5872 1729/fax 5871 1612) or from Employment National (361 Wyndham St, Shepparton; 03-5832 0300). Send an IRC for the information leaflet 'Guide to your Working Holiday'.

Searching the web for employment leads is especially productive in Australia. There are dozens of routes in to finding out about job vacancies. Before leaving home, you might like to register (free) with www.gapwork.com which is updated regularly and lists employers who hire working holidaymakers. The relatively new www.jobsearch.gov.au is a government source of information with details of the National Harvest Trail. One of the best sites is a free service by the Wayward Bus Company (www.waywardbus.com.au/seaswork.htm) which has an index of actual employers, hostels and pubs recommended for job-seekers and agents. If in Queensland check the adverts in *Queensland Country Life* magazine. Some properties also function as holiday ranches and they often take on domestic staff and guides.

Hard-working travellers can earn A$100 a day doing harvest work, although AS$9 an hour would be more typical. The cost of living in Australia is a lot lower than in Britain so those wages go further than it sounds if you convert them into sterling at the current rate (£1 is worth A$2.84 at the time of writing).

Anyone who is serious about earning their way over a long period by fruit picking should consider obtaining the small format specialist booklet *Fruit Picking around Australia* which is available for £6 from Pickpack, 114 Hazelton Way, Waterlooville, Hants. PO8 9DW (cheques payable to R. Wedd), or in Australia for A$10 from Pickpack (11 Coral St, Saunders Beach, Queensland 4818; payable to L. Hutchinson) or from campsites and bookshops in the relevant areas. Details can be found on www.cix.co.uk/~yama.fruit.

Some city-based employment agencies deal with jobs in outback areas, primarily farming, station, hotel/motel and roadhouse work. In Western Australia try Pollitt's (13th Floor, 251 Adelaide Terrace, 13th Floor, Perth 6000; tel 08-9325 2544) who say that experienced farmworkers and tractor drivers are paid £4.50-£5 (A$12-$14) an hour for 10-12 hour days, seven days a week at seeding time (April to June) and harvest time (October to December). Housekeeping, nannying and cooking positions are available for two to three months at a time throughout the year. The standard wage is £105 (A$300) a week after board, most of which can be saved. For work in outback roadhouses and hotels, previous experience in kitchen, food and beverage service is essential to earn £140 (A$400) a week after lodging. The three-month commitments enable travellers to experience the regional country towns while saving most of their earnings.

In urban areas the usual range of jobs exists (bar, restaurant, office and factory work) available through the many private employment agencies such as Bligh, Adecco and Drake Personnel. It is also worth investigating tourist areas such as the coastal and island resorts of Queensland for jobs in hotels, restaurants, etc. especially during the Australian winter from June to October.

One of the best sources of job information for working holidaymakers in Australia is the extensive network of backpackers' hostels, some of which employ young foreigners themselves and all of which should be able to advise on local possibilities. One such is Brook Lodge Backpackers (3 Bridge Street, Donnybrook, WA 6239; tel 08-9731 1520; e-mail brooklodge@iinet.net.au) in Western Australia, which provides accommodation and can arrange hourly or weekly contract seasonal work including seasonal work in the apple harvest between November and May. Details of lodges like this can be found on the internet at http://backpackingaround.com, a website set up by backpackers which carries job and visa information as well as links and info on accommodation around Western Australia. The group Hostelling in Homes (Gabba Guesthouse, 18 Withington St, East Brisbane, Queensland 4169; tel 1800-333244; www.homehostel.com) primarily arranges accommodation for paying clients with host families, though it can also arrange fruit-picking in some areas.

Either before you leave Britain or once you are in one of the major cities, get hold of the free 200-page booklet *Australia & New Zealand Independent Traveller's Guide* published by the London-based travel magazine *TNT* (14-15 Child's Place, London SW5 9RX; tel 020-7373-3377; www.i-t-g.co.uk); send s.a.e. with 80p stamp. It includes a section on work and some relevant advertisements as well as travel advice. The same company publishes specific pocket-sized regional guides for Sydney/NSW, Queensland, Victoria/Tasmania and the Outback, available free at airports, stations and backpacker hostels. They carry a certain number of classified ads for job-seekers and a section called 'Finding Work'.

You can advertise yourself as being available for work in a number of state and national newspapers through Smyth International of 1 Torrington Park, London N12 9GG. The *Sydney Morning Herald* is based at 201 Sussex Street, Sydney, NSW 2000 (www.smh.com.au). *The Australian* can be contacted at 46 Cooper Street, Surrey Hills, NSW 2010, and *The West Australian* at Newspaper House, 50 Hasler Road, Osborne Park, Western Australia 6017.

Copies of the above newspapers, plus information and application forms for visitor and working holiday visas may be obtained in the UK from the High Commission's designated agent, Consyl Publishing. For an application form and a free copy of 'Travel Australia', a newspaper aimed at those planning a working holiday in Australia, write to Consyl Publishing, 3 Buckhurst Road, Bexhill on Sea, East Sussex TN40 1QF (tel 01424 223111; e-mail consylpublishing@ btconnect.com; www.consylpublishing.co.uk); enclose an A4 stamped addressed envelope bearing at least 66p worth of stamps.

RED TAPE

Tourist Visa Requirements: All intending visitors require either a visa stamped in their passport or an Electronic Travel Authority (ETA) which is a paperless visa. As of July 1st 2001, ETAs are no longer available from the Australian High Commission and must be obtained through airlines, travel agents or specialist visa agencies. An ETA is valid for 12 months and covers multiple entries into Australia for no more than three months each. Private visa agencies and delegated travel agencies can issue an ETA over the phone for varying fees, usually between £10 and £25. Major airlines may offer a free ETA service if you purchase an air ticket through their reservations offices. The two main agencies are Visas Australia Company (PO Box 1, Nantwich, Cheshire CW5 7PB; 01270 626626/ www.visa-australia.co.uk) and Australian Visas Ltd (PO Box 170, Ashford, Kent TN24 0ZX; 01233 211800). Those with ETAs and visitor visas are not permitted to work.

Working Holiday Visas may be granted to single people or married couples without children aged 18-30, provided they have British, Irish, UK or Canadian nationality or are from one of a growing list of countries including Germany, Netherlands and Sweden.

The criteria for the issue of such visas are:
(a) prime purpose is a holiday in Australia;
(b) temporary entry for a specific period (not settlement) is intended;
(c) employment is incidental to the holiday purpose and would be intended to supplement holiday funds;
(d) full-time employment must not exceed 3 months with any one employer.

(e) possession of reasonable funds (currently £2,000 in the UK, but the amount varies from country to country and is liable to increase) for normal maintenance purposes for the initial part of the proposed holiday period and sufficient for airfare; (g) departure at the expiry of the authorised period of temporary stay in Australia. The allocation of the annual quota of visas starts in July; once the total has run out, applications are not considered until the start of the next round, so the best time to apply is in the northern summer. There is a non-refundable processing fee for a working holiday visa, currently £65 in the UK (subject to change). Current information is available by calling the Australian Immigration and Citizenship Information Line on 09065-508900 (calls are charged at £1 per minute).

The working holiday visa will be valid for 12 months after entry, which must be within 12 months of issue, and is non-renewable. During those 12 months you may leave and re-enter the country as many times as you wish. Full details are available on the Australian Immigration website www.australia.org.uk. Britons should apply in plenty of time to the High Commission in London (Australia House, Strand, London WC2B 4LA) or in the north to the Australian Consulate in Manchester (Chatsworth House, Lever St, Manchester M1 2DL; 0161-228 1344).

The first step is to get the working holiday visa application form from a specialist visa agent or Consyl Publishing (as above). The second step is to save at least £2,000 since you will have to submit bank statements with your application.

Agricultural Work

OUTBACK STAFF: P.O. Box 8042, Allenstown, QLD 4700, Australia (tel +61-7-49-274300; fax +61-7-4922-6923; e-mail outstaff@rocknet.net.au; www.rocknet.net.au/~outstaff). Outback Staff is an Australia-wide rural employment agency; they have jobs for farmers, tractor drivers, cotton workers, cooks and seasonal staff; and provide on-going support and back-up during your time working in Australia.
Farm Staff: numerous vacancies for personnel to operate farm machinery, drive tractors/harvesters, or work on irrigation schemes. Wages start at around £4-£5 per hour, applicants must have an agricultural background.
Cooks, Housekeepers, Nannies to work on outback farm stations. Wages between £100-£160 per week. Applicants should have experience with cooking housework and childcare.

All positions work 8-10 hours a day over a 5 or 7 day week. Farm workers are required all year, while cooks are needed between February and October. Minimum period of work two weeks. Board and lodging is usually included, but this depends on the location. Applicants should speak English.

Applications are invited at any time to the above address.

THE VISITOZ SCHEME: Springbrook Farm, MS188, Goomeri, 4601 Queensland, 4601 Australia (fax 0061-741-686-155; e-mail VISITOZSCHEME@bigpond.com; www.visitoz.org).
The VISITOZ scheme is the perfect introduction to Australia for those with Working Holiday Visas. They operate a scheme under which all those entitled to Working Holiday Visas find work in rural Australia as tractor drivers, stockworkers, horse riders, hospitality workers, on cattle and sheep stations, and mothers' helps and teachers. There are generally around 200 vacancies to choose from and employment is guaranteed. Wages vary according to the job being done, working hours, the State and the age of the worker; earnings are generally around

£140 per week with free board and lodging but have been known to reach around £500 per week.

Staff are needed around the year but working holiday regulations limit the time with any one employer to 3 months. Applicants must be aged 18-30 and all are assessed and/or trained for the job required. Participants in the scheme must pay for their own air fare, visa costs and the Visitoz training fee of £395 which also covers being met at the airport on arrival, 5 days on the training farm and help with the red tape once in Australia.

For further details contact Dan and Joanna Burnet at the above address by fax or e-mail; there is also a London contact, William, on 07966-528664 or wdtb@aol.com.

WILLING WORKERS ON ORGANIC FARMS (AUSTRALIA): Buchan 3885, Victoria, Australia (tel +61-03-5155 0218; fax +61-03-5155 0342; e-mail wwoof@net-tech.com.au; www.wwoof.com.au).

WWOOF Australia offers the chance to learn about organic farming and Australian culture by giving practical help on over 1400 farms and properties around Australia. Jobs may range from weeding to building. Applicants should note that WWOOF **is not a source of paid employment**, but food and accommodation is provided in exchange for 4-6 hours work per day. Positions available all year.

Write for a brochure, or send £20 if single (£23 for a couple), for the list and insurance.

Sports, Couriers and Camping

THREDBO RESORT CENTRE: Kosciusko Thredbo Pty Ltd, P.O. Box 92, Thredbo, NSW 2625, Australia (tel +61-2-6459 4100; fax +61-2-6459 4101; e-mail recruitment@thredbo.com.au; www.thredbo.com.au). Thredbo is Australia's premier ski resort, with a season from mid-June to the end of September. They employ over 600 staff in winter, and have a ski village population of over 4,200.

Ticket Sellers (5) to sell ski lift and ski school products. Applicants should be have cash handling, accurate balancing and computer skills/experience. Wages £650 per month.

Ski Hire Staff (8) to fit customers with skis and snowboards and hire out clothing and equipment. Should have some cash handling experience and be willing to work split-shifts. Wages £750 per month.

Food and Beverage Staff (10) should have passed Australian 'Responsible Service of Alcohol Course' and have previous experience of busy establishments.

Hours of work vary between 28-38 per week according to position. The period of work is from around 1 July to 28 September (depending on snow), with a minimum period of work of 12 weeks. Board and lodging is available for a cost of £45 per week.

Applications to the above address are invited from January and close in mid-April, with interviews in Sydney in early May.

Voluntary Work and Archaeology

CONSERVATION VOLUNTEERS AUSTRALIA (CVA): Head Office, PO Box 423, Ballarat, Victoria 3353, Australia (tel +61-3-5333 1483; fax +61-3-5333-2166; e-mail info@conservationvolunteers.com.au; www.conservationvolunteers.com.au). Conservation Volunteers Australia is Australia's largest practical conservation organisation. CVA welcomes everyone who is enthusiastic about the outdoors and hands-on conservation. Volunteers are part of a team of 6 to 10 people under the guidance of an CVA team leader. Projects undertaken by CVA include: tree planting, native seed collection, endangered flora and fauna surveys, constructing and maintaining walking tracks in national parks. Projects are run in every state and territory of Australia throughout the year and include some of Australia's most beautiful locations. CVA offers overseas volunteers the Conservaton Experience six weeks package. Volunteering with CVA costs £8.50 (A$23) a night which includes all meals, project related travel and accommodation.   For more information visit the website or e-mail or write to CVA.

CHRISTIAN WORK CAMPS AUSTRALIA: P.O. Box K164, Haymarket, NSW 2000, Australia.

Volunteers to take part in work camps which are held for two to four weeks each January and July. The camps are currently held in New South Wales, the Northern Territory and Far North Queensland. Volunteers must pay camp registration fees of approximately £23; additional expenses may include food and accommodation at a further £23, approx. per week. Volunteers are responsible for their own travel costs. For information on forthcoming projects send an International Reply Coupon to the above address.

Other Employment Abroad

AUSTRALIA WORK AND TRAVEL (AUSWAT) PROGRAMME: Council on International Educational Exchange (Council Exchanges), 52 Poland Street, London W1F 7AB (tel 020-7478 2022; fax 020-7734 7322; e-mail: auswat@councilexchanges.org.uk; www.councilexchanges.org). Council Exchanges is a worldwide organisation placing people in casual work, internships and teaching positions across the world.

The AUSWAT programme allows participants to travel in Australia, taking up work along the way to support themselves. Council Exchanges offers assistance at every stage, from obtaining the visa, to helping find work and accommodation in Australia. Ongoing services include mail receiving and holding, 24 hour emergency support, and access to office facilities and free internet at their resource centre in Sydney.

This programme is open to British, Canadian, Dutch and Irish passport holders resident in the UK, aged 18-30, who have not been on a working holiday to Australia before. Programme fee starts at £320 (and rises in increments for every months additional stay) and includes all services and 3 night's accommodation. Visa valid for 12 months from entry to Australia. Wide variety of work available, for up to 3 months per position.

Applications all year round, at least 9 weeks before planned departure for Australia.

CAMP COUNSELORS USA: UK Offices: Green Dragon House, 64-70 High Street, Croydon CR0 9XN (tel 020-8688 9051; e-mail Inquiry@ccusaweusa.co.uk; www.ccusa.com) and 27 Woodside Gardens, Musselburgh, nr. Edinburgh EH21 7LJ (tel 0131-665 5843; e-mail 101355.257@compuserve.com; ccusa.com).

Work Experience Down Under is a high quality programme that helps young people to work and travel in Australia or New Zealand for up to 12 months. For details contact the above addresses.

WORK AUSTRALIA: BUNAC, 16 Bowling Green Lane, London EC1R 0QH (tel 020-7251 3472; e-mail downunder@bunac.org.uk).
BUNAC offers a work and travel scheme to Australia for up to a year. The package includes a round trip flight, a working holiday visa, 2 nights' accommodation in Sydney, and orientation with guidance on jobs, housing, health, taxes, etc. plus back-up services. Departures from the UK are from June to March; participants in BUNAC's US programmes (Work America, Summer Camp USA, KAMP) can take a flight from California in early October.

Applicants must be aged 18-30 inclusive, *citizens of the UK, Ireland, Holland or Canada*, and will need to be able to show that they have reserve funds of at least £2,000. Programme costs in 2000 were between £1,500 (from London) and £1,600 (from California). For further details contact Work Australia at the above address.

New Zealand

New Zealand offers many opportunities just as its massive neighbour Australia does. The downside is that visas and work permits are necessary for any form of paid employment in New Zealand, the only exception being for Australians. These should normally be obtained before entry to the country, and a job offer must be held at the time of application.

The UK Citizens' Working Holiday Scheme allows Britons aged 18-30 to do temporary jobs in New Zealand for up to 12 months. The allocation has steadily risen and now stands at 8,000 working holiday visas which are granted annually on a first come first served basis starting September 1st. Information can be obtained from the New Zealand Immigration Service, Mezzanine Floor, New Zealand House, 80 Haymarket, London SW1Y 4TE (fax 020-7973 0370) in person, by phone on 09069 100100 (charged at £1 per minute) or via the internet at www.immigration.govt.nz.

To apply you need the right Application for Work Visa form, your UK passport, the fee of £30, evidence of a return ticket and evidence of NZ$4,200 (about £1,200). Sponsorship from a New Zealand citizen is not considered an acceptable substitute for proof of funds. Applications for the working holiday visa must be lodged in the UK. Other working holiday schemes are open to Irish, Canadian, Japanese and Malaysian nationals who must apply in their country of nationality. You do not need a job offer when applying as the scheme allows you to pick up temporary work while holidaying in New Zealand.

The expense of getting to New Zealand, together with the fact that wages are significantly lower than in Australia, means that many people who visit New Zealand to work are more concerned with the cultural than the financial aspects of their trip. Opportunities vary from region to region depending on the local employment situation.

Council: Exchanges in New York administers a *Work in New Zealand Programme* for American citizens, see the Council entry in the Worldwide chapter.

Worth reading is the *Independent Traveller's Guide – Australia & New Zealand* published bi-monthly by *TNT Magazine* which runs to around 200 pages of information, ideas and advice about travelling in Australia and New Zealand. To obtain a copy send an A4 SAE (70p) to: Independent Traveller's Guides, TNT/Southern Cross, 14-15 Child's Place, Earl's Court, London SW5 9RX (tel 020-7373-3377; www.i-t-g.co.uk).

If you want to place an advertisement stating that you are looking for work the *New Zealand Herald* is published by Wilson and Horton Ltd, P.O. Box 32, 46 Albert Street, Auckland (tel 9-379 5050; fax 9-373 6410; www. wilsonandhorton.co.nz).

RED TAPE

Visa Requirements: New Zealand has Visa Waiver agreements with 30 countries so citizens of the UK, Ireland, USA and most European countries do not need a visa for bona fide tourist or business visits of up to 3 months (6 months for UK citizens). On arrival, visitors must have valid passports, return tickets and evidence of sufficient funds (about £300 per month of stay). Renewals of permits will be considered to allow stays of up to a maximum of 12 months: approval is not automatic.

Residence Visas: People wishing to reside permanently in New Zealand can make a prior application to a New Zealand overseas post, or can apply while on a temporary permit in New Zealand.

Work Visas & Permits: Recent changes to immigration rules make it possible for people on working holidays to apply to extend their stay or even for residence without having to leave the country. Applicants with skills in demand may apply for a new work permit option that will be valid for up to six months at one of the seven Immigration Service offices in New Zealand. Permission may be given if there are no local residents available to take up the work offered.

American students are eligible to apply for a six-month work permit from Council or BUNAC USA to work between April 1st and October 21st. CCUSA at 2330 Marinship Way, Suite 250, Sausalito, CA 94965 (1-800-999-CAMP; outbound@campcounselors.com/ www.campcounselors.com/australia.html) runs a three-month work experience programme (June to September).

Au Pair: Not customary. Work permit required.

Voluntary Work: Work permit required.

However, it should be noted that the above rules are liable to sudden change; all visas, including visitor visas, are charged for. There is a charge for all permit applications. For further information, check the New Zealand Immigration Service website (www.immigration.govt.nz).

Agricultural Work

FARM HELPERS IN NEW ZEALAND: 50 Bright Street, Eketahuna, New Zealand (tel/fax 06-375-8955; e-mail Fhinz@xtra.co.nz; www.fhinz.co.nz).

FHINZ is a voluntary group of over 180 farms throughout New Zealand who offer free farm stays to visitors in exchange for 4 hours help per day. Board and lodging is provided in the family home in return for daily farm work dependent on season and type of farm. No experience is necessary and all equipment is provided. Most farms will collect visitors from the nearest town at no cost, and return them after the stay, which can be from 3 days to several months, depending on the needs of the farm. Visitors need to each have a membership booklet (revised every month), with full details of all the farms, the family and what kinds of work visitors will be helping with. These are $20 each, valid for 6 months and available either by mail order or through some agents. For more information *contact* the address above.

WWOOF: P.O. Box 1172, Nelson, New Zealand (tel/fax 03-5449890; e-mail wwoof-nz@xtra.co.nz; www.wwoof.co.nz).
Volunteer Farm Labourers for unpaid work on organic properties including orchards, nurseries, farms etc. in New Zealand. It must be stressed that these positions are unpaid, and that participants must pay for their own travel expenses; they do, however, receive free food and accommodation. Positions are available at any time of year. WWOOF runs 550 farms around New Zealand.

Applicants must be aged over 16 and must not be from countries whose nationals need special invitations to enter New Zealand. For further information *write* to Jane and Andrew Strange at the above address enclosing £10 membership fee.

Voluntary Work

INVOLVEMENT VOLUNTEERS NEW ZEALAND: P.O. Box 153, Helensville, New Zealand (tel 64-94-207859; fax 64-94-207858).
Involvement Volunteers is an organisation that places volunteers in the areas of social work, conservation, farming and education. Board and lodging is sometimes provided free of charge but at other times a small fee is charged. Minimum period of work 2-6 weeks all year round. Knowledge of English is required. There is a fee for placement. *Contact* the above address for further details.

Other Employment

BUNAC:16 Bowling Green Lane, London EC1R 0QH (tel 020-7251 3472; fax 020-7251 0215; e-mail downunder@bunac.org.uk; www.bunac.org).
BUNAC offers a work/travel scheme entitled *Work New Zealand*, which enables participants to spend up to one year working and travelling in the South Pacific. The programme is open to all students and non-students aged 18-30 *who hold a British passport*. Choose any type of job, anywhere in New Zealand. The package includes a round trip flight, stop-over in Bangkok, first night's accommodation and a 3-month tourist visa for Australia. For further information *contact* BUNAC at the above address or through their website www.bunac.org.

Useful Publications

ARCHAEOLOGY ABROAD: 31/34 Gordon Square, London WC1H 0PY.
Publishes bulletins in April and November containing information on digs abroad for subscribers preferably who have experience of excavation. The Archaeology Abroad Fieldwork Awards were set up in 2001 to promote participation in fieldwork outside the UK, all subscribers are eligible. For details send an sae.

CANNING HOUSE: The Hispanic and Luso Brazilian Council, 2 Belgrave Square, London SW1X 8PJ (Tel 0207-235 2303).
Literature includes *Guides to Employment and Opportunities for Young People* for Spain, Portugal or Latin America; these cost £4.00 each (made payable to the Hispanic and Luso Brazilian Council). Send a stamped addressed envelope to the above address for the current list of information leaflets.

CAREERS EUROPE: 4th Floor, Midland House, 14 Cheapside, Bradford BD1 4JA (tel 01274-829600; www.careerseurope.co.uk).
Careers Europe is the UK Resource Centre for International Careers and produces *Eurofacts* and *Global Facts* which are a series of international careers leaflets, and *EXODUS* which is a database of international careers information. This information is available via UK careers offices and other careers libraries.

CHRISTIAN VOCATIONS: St. James House, Trinity Road, Dudley, DY1 1JB (Tel 01384-233511; fax 01384-233032; e-mail info@ChristianVocations.org; www.ChristianVocations.org).
Publishes the *Short-Term-Service Directory*, a comprehensive source of information about short-term service options with a Christian emphasis in the UK and abroad, at a cost of £5.25 plus £1.75 post & packing (overseas postage is extra). For further details and information on their one-to-one advisory service contact them at the above address.

CO-ORDINATING COMMITTEE FOR INTERNATIONAL VOLUNTARY SERVICE (CCIVS): UNESCO, 1 rue Miollis, F-75732 Paris Cedex 15, France (tel +33-1-45-68-45-36; e-mail ccivs@unesco.org; www.unesco.org/ccivs).
CCIVS is an international non-governmental organisation created in 1948 under the aegis of UNESCO to promote and coordinate voluntary work worldwide. CCIVS has 140 member organisations present in more than 90 countries.

Publishes *How to be a Volunteer* in Europe, Africa, Asia and America a guide and useful address book, costing £3.50 or 7 International Reply Coupons. Other specialised publications include *Volunteering in Conflict Areas (£3.50), and How to Present a Project* (£3.50), post free.

CCIVS does not recruit volunteers directly so would be volunteers should contact CCIVS member organisations in their own country.

For a full list of publications, please send your request to the above address with one IRC.

ISCO PUBLICATIONS: 12A Princess Way, Camberley, Surrey GU15 3SP (tel 01276-21188; www.isco.org.uk).
Produce a booklet entitled *Opportunities in the GAP Year*, price £5.95 (plus

postage costs of £1.00 on orders up to £10.00), that gives advice to those with a spare year between leaving school and going to University; for details please contact ISCO at the above address.

OVERSEAS JOBS EXPRESS: 20 New Road, Brighton, Sussex BN1 1UF (tel 01273-699777; 01273-699778; e-mail editor@overseasjobsexpress.co.uk; www.overseasjobsexpress.co.uk).
A fortnightly newspaper for international job hunters covering more than 30 categories of work, from seasonal opportunities to permanent/contract work. Contains details of current vacancies and feature articles on work abroad, travel, migration etc.

PETERSON'S GUIDES: P.O. Box 67005, Laurenceville, NJ 08648-4764 (www.petersons.com). Leading publishers of books on employment and education in the US..
Summer Jobs for Students 2002; ($18.95). Covers opportunities in the US in detail. Available in the UK as *Summer Jobs USA* (see below)
Internships USA. ($26.95). A guide to career-related employment in the US. (Also see under Vacation Work below)
Petersons are also the US distributors of *Work Your Way Around the World* ($17.95), *Summer Jobs in Britain* ($17.95) and *Teaching English Abroad* ($17.95): see under Vacation Work below for details of these titles.

TRAVEL TRADE GAZETTE DIRECTORY:
This book contains comprehensive lists of the names and addresses of travel operators and is available for reference in large public libraries. The publishers are CMP Data and Information Services, Riverbank House, Angel Lane, Tonbridge, Kent TN9 1SE (tel 01732-377586; fax 01732-367301).

VACATION-WORK: 9 Park End Street, Oxford OX1 1HJ, (tel 01865-241978; fax 01865-790885; www.vacationwork.co.uk), publishes or distributes the following titles in the UK. Books marked (PET) are available in the USA from Peterson's Guides (see above). Those marked (SEV) can be obtained from Seven Hills Book Distributors, 49 Central Avenue, Cincinnati, Ohio 45202 (call toll-free 1-800 545 2005; there is a $3.50 charge for postage and packing).
Summer Jobs USA 2002; (£12.95). Covers opportunities in the US in detail. Published by Peterson's Guides in the US, where it is known as *Summer Jobs for Students* ($18.95). (PET)
Work Your Way Around The World (£12.95). Contains invaluable information on all the ways to find temporary work worldwide, both in advance and when abroad. (PET)
Taking a Gap Year (£11.95). A comprehensive guide for anyone planning a year off before or after college. (SEV)
Taking a Career Break (£11.95). An examination of the opportunities for those wanting a break from their job to embark on a fulfilling year out without destroying their career or their family. Filled with interviews with people who have successfully proved that Gap Years are not just for students. (SEV)
Working in Tourism – The UK, Europe & Beyond (£11.95). A comprehensive guide to short and long-term work in the booming tourist industry. (PET)
Working on Cruise Ships (£10.99) a complete guide to both short and long term work afloat. (SEV)
Working in Ski Resorts – Europe & North America (£10.99). Includes details on

both how to arrange a job with a British based ski operator and how to find a job after arriving in a ski resort. (SEV)

The International Directory of Voluntary Work (£11.95). A comprehensive worldwide guide to both residential and non-residential voluntary work. (PET)

Kibbutz Volunteer (£10.99). A unique publication giving full details of 200 different kibbutzim, the atmosphere of these fascinating communities and what you may expect when working in one. (SEV)

The Au Pair and Nanny's Guide to Working Abroad (£11.95). Explains how to get domestic work abroad, including a guide to agencies and country by country guides. (SEV)

Teaching English Abroad (£12.95). Covers both short and long term opportunities for teaching English abroad for both qualified and untrained teachers. (PET)

Internships USA 2001: (£17.95). Published by Peterson's Guides in the US ($26.95), it lists over 50000 opportunities for short term career-related work throughout America.

THE WORLD ATLAS OF WINE: by Hugh Johnson (Mitchell Beazley, £30); although primarily aimed at the wine-lover, this large book provides useful information on the location of vineyards around the world for those looking for work picking grapes. It may be available for consultation at public libraries. Mitchell Beazley also produce a number of other more pocketable books covering the wine regions of specific countries.

WORLD SERVICE ENQUIRY: Room 233, Bon Marché Centre, 241-251 Ferndale Road, London SW9 8BJ (tel 020-7346 5950 fax 020-7346 5955; e-mail wse@cabroad.org.uk; www.wse.org.uk).

World Service Enquiry is the information and advice activity of Christians Abroad, for people of any faith or none. WSE provides information on working overseas in the developing world on short or long-term basis for both skilled and unskilled people. A free Guide to voluntary opportunities in Europe and worldwide is available. The Guide gives ideas for alternative travel, information on work camps, gap-year activities and other voluntary placements. To receive a copy of the latest Guide please send an A5 SAE (44p) or you can read a version on-line at the above website. In addition WSE publish the Opportunities Abroad Directory for subscribers to their Opportunities Abroad service, which provides brief but useful information about agencies who are actively involved in providing staff for overseas projects. Full details of all World Service Enquiries services are available in the Guide or on-line.